REMAKING
NORTH AMERICAN
SOVEREIGNTY

RECONSTRUCTING AMERICA
Andrew L. Slap, series editor

Remaking North American Sovereignty

State Transformation in the 1860s

Jewel L. Spangler and
Frank Towers, Editors

Fordham University Press
New York   2020

Fordham University Press has no responsibility for the persistence or accuracy of URLs for external or third-party Internet websites referred to in this publication and does not guarantee that any content on such websites is, or will remain, accurate or appropriate.

Fordham University Press also publishes its books in a variety of electronic formats. Some content that appears in print may not be available in electronic books.

Visit us online at www.fordhampress.com.

Library of Congress Control Number: 2020902552

Printed in the United States of America

22 21 20   5 4 3 2 1

First edition

To our mentors:
Joyce Appleby, Steven Hahn, Christine Heyrman,
Rachel Klein, and Michael Johnson

Contents

Introduction: Sovereignty and the
Nation-State in Nineteenth-Century
North America
Frank Towers | 1

PART I   MAKING NATIONS

1   The United States from the Inside
Out and the Southside North
Steven Hahn | 25

2   Confederation as a Hemispheric
Anomaly: Why Canada Chose
a Unique Model of Sovereignty
in the 1860s
Andrew Smith | 36

3   Civil War and Nation Building
in North America, 1848–1867
Pablo Mijangos y González | 61

4   1860s Capitalscapes, Governing
Interiors, and the Illustration
of North American Sovereignty
Robert Bonner | 90

PART II   INDIGENOUS POLITIES

5   The Long War: Sustaining Indigenous
Communities and Contesting
Sovereignties in the Civil War South
Jane Dinwoodie | 107

6   Negotiating Sovereignty: U.S. and
Canadian Colonialisms on the
Northwest Plains, 1855–1877
Ryan Hall | 132

7   Indian Raids in Northern Mexico
        and the Construction of Mexican
        Sovereignty
        Marcela Terrazas y Basante | 153

PART III   THE COMPLICATIONS
            OF THE MARKET

8   State, Market, and Popular
        Sovereignty in Agrarian North
        America: The United States,
        1850–1920
        Christopher Clark | 177

9   Reconstructing North America:
        The Borderlands of Juan Cortina
        and Louis Riel in an Age of National
        Consolidation
        Benjamin H. Johnson | 200

10   City Sovereignty in the Era of the
        American Civil War
        Mary P. Ryan | 220

        Conclusion: Continental History
        and the Problem of Time and Place
        Frank Towers | 251

Acknowledgments   261
List of Contributors 263
Index   265

REMAKING
NORTH AMERICAN
SOVEREIGNTY

Introduction

Sovereignty and the Nation-State
in Nineteenth-Century North America

Frank Towers

Today's political map of North America took its basic shape in the continental crisis of the 1860s, marked by Canadian Confederation (1867), the end of the U.S. Civil War (1865), the restoration of the Mexican Republic (1867), and numerous wars and treaty regimes conducted between these states and indigenous peoples in that decade and the one that followed. This crisis transformed North America from a patchwork of foreign empires, republics, indigenous polities, and contested no-mans-lands into the nation-states of Mexico and the United States and the Dominion of Canada, a largely self-governing polity that nonetheless remained part of the British Empire.

That outcome seemed improbable as late as 1861 when the U.S. entered into a civil war and Mexico, which had just concluded its own, was invaded by a coalition of European powers. Meanwhile, indigenous states on the Great Plains held the upper hand, and British North America remained a combination of colonies and private company lands. In that moment, it was possible to imagine new nations arising, old empires returning, and balances of power reconfigured. By the end of the decade, Mexico and the United States had emerged from their wars intact and in many ways strengthened, and Canada became a unified dominion in control of most of its domestic affairs. On the Plains, waves of white settlers backed by armies and supplied by steamboats and railroads began to break the power of the Blackfoot, Comanche, and Apache, the dominant indigenous powers in the interior West. And, although Britain retained ultimate authority over Canada, other European empires made their final retreat from the continent, either through military defeat in the case of France's intervention in Mexico or through diplomatic negotiation as Russia did when it sold Alaska to the United States in 1867.

This volume explores this tumultuous history of North American state-making from a continental perspective that seeks to look across and beyond the traditional nation-centered approach to this period. Its chapters emerged from a conference of the same name held from July 30 through August 1, 2015, in Banff, Alberta, Canada. That conference brought together historians from Canada, Mexico, the United Kingdom, and the United States with the aim of cutting across these national literatures to find the continental dimensions of this history.[1]

As our title indicates, this is a history of "remaking" sovereignty, a process in which the players not only created new territorial boundaries but also asserted new powers for the governments claiming their spaces on the map. This introduction orients readers to this complex history by first exploring the meaning of key terms—in particular *sovereignty* and its historical attachment to the concept of the *nation-state*—and then previewing how our authors interrogate different themes of the mid-century struggles that remade the continent's political order. Those themes fall into three main parts: the character of the states made and remade in the mid-1800s; the question of sovereignty for indigenous polities that confronted the European settler–descended governments of Canada, Mexico, and the United States; and, finally, the interaction between capitalist expansion and North American politics, and with it the implications of state making for sovereignty's more diffuse meaning at the level of individual and group autonomy.

Central to this volume are the terms "sovereignty," "state," and "nation," and their relationship to the century's emerging governmental form, the nation-state. In common usage, sovereignty is typically associated with the powers of government and means "a right to decide and therefore to rule"; the state is a political association in control of a given territory and its population; and a nation denotes a people identified with a particular territory and united by shared traits such as language, descent, ideology, and culture. Nineteenth-century nationalists combined these terms into the political objective of the sovereign nation-state: a government whose powers are absolute within its territorial boundaries (a state with power over a nation, in this sense) and a people united in their identification with and subjection to that sovereign power (a nationality with a state of its own, in this second meaning).[2] These simple definitions are meant to assist readers seeking quick reference points, but they are only the starting point for untangling the relationship between the history of state transformation and the conceptual vocabulary used to describe it.

In fact, recent scholarship on the history of sovereignty has cast doubt on the utility of assigning it a fixed, dictionary-style definition, "because sovereignty is not a property that can be analysed in the abstract, separating it from the multiple discursive contexts in which it has been invoked."[3] Conventional definitions of sovereignty, like other keywords of contemporary politics, are themselves artifacts of nineteenth-century history. That is, their origins can be traced back to the arguments made by protagonists in that era's state-making conflicts.

Ideas about national sovereignty gained ground in the American and French revolutions of the late eighteenth century. According to France's 1789 *Declaration of the Rights of Man and Citizen*, "The principle of any sovereignty resides essentially in the Nation. No body, no individual may exercise any authority which does not proceed directly from the nation." In the following decades, nationalism—a political ideology grounded in national identity and popular sovereignty—grew in popularity on both sides of the Atlantic, as calls for self-rule for peoples sharing a common land and culture fueled demands to make new sovereign nation-states out of old empires. As the advocate of Italian unification Giuseppe Mazzini put it, "every nation a state, only one state for every nation."[4]

Acting within this broader ideological current, the political leaders who triumphed in 1860s North America identified the nation-state model of sovereignty as an end goal of their struggles. According to Canada's John A. Macdonald, "The true principle of a confederation lies in giving to the general Government all the principles and powers of sovereignty, and in the provision that all the subordinate or individual States should have no powers but those expressly bestowed upon them."[5] In his December 1, 1862, annual message to Congress, U.S. President Abraham Lincoln said, "A nation may be said to consist of its territory, its people, and its laws. The territory is the only part which is of certain durability. . . . That portion of the earth's surface which is owned and inhabited by the people of the United States is well adapted to be the home of one national family, and it is not well adapted for two or more." After the execution of French-installed monarch Maximilian I, Mexico's Benito Juárez declared, "[W]e recognize no foreign sovereigns, no judges, and no arbiters."[6] In making these claims for nation-state sovereignty, Macdonald, Lincoln, and Juárez provided a rationale for fighting secessionists at home while simultaneously asserting equal standing abroad with the European powers that dominated international politics.

Writing in the aftermath of these conflicts, political theorists took the systems worked out by the victors as ideal types for these categories. In one of the most influential examples, Germany's Max Weber defined the state as "a human community that (successfully) claims the *monopoly of the legitimate use of physical force* within a given territory."[7] As critics of this model observe, "Such a definition implied that sovereignty was the preserve of the ruler and by extension what came to be perceived as a 'government,' the existence of which derived directly from princely validation and attribution of responsibility." Working with this understanding of sovereignty, scholars "have traditionally reified the nation-state, and located its origins in the early modern era and even medieval developments" in Western Europe.[8] For historians, in particular, the idea of the nation-state has led them to try to find it, to look within national lineages for its origins and arrival. This emphasis on national history was part of nineteenth- and early twentieth-century government-sponsored professionalization of historical studies. That project was "intensely nationalistic" and focused on "politics at the state level and on diplomacy and the military to the exclusion of social and cultural history." Although moderated by later scholars, this tendency remains powerful. As Steven Hahn reminds us in his contribution to this volume, historians "often work with a structure and language of analysis that the dynamics of nation and sovereignty make credible."[9]

Now, well into the twenty-first century, academics and policy makers worry that transnational forces—such as multinational corporations, digital media, ethnic diasporas, and stateless terror networks—have compromised the sovereignty of the nation-state, which some see as receding into history as the dominant mode of world political organization. Doubt about the nation-state in the present has helped historians reconsider its vitality in the past, leading one scholar to argue that "'Strong States'—centralized states that monopolize violence and provide basic services—have never been the majority of polities in world politics."[10] This claim fits with a growing body of scholarship that shows how non-state actors, "invisible" sovereign states, and local power brokers prevented the consolidation of sovereign authority in the hands of a central governing authority (the nation-state). Seeing outside of the nation-centered history of sovereignty has required "the recognition that empires, federations, and other kinds of layered or divided sovereignty were more characteristic of political authority" prior to 1900 and "attention to the world beyond northern Europe to see how little respect was paid to the sovereignty of many of the world's peoples under the regime of empire."[11]

The first of these two critiques re-examines the European lineage of the international state system. Definitions of modern state sovereignty often trace back to ideas put forth by advocates of expanded monarchical power writing in the sixteenth and seventeenth centuries, such as France's Jean Bodin who argued that "the sovereign prince, who is the image of God, cannot make a subject equal with himself without self-destruction."[12] In asserting absolute powers for the monarch, Bodin not only offered an ideological rationale for undercutting rival authorities such as landed nobles and the Church, but also depicted this version of sovereignty as a historic break with an imagined feudal past. Yet although monarchs encouraged "exaggerated claims advanced upon their behalf by royal propagandists," the current view of historians is that "overlapping forms of sovereignty were characteristic even of the allegedly absolute monarchies of contemporary Europe."[13]

Perhaps the best example of the gap between claims for national sovereignty and reality is the Peace of Westphalia of 1648 that is often treated as the starting point for modern statehood. As the settlement of the sectarian Thirty Years War, the Peace of Westphalia supposedly recognized the sovereignty of individual states over their populations and borders, and treated them as the representatives of those nations in interstate relations. Dissatisfied with the use of Westphalia as a starting point, scholars have revisited the 1640s to show that treaties signed at Osnabrück and Münster (the Westphalian cities where the peace was made) never mentioned sovereignty, included only three of the contending powers in what had been a much wider multi-state conflict, and in no way ended the involvement of one government in the internal affairs of another, as witnessed by the endurance of multiple layers of sovereignty within the Holy Roman Empire's constituent states. As Andreas Osiander has argued, the outcome of the treaties was "a system of mutual relations among autonomous political units that was precisely not based on the concept of sovereignty." Thus, counter to the older narrative of modern state sovereignty taking hold in Europe in the 1600s, historians now agree that "Even the most cohesive Western European states needed centuries to define clear boundaries and to move from jurisdictional to territorial authority."[14]

A second path to rethinking the history of sovereign nation-states has been engagement with past politics outside of Europe and the role played by empires, not only Europe's but also those of Asia, Africa, and the Americas. These studies show empire's enduring significance and the overlap between imperial governing practices and those of sovereign nation-states.

Always imprecise, the terms "empire" and "nation" can be understood as poles on a continuum of political organization with most states falling somewhere in between. At the imperial end, elites residing at the core dominate subject peoples in peripheral zones. In practice, the core means a capital city, or cluster of cities and surrounding "home counties." Peripheries take many forms, ranging from shells of old empires replete with their own urban-rural hierarchies to underpopulated borderlands desolated by war. Empires are not only "large political units," but also "expansionist or with a memory of power extended over space . . . that maintain distinction and hierarchy as they incorporate new people." Common to all is a model of governance that encourages divisions of identity, economy, and culture so as to prevent politics from organizing around questions of common good.[15]

At the other extreme, the nation implies social solidarity, if not for all of its subjects then at least for all of its citizens. Empires are heterogeneous, nations uniform. As Jürgen Osterhammel puts it, "Unlike a nation state, which has a more or less matching national society, an empire is a political but not a social organization. There is no overarching imperial 'society.'" Power flows from the top down in an empire, but emanates from multiple points across the spectrum in a nation and is exercised uniformly across the territory.[16]

Several recent studies have shown the persistence of imperial forms inside new, self-proclaimed nation-states. Charles Maier argues that the nation-state only appeared on the world stage in the 1860s and then as the tool of established powers not popular insurgencies. Going farther than Maier in downgrading the significance of the nation-state, Osterhammel, along with Jane Burbank and Frederick Cooper, emphasize continuity with the past. In the nineteenth century, like the centuries preceding it, "empire remained the dominant territorial form of the organization of power." Even decolonization in the "mid-twentieth century was not a self-propelled movement from empire to nation state."[17] In such accounts, nationalism grows within empires, first as the ideology of the core and later as a means for resistance by the periphery, and nationalists often end up using imperial methods of rule to advance claims for political solidarity across the territory. This tendency was strongest in empires such as Napoleonic France and its antagonist Great Britain, both of which were "extending the remit of the state into everyday life," and "thus required legitimation beyond the original core" to raise the resources—labor, taxes, and crops—needed for the imperial project.[18]

In addition to showing the overlap between national and imperial forms of sovereignty, scholars have also shown the limits on central authority within both systems in the nineteenth century. For republics such as the United States and Mexico, federalism—the division of powers between national and regional administrative units as well as between competing legislative branches within each unit—aimed at preventing tyranny from the metropolitan center that had been the spark for revolution in the first place. However, the ideological inheritance of these anti-imperial foundings obscures the importance of divided powers to imperial governments themselves. In most empires, the central government concentrated on controlling key places (usually transportation corridors, plantation districts, and cities) but exerted weak or no authority elsewhere in their territorial domain—mountains and islands, for example. Dividing sovereignty served practical needs such as creating a de facto truce with regions that had the power to resist the center, and as a means for rewarding friends of the regime who wanted privileges not accorded to a uniform, and equal, citizenry. When the imperial state occasionally faced challenges to its coherence from divided sovereignty, it imposed a state of emergency that suspended rules and imposed extreme force through the military. These periodic emergencies acted as the necessary patch for the problems of divided sovereignty but were never intended, nor could they be sustained, as a permanent condition of imperial rule. On this point, historian Paul Kramer advises that viewing nation-states, such as the United States, through "an imperial lens" opens up a "historiography of spatial exceptions: extraordinary power exercised at and through the interstices of sovereignty, often underwritten by essentialisms of race, gender, and civilization."[19]

In light of these criticisms, the more useful way to understand sovereignty and related terms is through a closer look at their contingent, historically specific meanings. Arguing that "[s]overeignty is best understood as a set of claims made by those seeking or wielding power, claims about the superiority and autonomy of their authority," historian James Sheehan provides an alternative to the search for static definitions: "State-making, therefore, is the ongoing process of making, unmaking, and revising sovereign claims. The nature of this process constantly changes; what it means to be a state varies from time to time and place to place."[20]

Sheehan's emphasis on sovereignty as a claim about power—and the importance of historical context for understanding such claims—frees historians from the teleological imperative created by fixed definitions of the sovereign state—a way of thinking that encourages binaries of failed/successful states or modern/premodern ones. Giving priority to contingency and specificity, Part I of this volume, "Making Nations," examines the meaning of sovereignty in the states that won out in the struggles of 1860s North America from four different perspectives.

Steven Hahn shows the value of putting the West at the center of the history of the U.S. Civil War. His work joins a number of recent studies that counter the tendency of comparative and transnational studies of the United States to focus on the Atlantic and the ties between Europe and the Americas.[21] Hahn's reorientation westward also builds on themes developed by historians of the American Revolution who have connected the conflict on the Atlantic seaboard to the struggle for the Mississippi interior and the wave of revolutions against Spanish rule that followed in the early 1800s.[22]

Taking an "inside out" and "southside north" vantage point on the Civil War era, Hahn argues that it was in the interior that "the nation-state best revealed its imperial dispositions." Developed at length in his recent book *A Nation Without Borders*, Hahn makes the case for the simultaneity of nation-state and empire as governing forms and ideological goals. Within its territorial borders, the United States pursued a model of undivided sovereignty that led in seemingly contradictory directions, such as the simultaneous drive by President Abraham Lincoln to free slaves in the South and conquer indigenous states in the West. Although one project was emancipatory and the other subjugating, they shared in common the nation-state's goal of eliminating rival sovereignties be they claimed by Southern slaveholders or Plains Indians.[23]

Along with consolidating sovereignty within their borders, nationalists also moved outward to conquer new lands. The "imperial tendencies of emerging nation states," Hahn argues, produced a dynamic in which nation-makers "are perpetually and necessarily colonizing their own domains even as they prepare to find new ones." Thus, the same actors who pushed for federal supremacy within the United States' borders encouraged an imperial hodgepodge of multiple sovereignties and vectors of influence in the Pacific and Latin America. There, a mix of missionaries, capitalists and soldiers furthered the global reach of the United States but did so by excluding new zones of influence from the rights and responsibilities of full-fledged members of the nation-state. The outcome was "a world in which the borders of American nationhood were well secured while the borders of American power remained limitless."[24]

Whereas scholars focused on powerful nation-states such as the United States argue that those formations were *more* imperial than their rhetoric admitted, as noted previously, newer studies of powerful empires, such as Great Britain, have found those systems to have been *less* imperial, or, perhaps, less centrally directed, than their legends pretend. A survey of recent work on the British Empire concludes that scholarship has moved "away from the old historiographic binaries of British 'metropole' and colonial 'periphery' to visualize the empire as an interconnected zone constituted by multiple points of contact and complex circuits of exchange."[25]

This change in focus has been aided by scholarship on the "British world" that looks at the empire less as a political structure and more as a geographic space of "multiple metropoles and peripheries" shaped by the "phenomenon of British migration and mass settlement." Focused primarily on the settler-colonies of Australia, Canada, New Zealand, and South Africa, British world studies highlight the significance of non-state actors, such as chartered companies, merchants, and settler militias. The impact of these autonomous actors shows the limits of London's power over the system it claimed to control. These informal agents of empire gained room to maneuver from a governmental framework that devolved powers to smaller administrative units in what James Belich has termed a "cloning system" that gave local officials more autonomy to carry out the work of conquest.[26]

In this volume, such understandings of empire inform Andrew Smith's chapter on the decision of Canadians to choose Confederation and the maintenance of their imperial ties over either independence or merger with the United States. "The fact that many political actors throughout history and in the present have been satisfied with governance systems that involve layered or quasi- sovereignty," Smith writes, "helps us to understand why the creators of the Canadian constitution of 1867 did not believe it was desirable for the new nation to have external sovereignty." The flexibility of the imperial framework appealed to Canadians who worried about the excesses of democracy as exemplified by the secession of the southern states in reaction to a heated presidential election.

Although indebted to British world studies, Smith recommends "a more hemispheric approach to the writing of Canadian history" that looks to the south. Bringing insights from U.S. historiography to bear on recent studies of British identity, Smith finds an additional motive for Confederation: according to Smith, defending Britishness against "an ethnic-nationalist definition of U.S. citizenship." The use of "the term 'British' as both an ethnic label and a more inclusive legal concept that corresponded to the category of British nationality," gave important protections to nonwhite and non-Protestant Canadians that they worried might be lost after annexation to the bellicose United States, which had shown its hand in anti-Catholic attitudes in its conquest of Mexico. The continental dialog over empire and nationhood, therefore, spurred "advocates of the rival British identity for Canada [to promote] an inclusive, civic-nationalist definition of Britishness that attracted many whites who were not of British ancestry."

Unlike Hahn, who looks at the United States from its colonized borders, and Smith, who foregrounds the British Empire's efforts to hold distant settler-colonies together, the comparison by Pablo Mijangos y González of the winners of the civil wars of the 1860s brings out their liberal-nationalist tendencies. Mijangos y González begins with the anti-imperial revolutions waged by Mexico and the United States. Because "neither Mexico nor the United States arose truly as *nations*, but rather as immense aggregations of autonomous territories," divided sovereignty characterized their post-revolutionary political orders. In each country a powerful anti-republican interest—slavery in the United States and the Catholic Church in Mexico—maneuvered to secure its privileges from rising democratic tides.

By destabilizing earlier equilibriums, Mijangos y González argues that the 1848 U.S. conquest of northern Mexico "led to a serious constitutional crisis in both countries." In Mexico, conservatives tried to solidify their power through a stronger central government and added authority for the Church. That bid for power resembled slaveholders' attempts to gain new protections for slavery by adding new slave states, annexing Cuba, and strengthening their ability to take slaves to federally administered territories in the West. The overreach of both projects produced strong popular reactions and then civil wars won by the supporters of democracy and nationalism. Mijangos y González concludes that the governments that followed were "characterized by a simultaneous affirmation of individual liberties and of state power, essential conditions for capitalistic expansion in the region during the following decades."

Mijangos argues that these postwar settlements also made nations. In Mexico, for example, "the nation-state created a *patria* for which it was worth dying, a sort of civic religion endowed with its own pantheon of saints, calendar of feasts, and civic edifices adorned with statues." From this conclusion Mijangos y González goes farther. Looking at what Canadian Confederation meant in light of the convulsions to its south, he shows that Canada not only avoided devastating civil war and occupation, but it also achieved the "creole dream" of autonomy within the empire that had been the original demand of revolutionaries in the republics to its south.

Similar to Mijangos y González, Robert Bonner finds democratic nationalism as the common theme of state making in Canada, Mexico, and the United States. And, like Mijangos y González, his analysis focuses on the self-presentation (the claims made in their own behalf) of the winners in these struggles. Looking at public commemorations, print narratives, and public architecture in the capitals of Ottawa, Washington, and Mexico City, Bonner argues that "one important shared feature concerned the visual link made between the most effective forms of sovereignty and tranquil spaces where the governing ideal was grounded in consent and deliberation rather than command and martial violence." Notwithstanding imperial tendencies on their edges, at their cores the three republics' leading supporters emphasized popular sovereignty and the majesty of democratic nationalism as the lasting achievements of 1860s state making. "While governing hubs imposed themselves on faraway populations with new force in the era of Leviathan 2.0," Bonner writes, "such endeavors did not figure in the most potent sovereign imaginaries then being circulated. Beyond the 1860s, the blunt iron that had secured national rulership across the continent tended to be visually cloaked by velveted interiors, as years of North American upheavals gave way to a critical period of geopolitical consolidation."

Bonner's essay speaks to a central contradiction of nation-states. Whereas new histories of nation and empire portray the mid-nineteenth-century state as less a leviathan with one head than an unruly hydra whose powers were always fragmentary, for the leaders of these nationalist victories, power was not only real but wielded in the name of the people, not the hegemons. In their stated aims, Juárez, Lincoln, and Macdonald had either restored popular government or, in Canada, increased its voice, and, they could each cite as proof costly struggles against aristocratic forces, be they French imperialists, southern slaveholders, or British anti-republicans.

The essays in Part II of this volume, "Indigenous Polities," investigate how this impression changes when one looks at North America's nation-states from the perspective of the native populations they sought to conquer rather than the powerful imperial influences they fought against. Until recently, the history of those conflicts has been isolated from the study of Canadian Confederation, Mexican Restoration, and American Reunion. That disconnect between wars waged by European Americans against Native Americans and wars between different factions of European Americans has been a byproduct of conventional definitions of national sovereignty, which have struggled to capture the diplomatic history of indigenous polities. As Brian DeLay writes, "Assumptions about the supposedly cramped and conditional nature of indigenous sovereignty have undoubtedly contributed to the field's enduring disinclination to treat Indian relations as foreign relations." The result has been a tendency to write about indigenous North Americans as subjects—often unwilling and resisting ones, but subjects nonetheless—within the histories of the settler-states that ultimately triumphed. DeLay points out that this perspective telescopes the political history of the continent to a late-nineteenth-century end point when conquest was seemingly complete. Prior to that time, "nineteenth-century North America [had] an international system comprised of a growing continental hegemon, a handful of rival states, and hundreds of sovereign indigenous polities."[27]

DeLay's argument fits with an intellectual turn away from narratives of indigenous histories as stories of declension—that is, the decline of once proud and vibrant indigenous societies—toward narratives of resilience that highlight the ways that native peoples adapted, resisted, and asserted their political power in the face of European invasions. This project has found expression in studies that "fac[e] east from Indian country" toward the Atlantic seaboard; comprehend the

Great Lakes as a "middle ground"; "turn the telescope around" on the history of the Great Plains; and look "out from Hawaii's shore" to understand the Pacific. Common to these efforts is an argument for the strength of indigenous polities and the integrity of their sovereign claims in the nineteenth century.[28]

Following in this vein, Jane Dinwoodie's contribution to this volume examines the persistence of Native American sovereignty in the southeastern United States long after the Removal Act of 1830 and the Trail of Tears supposedly extinguished those claims. Working with more nuanced definitions of sovereignty, Dinwoodie shows how indigenous "non-removed groups were more like maroon communities—physically located within, but distinct from American power within the South—or like some of the many semi-sovereign groups partially or incompletely absorbed into the sphere of the 'imperial nation-state' as it headed westwards during the Civil War and Greater Reconstruction." In recasting the problem of sovereignty east of the Mississippi, Dinwoodie demonstrates how despite the new attention to the significance of the West in 1860s North America, the resilience of indigenous states extended beyond the native empires of the Plains.

As Mijangos y González and Bonner show, when viewed in their relationship to European powers, North America's settler-descended polities stood out as defenders of liberal nationalism against old regime imperialism and aristocracy.[29] In contrast, the behavior of these same polities toward indigenous Americans makes it easier to see how "most contemporary nation-states are also colonial ones."[30] In a near endless series of wars against North America's original inhabitants, settler-colonial polities combined some of the worst tendencies of egalitarian nation-states—drawing a sharp line between citizen insiders and outside others—with those of imperial hegemons, namely their propensity to colonization and conquest. One study of settler-colonialism in the United States argued that it went hand-in-hand with nation building. Wars against indigenous Americans not only secured land and resources but also promoted the cultural "inclusions and exclusions" that "enable settler communities to cohere," thus providing a different explanation for the growth of nationalism within imperial systems.[31] Despite tensions between metropolitan and colonial societies, settler identification with the ethnic core group of ancestral European empires was, in fact, a pre-condition for devolving sovereignty to far-flung administrative provinces or fully independent nations.[32]

In the 1860s, the confrontation between militarily powerful indigenous polities and determined settler-nationalists was most evident on the Plains. In this volume, essays by Marcela Terrazas y Basante and Ryan Hall show what Hall

terms "remarkably similar approaches to expansion" undertaken by white settler-states to subdue native polities. For settler states, the aim of wars against
indigenous polities was what Terrazas y Basante describes as "territorialization,"
or "the desire of the respective elites to achieve the presence and effective control
of the state over territory and the flow of people and goods." Meanwhile, indigenous nations "never saw the treaties as representing a transformation of sovereignty." In Hall's study of the Blackfoot's dealings with the U.S. and Canadian
governments, he argues that "the treaty councils were negotiations about the extent of their own inherent sovereignty over their homelands," not surrenders to a
new concept of the nation-state as the absolute sovereign over the people within
its borders.[33]

Along with highlighting the strength of indigenous polities and the anti-
liberal side of the triumphant European-descended republics, increased attention to the continent's interior offers a North American example of "entangled
state-building" or "a transnational process in which emerging states approach
developmental equilibrium as a result of shared historical experiences and global
economic trajectories." This method does not do away with the state as an analytical unit, but it looks beyond national borders and imperial cores as the frames
inside which state-making unfolded.[34]

Applied to North America, this outlook shares much in common with calls for
an "integrative history of the continent" that have been especially strong among
specialists in borderlands studies.[35] In the borderlands, "visions of empires and
nations often foundered and the future was far from certain," and even after
states agreed on political boundaries, "borders formalized but did not foreclose
the flow of people, capital and goods."[36] Studying the history of North America
from its borderlands "emphasizes the contingency of nations in opposition to the
seeming inevitability of the nation-state as the form of government, and nationalism as the currency of group belonging."[37]

Therefore, in addition to looking at the question of sovereignty as a continental, state-making problem, this volume also considers sovereignty's more diffuse meaning as a question of self-government and national attachment. How,
for example, did new understandings of national identity and new definitions
of citizenship come to pass in the 1860s and 70s, and in what ways did these
transformations in group loyalty and legal status cross political boundaries?
These questions take into account the transnational character of social identities, particularly race and gender, in what Elliott West once termed the "Greater
Reconstruction" of nationality in the mid- 1800s.[38] The reality of porous borders
and multiple sovereigns means that a full accounting of how North America's

nation-states came about should consider sovereignty's implications for identity and power beyond the state's officials and institutions. Doing so moves sovereignty outside of the formal boundaries of the state to consider it "as integrating a spectrum of meanings and operations," which include "the attempt to control natural, human, and material forces."[39]

The essays in Part III of this volume, "The Complications of the Market," focus on this meaning of sovereignty by exploring the links between state-making and capitalism. Transnational movements of people and commodities were critical to changing collective identity and state structures. On one hand, migration and new trading patterns encouraged bids for independent sovereign states from Manitoba to the Yucatan. On the other, new technologies such as the railroad, telegraph, and improved firearms, as well as new means of tapping global capital to finance these undertakings, helped established powers to overcome these insurgencies. With these patterns in mind, the question of sovereignty extends to global trade in commodities like cotton and guns and the renegotiation of labor relationships such as the U.S. abolition of slavery in 1865.[40]

Christopher Clark brings attention back to the core economic enterprise of the nineteenth century: agriculture. His essay on the freehold ideal in the United States argues for the democratic potential of small farmer politics, which pursued state policies that would widely distribute productive land among the citizenry. This was the democratic-egalitarian side of settler-colonialism. And, as Clark argues, it dominated American political economy in the latter half of the nineteenth century. One of the contradictions of American territorial settlement was the simultaneous drive to exploit resources for the market and the aim of many of those actively engaged in settlement to shield themselves from the market's dangers by acquiring land on the frontier. Clark shows how the vision of freehold farming as the basis for American political economy had an inherent tension not from the dangers of the market overwhelming the small farm but from the family farm running out of labor to uphold its own productive capacity. Labor, not land, was the problem confronting the freehold vision, as he argues in a provocative re-reading of late nineteenth-century small farmers' calls for state intervention.

This was a Janus-faced project. As Clark writes, "The freehold ideal . . . offered 'sovereignty' over the land and substantial equality to those owning property," but these same nonstate actors, empowered by fragmented sovereignty, composed the "grassroots movements that demanded state and federal assistance to clear obstructions from their path." Those obstructions were indigenous polities with a rival claim to settler lands.

If capitalism empowered freehold farmers in the West, it had surprisingly little traction for would-be secessionists in the same region where nationalist dreams of sovereign government by and for the people ran up against the reality of entrenched power and vested interests, a point brought out in this volume in Benjamin Johnson's comparisons of failed republican revolutions in Manitoba and south Texas. "Despite their distinct genealogies, reigning ideologies, and legal systems," Johnson says of Canada, Mexico, and the United States, "all three of these states were intent on extinguishing competing sovereignties in the territory that they claimed as their own." That drive for absolute sovereignty meant that secessionist movements embodying the same principles that those states claimed as their own would never be allowed to part on good terms. Interestingly, Johnson finds in the rebel movements of Louis Riel and Juan Cortina arguments for self-determination made in liberal capitalist terms rather than ethnic-nationalist ones. As proponents of secessionist republics, Cortina and Riel bore some resemblance to the movement for freehold sovereignty described by Clark, but in trying to make a formal break with established states they encountered those governments' hard limits.

Capitalism was also at the heart of municipal battles over property rights in post-war San Francisco, the subject of Mary Ryan's closing essay to this book. Ryan draws on geographer John Agnew's critique of the "'Territorial Trap,' whereby history is seen to transpire only in relation to institutional boundaries, usually those of the nation, where power descends from a single center of government, most often the capital of the centralized state." Building from this blueprint, she draws attention to the local level of government where sovereignty "was particularly ambiguous and unstable in the era of the American Civil War." Ryan shows how "at this level of sovereignty the most contentious issue was not slavery but property, not labor but land."

The "tidal wave of land and lot seekers" that followed the Gold Rush to San Francisco pursued their real estate fortunes in a complicated, ambiguous array of property claims descended from the former Mexican authorities and amended by the newly installed American ones. With a federal government distracted by the sectional conflict, land law in San Francisco was made primarily by local actors who "arrogated 'sovereign' authority unto themselves" such that "governance was the work of a succession of self-appointed and competing town councils, given little direction from Washington or anywhere else."

This pattern fits with the big-picture studies of the limits on state sovereignty discussed previously. Despite grand claims for uniform rule across its territory, central governments yielded considerable authority to local administrative units. In the case of San Francisco, local actors were by no means unified. Long-established Californio families fought to maintain land claims granted by Mexico before 1848. Newly installed city officials sought to divide and sell land into small, gridded plots so as to maximize tax revenue. Squatters invoking "an inalienable right to free land in the West" also made their mark, sometimes violently, on the property map. In asserting a political right to the land based on citizenship and ethnicity, Ryan's squatter sovereigns advanced arguments similar to Clark's freehold farmers and Johnson's secessionists, but they did so in pursuit of speculative profit-taking not productive agriculture or liberal nationalism. Their story shows how the market's incentives could quickly turn an egalitarian plan for productive land development into an unequal scramble to maximize personal advantage at the expense of one's neighbors.

Ryan concludes that the volatile relationship between state making and capitalism maximized the power of opportunists on the margin of empire at the expense of the central government: "All these real estate transactions demonstrated, among other things, that wily individuals could capitalize on the uncertainties of sovereignty during the transition from Mexican to U.S. governance. If power rested anywhere amid the chaos of the Gold Rush, it was on the ground at the time and in the place where savvy pioneers could take advantage of local political opportunities."

Ryan's point can be applied more broadly to the study of North American state making in the nineteenth century. No matter the pretensions of would-be nation builders, the practical exercise of sovereignty on the ground often fell short of their assertions about the sovereign power of the state. This insight returns to the problem of defining sovereignty and the value gained by studying state-making in mid-nineteenth-century North America as an interconnected, continental history.

As noted previously, sovereignty can be understood as a historically contingent claim about power and authority. Thinking about sovereignty as a political argument advanced by those seeking to rule (as opposed to an abstract definition of how power and authority are exercised) helps to situate the nation-state model of sovereignty as one of many competing claims made by North Americans at the time. This volume's comparative and cross-border studies of these competing claims sheds new light on the character of the nation-states that won out. It also examines rival claims to state sovereignty, particularly those advanced by indigenous polities whose fates were entangled with those of the settler-colonial powers they confronted. This transnational and comparative perspective also opens up the interplay between sovereign claims on the state and the logic of liberal capitalist economics. Taken together, these essays show that although often told as separate histories, state-making in Canada, Mexico, and the United States connected the peoples of the continent to each other and to the larger world. It is the aim of this volume to open up those connections and examine their significance for the momentous struggles that set North America on a path of political and economic development that continues to shape its present.

Notes

1. In addition to this volume, essays from the Banff conference appear in revised form in "Crises of Sovereignty in the 1860s: A Special Issue" in *The Journal of the Civil War Era* 7, no. 4 (December 2017) and *Continent in Crisis: Transnational Histories of the Civil War Era*, ed. Jewel L. Spangler and Frank Towers (New York: Fordham University Press, forthcoming).

For other recent transnational approaches to the 1860s, most of them related to the U.S. Civil War, see *The Civil War as Global Conflict: Transnational Meanings of the American Civil War*, ed. David T. Gleeson and Simon Lewis (Columbia, S.C.: University of South Carolina Press, 2014); *The Transnational Significance of the American Civil War*, ed. Jörg Nagler, Don H. Doyle, and Marcus Gräser (New York: Palgrave Macmillan, 2016); *American Civil Wars: The United States, Latin America, Europe and the Crisis of the 1860s*, ed. Don H. Doyle (Chapel Hill: University of North Carolina Press, 2017); *Reconstruction in a Globalizing World*, ed. David Prior (New York: Fordham University Press, 2018). Exceptions to the U.S.-centered trend are *El Poder y la Sangre: Guerra, Estado y Nación en la Década de 1860*, ed. Guillermo Palacios and Erika Pani (Mexico, D.F.: Colegio de Mexico, 2014) and *Globalizing Confederation: Canada and the World in 1867*, ed. Jacqueline Krikorian, Marcel Martel, and Adrian Shubert (Toronto: University of Toronto Press, 2017).

Because this volume includes authors based in four different national academies, readers will find somewhat different usage of familiar terms across the essays. Those differences have been left in place as a better alternative to imposing a uniform standard that ultimately goes back to one particular national standard. Further to this point, the terms "Blackfoot" and "Blackfeet" refer to the same people, but in their legal designations, the Canadian usage is Blackfoot, and the U.S. usage is Blackfeet. This introduction uses Blackfoot.

The author thanks Jewel Spangler, Ryan Hall, Pablo Policzer, and the anonymous reviewers of this manuscript for their insights.

2. Terry Nardin, "The Diffusion of Sovereignty," *History of European Ideas* 41, no. 1 (2015), 89–102, 91 (quotation). For recent scholarly overviews of these concepts see Zvi Ben-Dor Benite, Stefanos Geroulanos, and Nicole Jerr, eds., *The Scaffolding of Sovereignty: Global and Aesthetic Perspectives on the History of a Concept* (New York: Columbia University Press, 2017); Hent Kalmo and Quentin Skinner, eds., *Sovereignty in Fragments: The Past, Present and Future of a Contested Concept* (Cambridge: Cambridge University Press, 2010); John Breuilly, ed., *The Oxford Handbook of the History*

of Nationalism (Oxford: University Press, 2013); Sarah A. Binder, R. A. W. Rhodes, and Bert A. Rockman, eds. *The Oxford Handbook of Political Institutions* (Oxford: Oxford University Press, 2006), esp. Bob Jessop, "The State and State Building," 111–31.

3. Kalmo and Skinner, *Sovereignty in Fragments*, 5.

4. Don H. Doyle, *The Cause of All Nations: An International History of the American Civil War* (New York: Basic Books, 2015), 282; Jürgen Osterhammel, *The Transformation of the World: A Global History of the Nineteenth Century*, trans. Peter Camiller (Princeton, N.J.: Princeton University Press, 2014), 404 (first quotation); E. J. Hobsbawm, *Nations and Nationalism Since 1780: Programme, Myth, Reality* (Cambridge: Cambridge University Press, 1992), 101 (Mazzini quoted).

5. John A. Macdonald, Remarks in House of Assembly, April 19, 1861 in Joseph Pope, ed., *Memoirs of the Right Honourable Sir John Alexander Macdonald, First Prime Minister of the Dominion of Canada* (Ottawa: J. Durie, 1894), 229.

6. Juárez quoted in Paul Vanderwood, "Betterment for Whom? The Reform Period, 1855–1875," in Michael C. Meyer and Paul Beezley, eds., *The Oxford History of Mexico* (New York: Oxford University Press, 2000), 391.

7. Max Weber, "Politics as a Vocation," in H. H. Gerth and C. Wright Mills, trans. and ed., *From Max Weber: Essays in Sociology* (New York: Oxford University Press, 1946), 78.

8. Robert Oresko, G. C. Gibbs, and H. M. Scott, Introduction to *Royal and Republican Sovereignty in Early Modern Europe: Essays in Memory of Ragnhild Hatton*, ed. Oresko, Gibbs, and Scott (Cambridge: Cambridge University Press, 1997), 5.

9. Stephen Krasner, *Sovereignty: Organized Hypocrisy* (Princeton, N.J.: Princeton University Press, 1999), 20; Georg G. Iggers, Q. Edward Wang, and Supriya Mukherjee, *A Global History of Modern Historiography, 2nd Edition* (Routledge: New York, 2017), 103 (quotation). For individual chapters, see the table of contents to this volume.

10. Arjun Chowdhury, *The Myth of International Order: Why Weak States Persist and Alternatives to the State Fade Away* (New York: Oxford University Press, 2017), 3 (quotation). Studies doubting the survival of the nation state include Joseph A. Camilleri, ed., *The End of Sovereignty? The Politics of a Shrinking and Fragmenting World* (Aldershot, England: Elgar, 1992); Christian Jopke, ed. *Challenge to the Nation State: Immigration in Western Europe and the United States* (New York: Oxford University Press, 1998); Jürgen Habermas, *The Postnational Constellation: Political Essays*, trans. and ed. by Max Pensky (Cambridge, Mass.: MIT Press, 2001); Richard N. Rosecrance and Arthur Stein, eds., *No More States? Globalization, National Self- Determination, and Terrorism* (Lanham, Md.: Rowman and Littlefield, 2006); John Agnew, *Globalization and Sovereignty* (Lanham, Md.: Rowman and Littlefield, 2009); Jean L. Cohen, *Globalization and Sovereignty: Rethinking Legality, Legitimacy, and Constitutionalism* (New York: Cambridge University Press, 2012); Zygmunt Bauman and Carlo Bordini, *State of Crisis* (Cambridge: Polity Press, 2014); David A. Rezvani, *Suppressing the Sovereign State: The Wealth, Self-Rule and Security Advantages of Partially Independent Territories* (Oxford: Oxford University Press, 2014), 222.

11. David Armitage, *Foundations of Modern International Thought* (New York: Cambridge University Press, 2013), 27 (quotation). For a recent summary and example of this scholarship, see James Pickett, "Written into Submission: Reassessing Sovereignty

through a Forgotten Eurasian Dynasty," *The American Historical Review* 123, no. 3 (June 2018), 817–45.

12. Jean Bodin, *The Six Books of the Commonwealth*, abridged and trans. M. J. Tooley (Oxford, UK.: Basil Blackwell, 1967), 42. Online at https://www.constitution.org/bodin/bodin.txt.

13. Quotations in Oresko, Gibbs, and Scott, Introduction, 3; and Pickett, "Written into Submission," 840. Also see Kathleen Davis, *Periodization and Sovereignty: How Ideas of Feudalism and Secularization Govern the Politics of Time* (Philadelphia: University of Pennsylvania Press, 2008), 44–50.

14. Andreas Osiander, "Sovereignty, International Relations, and the Westphalian Myth," *International Organization* 55, no. 2 (Spring 2001), 265–68, 270 (first quotation); James J. Sheehan, "The Problem of Sovereignty in European History," *The American Historical Review* 111, no. 1 (Feb. 2006), 6 (second quotation); Benno Teschke, *The Myth of 1648: Class, Geopolitics, and the Making of Modern International Relations* (London: Verso, 2003), 238–45.

15. Jane Burbank and Frederick Cooper, *Empires in World History: Power and the Politics of Difference* (Princeton, N.J.: Princeton University Press, 2014), 8.

16. Osterhammel, *The Transformation of the World*, 425. Also see Ernest Gellner, *Nationalism* (London: Wiedenfeld and Nicholson, 1997); Anthony D. Smith, *Nationalism and Modernism* (New York: Routledge, 1998); John Breuilly, *Nationalism and the State*, 2nd ed. (Chicago: University of Chicago Press, 1993); Hobsbawm, *Nations and Nationalism*.

17. Osterhammel, *The Transformation of the World*, 421; Burbank and Cooper, *Empires in World History*, 7–8, 413 (quotation).

18. John Breuilly, "Modern Empires and Nation States," *Thesis Eleven* 139, no. 1 (2017), 11–29, 19 (quotation).

19. Lauren Benton, *A Search for Sovereignty: Law and Geography in European Empires, 1400–1900* (New York: Cambridge University Press, 2009); Lisa Ford, *Settler Sovereignty: Jurisdiction and Indigenous People in America and Australia, 1788–1836* (Cambridge: Harvard University Press, 2010); Paul A. Kramer, "Power and Connection: Imperial Histories of the United States in the World," *American Historical Review* 116 (December 2011): 1356.

20. Sheehan, "The Problem of Sovereignty in European History," 3.

21. Heather Cox Richardson, *West from Appomattox: The Reconstruction of America after the Civil War* (New Haven: Yale University Press, 2007); Adam Arenson and Andrew Graybill, eds., *Civil War Wests: Testing the Limits of the United States* (Oakland: University of California Press, 2015); Ari Kelman, *A Misplaced Massacre: Struggling over the Memory of Sand Creek* (Cambridge: Cambridge University Press, 2013); Virginia Scharff, ed., *Empire and Liberty: The Civil War and the West* (Oakland: University of California Press, 2015); Stacey Smith, *Freedom's Frontier: California and the Struggle Over Unfree Labor, Emancipation, and Reconstruction* (Chapel Hill: University of North Carolina Press, 2013).

22. Alan Taylor, *American Revolutions: A Continental History, 1750–1804* (New York: Norton, 2016); Elizabeth A. Fenn, *Encounters at the Heart of the World: A History of the*

Mandan People (New York: Hill and Wang, 2014); Caitlin Fitz, *Our Sister Republics: The United States in an Age of American Revolutions* (New York: Norton, 2016); Kathleen Duval, *Independence Lost: Lives on the Edge of the American Revolution* (New York: Random House, 2015).

23. Steven Hahn, *A Nation Without Borders: The United States and the World in an Age of Civil Wars, 1830–1910* (New York: Penguin Random House, 2016), 270–316.

24. Hahn, *A Nation Without Borders*, 399, 517.

25. Gary B. Magee and Andrew S. Thompson, *Empire and Globalisation: Networks of People, Goods, and Capital in the British World, c. 1850–1914* (Cambridge: Cambridge University Press, 2010), 23.

26. Carl Bridge and Kent Fedorowich, eds., *The British World: Diaspora, Culture and Identity* (London: Frank Cass, 2003), 2; James Belich, *Replenishing the Earth: The Settler Revolution and the Rise of the Anglo-World, 1783–1939* (New York: Oxford University Press, 2009), chapter 5; John Darwin, *The Empire Project: The Rise and Fall of the British World System, 1830–1970* (New York: Cambridge University Press, 2009); Phillip Buckner and R. Douglas Francis, eds. *Canada and the British World: Culture, Migration, and Identity* (Vancouver: University of British Columbia Press, 2011).

27. Brian DeLay, "Indian Polities, Empire, and the History of American Foreign Relations," *Diplomatic History* 39, no. 5 (2015): 927–42, 935, 940.

28. Daniel K. Richter, *Facing East from Indian Country: A Native History of Early America* (Cambridge: Harvard University Press, 2001); Richard White, *The Middle Ground: Indians, Empires, and Republics in the Great Lakes Region, 1650–1815* (New York: Cambridge University Press, 1991); Pekka Hämäläinen, *Comanche Empire* (New Haven: Yale University Press, 2008); David Chang, *The World and All the Things Upon It: Native Hawaiian Geographies of Exploration* (Minneapolis: University of Minnesota Press, 2016).

29. Also see Doyle, *The Cause of All Nations*; Andre M. Fleche, *The Revolution of 1861: The American Civil War in the Age of Nationalist Conflict* (Chapel Hill: University of North Carolina Press, 2012); Patrick, J. Kelly, "The North American Crisis of the 1860s," *Journal of the Civil War Era* 2, no. 3 (September 2012): 337–68; Andrew Zimmerman, "From the Rhine to the Mississippi: Property, Democracy, and Socialism in the American Civil War," *Journal of the Civil War Era* 5, no. 1 (March 2015), 3–37.

30. Roger C. A. Maaka and Chris Andersen, *The Indigenous Experience: Global Perspectives* (Toronto: Canada Scholars' Press, 2006), 10.

31. Walter Hixson, *American Settler-Colonialism: A History* (New York: Palgrave MacMillan, 2013), 9.

32. Jack P. Greene, "Introduction: Empire and Liberty," in Jack P. Greene, ed., *Exclusionary Empire: English Liberty Overseas, 1600–1900* (New York: Cambridge University Press, 2010), 22. Also see Aziz Rana, *The Two Faces of American Freedom* (Cambridge: Harvard University Press, 2010).

33. Also see David G. McCrady, *Living with Strangers: The Nineteenth-Century Sioux and the Canadian-American Borderlands* (Lincoln: University of Nebraska Press, 2006); Brian DeLay, *War of a Thousand Deserts: Indian Raids and the U.S.-Mexican War* (New Haven: Yale University Press, 2008).

34. Melissa Macauley, "Entangled States: The Translocal Repercussions of Rural Pacification in China, 1869–1873," *American Historical Review* 121, no. 3 (2016), 758 (quotation).

35. Ramón Gutiérrez and Elliott Young, "Transnationalizing Borderlands History," *The Western Historical Quarterly* 41, no. 1 (Spring 2010): 26–53; Raul Ramos, "Chicano/a Challenges to Nineteenth Century History," *Pacific Historical Review* 82, no. 4 (November 2013): 566–80.

36. Pekka Hämäläinen and Samuel Truett, "On Borderlands," *The Journal of American History* 98, no. 2 (September 2011): 338–61, 340 (quotation); Jeremy Adelman and Stephen Aron, "From Borderlands to Borders: Empires, Nation-States, and the Peoples in Between in North American History," *The American Historical Review* 104, no. 3 (June 1999): 814–41, 840 (quotation).

37. Benjamin H. Johnson and Andrew R. Graybill, eds., *Bridging National Borders in North America: Transnational and Comparative Histories* (Durham, N.C.: Duke University Press, 2010); Rachel St. John, *Line in the Sand: A History of the Western U.S.-Mexico Border* (Princeton, N.J.: Princeton University Press, 2011).

38. Elliott West, "Reconstructing Race," *Western Historical Quarterly* 34 (Spring 2003): 7–26.

39. Benite, Geroulanos, and Jerr, eds., *The Scaffolding of Sovereignty*, 6.

40. Brian DeLay, "How Not to Arm a State: American Guns and the Crisis of Governance in Mexico, Nineteenth and Twenty-First Centuries," *Southern California Quarterly* 95, no. 1 (2013): 5–23; Sven Beckert, *Empire of Cotton: A Global History* (New York: Vintage Books, 2014); Jay Sexton, "Steam Transport, Sovereignty, and Empire in North America, 1850–1885," *The Journal of the Civil War Era* 7, no. 4 (December 2017): 620–47; Richard White, *The Republic for Which It Stands: The United States During Reconstruction and the Gilded Age, 1865–1896* (New York: Oxford University Press, 2017).

I

MAKING NATIONS

1   The United States from the Inside Out and the Southside North

Steven Hahn

Among the things that putatively sovereign states do, especially nation-states that claim a more extensive sovereign authority than their predecessors, is to construct a history that affirms their lineage and integrity, and deepens a sense of belonging among the citizens/subjects within their borders. This history usually owes to popular movements that helped bring them into being, and it is further elaborated by festivals and commemorations meant to establish origins, recognize important struggles and heroic figures, and celebrate triumphs. So powerful can these stories be that they are not only central to the framing of quotidian events but they also organize the making of formal—scholarly—historical narratives, which in turn become well entrenched. That professional history writing has accompanied the rise and consolidation of many nation-states is no accident; as self-designated architects of change and modernity, the bourgeoisie—whose project nation-state building usually is—sees history as its own validation.

In saying this, I'm not trying to suggest that professional historians are the mere acolytes and interpreters of nation builders—though they certainly have played these roles—but rather that we often work with a structure and language of analysis that the dynamics of nation and sovereignty make credible. In the United States, we tell the country's history—whatever our assessments of the whos and whys—mainly from the perspective of the Atlantic, the Northeast, and the nation-state, and we regard alternative geographies as "regions" or "peripheries," usually in some state of backwardness and crisis for which the "center" or the "core" is meant to provide the fix. The great dramas—especially the political dramas—of the nineteenth century are about the various challenges and obstacles to a national sovereignty, about competing sovereignties and their eventual defeats, whether they were slaveholding, Native American, Mormon, or some other.

It is true of course that over the last couple of decades, numbers of imaginative historians have attempted to confound these vectors and hierarchies of power:

Some, to borrow from Daniel Richter, have done so by "looking east from Indian country";[1] some have done so by exploring what have come to be known as "borderlands";[2] many have done so by studying localized episodes and developments that run against the hegemonic discourses and ambitions of the center.

Yet while these studies have complicated the narrative structure of American historical writing, it is not clear that they have offered the materials of an alternative. It is one thing to show that the struggle for power on the North American continent was far more massive and contingent than we had long assumed, or that the sovereign claims of the state were always far easier to proclaim than enact. But it is quite another to take the larger interpretive measure of these recognitions and to demonstrate what we really get by embracing them. "Borderlands" history, for example, has mostly been a feature of "Western" history and thereby reinforces the very conceptual hierarchies it hoped to dismantle.

Can we write the history of a country at least in good part from the perspective of what would become the "interior" or the "peripheries," or the "margins"; or even from outside of what would become its sovereign boundaries? Can we write a history of the United States—a sustained history of the United States—looking north from the South or east from the West, or from Canada or Mexico or the Caribbean? Can we write such a history, as is suggested a bit playfully in the title to this essay, "from the inside out and the southside north?" To be honest, I'm really not sure. It would be difficult and complicated for all sorts of reasons, some of which are obvious. And, perhaps, in the end it would not be all that useful. But in conceiving of such a history, we may also call into question many of our interpretive presumptions about the past. And that is a good thing.

Let's take a large issue such as the development of capitalism. There seems to be a good deal of agreement these days that the expansion of capitalism was a central force in the European settlement of the North American continent, especially in a broad crescent extending from the Chesapeake through the lower Mississippi Valley. There, slave plantations producing staple crops began to take hold in the late seventeenth and early eighteenth centuries—as they were also doing in the Caribbean—and in many ways drove the ramification of trade networks, the accumulation of capital, the commodification of the labor force, and, in some cases, the factory-like organization of agricultural operations. By the nineteenth century, according to recent accounts, cotton plantations of the Deep American South were not only fueling the economic growth of the entire country but also seemed to embody the very essence of capitalism itself.[3]

It was not very long ago that a lively debate took place among historians about these very issues: about the timing and reach of capitalist development in North America, about whether either the farming economies of New England and the Middle Atlantic, or the slave plantations of the Atlantic and Gulf coasts were to be regarded as capitalist in their productive relations or dynamics of exchange. Although it no longer seems to have much traction, this debate raised serious questions about what capitalism was and is (a system of production, of exchange, both), what sort of history it had, and how much it fed off and was possibly reshaped by alternative or antagonistic social formations. At the very least, it reminded us—as students of peasant societies have long known—that market exchanges and even long-distance trade can thrive in many different contexts, and that the development of capitalism encountered assorted obstacles and was beset with contingencies. Capitalism was not just a juggernaut steadily sweeping all before it.[4]

One of the reasons that we have pretty much abandoned a critical interrogation of capitalist development is the importance of what we have come to call "Atlantic history." There is, of course, much to recommend such a perspective. Atlantic history has taken the history of North America—and other parts of the hemisphere—out of the narrow frame in which it had long been encased, and placed it in an early-modern global setting of movement, contact, conquest, predation, and expansion. It is a large and capacious framework. The problem is that we effectively look out from the Atlantic, west in the case of North America, and generally consider what is being hatched in the Atlantic world as the dynamic and consequential part of the story—certainly for the long term. Because the Atlantic vibrated with powerful states, formidable mercantile and slaving communities that tapped the trade of four continents, and nodes of early industrial and proto-industrial enterprises, it is easy to see capitalism, at least in nascent form, washing across multiple shores. Indeed, it is quite logical to imagine the Atlantic itself as a creation of capitalism, and, given its many connections and bulwarks, as a force almost destined to transform all before it.

But what if we shift our vantage point from the Atlantic to the North American and hemispheric interior? What if we were to begin with the vast array of social formations already in motion: with their distinctive hierarchies, gender and labor relations, property regimes, political ambitions, and trading patterns? Here we might remember the challenges that Steve Stern for Latin America and Dipesh Chakrabarty for South Asia offered up some years ago, as they interrogated how the analytical categories of modernity that have framed the Euro-Atlantic world have in turn given shape to how we understand the process of development else-where—and, needless to say, they wonder seriously about them.[5] Here, too, we might think of John Tutino's book *Making a New World*, which finds the origins of capitalism not in England or continental Europe but in the sixteenth-century Mexico Bajio and in its silver trade with China—a connection Tom Bender has drawn our attention to as well.[6]

Thanks to the remarkable work of historians of North American Native socie-ties, we have an emerging picture of economically dynamic, politically aggressive, and ever-changing constellations of power. Agricultural, pastoral, equestrian—and, increasingly, combinations of these—Native peoples traded goods and cap-tives, raided over extensive territories, brought rivals to heel, created divisions of labor, produced hierarchies of their own based on forms of recognized wealth and status, and understood different types of use and property claims, not to mention their own ideas about time, space, and spirituality.[7] But, to my knowl-edge, no one suggests that these are to be seen as protean forms of capitalism, even as "middle grounds" of contact came into being (though Richard White in *Roots of Dependency* recognizes such a frame of reference).[8]

On the one hand, this ought to remind us of the complex world of production and exchange systems that capitalism was born into, giving the lie to the notion of linear developmental modes that, in one form or another, can be identified in classical political economy, Marxism, and modernization theory. On the other hand, for those interested in the development of capitalism in North America—and elsewhere—this implies large-scale and long-term struggle, rather than a se-ries of relatively brief and almost inevitable transitions. What Frederick Jackson Turner and the U.S. Census Bureau regarded as the end of the "frontier" in the 1890s might also, or more usefully, be understood as the point at which capi-talism completed its prolonged conquest of the continent, very much requiring interventions of all sorts on the part of a new nation-state.

Some of the same dis- and re-orientation would be in evidence if we took up yet another large issue: slavery. It is fair to say that the development of African-descended slave systems in the Western Hemisphere has been of central impor-tance in shaping how we have come to think of historical research and writing. Since the time of Eric Williams and Frank Tannenbaum, writing in the 1940s, the field has had many of the characteristics we associate with "cutting edge" scholar-ship of the present: It was transnational and comparative in its geographical per-spective. It was "Atlantic" in its many networks and contact points. It was taken up with the ways in which domination and race were constructed in different societies. And it was concerned with the relationship between the rise and fall of slave regimes and the advance of both capitalism and modern nation-states. In fact, it is arguable that the slavery literature of the 1940s, 1950s, and 1960s was much richer and more nuanced in these regards than it has been over the past decade or so.[9]

What's more, the study of African-descended slave systems not only provides us with geographies but also supplies important chronologies—indeed chronologies that have played critical roles in periodizing the past three or four centuries. One could say that the "problem of slavery" in its various phases has become one of the main principles that organizes our notions of the coming and meaning of modernity. What we call the "age of emancipation," stretching from the American and Haitian Revolutions on the one end to the abolition of slavery in Cuba and Brazil on the other, is perhaps the defining development of the Atlantic world in the nineteenth century, and closely tied in our telling to the building of new empires, the hegemony of liberal ideas, and the international extension of the capitalist economy. A good number of us have written many pages discussing what we see as the implications of this process.[10]

But what if we were to place African-descended slavery into a broader context of captive economies and forced labor regimes that spanned the hemisphere, from the Andes up through the Great Plains. These regimes underwent a variety of transformations from the time of European contact—and of course came to involve Europeans both as captors and captives. Like the slave systems with which we are most familiar, these involved the trade of captives and slaves, the exploitation of their labor for various services including the production of material goods, and their use as symbols of social prestige. Although it is very difficult to determine the numbers involved—and they obviously changed dramatically over time—the geographical expanse of what have been recognized as slave and captive "systems" was very considerable. At the same time, unlike African-descended slavery, these involved forms of adoption, intermarriage, and fictive kinship rituals that reconfigured the social and ethnic composition of Native bands and bore resemblance to the captive slave societies to be found in West and West Central Africa, as well as to some in the Indian Ocean world. The picture is, in fact, one of the Atlantic slave economies being surrounded by slaving and captive systems, a few with direct relations to it. What are we to make of this?[11]

And what of the chronologies? Needless to say, they are very different both as to origins and abolitions, although putting Native captive economies into the history of North American African-descended slavery not only stretches the age of emancipation but also emphasizes the imperial dimension that is attached to

it, but often overlooked: that is to say the ways in which colonialism and abolitionism would reinforce one another. The Thirteenth Amendment, it is worth
remembering, ended slavery not simply in the United States but in any territory
subject to "their jurisdiction," and the Andrew Johnson administration together
with the Republican-dominated Congress moved against Indian slavery and
debt-peonage, with which it had a complex connection. Even so, captive raiding
and trading continued for some time in the southwestern borderlands. European
colonial powers—the British, French, and Italians most notably—prided themselves on abolishing slavery on the African continent in the late nineteenth and
early twentieth centuries, much as the United States did in the Philippines during
its invasion and occupation there. At the very least, the rise and fall of slavery in
North America looks very different once the Native experience is included.[12]

The Atlanticist orientation of much United States history, at least through the
nineteenth century, has not only shaped our understanding of capitalist development and the slave system; it has also framed our interpretation of major political struggles that erupted. Consider, for example, the massive one that exploded
into the Civil War. Here we are accustomed to talking about "sectionalism," about
"North" and "South," about "slave" and "free" labor, plantations and family farming. Indeed, even though we know full well that the central issues eventuating in
the slaveholders' rebellion had to do with the fate of the trans-Mississippi West,
the West's role in the lead up to the war is largely as an imagined space to be filled
either by slaveholders or other white migrants. Then the West pretty much drops
out of our treatments of both the War and what we call Reconstruction.[13]
    Yet if we were to look at this problem from the inside out, from the interior
east and west, a different sense of what was at stake may in fact emerge. I'm
especially interested in the significance of the Mississippi Valley, not just as an
artery of trade and site of political influence, or as a region to be assimilated to
the sectional conflict as we have come to understand it, but as an entire developmental zone competing for continental, if not hemispheric, hegemony. Linking
Chicago, St. Louis, New Orleans, and possibly Havana—and by extension linking powerful real estate, merchandising, railroad, and slaveholding concerns—
the Mississippi Valley was, particularly for many Democrats, North and South,
the potential center of an agro-commercial empire that would expand into the
Caribbean basin as well as into the Southwest.[14]
    Deep South planters had an ambitious imperial vision both to secure and
extend slavery and the slave regime over which they presided. They spoke aggressively about annexing Cuba and taking hold of much of Mexico, and a few

cast their eyes toward Brazil either as a possible slaveholding ally or as a site of colonialism. Some hoped to re-open the African slave trade to help bring the vision into reality. As Secretary of War, Jefferson Davis went so far as to import North African camels to test their usefulness in transporting supplies in desert climates. New Orleans, its wharves stacked with cotton bales, was the staging ground for all sorts of imperial adventurism, from the Texas Revolution to the U.S.-Mexican War to filibustering expeditions to Cuba and Central America. This was the world that Deep South slaveholders wished to make.[15]

But the Deep South slaveholders were by no means alone. Stephen Douglas became one of their important allies, not because he supported the expansion of slavery per se but because the empire he imagined could accommodate different forms of labor and property relations. Although Lincoln's "house divided" warning best remains in our memories, Douglas mocked him for it and accused him of advocating "uniformity," of attempting to undermine what had been the source of American might and the likely future of hemispheric power.[16] The Mississippi River tapped the agricultural production of the American interior—raised by slave and free labor—that would feed and clothe the world. The plains of east-central Texas, as annexationists had insisted, would secure the dominance of American cotton on the international market. And New Orleans would emerge as the great port city of the Western Hemisphere. Until fairly late in the game, that is, it was the Mississippi Valley, not the "South," that vied with the Northeast for continental supremacy. And, had the war ended differently, it is conceivable that the Mississippi Valley could have become the pivot around which the country—or what was left of it—continued to turn.

Not surprisingly, Stephen Douglas championed the construction of the Illinois Central Railroad, planned to link the Gulf of Mexico to the Great Lakes by way of Chicago where, it should be said, he had substantial real estate investments. But the Illinois Central was, in Douglas's mind, part of a sprawling transportation network extending west to the Pacific and perhaps south to the Isthmus of Panama, securing what he called an "ocean bound republic."[17]

This brings us to the importance of the Pacific to the history of eighteenth- and nineteenth-century North America. The Pacific's importance is not readily apparent given the Atlantic framework that has governed the telling of early-ish North American history. But, in truth, much of the political and economic dynamic of this extended time period is lost without taking the Pacific—as goal, destiny, and gateway—into significant account. From the first days of the republic, power in the Pacific had been central to the continental ambitions of American leaders and policy-makers. Well aware of the thriving trade in east and south Asia—and of the intense jockeying between the British, French, Spanish, and Dutch—they saw the Pacific as a vast source of economic enrichment and the Pacific coast of North America as the door to its riches. New England merchants had been active in the ports of Asia and the Indian Ocean since the 1780s, involving themselves in the lucrative trade, disrupting the operations of the British East India Company, and accumulating capital, some of which would find its way into New England textile mills. By the late 1830s, whaling vessels from New Bedford, Nantucket, and Martha's Vineyard were busy in the northern Pacific, and Hawai'i was already showing the influence of the American Northeast. Jefferson's eyes were firmly on the Pacific when he issued instructions to the Lewis and Clark expedition, hoping to find waterways across the continent, and his views were shared by virtually all of his successors, especially those from John Quincy Adams to James K. Polk.[18]

The purchase of the Louisiana Territory, the annexation of Texas, and the invasion of Mexico during the 1840s—three of the signal political events of the nineteenth century—were driven in good part by the objective of gaining control of the harbors stretching from San Diego in the south to the Strait of Juan de Fuca to the north. So concerned was antislavery Senator William Seward that California be quickly brought into the Union as a state, thereby securing its ports, that he claimed to be ready, if necessary, even to accept the legality of slavery there. It was the New Yorker Seward who envisioned a new type of commercial empire, and when the defeat of Civil War–era rebellions in the South and West completed the continentalism he so desperately sought, he emerged as an architect of United States relations with Asia—in many ways anticipating the framework of the "Open Door"—that control over the Pacific coast made possible.[19]

In this regard and others, attempting to view the history of North America and the United States from the "inside out" and the "southside north" lends range and substance to battles we allude to but generally do not believe are very central to the nineteenth century, and enables us to make connections that have long been difficult to conceive. Rather than seeing a War of the Rebellion between 1861 and 1865, we may see "wars of the rebellions" (what we've come to call the Civil War certainly being the most consequential) over a more extended period, recognizing many challenges to the sovereignty that the federal government claimed. These include separatist movements in the lower Mississippi Valley and on the Canadian border; Native resistance to federal power and presumed authority; the Mormon "war" of the 1850s; and secessionist sentiment on the Pacific coast, in the Midwest, and in New York City. We may, as well, come to understand Reconstruction as a large state-building project that linked the South and the West and influenced the way historians would then write about the country's history.

An "inside out" and "southside north" perspective may also allow us to see that it was in the South and West that the patterns of development most important to nineteenth-century American capitalism were dramatically in evidence, that there the nation-state best revealed its imperial dispositions, and that there the most determined and enduring oppositional movements had their bases. And looking further to the inside and the south, we may even see that it was in the great Mexican Revolution—mostly ignored by scholars of the United States— that the long nineteenth century first gave way to the twentieth.

Notes

1. Daniel Richter, *Facing East from Indian Country: A Native History of Early America* (Cambridge: Harvard University Press, 2003).

2. See, for example, Stephen Aron, *American Confluence: The Missouri Frontier from Borderland to Border State* (Bloomington: Indiana University Press, 2009); Andrés Reséndez, *Changing National Identities at the Frontier: Texas and New Mexico, 1800–1850* (New York: Cambridge University Press, 2004); Andrew J. Torget, *Seeds of Empire: Cotton, Slavery, and the Transformation of the Texas Borderlands* (Chapel Hill: University of North Carolina Press, 2015); Samuel Truett, *Fugitive Landscapes: The Forgotten History of the U.S.-Mexico Borderlands* (New Haven: Yale University Press, 2008).

3. See Edward Baptist, *The Half Has Never Been Told: Slavery and the Making of American Capitalism* (New York: Basic Books, 2014); Sven Beckert, *Empire of Cotton: A Global History* (New York: Knopf, 2015); Seth Rockman, *Scraping By: Wage Labor, Slavery, and Survival in Early Baltimore* (Baltimore: Johns Hopkins University Press, 2009); Sven Beckert and Seth Rockman, eds., *Slavery's Capitalism: A New History of American Economic Development* (Philadelphia: University of Pennsylvania Press, 2016).

4. See, for example, Eugene D. Genovese, *The Political Economy of Slavery: Studies in the Economy and Society of the Slave South* (New York: Pantheon Books, 1965); Christopher Clark, *The Roots of Rural Capitalism: Western Massachusetts, 1780–1860* (Ithaca: Cornell University Press, 1992); Allan Kulikoff, *The Agrarian Origins of American Capitalism* (Charlottesville: University of Virginia Press, 1992); James A. Henretta, *The Origins of Capitalism: Collected Essays* (Boston: Northeastern University Press, 1991); Steven Hahn and Jonathan Prude, eds., *The Countryside in the Age of Capitalist Transformation: Essays in the Social History of Rural America* (Chapel Hill: University of North Carolina Press, 1985). More recently, see Daniel Richter's, *Before the Revolution: America's Ancient Pasts* (Cambridge: Harvard University Press, 2013).

5. Steve J. Stern, "Feudalism, Capitalism, and the World System in the Perspective of Latin America and the Caribbean," *American Historical Review* 93 (October 1988): 829–72; Dipesh Chakrabarty, *Provincializing Europe: Postcolonial Thought and Historical Difference* (Princeton: Princeton University Press, 2007).

6. John Tutino, *Making a New World: Founding Capitalism in the Bajío and Spanish North America* (Durham, N.C.: Duke University Press, 2011); Thomas Bender, *A Nation Among Nations: America's Place in World History* (New York: Hill and Wang, 2006), 28–33. While I do not find Tutino's account convincing, I do find it thought-provoking.

7. Pekka Hämäläinen, *The Comanche Empire* (New Haven: Yale University Press, 2009); James F. Brooks, *Captives and Cousins: Slavery, Kinship, and Community in the Southwest Borderlands* (Chapel Hill: University of North Carolina Press, 2002); Brian DeLay, *War of a Thousand Deserts: Indian Raids and the U.S.-Mexican War* (New Haven: Yale University Press, 2008); Ned Blackhawk, *Violence Over the Land: Indians and Empires in the Early American West* (Cambridge: Harvard University Press, 2006).

8. Richard White, *Roots of Dependency: Subsistence, Environment, and Social Change Among the Choctaws, Pawnees, and Navajos* (Lincoln: University of Nebraska Press, 1988); Richard White, *The Middle Ground: Indians, Empires, and Republics in the Great Lakes Region, 1650–1815* (New York: Cambridge University Press, 1991).

9. See Eric Williams, *Capitalism and Slavery* (Chapel Hill: University of North Carolina Press, 1944); Frank Tannenbaum, *Slave and Citizen: The Negro in the Americas* (New York: Vintage Books, 1946).

10. The work of David Brion Davis has been central to the construction of this framework. See his *The Problem of Slavery in Western Culture* (Ithaca: Cornell University Press, 1967); *The Problem of Slavery in the Age of Revolution, 1770–1823* (Ithaca: Cornell University Press, 1975); *The Problem of Slavery in the Age of Emancipation* (New York: Knopf, 2014); Christopher Brown, *Moral Capital: Foundations of British Abolitionism* (Chapel Hill: University of North Carolina Press, 2006).

11. See especially Andrés Reséndez, *The Other Slavery: The Uncovered Story of Indian Enslavement in America* (Boston: Houghton Mifflin Harcourt, 2016).

12. Reséndez, *The Other Slavery*, 241–321; Michael Salman, *The Embarrassment of Slavery: Controversies over Bondage and Nationalism in the American Colonial Philippines* (Berkeley: University of California Press, 2001).

13. The limits of this perspective have been increasingly apparent to scholars and important new work is underway. See Adam Arenson and Andrew Graybill, eds., *Civil War Wests: Testing the Limits of the United States* (Berkeley: University of California, 2015); Virginia A. Scharff, ed., *Empire and Liberty: The Civil War and the West* (Berkeley: University of California, 2015); Stacy L. Smith, *Freedom's Frontier: California and the Struggle Over Unfree Labor, Emancipation, and Reconstruction* (Chapel Hill: University of North Carolina Press, 2013); Kevin Waite, "Jefferson Davis and Proslavery Visions of the Far West," *Journal of the Civil War Era* 6, no. 3 (Fall 2016).

14. I develop this argument in *A Nation without Borders: The United States and Its World in an Age of Civil Wars, 1830–1910* (New York: Viking, 2016).

15. See especially Matthew Karp, *This Vast Southern Empire: Slaveholders at the Helm of American Foreign Policy* (Cambridge: Harvard University Press, 2016); Robert May, *The Southern Dream of a Caribbean Empire* (Baton Rouge: Louisiana University Press, 1973); Walter Johnson, *River of Dark Dreams: Slavery and Empire in the Cotton Kingdom* (Cambridge: Harvard University Press, 2013); Robert E. May, *Slavery, Race, and Conquest in the Tropics: Lincoln, Douglas, and the Future of Latin America* (New York, 2013).

16. Readers would do well to re-examine the Lincoln-Douglas debate on this account, overlooked as this matter usually is.

17. Robert W. Johannsen, *Stephen A. Douglas* (New York: Cambridge University Press, 1973).

18. James R. Fichter, *So Great a Proffit: How the East Indies Trade Transformed Anglo-American Capitalism* (Cambridge: Harvard University Press, 2010); David Igler, *The Great Ocean: Pacific Worlds from Captain Cook to the Gold Rush* (New York: Oxford University Press, 2013); Nicholas Thomas, *Islanders: The Pacific in the Age of Empire* (New Haven: Yale University Press, 2011).

19. E. N. Paolino, *Foundations of the American Empire: William Henry Seward and United States Foreign Policy* (Ithaca: Cornell University Press, 1973).

2

Confederation as a Hemispheric Anomaly

Why Canada Chose a Unique Model of Sovereignty in the 1860s

Andrew Smith

In the early 1770s, virtually all of the Western Hemisphere was subject to or claimed by a European sovereign.[1] The Atlantic Revolutions that began in the Thirteen Colonies in the 1770s swept away this system of sovereignty.[2] By the 1860s, the British North American colonies were a hemispheric anomaly in the sense that they were the only large regions of the American mainland that were still part of a European colonial empire. In other words, the model of sovereignty in place in present-day Canada was distinctive among the large countries of the hemisphere. As has been demonstrated elsewhere, the federation of the British North American colonies between 1867 and 1873 was intended to preserve this rather unusual status.[3] In an earlier monograph, the author advanced an essentially economic explanation for why Canadians opted to remain part of the British Empire.[4] This approach was designed to address a gap in the classic works on Confederation, which had focused on high politics and tended to downplay corporate interests.[5] This essay supplements my earlier economic explanation by integrating culture and race into the analysis. I will suggest that in explaining why the political classes of British North America chose not to establish a fully sovereign state in the 1860s, we need to consider developments elsewhere in the Americas.

The hemispheric approach adopted here has several key elements. First, it is comparative and seeks to understand the experience of present-day Canada in light of parallel developments in other Western Hemisphere countries. Second, it is interested in the connections between Canada and these countries. In this sense, it is similar in spirit to Caitlin Fitz's new book, *Sister Republics*, which shows that many in the nineteenth-century United States paid close attention to and felt a strong sense of affinity with the nations of Latin America.[6] There were substantial trade ties between present-day Canada and Latin America and even an attempt, in 1866, to negotiate a free trade agreement linking British North America and the other monarchical territories of the western hemisphere.[7]

Moreover, as is shown later in the chapter, Canadians in the 1860s were aware of political developments in Latin America and referenced them in the Canadian constitutional debates of that decade. Because many Canadians in the 1860s adopted a hemispheric approach, it behooves the historians who study them to follow suit. Third, the hemispheric approach developed here involves highlighting race and class. Recent comparative research on the century after the Atlantic Revolutions suggests that the politics of nation building in many Western Hemisphere countries was connected to the question of how far to apply the "contagious" ideas of liberty and equality, which had originally been used by white colonial elites opposed to the policies of European monarchies, to other ethnic and socio-economic groups.[8] In the United States, Brazil, Cuba, Mexico, Argentina, and other New World countries in the nineteenth century, a central issue was whether poor whites and the descendants of Africans and Amerindians were to be considered full citizens, or indeed citizens at all.[9] This dynamic was the common denominator linking the politics of nation building in these countries. If we accept that the centrality of such struggles to political life was a common experience for New World societies, it is logical to integrate race and class into our hemispheric approach. This chapter attempts to do so for present-day Canada.

In the last two decades, many Canadian historians have enthusiastically adopted a British World perspective. This approach to historical writing emphasizes Canada's links to, and close identification with, the British Empire, and has resulted in the publication of a number of important works that either compare the experience of Canada with that of Australia and New Zealand or examine relations between Canada and these countries as well as Britain.[10] The British-World approach is certainly helpful in understanding many aspects of Canadian history. Indeed, the present author has applied the British World approach in research published in history and political-science journals.[11] However, to achieve a more comprehensive understanding of the motives of the creators of the Canadian constitution of 1867, we must place British North America in the 1860s in a hemispheric context as well as in a British imperial one. Doing so helps to explain why the creators of the 1867 constitution opted for a model of layered sovereignty that fell well short of full independence and which involved Canada's continued membership in the British Empire.

Sovereignty

The definition of "sovereignty" has been contested by scholars working in law, international relations, and other disciplines.[12] For Canadians who grew up in the late twentieth century, the word acquired a particular set of associations because advocates of Quebec independence labeled their preferred constitutional order as "sovereignty" or "sovereignty-association" rather than the less ambiguous term "independence."[13] The working definition of sovereignty adopted in this chapter is: "a normative conception that links authority, territory (population, society) and recognition" in international society.[14] Sovereignty, in this definition, relates to both internal sovereignty (control over subjects and a monopoly over the legitimate use of force) and external sovereignty and the juridical personhood of the state in the eyes of the international community.[15] It is worthwhile making several observations about sovereignty. First, the concept of sovereignty is relatively novel in Western political thought and only slowly diffused from Europe to the rest of the world. As David Armitage's global history of the U.S. Declaration of Independence has demonstrated, the global adoption of this norm was slow, and many nineteenth-century people remained satisfied with governance systems in which sovereignty was amorphous and shared. Second, sovereignty is a matter of degrees, not absolutes, as the legal histories of the British Empire-Commonwealth and, more recently, the European Union, have demonstrated.[16] Third, we must avoid the trap of thinking that sovereignty is necessarily normative, an idea that is promoted by nationalists of various types, not to mention advocates of "economic sovereignty," "tribal sovereignty," "American exceptionalism," and, more recently, British withdrawal from the European Union. The fact that many political actors throughout history and in the present have been satisfied with governance systems that involve layered or quasi-sovereignty helps us to understand why the creators of the Canadian constitution of 1867 did not believe it was desirable for the new nation to have external sovereignty.

The Canadian constitution of 1867, which was an act of the British parliament, produced a state that was quasi-sovereign in that it possessed a degree of internal sovereignty while not yet enjoying juridical personhood in the eyes of the international community.[17] In 1865, a Canadian politician accurately described the powers of the British parliament over the colonies, remarking that is has "sovereign and uncontrollable authority in making, confining, enlarging, restraining, repealing, revising and expounding of laws."[18] Somewhat confusingly, British North Americans in the constitutional moment of the 1860s referred to both the tripartite British parliament and the person of Queen Victoria as the "sovereign" power in the empire. This confusion stemmed from the common practice of referring to monarchs as "sovereigns," even though only the King/Queen-in-Parliament has been sovereign since 1688.[19]

Regardless of this terminological confusion, most Canadian legislators agreed that the state of affairs whereby ultimate sovereignty (that is, the right to alter the constitution) lay (somewhere) in London should continue. When a politician declared during the debates on Confederation that "our first act should have been to recognize the sovereignty of Her Majesty" he was cheered by his fellow legislators.[20] When discussing the division of powers between the future federal and provincial governments, the prevailing view was that most sovereign powers should be exercised by the national government: The U.S. system of states' rights and state sovereignty should be avoided at all costs.[21] During the debates on the proposed constitution, one legislator opined that the future federal government should be "armed with a sovereignty which may be worthy of the name." He remarked that "all good governments . . . have somewhere a true sovereign power. A sovereign which ever eludes your grasp, which has no local habitation, provincial or imperial, is in fact no government at all."[22] Sovereignty, strong government, and centralization were linked in the eyes of most of the creators of the 1867 constitution. The creators of the 1867 constitution rejected the idea of popular sovereignty,[23] which is one of the reasons the proposed union of the colonies was not put to the electorate in referenda, in sharp contrast to the practice adopted prior to the federation of the Australian colonies a generation later.[24]

Sovereignty and Canadian Constitutional Politics in the 1860s

Had British North Americans expressed a clear preference for independence in the 1860s, the British parliament almost certainly would have granted this request, thereby terminating its sovereignty over northern North America. In 1837–38, British troops had brutally crushed a republican rebellion in Lower Canada just as they had earlier tried to crush the American Revolution and would subsequently crush anti-British risings in India and elsewhere. Then, in the 1840s, the British gave internal home rule ("Responsible Government") to their colonies of white settlement in North America and Australasia.[25] By the 1860s, Britain had abandoned any notion of holding on to her remaining North American colonies by force. Indeed, a sizeable proportion of the British political class now thought that continued British sovereignty over the country's North American colonies was a net burden for the British taxpayer.[26] Indeed, some of the more strident "Little Englanders" in Britain believed that Canada and other costly overseas possessions should be forced to be independent.[27] These individuals, who had a low-tax limited-government ideology similar to that of present-day

U.S. libertarians, actually had some influence over the course of British government policy in the 1860s. In 1864, for instance, Britain actually gave up control
of an overseas territory over the objections of its inhabitants: In that year, the
British handed the United States of the Ionian Islands over to the Greek government, which promptly incorporated this territory into the Kingdom of Greece.[28]
The Little Englanders were a sizeable minority within the Liberal governments
led by Palmerston (1859–64) and Gladstone (1868–74).[29] Moreover, most of the
leading Conservative and Liberal politicians in Britain in the 1860s declared that
the North American colonies could become independent, albeit only if they so
wished. In 1865, a British government lawyer named Henry Thring even went so
far as to draft a statute that would have granted independence to any colony of
white settlement in which the elected legislature had passed two successive resolutions requesting it.[30] Unfortunately, for Britain's Little Englanders, the people
of British North America, or at least the articulate political classes of the region,
were generally opposed to leaving the British Empire and Thring's bill was never
passed, let alone used. In the face of British North American opposition to becoming fully independent, the British felt compelled to retain a degree of sovereignty over these territories. As the *Edinburgh Review*, an influential journal, put
it: "Retainers who will neither give nor accept notice to quit our service must, it
is assumed, be kept on our establishment."[31]

As has been shown in other publications, the federation of the British North
America colonies in the 1860s was intended as a means of keeping the colonies British.[32] That the intention of the creators of the 1867 constitution was to
strengthen rather than to diminish the colonies' ties to Britain is suggested by
the arrangement of the Quebec Resolutions of 1864, which were a draft outline
of the constitution of 1867. The very first of these resolutions declared the delegates' belief that the "present and future prosperity of British North America will
be promoted by a Federal Union under the Crown of Great Britain." The third
resolution stated that "in framing a Constitution" the delegates' decision-making
had been shaped by their wish to perpetuate the connection with the mother
country and to replicate her political institutions "so far as our circumstances
will permit."[33] At an October 1864 banquet given to honor the drafters of these
resolutions, a local merchant named Abraham Joseph, saluted the loyalty of the
delegates to the Empire. Joseph declared that the merchants of Quebec City, "desired a union under one flag and that flag the good flag of old England. (Cheers)."
Joseph, it should be noted, was a Sephardic Jew and his loyalty to the mother
country demonstrates that Britishness in the Canada of the 1860s could be an
inclusive civic nationalist identity, an issue discussed later in the chapter.[34]

Observers in the United States agreed that the federal constitution drafted at the 1864 Quebec City conference was a measure that would help to keep Canada in the Empire.[35] The *New-York Tribune* condemned the delegates in Quebec City for their "submissiveness" to England, noting that they had been "very anxious to affirm their loyalty to the British Crown."[36] Some in the United States saw the proposed federation of the North American colonies as a threat to America's republican institutions. For instance, the *New York Herald* denounced England for planning to foist a Brazilian-style hereditary viceroy on the poor people of British North America.[37] The *New York Times* also recognized that the promoters of Confederation wished to draw closer to Britain, although it sneered that "the 'monarchical principles' on which it is ostensibly said that the new Federation is to be based" did not extend so far as to induce Canadians to pay for a large standing army in peacetime.[38] The *Advertiser*, a newspaper in the border town of Calais, Maine, regarded the plan to federate British North America as unimportant because it would involve no change to the colonial status of the provinces. It remarked that the colonists "do not propose to separate themselves from Great Britain. If they did the movement would be one of great significance. And so long as they remain as Provinces it is of not the slightest political consequence whether they unite or remain separate."[39]

Monarchism and Canadian Political Culture in a Hemispheric Perspective

Most contemporaries recognized that the aim of Confederation was to keep the colonies within the British Empire. Canadians' evident loyalty to the Crown was driven, in part, by a belief in the benefits of monarchical political institutions over their republican alternatives. This belief that blended constitutions that included monarchical institutions were generally superior was seen in the ideas of Thomas D'Arcy McGee. In the 1840s, he had participated in an armed uprising that sought to create a sovereign Irish republic.[40] He became a fervent advocate of the British connection after arriving in Montreal. In the 1860s, McGee waxed poetic on the great blessings British sovereignty had brought to Canada. Given that the republican experiment that had begun in 1776 was being severely tested at this time, McGee's argument resonated with many of Queen Victoria's subjects in northern North America.[41] In 1863, he proposed a permanent viceroy for Canada on the Brazilian model, suggesting that one of Queen Victoria's younger sons should become Canada's king.[42] McGee's decision to use Brazil as a constitutional model shows that at least some Canadians in the 1860s were thinking in hemispheric terms. In speeches in the Canadian parliament, McGee denounced

the republican institutions of the United States and proclaimed his preference for
the ancient establishment of monarchy. In 1858, he declared that "my native dis-
position is reverence towards things old and veneration for the landmarks of the
past." He explained away his flirtation with republicanism as due to the excesses
of British rule in Ireland. He also declared that he was "as loyal to the institutions
under which I live in Canada as any Tory of the old or the new school."[43]

McGee believed that without the stabilizing forces of monarchy and active
government, New World societies would inevitably degenerate into anarchy
as individuals in the Western Hemisphere lacked the customary and legal re-
straints common in the more hierarchical societies of Europe. In his 1865 book
on federal government, he observed that the people of Canada, "like all other
American communities (when compared with European countries) have necessarily very decided democratic tendencies within them." By democracy, McGee
meant an unruly mob. It was, he said, the task of the present generation of British North Americans to see that "authority is exalted" and that the best way of
doing so was to strengthen the power of the central executive in any future British North American federation. "Executive impotency" should be avoided. Although McGee conceded that the U.S. Constitution of 1789 was "a vast advance
on the previous Articles of Confederation" it nevertheless provided for too weak
a government due to the compromises nationalist statesman such as Alexander
Hamilton had been forced to make with "state jealousy" and the "wild theories of
the demagogues of the day," by which he meant Thomas Jefferson. Again adopting a hemispheric frame of reference, McGee regarded the Empire of Brazil as
perhaps the best-governed nation in the hemisphere, attributing that country's
relative peace and stability to its monarchical institutions.[44] The fact the Brazil's
prosperity was based on slavery went unmentioned by both McGee and by the
British North American politicians who visited that country in early 1866 on a
trade mission.[45] Like many British North Americans, they were largely indiffer-
ent to the question of the rights of people of African descent and the struggles
then underway throughout the hemisphere about those rights

Evidence for Popular Support for Remaining Within the British Empire

Elite opinion in British North America in the 1860s was generally hostile to the
idea of a complete break with Britain. It is hard to assess with a high degree of
certainty the extent to which this attitude was shared by non-elite Canadians
(for example, farmers, lumberjacks, petty traders, and members of the emerging urban working class), as methodical public opinion polling did not reach

Canada until the 1930s. However, as far as we can tell, most ordinary colonists shared the elite's belief that remaining in the British Empire was normative. On the eve of the 1864 constitutional convention in Quebec City, reporter Charles MacKay assessed colonial attitudes to the British connection for the readers of the *Times of London*. He said that of the three basic options open to the colonists (for example, joining the United States, becoming an independent republic, or remaining within the Empire), the vast majority of Canadians favored the latter. MacKay based this statement on conversations he had had all over the Province of Canada. In the course of a 1,200 mile journey through the colony, he had "interchanged ideas" on this issue with men at all levels of society, from stagecoach drivers and farmers to merchants and "members of the legislature of every political party." MacKay said that the desire to remain British subjects was shared by French Canadians, descendants of the old United Empire Loyalists, and more recent immigrants from the British Isles, the three main groups in the Canadian electorate. MacKay summed up the situation: "Canadian loyalty is not a thing of light account."[46] The English novelist Anthony Trollope observed in 1862 that "the loyalty of both the Canadas to Great Britain is beyond all question."[47] A newspaper in Glasgow came to similar conclusions in 1865: "Mr. Howe, Lord Monck, the members of the Canadian Ministry who lately visited this country, every politician, traveller, or journalist of the slightest note, concur in stating that the people of British North America are almost without exception loyal to their Queen."[48]

In an address to the Mechanics' Institute in New Brunswick, Nova Scotia's Charles Tupper said that "the day has long since passed when the idea of annexation to our republican neighbours, or of the formation of an independent republic, was entertained by any portion of these provinces."[49] Individuals in all regions of British North America expressed annoyance when British people discussed the utility of forcing the colonies to leave the British Empire. Thomas Gladwin Hurd of Toronto sent an acerbic letter to a London newspaper to remind it of the many donations to British patriotic funds that had been remitted from Canada: "I do trust when English journals discuss matters colonial, especially Canadian, they will remember that we too are Englishmen. The Irish famine, the Crimean War, the Indian mutiny, attest our loyalty. Any national calamity and our purse was opened."[50] In Hurd's eyes, colonial donations to British patriotic funds demonstrated that the people of the colonies were *bona fide* "Englishmen," a term he carelessly used, like so many contemporaries, to denote any British subject.[51] Although he did not mention it, Canadians had also formed a regiment to help suppress the recent uprising against British rule in India.[52]

Identification with Britain was, of course, stronger in some localities than in others. Richard Cartwright, a politician first elected to the Canadian parliament in 1863, discussed this issue in his memoirs. He recalled that attitudes toward the United States had been much more positive in western Upper Canada than in the old United Empire Loyalist settlements along the Saint Lawrence River. In his parliamentary constituency, Lennox and Addington, many voters were the grandsons of the pro-British refugees who left the Thirteen Colonies during the American Revolution. In such communities, there was a strong sense of loyalty to Britain. Cartwright's own grandfather was one of these refugees. In regions of Canada that were settled in the nineteenth century, the political culture was quite different: Cartwright recollected that when a business trip took him to the area west of Toronto in 1856, he had been surprised and even "disgusted" by the widespread "sentiment in favour of union with the United States."[53] Many farmers and others in that region thought that joining the United States would bring prosperity.

Opposition to the Prevailing Desire to Remain Within the British Empire

While it appears that a majority of British North Americans wished to remain part of the British Empire, there was nevertheless substantial dissent from this view. Some wished to become part of the United States, the Great Republic. Others wished to form an independent Canadian republic, an option that would have brought Canada into line with the many small independent republics that had emerged out of Spain's empire in the western hemisphere. Advocates of the latter option had few allies outside of Canada. However, those Canadians who favored so-called "continental union" had allies in Washington, at least for a brief period in the 1860s.

For context, it should be remembered that in the late 1840s, a large section of the English-speaking business community in Montreal had signed a petition that had called for Canada to become a U.S. state. This petition was also supported by Louis-Joseph Papineau, who had led Lower Canada's failed republican rising in 1837–38.[54] The wave of Annexationist sentiment represented by the Manifesto had largely dissipated by the end of 1850, in part because the United States government made it very clear that it was unwilling to consider annexing Canada. The United States had just conquered much of Mexico and was too busy consolidating its rule there to undertake northward expansion as well. Moreover, Washington was unwilling to consider admitting northern territories that would upset the delicate Congressional balance between slave and free states. Southern congressmen were downright hostile to the proposed annexation of Canada.[55] This deadlock persisted throughout the 1850s, when the southern-dominated Democratic Party controlled the White House and the Senate.

In the aftermath of the election of Abraham Lincoln, a Republican, in November 1860, many southern states left the Union and recalled their congressional representatives. This change in the sectional balance in the Senate allowed for the issue of the acquisition of Canada to be re-opened. In January 1861, as state after state in the Lower South announced its secession, the *New York Herald* proposed that the northern states let the South depart in peace and instead concentrate on annexing British North America as compensation. The editor of the *Herald*, who had once lived in the North American colonies, reasoned that a union between the free-soil states and the slavery-free British provinces would be a more natural one than the former union between North and the slave-holding South.[56]

Some senior Republicans supported this idea. Lincoln's Secretary of State, William Henry Seward, proposed the annexation of Canada in a confidential memorandum for the President in early April 1861, shortly before the first shots of the Civil War were fired at Fort Sumter.[57] Seward, who was from New York State, had first advocated the peaceful acquisition of Canada in an 1857.[58] In 1857, he had condemned the Southerners' opposition to annexing Canada, declaring that it would have been better had the United States expanded northward into British America rather than southward into Mexico. Speaking of his recent tour of Canada and Labrador, he said that he had found the "inhabitants vigorous, hardy, energetic, perfected by the Protestant religion and British constitutional liberty." Seward condemned the current policy of the Democratic administration, which involved "spurning vigorous, perennial, and ever growing Canada while seeking to establish feeble states out of decaying Spanish provinces on the coast and in the islands of the Gulf of Mexico."[59] He was alluding to the faction of the Democratic Party that then supported filibustering expeditions and other measures designed to bring Caribbean basin territories into the United States as slave states.[60] Campaigning for Lincoln in Minnesota in September 1860, Seward had praised the rapid economic progress of the British North American colonies, declaring that their "enlightened" governments were "building excellent States to be hereafter admitted into the American Union."[61]

The start of the Civil War in 1861 put the issue of northward expansion on hold. Few Canadians wished to join a country that was racked by civil war. After the surrender of the Confederacy in April 1865, Canadian interest in annexation quickly revived, due in part to Washington's announcement of its intention to abrogate the 1854 Reciprocity Treaty, which had given colonial natural products duty-free entry into the Republic. In the summer and autumn of 1865, there was a lively debate in Canada on the advisability of joining the United States. The *Montreal Trade Review* observed that a rapid change in Canadian thinking about Annexation had taken place since the capture of the Confederate capital of Richmond in March: "What was three months ago regarded as rank disloyalty is now the most frequent topic of discussion and advocacy."[62] In 1865, the *Globe* attacked two other newspapers in Upper Canada, the *Galt Reporter* and the *St. Catharines Post*, for supporting Annexation on the grounds it would improve local economic conditions. In an editorial written in response to a piece in the *Galt Reporter*, the *Globe* stated that it was a fallacy to suppose that Confederation, Annexation, or any other constitutional change would restore prosperity. The *Globe* said that the previous autumn's poor harvest would have been bad under any political system. It compared the Galt newspaper to a "quack" doctor selling a cure-all pill.[63]

Observers in the United States agreed that the sudden wave of Canadian interest in joining the United States was driven by purely economic considerations. A Maine newspaper said in August 1865 that economic considerations would eventually force the colonists into the United States: "It is self-interest, and that alone, which will decide the question."[64] In August 1865, the *Philadelphia North American* noted that a number of "subjects of Her Majesty" had come out in favor of the scheme.[65] The *Milwaukee Daily Sentinel*, which thought that Rupert's Land should be joined to the United States, published a letter from a correspondent in Hamilton, Upper Canada who ridiculed the *Globe's* claims that there were no Annexationists in Canada. He wrote that were Queen Victoria to "travel incognito through our fair western provinces," she would find that many of her subjects leaned in the direction of Annexation, "notwithstanding a great deal of affection and respect for herself."[66]

The discussion of "continental union" was encouraged by John F. Potter, the United States Consul-General in Montreal. In 1866, the Massachusetts Congressman Nathaniel P. Banks introduced a bill to provide for the admission of the eastern British North American colonies as states, each with two senators. According to this bill, Rupert's Land was to be given the status of a territory similar to Dakota.[67] Congressman Banks does not appear to have regarded the incorporation of a predominantly French-speaking territory (Lower Canada) into the United States as problematic, an attitude that can be related to his earlier experiences as military governor of Louisiana, a state in which linguistic politics had become connected with the racial politics of Reconstruction during the 1864 state constitutional convention.[68]

Historian Joe Patterson Smith maintains that the strongest proponents of annexing Canada were Radical Republicans and that their interest in Canada was connected to their ongoing struggle with President Andrew Johnson over Southern Reconstruction. The Radical Republicans favored a prolonged military occupation and the far-reaching restructuring of southern society so as to improve the position of African Americans. They came into conflict with Johnson, the profoundly racist Tennessee Democrat who had inherited the White House after Lincoln's assassination. Johnson wanted to end the military occupation of the South, rehabilitate the former rebels quickly, and give the plantations back to their old owners, minus the slaves. The conflict between these two agendas came to a head in 1868, when the Radical Republicans impeached Johnson.[69] According to Smith, a number of the Radical Republicans thought that the Annexation of the British provinces would strengthen their political power by adding to the number of non-Southern states in Congress. This was certainly the reasoning of Joseph Medill, the Canadian-born editor of the *Chicago Tribune*.[70]

A few businessmen in Canada, most notably Orrin S. Wood, the chief executive of the dominant telegraph firm, endorsed the continental union concept. He was fired by the firm's board of directors for publicly advocating Canada's peaceful incorporation into the United States.[71] Many of the Canadians who opposed Canada's continued membership in the British Empire were trade unionists or self-described socialists who opposed the power of the bourgeoisie. In 1864, the labor activist T. Phillips Thompson proposed that the British North American colonies unite under a republican constitution. Thompson did not want the British North American colonies to become part of the United States, and instead envisioned a separate sovereign nation freed of the entanglements of the British Empire. Thompson took issue with Thomas D'Arcy McGee's view that Canada could become sovereign while still remaining part of the British Empire and subject to the jurisdiction of the imperial parliament. McGee had argued that the North American colonies "should advance to sovereignty" as the "youth should grow to manhood, but there is not inevitable inference to be drawn that sovereignty should include separation." McGee had given the Holy Roman Empire as an example of an institution that combined sovereignty with close ties. Thompson regarded McGee's vision of the constitutional future as quixotic.[72]

Thompson appears to have thought that his vision of a just and egalitarian society required the attainment of full sovereignty by the people of British North America and republican political institutions. The chief problem with monarchy, he felt, was that it was linked to aristocracy and inequality more generally.

Thompson regarded the various recent proposals for the creation of a Canadian order of nobility as highly undesirable, observing that "already we have too much of the aristocratic feeling" and Canada's elites looked down on "the farmer and the mechanic." In his view, it should be "our aim to repress rather than encourage this feeling, which the establishment of an aristocracy would assuredly tend to strengthen and develop."[73] As did his opponent McGee, Thompson adopted a hemispheric frame of reference, doing so when he noted that in addition to being the only monarchy in South America, Brazil was the sole nation on that continent that still permitted slavery.[74] Thompson stressed that he favored a union of the British North American colonies but insisted that it have a republican form of government, not a hereditary head of state.

In the 1860s, one of the leading proponents of Canada's incorporation into the United States was Médéric Lanctot, a French Canadian socialist. Lanctot was born in 1838, shortly after his father was transported to Australia for his participation in the 1837–38 Rebellion in Lower Canada. When Lanctot senior returned from his exile in 1845, he inculcated republicanism and hatred of the British Empire in his son. In the late 1850s, Médéric became a member of the *Institut Canadien*, an organization that was condemned by the Catholic Church as a nest of radical free thinkers because it had books on the Index in its library. In 1862, he traveled to Paris, where he immersed himself in the radical political movements that would later help to establish the short-lived Paris Commune. After 1864, Lanctot devoted himself to two causes: fighting the proposed Confederation of British North America and campaigning against Big Business. In 1867, Lanctot announced that it was time to form a union that would represent all workers in society, rather than simply those in a particular craft or workplace. Lanctot's *Grande Association de Protection des Ouvriers du Canada* took up the cause of bakery workers, holding large protests in Montreal at which the 1837 rebels' red-white-green flag was displayed prominently. Lanctot also attacked the way in which the Grand Trunk, a British-owned railway, was treating its workers. Lanctot's socialism was linked to his nationalism and republicanism: In his eyes, improving the lot of Canada's workers required independence from Britain.

In 1868, Lanctot established *L'Association de l'Indépendance pacifique du Canada*, which sought the creation of a Canadian republic through non-violent means. He soon abandoned this goal and became an advocate of Canada's incorporation into the U.S. Republic. In 1869, he organized a convention of Annexationists in Detroit that attracted delegates from both Canada and French-speaking communities in the United States.[75] In the Detroit River area and other regions in which the Canada-U.S. boundary bisected French-speaking communities, the Annexationist project was popular, perhaps because Canada's incorporation into the U.S. customs union would have eliminated the practical inconveniences caused by the border. After evidence of his conversion to Protestantism was published in 1869, many of Lanctot's Roman Catholic supporters deserted him.[76] His political career thus suddenly ended, Lanctot spent his final years editing an obscure newspaper in Hull, Quebec, where he worked on a treatise on the relations of labor and capital.[77]

In the twenty-first century, it seems curious that a Canadian socialist would favor his country's annexation by the United States, given the strength of anti-Americanism on the left of the Canadian political spectrum. Knowing how international observers in the 1860s viewed U.S. society is necessary if we are to understand the reasoning of Lanctot and the other Canadians who evidently supported this option. We should remember that neither the United States nor the Republican Party of the 1860s represented the same values as the United States and the Republican Party of the present. In the nineteenth century, many trade unionists, Chartists, and other left-wing people in Britain and Continental Europe admired the United States as a beacon of democracy and equality.[78] Many European advocates of democracy saw the U.S. Civil War as a struggle between the democratic North and the aristocratic South. Karl Marx cheered for Lincoln and the Republicans during the Civil War and regarded the North as the progressive force in the conflict. Marx attacked the many conservative newspaper editors in Britain who advocated a peaceful resolution of the differences between the free and slave states. He did so on the grounds that such a resolution would have provided for the survival of slavery.[79]

In the nineteenth century, conservative Canadians disliked the United States because it was irreligious, not because it was too religious. They remembered that Thomas Jefferson, the author of the Declaration of Independence and the phrase "separation of church and state" was an Enlightenment Deist. They were horrified to learn that James Polk, who had been President in the 1840s, had not been baptized while in office and only received that sacrament on his deathbed. In Britain or any other European monarchy, it would be unthinkable to have had an unbaptized head of state.[80] In 1870, the *Halifax Morning Chronicle* reported that the emancipation of women had proceeded more quickly in the United States than in other western countries. Speaking of the "new woman," the paper said that "British air is fatal to her mental growth and even continental Europe with all its moral latitude affords no congenial school" for the modern woman who wishes to qualify as a lawyer or doctor.[81] There was some truth in the *Morning Chronicle's* observation. The first woman to qualify as a doctor in the United

States did so in 1849. She later returned to her native Britain, where she struggled to have her qualifications recognized.[82] In short, there were valid reasons for the tendency of many Canadians and Europeans to regard the United States as a progressive rather than a conservative society. Given this context, many advocates of continental union were on the left of the Canadian political spectrum.

Why Did Most Canadians Support Remaining in the British Empire Rather Than the Alternatives?

British North Americans who advocated joining the United States or republican nationhood were a small minority. We therefore need to explain why so many British North Americans in the 1860s supported remaining in the British Empire when other constitutional options were open to them. First, their status as British subjects offered them a degree of military protection against the Army of the United States and the Fenians, an Irish-American paramilitary organization that attacked the Canadian border in the 1860s.[83] This status also offered British colonial subjects considerable consular protection when they traveled abroad, as the recent Don Pacifico affair has vividly illustrated.[84] Second, the American Civil War had discredited the U.S. experiment with democracy and republicanism in the eyes of many Canadians. The U.S. concept of state sovereignty was widely regarded in Canada as the cause of the Civil War, which is one of the reasons the Canadian constitution of 1867 provided for a very strong central government and weak sub-national governments.[85] Third, Canadians were aware of the chaos in other republican countries in the Western Hemisphere. Only the Empire of Brazil stood out as a beacon of stability in a sea of republicanism, as McGee argued. One can well understand why McGee's interpretation of events elsewhere in the hemisphere would have reinforced his monarchism. In 1864, as British North America's political leaders were about to frame their plan for a federation within the British Empire, the War of the Triple Alliance was breaking out in Latin America. This conflict pitted Paraguay, a former Spanish colony, against two other former Spanish colonies, Argentina and Uruguay, along with Brazil. When the war concluded in 1870, perhaps 400,000 were dead.[86] This conflict was reported in Canadian newspapers and likely would have reinforced the idea that the republics of Latin America were a hotbed of instability and violence. Canadians already had a negative view of republican institutions thanks to the recent civil war in the United States.[87] Those Canadians who adopted a hemispheric frame of reference had additional data points to support their existing political views, monarchical or republican.

In accounting for the widespread nature of the preference in favor of remaining in the Empire, we also have to integrate race and ethnicity into our analysis. As was mentioned previously, there were some in the United States, particularly the Radical Republicans, who would have welcomed the British North American provinces into the United States. However, there were many who were opposed to this option. In some cases, this opposition was rooted in an ethnic-nationalist definition of who could be a U.S. citizen. As Eric Foner has noted, the battle over ratification of the Reconstruction Amendments exposed the deep division between two conceptions of the nation, one civic, the other ethnic. The ethnic nationalist definition of U.S. citizenship, of course, did not include African Americans or Asian immigrants, but it also excluded, albeit less virulently, non-Protestants and those who were not of Anglo-Saxon or closely related stock.[88] British North Americans who were not of Anglo-Celtic ancestry were able to observe this pattern, which helps to explain why so many of them wished to remain under British sovereignty.

British North America in the 1860s had a large population of non-Protestant, non–Anglo-Celtic people, namely the French Canadians. Although many regions of British North America were overwhelmingly white, Protestant, and Anglo-Celtic, some in the United States perceived Canada as a motley crew of non–Anglo-Saxon, biologically inferior people. This was certainly the view that *Frank Leslie's Illustrated Newspaper* in New York took in an editorial on whether the incorporation of Canada into the United States was desirable. This editorial said that it was opposed to any further "territorial aggrandizement" by the United States save for the annexation of the slave colony of Cuba. Canada, the editor reasoned, had too many non–Anglo-Saxon people living in it to be worthy of "admission into the Union." This editorial, which strangely did not specify what was to happen to the existing population of Cuba, claimed that so much "incongruous rubbish" had already entered the United States as to make the annexation of "squalid hyperboreans" undesirable. The United States had "enough nigger, Irishman, German, and Chinaman to digest, without imperilling health still further by the deglutition of the creature called 'Canuck.'" The editor asserted the United States was, in any event, preoccupied with re-asserting its authority over the restive white population of the erstwhile Confederate States and could ill afford to expand northward: "We are 'engaged' for many years to come, with sundry raven-tressed ladies to the south of us. So the girls of frosty hair must wait their turn." The paper recommended that instead of trying to join the United States, Canadians should, as an interim measure, sever their ties with Britain and become an independent republic.[89]

A more restrained newspaper editor in the Lake Erie port of Cleveland, Ohio, alluded to Canada's diversity in an 1865 editorial on the proposals to make Canada a state. This editorial flatly declared that all of the recent discussions of Annexation of Canada were "idle utterances." The paper reasoned that while it might be desirable for the United States to obtain "control of the St. Lawrence outlet to the ocean," annexing Canada would not otherwise be in the interests of the Republic given that doing so would force the United States to confront the difficulties of "harmonizing the conflicting interests" of the various provinces and "assimilating peoples of opinions and prejudices as widely diverse as those of the North and the South just previous to the war." This statement was an allusion to the French-English tension, which was arguably the main driver of constitutional change in 1860s Canada, as the union between French-speaking Lower Canada and English-speaking Upper Canada was then under strain. Relations between Francophones and Anglophones were tense at this juncture as a result of disputes over the allocation of seats in the legislature and the highly sensitive issue of state funding for denominational schools, a matter that pitted Protestants against Roman Catholics.[90] The paper pointed out that the United States already had abundant land and hardly needed more. It also said that while parts of Upper Canada might be induced to join the union, the population in the rest of British North America was firmly opposed to the concept.[91]

The evident reluctance of some Anglo-Saxon Protestants in the United States to take over a territory associated with Roman Catholicism and the French language is part of a broader pattern. U.S. historians often associate the ideology of Anglo-Saxon supremacy with Manifest Destiny and the desire to engross as much territory as possible. The reality was more complicated: As Eric T. Love demonstrated in Race Over Empire, a sense of superiority over non-white and non–Anglo-Saxon people prompted many in the United States to recoil from proposals to annex particular territories. Indeed, this sentiment contributed to the decision of Congress to block the territorial expansion plans of the Grant administration. The politics of race influenced U.S. hemispheric diplomacy in the Reconstruction Era, when U.S. legislators considered proposals to annex Alaska, the Virgin Islands, and part of the island of Santo Domingo.

With the exception of the purchase of Alaska in 1867 and the acquisition of the unpopulated Midway Islands, most of these proposed expansions of U.S. territory failed, in part because of Congressional opposition to including additional non-white majority territories in the United States. The predominant view in the North was that the country already had enough problems connected to the semitropical and racially mixed states of the former Confederacy.[92] Similarly, in the

1840s when the United States was seriously considering annexing all of Mexico, rather than just its sparsely populated northern third, anti-Catholic sentiment and fear of the future power of a Catholic voting bloc contributed to the defeat of the so-called "All Mexico" option.[93]

An ethnic-nationalist definition of U.S. citizenship was liable to antagonize potential supporters of continental union in Canada. Indeed, we know that the anti-Catholic, anti-Irish chauvinism rampant in the United States in the 1850s converted the aforementioned Thomas D'Arcy McGee from a republican into an ardently loyal subject of Queen Victoria.[94] Speaking during a somewhat earlier wave of anti-Catholic sentiment in the United States, a French-speaking Roman Catholic legislator famously declared that "le dernier coup de canon tiré pour le maintien de la puissance anglaise en Amérique le sera par un bras canadien" (the last cannon shot in defense of British power in the America would be fired by a French-Canadian hand).[95] Advocates of a British identity for Canada were promoting an inclusive, civic-nationalist definition of Britishness that attracted many whites who were not of British ancestry. In 1861, John A. Macdonald declared that he considered "every man who says that he is in favour" of the British connection as belonging "to my party, whatever his antecedents may have been."[96] Macdonald was speaking a year after the visit by the Prince of the Wales, which had been intended, in part, to reinforce the loyalty to Britain of Canada's diverse population. During the Prince's visit, care had been taken to include every major ethnic group in the associated events and to avoid associating the Prince with the anti-Catholic Orange Order.[97]

We should remember that contemporaries used the term "British" as both an ethnic label and a more inclusive legal concept that corresponded to the category of British nationality. Britishness was an elastic concept partly because it was a relatively recent invention and one that an immigrant German dynasty had used to unite the ethnic nations of the British Isles after 1714.[98] Since the Conquest, the British had cultivated the allegiance of the French Canadians, the so-called "new subjects." This strategy paid massive dividends, for during the invasions by Continental and U.S. forces in 1775 and 1812, the lay and clerical elites of French Canada had remained loyal to the Crown.[99] Given this context, it is not surprising that French Canadians and other Canadians who were not of British ethnicity regarded the retention of British colonial status as the "least bad" option.

Conclusion and Directions for Future Research

The course of Canadian political history in the 1860s resulted in a constitutional settlement whereby British North America remained under British sovereignty.

The other options that were open to British North Americans in the 1860s, becoming an independent republic or joining the United States, remained roads not taken. As the older historiography on Canada in the 1860s has shown, a host of factors helped to produce this outcome. This chapter has sought to integrate the politics of race and ethnicity into our understanding of why present-day Canada remained part of the British Empire. The author does not claim that the politics of race and ethnicity were the only, or even the most important, set of factors that kept Canada within the British Empire. However, it is important to recognize that contemporary ideas about racial and ethnic hierarchies did shape the drawing of the political map of northern North America in the 1860s in a fashion that has not been acknowledged by previous scholars. By bringing race back into the story of Canadian Confederation in the 1860s, we can develop a better understanding how the Canadian federation was created and the subsequent evolution of the Canadian nation-state.

The previous pages have shown that British North Americans in the 1860s were conscious of developments elsewhere in the hemisphere, not just in the United States but also in Latin America as well. If we are to understand Canadian constitutional politics in the 1860s, we must use a hemispheric framework. This paper is therefore a call for a more hemispheric approach to the writing of Canadian history. In a sense, it is a gentle critique of the tendency of many Canadian historians to ignore developments elsewhere in the Americas. One could argue that the longstanding tendency of Canadian historians to overlook, or at least downplay, their country's connections to the rest of their hemisphere has likely been reinforced by the advent of the British World research paradigm. While there are clearly many advantages that come from using a British World approach, historians of Canada should also engage with the histories of and historians in the Caribbean and Latin America. By adopting a hemispheric perspective, Canadian historians will be able to generate a fresh scholarly perspective on a wide range of important research topics.

Notes

1. Lauren Benton, *A Search for Sovereignty: Law and Geography in European Empires, 1400–1900* (Cambridge: Cambridge University Press, 2009); Jack P. Greene, "Negotiated Authorities: The Problem of Governance in the Extended Polities of the Early Modern Atlantic World," in *Negotiated Authorities: Essays in Colonial Political and Constitutional History* (Charlottesville: University of Virginia Press 1994), 1–24. I would like to thank Jay Sexton and Marise Bachand for commenting on earlier drafts of this paper.

2. John Lynch, ed. *Latin American Revolutions, 1808–1826: Old and New World Origins* (Norman: University of Oklahoma Press, 1994).

3. Andrew Smith, "The Reaction of the City of London to the Quebec Resolutions, 1864–1866," *Journal of the Canadian Historical Association / Revue de la Société historique du Canada* 17, no. 1 (2006): 1–24.

4. Andrew Smith, *British Businessmen and Canadian Confederation: Constitution Making in an Era of Anglo-Globalization* (Montreal and Kingston: McGill-Queen's Press, 2008).

5. Donald Creighton, *The Road to Confederation: The Emergence of Canada, 1863–1867* (Toronto: Houghton Mifflin, 1965); W. L. Morton, *The Critical Years: The Union of British North America, 1857–1873* (Toronto: McClelland & Stewart, 1964); Peter B. Waite, *The Life and Times of Confederation* (Toronto: University of Toronto Press, 1962).

6. Caitlin Fitz, *Our Sister Republics: The United States in an Age of American Revolutions* (New York: Norton, 2016).

7. Andrew Smith and Kirsten Greer, "Monarchism, an Emerging Canadian Identity, and the 1866 British North American Trade Mission to the West Indies and Brazil," *Journal of Imperial and Commonwealth History* 44, no. 2 (2016): 214–40.

8. Lester D. Langley, *The Americas in the Age of Revolution, 1750–1850* (New Haven: Yale University Press, 1996), 58, 176, 232.

9. A. W. Marx, *Making Race and Nation: A Comparison of South Africa, the United States, and Brazil* (Cambridge: Cambridge University Press, 1998); Mara Loveman, *National Colors: Racial Classification and the State in Latin America* (Oxford: Oxford University Press, 2014); Edward Telles and René Flores, "Not Just Color: Whiteness, Nation, and Status in Latin America," *Hispanic American Historical Review* vol. 93, no. 3 (2013): 411–49.

10. Phillip Buckner and R. Douglas Francis, eds. *Canada and the British World: Culture, Migration, and Identity* (Vancouver: University of British Columbia Press, 2011); Katie Pickles, "Transnational History and Cultural Cringe: Some Issues for Consideration in New Zealand, Australia and Canada," *History Compass* 9, no. 9 (2011): 657–73.

11. Andrew Smith, "Thomas Bassett Macaulay and the Bahamas: Racism, Business and Canadian Sub-Imperialism," *Journal of Imperial and Commonwealth History* 37, no. 1 (2009): 29–50; Andrew Smith and Jatinder Mann, "A Tale of Two Ex-Dominions: Why the Procedures for Changing the Rules of Succession Are So Different in Canada and Australia," *Commonwealth & Comparative Politics* 52, no. 3 (2014): 376–401.

12. Jayan Nayar, "On the Elusive Subject of Sovereignty," *Alternatives: Global, Local, Political* 39, no. 2 (2014): 124–47; Hent Kalmo and Quentin Skinner, eds, *Sovereignty in Fragments: The Past, Present and Future of a Contested Concept* (Cambridge: Cambridge University Press, 2010).

13. Stéphane Dion, "The Dynamic of Secessions: Scenarios After a Pro-Separatist Vote in a Quebec Referendum," *Canadian Journal of Political Science* 28, no. 3 (1995): 533–51; Claude Ryan, *Consequences of the Quebec Secession Reference: The Clarity Bill and Beyond* (Montreal: CD Howe Institute, 2000).

14. Eiki Berg and Ene Kuusk, "What Makes Sovereignty a Relative Concept? Empirical Approaches to International Society," *Political Geography* 29, no. 1 (2010): 40.

15. Jean L. Cohen, *Globalization and Sovereignty: Rethinking Legality, Legitimacy, and Constitutionalism* (Cambridge: Cambridge University Press, 2012), 26–27.

16. Carl Schmitt, *Political Theology: Four Chapters on the Concept of Sovereignty* (Chicago: University of Chicago Press, 1985); Daniel Philpott, "Sovereignty: An Introduction and Brief History," *Journal of International Affairs* 48, no. 2 (1995): 353; Terry Nardin, "The Diffusion of Sovereignty," *History of European Ideas* 41, no. 1 (2015): 89–102; David Armitage, *The Declaration of Independence: A Global History* (Cambridge: Harvard University Press, 2007).

17. Philip Noel-Baker, *The Present Juridical Status of the British Dominions in International Law* (London: Longmans, Green, 1929).

18. *Parliamentary Debates on the Subject of the Confederation of the British North American Provinces, 3rd Session, 8th Provincial Parliament of Canada* (Quebec: Hunter, Rose & Co., parliamentary printers, 1865), 220.

19. Noel Cox, "The Theory of Sovereignty and the Importance of the Crown in the Realms of the Queen," *Oxford University Commonwealth Law Journal* 2, no. 2 (2002): 237–55.

20. *Parliamentary Debates on the Subject of the Confederation*, 33.

21. *Parliamentary Debates on the Subject of the Confederation*, 433, 440.

22. *Parliamentary Debates on the Subject of the Confederation*, 539.

23. Bruce W. Hodgins, "Democracy and the Ontario Fathers of Confederation," in *Profiles of a Province: Studies in the History of Ontario*, ed. Edith G. Firth (Toronto: Ontario Historical Society, 1967), 83–91.

24. Helen Irving, "Sister Colonies with Separate Constitutions: Why Australian Federationists Rejected the Canadian Constitution," in *Shaping Nations: Constitutionalism and Society in Australia and Canada*, ed. Linda Cardinal and David Headon (Ottawa: University of Ottawa Press, 2002), 27–38.

25. Phillip Buckner, *The Transition to Responsible Government: British Policy in British North America, 1815–1850* (Westport, Conn.: Greenwood Press, 1985); Peter Cochrane, *Colonial Ambition: Foundations of Australia's Democracy* (Victoria, Au.: Melbourne University Press, 2006).

26. Bernard Semmel, *The Liberal Ideal and the Demons of Empire: Theories of Imperialism from Adam Smith to Lenin* (Baltimore: Johns Hopkins University Press, 1993), 17–38.

27. William Harbutt Dawson, *Richard Cobden and Foreign Policy* (London: Allen & Unwin, 1926), 189–90. For Canadian reaction to Little Englandism, see Donald Creighton, "The Victorians and the Empire," *Canadian Historical Review* 19 (1938): 138–53.

28. Bruce Knox, "British Policy and the Ionian Islands, 1847–1864: Nationalism and Imperial Administration," *English Historical Review* 99 (1984): 503–529.

29. John S. Galbraith, "Myths of the 'Little England' Era," *American Historical Review* 67, no. 1 (1961): 34–48; Bernard Porter, *The Absent-Minded Imperialists: Empire, Society, and Culture in Britain* (Oxford: Oxford University Press, 2004), 84–114.

30. Henry Thring, *Colonial Reform: Provisions Intended as Suggestions for a Colonial Bill* (1865; repr., London: King, 1903). Thring's surviving personal papers, which are held by the Royal College of Music, do not shed light on why he was asked to prepare

this draft legislation. As other historians have noted, British ideas about which colonies deserved Responsible Government and the theoretical right to leave the Empire were essentially racial. Catherine Hall, Keith McClelland, and Jane Rendall, *Defining the Victorian Nation: Class, Race, Gender and the British Reform Act of 1867* (Cambridge: Cambridge University Press, 2000).

31. Quoted in Ged Martin, *Britain and the Origins of Canadian Confederation, 1837–67* (Vancouver: University of British Columbia Press, 1995), 173.

32. See Smith, "Reaction of the City of London."

33. "Quebec Resolutions," in *Confederation: Being a Series of Hitherto Unpublished Documents Bearing on the British North America Act*, ed. Sir Joseph Pope (Toronto: Carswell, 1895), 38–52.

34. "Confederation of British America," *Daily News*, November 3, 1864, 3; Annette R. Wolff, "Abraham Joseph," *Dictionary of Canadian Biography*, http://www.biographi.ca/en/bio/joseph_abraham_11E.html.

35. Andrew Smith, *British Businessmen and Canadian Confederation: Constitution-Making in an Era of Anglo-Globalization* (Montreal: McGill-Queen's University Press, 2008), 91–108.

36. "The Canadian Federation," *New-York Tribune*, October 20, 1864, 4.

37. In its reply to the *New York Herald*, the *Toronto Globe* stated that people in British North America would decide for themselves whether the federation's chief magistrate would be named "Governor," "Viceroy," "President," or "King." "English Designs on America," *Toronto Globe*, September 15, 1864, 2.

38. "The Canadian Confederation: Imperial Designs," *New York Times*, October 23, 1864, 4.

39. Quoted in "Confederation: What Our Neighbours Think," *Saint John Weekly Telegraph*, December 7, 1864, 3.

40. David Wilson, *Thomas D'Arcy McGee: Passion, Reason, and Politics, 1825–1857* (Montreal and Kingston: McGill-Queen's University Press, 2008), 259, 328, 4.

41. Thomas D'Arcy McGee, *The Crown and the Confederation: Three Letters to the Hon. John Alexander McDonald, Attorney General for Upper Canada* (Montreal: J. Lovell, 1864).

42. McGee, "A Plea for British American Nationality," *British American Magazine* 1 (August 1863), 337–45, 342. For the possibility that Canada might acquire a permanent hereditary viceroy chosen from among Victoria's sons, see "The Vice-Royalty," *Saint John Morning News*, October 21, 1864, 2.

43. Thomas L. Connolly, *Funeral Oration on the Late Hon. Thos. D'Arcy McGee: Delivered in the Metropolitan Church of St. Mary's, Halifax, Nova Scotia on Friday 24th April, A D. 1868* (Halifax, N.S.: Compton, 1868), 12.

44. Thomas Darcy McGee, *Notes on Federal Governments, Past and Present* (Montreal: Dawson, 1865), 51, 52, 44, 34.

45. Andrew Smith and Kirsten Greer, "Monarchism, an Emerging Canadian Identity, and the 1866 British North American Trade Mission to the West Indies and Brazil," *Journal of Imperial and Commonwealth History* 44, no. 2 (2016): 214–40.

46. "Canada and the Canadians," [London] *Times*, October 22, 1864, 9.

47. Anthony Trollope, *North America* (London: Chapman & Hall, 1862), 256.

48. *Glasgow Herald*, September 5, 1865.

49. Charles Tupper, *Recollection of Sixty Years in Canada* (Toronto: Cassell and Company, 1914), 24.

50. "Canada and Her Position," *Lloyd's Weekly Newspaper*, July 28, 1861.

51. See "Return of Amount Contributed by Colonies Towards Patriotic Fund; Number of Russian Guns, taken during late war, distributed as Trophies amongst Colonies," [Great Britain] *Parliamentary Papers*, 1857–58, Command Paper No. 65, 3–4.

52. J. Mackay Hitsman, "How Successful was the 100th Royal Canadians," *Military Affairs* 31, no. 1 (1967); David L. Stone, "Perceptions of an Imperial Crisis: Canadian Reactions to the Sepoy Mutiny, 1857–8," M.A. Thesis (University of British Columbia, 1984).

53. Richard Cartwright, *Reminiscences* (Toronto: W. Briggs, 1912), 20.

54. L. B. Shippee, *Canadian-American Relations, 1849–1874* (New Haven: Yale University Press, 1939), 1–12; Jacques Monet, "French Canada and the Annexation Crisis, 1848–1850," *Canadian Historical Review* 47, no. 3 (1966): 249–64; Ged Martin, "The Canadian rebellion losses bill of 1849 in British politics," *The Journal of Imperial and Commonwealth History* 6, no. 1 (1977): 3.

55. Shippee, *Canadian-American Relations*, 17–20; Cephas D. Allin and George M. Jones, *Annexation, Preferential Tariff and Reciprocity* (Toronto: Musson 1912), 99.

56. Shippee, *Canadian-American Relations*, 183.

57. Robin W. Winks, *Canada and the United States: The Civil War Years* (Baltimore: Johns Hopkins University Press, 1960), 4–5, 33–34; Glyndon G. Van Deusen, *William Henry Seward* (New York: Oxford University Press, 1967), 535–37.

58. Shippee, *Canadian-American Relations*, 184.

59. "Reflections on the Future of British America by Hon. W. H. Seward," in Henry Youle Hind, *Explorations in the Interior of the Labrador Peninsula the Country of the Montagnais and Nasquapee Indians*, Vol. 2 (London: Longman, Green, Longman, Roberts & Green, 1863), 252.

60. George C. Herring, *From Colony to Superpower: U.S. Foreign Relations Since 1776* (New York: Oxford University Press, 2008), 228–29; Robert E. May, *Manifest Destiny's Underworld: Filibustering in Antebellum America* (Chapel Hill: University of North Carolina Press, 2002); Gavin B. Henderson, "Southern Designs on Cuba, 1854–1857 and Some European Opinions," *Journal of Southern History* 5, no. 3 (1939): 371–385.

61. Shippee, *Canadian-American Relations*, 184.

62. "The Effect on Canada," *The Trade Review*, April 7, 1865, 141.

63. "Gloomy Minds," *Toronto Globe*, May 17, 1865, 2. See D. F. Warner, *The Idea of Continental Union: Agitation for the Annexation of Canada to the United States, 1849–1893* (Lexington: University of Kentucky Press, 1960), 43.

64. "Canada and Annexation," *Bangor Daily Whig and Courier*, August 16, 1865.

65. "Canadian Sorrows," *North American and United States Gazette*, August 4, 1865.

66. "Letter from 'One of Them,' of Hamilton, Upper Canada," *Milwaukee Daily Sentinel*, July 29, 1865, and "The Annexation of Canada," August 8, 1865.

67. Fred Harvey Harrington, *Fighting Politician: Major General N. P. Banks* (1948; repr., Westport, Conn.: Greenwood Press, 1970), 179.

68. Shirley Brice Heath, "Language and Politics in the United States," *Georgetown University Round Table on Languages and Linguistics* ed. Muriel Saville-Troike (Washington, D.C.: Georgetown University Press, 1977), 267–96.

69. Kenneth M. Stampp, *The Era of Reconstruction, 1865–1877*, 1st ed. (New York: Knopf, 1965), 119–85. Eric Foner, *Reconstruction: America's Unfinished Revolution, 1863–1877* (New York: Harper & Row, 1988), 218–80.

70. Joe Patterson Smith, "American Republican Leadership and the Movement for the Annexation of Canada in the Eighteen-Sixties," *Report of the Annual Meeting of the Canadian Historical Association* 14, no. 1 (1935), 67–75, esp. 71–72.

71. Wood returned to the United States after his dismissal. See O. S. Wood to President and Directors, July 15, 1865, in Montreal Telegraph Company papers in Canadian National Railways Company Fonds, R231-386-4-E, sub-sub-series in Library and Archives Canada, Ottawa.

72. T. Phillips Thompson, *The Future Government of Canada: Being Arguments in Favour of a British American Independent Republic* (St. Catharines: Herald Press, 1864), 9.

73. Thompson, *Future Government of Canada*, 13.

74. Thompson, *Future Government of Canada*, 9.

75. Télésphore Saint-Pierre, *Histoire des Canadiens du Michigan et du Comte d'Essex* (Montreal: La Gazette, 1895), 235–46; Jean Hamelin, "Médéric Lanctot," *Dictionary of Canadian Biography*, http://www.biographi.ca/en/bio/lanctot_mederic_10E.html.

76. Hamelin, "Médéric Lanctot."

77. Médéric Lanctot, *Association du Capital et du Travail* (Montreal: J. Wilson, 1872).

78. Murney Gerlach, *British Liberalism and the United States: Political and Social Thought in the late Victorian Age* (Basingstoke: Palgrave, 2001); Henry Pelling, *America and the British Left; from Bright to Bevan* (London: A. & C. Black, 1956), 1–24.

79. Marx, "The North American Civil War," in Karl Marx and Frederick Engels, *Collected Works, Volume 19* (New York, International Publishers, 1984), 32–42.

80. S. F. Wise, "The Annexation Movement and Its Effect on Canadian Opinion, 1837–67," in S.F. Wise and Robert Craig Brown, *Canada Views the United States: Nineteenth Century Political Attitudes* (Seattle: University of Washington Press, 1967), 47–51.

81. "The New Woman," *Halifax Morning Chronicle*, May 3, 1870.

82. Mary Ann Elston, "Blackwell, Elizabeth (1821–1910)," in *Oxford Dictionary of National Biography* (Oxford: Oxford University Press, 2004).

83. Hereward Senior, *The Last Invasion of Canada: The Fenian Raids, 1866–1870* (Toronto: Dundurn, 1991); Phillip Buckner, "British North America and a Continent in Dissolution: The American Civil War in the Making of Canadian Confederation," *The Journal of the Civil War Era* 7, no. 4 (2017): 512–40.

84. Abigail Green, "The British Empire and the Jews: An Imperialism of Human Rights?" *Past & Present* 199, no. 1 (2008): 175–205.

85. Garth Stevenson, *Ex Uno Plures: Federal-Provincial Relations in Canada, 1867–1896* (Montreal and Kingston: McGill-Queen's Press, 1993).

86. Harris Gaylord Warren, *Paraguay and the Triple Alliance: The Postwar Decade, 1869–1878* (1978; repr., Austin: University of Texas Press, 2014), 31–32.

87. S. F. Wise, "The Annexation Movement and Its Effect on Canadian Opinion."

88. Eric Foner, "Who Is an American? The Imagined Community in American History," *Centennial Review* 41, no. 3 (1997): 425–38.

89. "Canadian Independence," *Frank Leslie's Illustrated Newspaper*, August 7, 1869.

90. Robert Vipond, "1867: Confederation" in *The Oxford Handbook of the Canadian Constitution*, ed. Peter Oliver, Patrick Macklem, and Nathalie Des Rosiers (Oxford: Oxford University Press, 2017); David E. Smith, *The Constitution in a Hall of Mirrors: Canada at 150* (Toronto: University of Toronto Press, 2017), 66.

91. "Canadian Annexation," *Daily Cleveland Herald*, June 6, 1865.

92. Eric Tyrone Lowery Love, *Race Over Empire: Racism and U.S. Imperialism, 1865–1900* (Chapel Hill: University of North Carolina Press, 2004).

93. John Douglas Pitts Fuller, *The Movement for the Acquisition of All Mexico, 1846–1848* (Baltimore: Johns Hopkins University Press, 1936); John C. Pinheiro, "'Religion without Restriction': Anti-Catholicism, All Mexico, and the Treaty of Guadalupe Hidalgo," *Journal of the Early Republic* 23, no. 1 (2003): 69–96.

94. Wilson, *Thomas D'Arcy McGee*, 321–28.

95. Étienne-Paschal Taché speech on the Militia Bill, April 24, 1846, quoted in Jacques Monet, *The Last Cannon Shot: A Study of French-Canadian Nationalism 1837–1850* (Toronto: University of Toronto Press, 1969). Translation by author.

96. Macdonald, "Remarks on the Composition and Policy of the Brown-Dorion Government," in *Address of the Hon. John A. Macdonald to the Elders of the City of Kingston* (Kingston, Canada: West 1861), 95.

97. Ian Radforth, *Royal Spectacle: The 1860 Visit of the Prince of Wales to Canada and the United States* (Toronto: University of Toronto Press, 2004).

98. Linda Colley, *Britons: Forging the Nation, 1707–1837* (New Haven: Yale University Press, 1992).

99. Donal Lowry, "The Crown, Empire Loyalism and the Assimilation of Non-British White Subjects in the British World: An Argument Against 'Ethnic Determinism,'" *Journal of Imperial and Commonwealth History* 31, no. 2 (2003): 96–120.

3

Civil War and Nation Building in North America, 1848–1867

Pablo Mijangos y González

B etween 1848 and 1867, North America was the setting of an intense political, economic, and social realignment that made possible the defini-
tive consolidation of the nation-state as the sovereign form of political
organization in the region.[1] In Mexico, the Liberal Party, led by Benito Juárez,
put an end in 1867 to a lengthy civil war; this was initially provoked by profound
disagreements over the 1857 Constitution, though it later evolved into an international conflict due to a failed imperialist experiment by Napoleon III of France.
North of the Rio Grande, in 1865, the United States finally imposed its will upon
the separatist southern Confederacy, a military victory that would soon be accompanied by the freeing of four million slaves and the introduction of a new
model of citizenship and civil rights with the Thirteenth and Fourteenth Amendments to the Constitution. Finally, in British North America, 1867 marked the
start of the Canadian Confederation, the only state in the region to arise without
a violent rupture with the mother country and the only one not to experience a
civil war.

Although these three histories run in parallel and have similar outcomes, until recently the historiographies of Mexico and the United States have paid scant
attention to the regional dimension of their respective processes of nation building. While a recent wave of transnational studies on the 1860s, most of them
focused on the relationship between the United States and the world, have begun
to change this picture, in general, Mexico's Reform War and the U.S. Civil War
are narrated from a fundamentally national perspective, focusing on particular
themes of each conflict: church-state relations in Mexico; the dispute over slavery
in the United States.[2] Regional and international dimensions make an appearance in terms of the highly important diplomatic factors in both wars, or in the
rare essays that compare them with similar conflicts in other parts of the world.
For Mexico, the usual reference point consists of those Hispanic American republics that experienced a similarly tempestuous nineteenth century, or perhaps

the different clashes between the Catholic Church and the liberal revolutions taking place in Europe; for the United States, two typical points of comparative reference are the emancipation of the serfs in Russia and Italy's national unification (both in 1861).[3] Canadian historiography is quite distinct, for the emergence of the Confederation is incomprehensible without considering its belonging to the British Empire and its problematic proximity to the United States, although it is rare that Mexico's territorial loss to the United States of 1848 gains mention as a relevant factor.

This essay outlines a regional and comparative history of the emergence of North American nation-states during the mid-nineteenth century, attempting to highlight common challenges and solutions—and reciprocal influences—between the region's distinct countries. It is undertaken with an awareness that a study with such aims may prove superficial in light of the tremendous density of each national history involved, but a broader perspective may help us better understand the context, the dynamics, and the principal triggers of the great political transformations of the 1860s. As Mauricio Tenorio notes in his perceptive invitation to imagine North America as having a common history, there is no "theme or issue in U.S., Canadian, or Mexican history that can be understood only in terms of a national history," and this traumatic era is undoubtedly no exception.[4] This essay therefore begins by analyzing the U.S. and Mexican cases, wherein civil wars definitively shaped the nation-state, in order to later compare both processes with the history of the Canadian Confederation, whose emergence took place in a more pragmatic, gradual, and peaceful manner. Although it tries to emphasize the complex interaction between political, social, and economic spheres, this analysis has as its fundamental axis the successive "constitutional pacts" that governed the difficult adaptation of the North American peoples to the demands of liberal capitalism and representative government. As will shortly be seen, political violence was neither the only nor the most efficient means for constructing modern states in the region.

In their movement toward becoming capitalist economies and representative democracies, this essay argues, Mexico and the United States followed a path of constitutional revolution, whereas Canada, which had neither a revolution against its imperial parent nor a civil war between antagonistic regions, managed to reach a similar end point through a different process of constitutional gradualism overseen by Great Britain. In Mexico and the United States, the ruptures produced by revolutions against empires, then a war with one another, and finally civil wars within each polity produced an intense nationalism and, by the late 1860s, a decisive consolidation of nation-state government. However, despite the persistence of deep-seated regional divisions in post-Confederation Canada, its peaceful route to the "creole dream" of belonging to a powerful empire while retaining local self-government nonetheless produced a national attachment to the liberal constitutional order that resembled the achievement of the winners of the civil wars in Mexico and the United States.

Mexico and the United States: The Path of Civil War

It would not be outlandish to claim that the signing of the Treaty of Guada-lupe Hidalgo on February 2, 1848, was the most important event to take place on the North American continent during the nineteenth century. By this treaty, Mexico ceded to the United States a vast and scarcely populated territory, from the Gulf of Mexico to the Rocky Mountains and the Pacific Ocean, which would very soon awaken great expectations of economic prosperity, especially follow-ing the discovery of gold in California. As various writers and political actors of the era well recognized, the Treaty of Guadalupe Hidalgo was a real watershed in the evolution of both countries. In Mexico, Mariano Otero observed that the humiliating defeat at the hands of an invader had revealed the absence of civic ties befitting a nation; in the United States, Ralph Waldo Emerson warned that the recently annexed territory contained a strong dose of "arsenic" that would end up destroying the young imperial republic.[5] Indeed, in both countries, the changes of 1848 triggered a lengthy political crisis that would lead to the erup-tion of civil wars a decade or so later (1858 in Mexico, 1861 in the United States). To what extent did these crises respond to similar causes, if we take into account that the problem of slavery did not exist in Mexico and that the relationship be-tween civil and religious authority was not an important cause of division in the United States?

These political crises were similar in that the Treaty of Guadalupe Hidalgo required a radical reformulation of the constitutional pacts adopted following the independence of both countries. To understand the similarity—and the fra-gility—of these pacts, it is necessary first to highlight the parallels between the American Revolution and Mexican independence.[6] In both cases, the process of rupture began with wars between imperial European monarchies during the eigh-teenth century, as a result of which colonial control was increased over respective territories in the Americas. Successive imperial reforms provoked increasing un-ease in the American colonies, in turn prompting demands for greater autonomy and equality within the framework of their respective imperial constitutions, al-though at notably different times: While in the British colonies these demands grew loud in the 1770s, in New Spain they did not become forceful until 1808, in the midst of a crisis provoked by the Napoleonic usurpation of the Spanish crown. In each case, the imperial response was equally negative, which led to the radicalization of the colonies, the eruption of wars against the mother country, and finally to independence. What is important here is that neither Mexico nor the United States arose truly as *nations*, but rather as immense aggregations of autonomous territories that shared commercial and self-defense interests, along with certain cultural traits. Thus, their first constitutional pacts were designed to maintain unity among a highly diverse group of political communities, by giving ample powers of self-government to signatories to each pact, and also by committing to act with great moderation toward two deep-rooted institutions: in the United States slavery, and in Mexico the Catholic Church.[7]

Certainly the initial trajectory of each republic was quite distinct. Except for the War of 1812 with Great Britain, the United States enjoyed a favorable international context and managed to consolidate a functional and democratic political system, which in turn served as the framework for an enviable rate of economic growth, visible in the increase in the population, the endless arrival of European immigrants, the proliferation of farms and agricultural enterprises, the development of modern means of communication such as railroads and the telegraph, the growth and industrialization of the commercial hubs of the North, and the full integration of the Southern plantations with the North Atlantic economy as the principal suppliers of cotton to the British textile industry.[8] However, this successful specialization of economies sharpened the differences between the Northern and Southern states, which, during the 1820s and 1830s, put to the test the strength of the constitutional pact signed at Philadelphia. The heart of the conflict had precisely to do with the two key elements of the constitutional pact: the autonomy of the states and respect for the South's "peculiar institution" of slavery, which had gained a second wind thanks to the success of U.S. cotton in Europe. Regarding slavery, in 1820, Congress renewed its policy of moderation via the so-called Missouri Compromise, which prohibited slavery in the Louisiana Purchase lands north of the 36°30' latitude line. As for states' rights, the conflict blew open in 1832, when South Carolina affirmed its right to unilaterally "nullify" those federal laws that, in the judgment of the local legislature, were contrary to the Constitution. Triggered by the imposition of customs tariffs harmful to the South, this episode did not escalate, due to a lack of support from neighboring states and the political talents of President Andrew Jackson, but it was a dangerous sign of the limits of the U.S. constitutional equilibrium.[9]

The performance of the Mexican federation was diametrically opposite.[10] With little international backing and the permanent fear of a war of reconquest by Spain and the Holy Alliance, the first Mexican governments channeled much of their budgets to the strengthening of the army, building up an ever greater debt burden and using up the scarce financial resources that had survived the war of independence. In the absence of public or private investment, development of communications and infrastructure was non-existent, and the old viceregal economy fragmented into mutually isolated markets. Yet worse, conflicts between the center and the provinces, and between distinct political factions, were ever more frequent and intense, and between 1833 and 1835 they affected the two key points of Mexico's constitutional pact: provincial autonomy and the Catholic Church as a crucial factor of social unity. While the Church managed to maintain its privileged status thanks to annulment of the anticlerical reforms of Valentín Gómez Farías, the first federal model ended up being substituted for a centralist one in 1836. Although the new regime maintained some spaces for provincial autonomy (for example, through local participation in the makeup of departmental assemblies), it failed to stabilize Mexican public life, and it ended up provoking separatist rebellions in various northern and southeastern provinces. The rebellion and eventual independence of Texas, occupied by Anglo-American colonists, made way for a potentially devastating conflict with the United States, which finally erupted in 1846. In the midst of this international war, the federalists (as Mexican advocates of states' rights were known) managed to regain control of the central government and drove the restoration of the constitutional pact of 1824, adding the option that a combined majority of state legislatures could annul any law passed by the national congress.[11]

After the disastrous war that pitted U.S. strength against Mexican weakness, the context and terms of political debate were radically altered in both countries. If during the early stages of independence the principal challenge had been to maintain unity via the generous ceding of power to the provinces and the commitment not to touch delicate issues such as slavery or clerical privilege, as of 1848 the goal consisted more of creating a unified state with the powers necessary to confront the multiple challenges arising from the Treaty of Guadalupe-Hidalgo. This swift change in priorities in turn demanded a profound revision of the prevailing constitutional pacts, which could not be done without a broad social consensus, nor without first resolving the latent tensions of early commitments to states' rights. Hence, the 1850s resumed the history of distinct failed efforts to construct a new constitutional arrangement in Mexico and the United

States, a history that also coincided with the rise and spread of liberal nationalism after the European revolutions of 1848.

In the case of the United States, the sudden conquest of more than three-quarters of a million square miles, preceded by the acquisition of Oregon in 1846, necessitated a revision of the rules governing the occupation and eventual incorporation of new territories into the Union, along with a broadening of the federal government's room to maneuver—without the government's help, it would be impossible to undertake the infrastructure projects needed to bind new territories to the existing states.[12] To what extent did these challenges jeopardize the U.S. constitutional pact? At heart, revising the rules of western expansion meant revising the compromise over the privileged position of Southern slavery. To be sure, the U.S. Constitution had proven its adaptability to change either through amendment or Supreme Court ruling, but the war with Mexico put new, unbearable strain on the federal compromises worked out between 1787 and 1821 in regards to the balance of sectional power. Although the Southern states increasingly claimed to have a singular identity and lifestyle, at the same time they found themselves tied to the North by a great variety of financial, commercial, religious, and even family ties, and so they demanded that their institutions be fully recognized and authorized throughout the *nation*.[13] Faced with such demands, the population of the North invoked the superiority of a lifestyle based on free labor, which in its fullest form required an abundant availability of land and a legal framework that guaranteed free and fair competition between property-holding citizens.[14] That is, while the South demanded the right to carry their system of slave-holding plantations into the new territories, the North insisted on respect for the Missouri Compromise to facilitate the expansion of free labor and its protection against the oligarchic power of the cotton barons. Amidst these contrary demands, the creation of a strong federal power was a very risky bet for all actors involved, for if that power should fall squarely into the hands of the North it might jeopardize Southern self-determination, and if it should come into the hands of the South it might impose the privileges of slave-holding throughout all territory incorporated into the United States, with inevitable harm to the liberties of Northern citizens.

While to the north of the Rio Grande the nation-state was a dangerous instrument without which the gains of 1848 could not be adequately administered, in Mexico it was an indispensable mechanism—yet an equally problematic one—for repairing the dramatic failures of the war.[15] First of all, the country's northern states and new frontiers needed to be populated, and that required a national strategy to foster colonization in those territories. As for Mexico's well-populated heartland, there was a great need to clean up and modernize bureaucracy at all levels, to create a more effective system of taxation, to restore public order and the safety of people and property, and above all to stimulate economic growth by means of investment in infrastructure and the elimination of those corporate (ecclesiastical and communal-landholding) privileges that were believed to have hampered agricultural productivity. Just as in the United States, these challenges put at risk the existing constitutional pact, in this case a republic conceived as federal and Catholic. Colonization projects, for example, required the strengthening of the national government vis-à-vis the states and moreover the establishing of a regime of religious tolerance for foreign immigrants, to which the clergy and much of public opinion were opposed. Implementing a more effective tax system and reforming the bureaucracy could cast doubt on the autonomy of provincial powers, and the attack on corporate privileges would inevitably revive conflict with the clergy, whose leaders increasingly invoked the sovereignty and freedoms of the Catholic Church.[16]

Thus the Treaty of Guadalupe Hidalgo rapidly led to a serious constitutional crisis in both countries. In the United States, the Democratic senator Stephen A. Douglas tried to put a stop to this crisis via the doctrine of "popular sovereignty," which reserved the right to decide upon the expansion and legality of slavery to the inhabitants of the new territories. But this doctrine collapsed following the violent confrontation between Northern and Southern migrants in the Kansas territory in 1855, and more so after the fateful Supreme Court decision in the case of *Dred Scott v. Sandford*, which among other things denied Congress the ability to impose limits upon the expansion of slavery, thereby destroying the Missouri Compromise.[17] In Mexico, meanwhile, the last administration of Antonio López de Santa Anna tried to remedy the crisis by dictatorially imposing a strong and centralized bureaucracy, favorable to the clergy and free of legislative checks and balances.[18] But this solution created huge dissatisfaction in the provinces, which suddenly lost autonomy to corrupt authorities that lacked any local roots. In response, many provincial leaders subscribed to the Plan of Ayutla, a revolutionary program that offered to restore a federal republic under liberal principles. The victorious revolution that followed would impose in 1857 a new constitution, which revived the federal model but also created a stronger national government founded upon the principle of popular sovereignty, decreed the end of corporate privileges, omitted any mention of the Catholic character of the republic, and granted federal authorities ample powers of intervention in Church affairs.[19]

Both in the United States and in Mexico, constitutional crisis and debate took place in an atmosphere of great ideological tension and growing hostility between interested parties, which closed the possibility of a new compromise and opened the terrible gates of civil war. As Thomas Bender observes, the ideal of a unified and homogenous nation, so common to the romantic liberalism of the European revolutions of 1848, made the coexistence of distinct political projects within a common constitutional framework impossible.[20] Abraham Lincoln recognized this in his famous speech of June 16, 1858: "A house divided against itself"— wherein one half was slave and the other free—"cannot stand."[21] The same thing happened in Mexico, when the bishops forbade their faithful (the great majority of the population) from taking an oath of allegiance to the 1857 Constitution because of its opposition to the rights and freedoms that the Church ought to enjoy in a confessional republic. If it had been possible to reconcile republican citizenship with loyalty to the Catholic faith for more than thirty years, to the point of considering this religious tradition to be the only tie uniting all Mexicans, as of 1857 believers ought to choose between eternal salvation and the fulfilling of civic obligations. The clash between the bishops and the liberal government was shattering; the dilemma divided society "even in the very heart of families" and in many towns there were riots against those authorities that dared to host swearing-of-allegiance ceremonies.[22]

At the outbreak of the civil wars (January 1858 in Mexico, April 1861 in the United States), rebel groups in both countries cited the rights and compromises that had structured the first constitutional pacts. The Southern separatists, for example, justified secession as an irrevocable right of the states that formed the republic; it was being exercised against federal attempts to decide the future of "our domestic institutions."[23] Mexican conservatives, meanwhile, demanded "institutions analogous to our practices and customs" and affirmed their desire to establish "an order of things that banished from memory the days of persecution and bitterness that the Mexican church has endured."[24] However, the particular dynamic of these conflicts necessitated a mass mobilization of economic and human resources and made inevitable the strengthening of the contending governments; this finally gave rise to a constitutional revolution in both countries. Broadening James McPherson's thesis regarding the United States, one may posit that the national governments of both Mexico and the United States—the principal fruit of the civil wars—would be characterized by a simultaneous affirmation of individual liberties and of state power, essential conditions for capitalistic expansion in the region during the following decades.[25] It is worthwhile analyzing this "constitutional revolution" more closely.

To be sure, in Mexico, the 1857 Constitution predated the civil war, and thus it may seem that the constitutional revolution was the cause—and not the effect—

of the armed conflict. To reach this conclusion, however, one must ignore the truly constitutional dimension of the decrees issued by the liberal government of Benito Juárez in Veracruz between July 1859 and December 1860, better known as the Reform Laws.[26] As is suggested in the presidential manifesto of July 7, 1859, the Reform Laws sought to define a new paradigm under which the 1857 document could finally operate: Constitutional rule, the document states, would only be possible through the removal of the "diverse elements of despotism, hypocrisy, immorality, and disorder" that had supposedly impeded the consolidation of a liberal regime in Mexico.[27] While the 1857 Constitution had preserved the old interdependence between Church and State (Article 123), the Reform Laws declared "the most perfect independence between the affairs of state and those purely of the Church." Once individual conscience had been protected and limits between secular and religious authority marked out, the state assumed control over acts involving civil status (starting with marriage, now seen as a contract) and decreed the nationalization and sale of Church properties, thus accelerating the shift to a national regime of individual private property that began in 1856 with the Disentailment of Rural and Urban Properties Law ("Lerdo Law").[28]

The simultaneous strengthening of the state and of individual liberties played out similarly in the United States. Beginning with the assumption of ample wartime powers in order to finance the federal army and suppress rebellion in the South, the Lincoln government set the legal foundations for definitively integrating new territories into the republic, both by providing subsidies and concessions for the building of the transcontinental railroad (the Pacific Railroad Acts, 1862 and 1864) and by awarding possession of public lands in the west to any settlers who should cultivate them for at least five years (the Homestead Act, 1862).[29] However, the most decisive measures were adopted after the war. On December 18, 1865, the Thirteenth Amendment to the Constitution was ratified, by which slavery was prohibited throughout the republic.[30] Considering the economic value of the four million slaves emancipated, this amendment implied the confiscation of almost $3 billion from an export-oriented elite that owned and administered almost a third of U.S. territory.[31] Foreseeing Southern resistance to the civil recognition of four million ex-slaves, Congress had to adopt a second and more overarching amendment, which turned the national state into the primary guarantor of individual rights.[32] This would be the Fourteenth Amendment, finally ratified in July 1868:

> All persons born or naturalized in the United States, and subject to the jurisdiction thereof, are citizens of the United States and of the State wherein

they reside. No State shall make or enforce any law which shall abridge the privileges or immunities of citizens of the United States; nor shall any State deprive any person of life, liberty, or property, without due process of law; nor deny to any person within its jurisdiction the equal protection of the laws. ... The Congress shall have power to enforce, by appropriate legislation, the provisions of this article.[33]

In his famous address after the Battle of Gettysburg on November 19, 1863, Lincoln described the Civil War as "a new birth of freedom."[34] And effectively the civil wars indeed gave birth to national states legitimized by the uncompromising defense of individual freedoms against provincial and corporate powers. In this sense, the civil wars also allowed the formation of new *national* identities, a process that would take several more decades to complete. Prior to the 1860s, neither in Mexico nor in the United States did there exist a feeling of national identity that could compete with local, ethnic, or religious loyalties: Mariano Otero admitted this in 1848, as did General Robert E. Lee in 1861 ("I shall never bear arms against the Union, but it may be necessary for me to carry a musket in the defense of my native state, Virginia"). However, the civil wars transformed these unions of states into something more than a pact cemented in defense of common interests. As David Brading observes with respect to the romantic liberalism of Mexico's Reform era, the "Great National Decade" contributed to emphasizing the mystique of sacrifice and "the priority of political action over private concerns." Victorious against enemies both internal and external (the conservatives and the invading French of the 1860s), the nation-state created a *patria* for which it was worth dying, a sort of "civic religion endowed with its own pantheon of saints, calendar of feasts, and civic edifices adorned with statues."[35] The perennial centrality of Benito Juárez and Abraham Lincoln in the Mexican and American public imaginary is clear evidence of the enormous cultural change created by and owing to the civil wars of the mid-nineteenth century.

Canada: The Fulfillment of the "Creole Dream"

What about Canada, however? To what extent does it fit into this story? During the first half of the nineteenth century, while the British provinces of North America (those that would become Canada) faced similar challenges to those of Mexico and the United States, such as sectional division, porous and hard-to-defend borders, or the establishment of a harmonic coexistence between church authorities and civil powers, its history is distinguished by an absence of great armed conflicts and even more so by the pragmatism of its leaders and the gradual and successful adaptation of its governing regime. Undoubtedly, Canada's point of departure was quite distinct: In contrast with the thirteen colonies that united against the mother country in 1776, the provinces of Quebec and Nova Scotia remained loyal to Great Britain, and very soon they gained the right whereby taxes collected locally would be destined solely for local needs. Before long, a massive arrival of refugees from the United States led to the creation of two new provinces, Upper Canada (Ontario) and New Brunswick, and in 1791, the British Crown authorized the election of representative assemblies in all its North American provinces, likewise allowing the persistence of French civil law and the privileges of the Catholic Church in Quebec.[36]

This notable leeway for self-government, along with protectionist measures favorable to colonial products, the fear of the nascent republic to the south, and the constant flow of British immigrants during the following decades, reinforced ties between the Crown and its Canadian provinces. One might therefore say that British North America was the fulfillment of the "creole dream," that American desire to share nation and monarchy with the mother country while enjoying autonomy at the same time (as extolled, for example, in Mexico's cusp-of-independence Plan of Iguala in 1821).[37] Free from the republicanism of their neighbors, the North American subjects of the British Crown considered that, in actual fact, the imperial constitution awarded them true political liberties, and even the Catholic bishops of Quebec recognized that Great Britain had providentially saved them from the "horrors of the [French] revolution and atheism."[38] And the rules of belonging to the great imperial commonwealth were sufficiently flexible to allow a North American coexistence of very distinct ethnic and religious communities: More than a cultural identity, their principal unifying bond was loyalty to British constitutional values and institutions, such as parliamentary monarchy, individual freedoms, respect for private property, local autonomy, and the legal defense of rights. (That said, one should not overlook the importance of the European provenance of the vast majority in the North American provinces, which explains the visible differences between the Canadian colonial experience and that of India or Africa, where imperial rule had a more overt, "civilizing" mission.)[39]

This imperial constitutional pact, however, had a weak point, which was the scant collaboration between local assemblies and provincial governors, the latter being designated directly by the mother country. Tensions between these powers gave way to rebellions in Quebec and Ontario in 1837, although these uprisings did not enjoy enough popular support and were suppressed with relative ease.[40]

Just as occurred in Mexico between 1833 and 1836, or in the United States during the Nullification Crisis of 1832, the rebellions of 1837 put the viability of the existing regime to the test and made its revision imperative. To that end, Prime Minister William Melbourne arranged an extraordinary visit by the Earl of Durham, Governor General of British North America, who in the end proposed that Quebec and Ontario be combined into a single province; in his view, the principal cause of Canada's problems was the presence of "two nations warring in the bosom of a single state." Although his proposal revealed a certain hardening of colonial policy—its real objective was the cultural absorption of the francophone population via the forced integration of Quebec and Ontario into a single Province of Canada, created in 1841—in actual fact, the union was carried out with a prudent pragmatism because the Crown also instructed the provincial governors to choose their ministers from among the leaders of majority factions in the local assemblies. Thus was founded a principle of parliamentary collaboration that would be formally recognized in 1848.[41] As a result, the imperial pact could be renewed without diminishing British authority and with an even greater autonomy for Canada's provinces.

Although the introduction of "responsible government" seemed to resolve British North America's main problems, two events took place in the late 1840s that forced yet another revision of the constitutional regime.[42] The first was the U.K. imperial free trade decree of 1846, which canceled tariff protections for colonial products and thereby severely affected the interests of those merchants and businessmen dependent on preferential access for their exports to the British market. The second, more decisive, event was the sudden territorial expansion of the United States thanks to the Treaty of Guadalupe Hidalgo in 1848. Although distrust of the republic to the south dated far back, Canadians understood that their economic future was inevitably linked to that of its neighbor, and there even arose opinions favoring eventual U.S. annexation of Britain's provinces. These recommendations failed, but through the course of the 1850s it became clear that the provinces needed to act in a coordinated manner to advance the integration of their respective markets and to develop canals and railroads, without which they could not hope to adapt to the new Atlantic economy, nor avoid U.S. colonization of Manitoba and British Columbia in the west. As though that were not enough, the growing demographic imbalance between the English- and French-speaking populations was making the joint government of Quebec and Ontario ever more difficult; it heralded a possible sectional and even religious conflict, similar to those of the United States and Mexico.

At this difficult crossroads a mere readjustment of local autonomies, as had occurred in the past, was not going to be enough. There was need for a new arrangement that combined representative government with the establishment of a *national* authority, and such an arrangement was precisely that of the Canadian Confederation, which began to be considered as of 1858.[43] It is important to emphasize that among the main advocates of the Confederation were the parliamentary leaders of the Province of Canada, where Anglo-French rivalry and clashes between parties often paralyzed legislative work. How was such a deal possible among leaders of opposing groups? While the pragmatism and political abilities of those leaders no doubt helped, a decisive factor may well have been the shared constitutional culture of the two "nations" that were supposedly "at war" within the same state. As opposed to Mexico and the United States, which were witnessing struggles for the absolute triumph of one national project over another, in the British provinces sectional projects and religious identities were being subordinated to a broader and more flexible political identity, defined by devotion to British constitutional values and institutions. So the challenge was not to create a state that was uniform in its laws and culture, but to build through negotiation a Canadian state that, without abandoning the Commonwealth, should facilitate governmental action, integration and defense of the provinces, economic progress, and the preservation of local interests and identities—in other words, the kind of strong and pluralistic state that could not be consolidated by peaceful means in mid-century Mexico and the United States.

Initially the federative proposal faced resistance on two fronts. First of all, many businessmen denounced the Confederation as a device designed to benefit the railroad consortia and their political allies with government subsidies drawn from public debt and higher tax rates. Charles Fox Bennett, a prestigious Newfoundland merchant opposed to the growing interventionism of local parliaments, even came to propose the abolition of "responsible government" because "previously to the introduction of the Local Legislature, this Colony was free from taxation."[44] Second, and closely related to this, most of the population of the Atlantic provinces rejected the federative proposal because they feared a grave loss of autonomy within a future national parliament dominated by Quebec and Ontario. At most, opponents of the Confederation were disposed to accept a customs and commerce reciprocity treaty between the British colonies, similar to the German *Zollverein*. Once again, war would be the decisive factor in the consummation of a contested political change, but in this case it would be a foreign civil war, having broad repercussions at a continental level. In 1864, with the defeat of the Confederate States of America on the horizon, the political leaders of Quebec and Ontario requested a new consideration of the federative proposal as the best bulwark against the United States, which was exhibiting an ever-more overwhelming military might. In the words of George Brown, one of the most influential members of the united provinces' government, "Unless we are willing to live at the mercy of our neighbors, we, too, must put our country in a state of efficient preparation."[45] The sense of urgency intensified due to frequent and violent raids by radical Irish Fenians,[46] along with Great Britain's growing disdain for its autonomous North American provinces. While the *Chicago Tribune* called for avenging Britain's dubious conduct of neutrality during the Civil War by annexing its North American colonies "as quickly as a hawk would gobble a quail," the Empire's finance minister, Benjamin Disraeli, lamented the excessive costs of continuing to defend militarily "a colony which does not permit us even to govern it!"[47]

Hence a difficult mix of international circumstances accelerated the political transition. The Canadian Confederation emerged though the Imperial Law of British North America (a.k.a. the Constitution Act), approved by the U.K. parliament on March 29, 1867—just a few weeks before Maximilian of Habsburg, the French-imposed Emperor of Mexico, capitulated at Querétaro.[48] "Confederation" in this case is a misnomer, as it did not involve a cooperative accord between sovereign provinces, as had occurred in Mexico and the United States after independence. On the contrary, the Imperial Law of 1867 established that the new "Dominion of Canada" would consist of four provinces—Ontario, Quebec, Nova Scotia, and New Brunswick—to be granted autonomy in local matters while being subordinated to a federal, two-chamber parliament. The superiority of this federal parliament was evident in the listing of its ample powers (fiscal, commercial, financial, migratory, and in defense and communications, to name the most important) and in the principle whereby powers not held exclusively by provincial legislatures should be understood as belonging to the confederation. To ensure this government's strength and unity, the 1867 law allowed the governor general to name his council of ministers (including the true holder of executive power, the prime minister) from among the leaders of the House of Commons, as per the tradition of "responsible government." Upon these principles, and similar to what occurred in Mexico and the United States at the end of their civil wars, the Constitution of the Dominion of Canada created an authentic liberal state—theoretically subject to the British Crown but actually directed by a powerful parliamentary government—able to foster the expansion and capitalistic development of a new *nation*.

One may question the use of the terms "state" and "nation" to refer to the Canadian Confederation created in 1867. Without wishing to engage a theoretical discussion beyond the bounds of this essay, it is worth making a couple of observations. First, it is beyond doubt that the Canadian Confederation was born as a true liberal state, ruled by principles of self-government, individual rights, and constitutional division of powers. Although the British Crown would continue to be sovereign over its Canadian "Dominion," in practice the authorities of the Confederation would exercise those powers that characterize any modern state: setting and collecting taxes; prosecuting, judging, and punishing criminals; defining and standardizing internal laws; organizing the territory's defense; regulating immigration, trade, and property rights; and so on. A more difficult task would be to determine whether the Dominion succeeded in becoming a true national community, above all given the development and future radicalization of Quebecois nationalism. If one assumes, as per the criteria of nineteenth-century Romanticism, that every nation ought to be based on some form of racial, ethnic, linguistic, or religious unity, Canada is indeed a legal construct that broaches multiple, conflictive national identities. But if one understands a nation as a community based on loyalty and daily adhesion to shared institutions and rights, the Canadian Confederation is a clear and successful historical example of the "constitutional patriotism" that is often presented today as an alternative to the exclusive nationalisms of the twentieth century.[49] As Mauricio Tenorio astutely puts it, "Canada is the liberal nation that has managed to tackle in a relatively peaceful fashion the experiments [of political and social coexistence] attempted by the United States and Mexico."[50]

Final Observations

What preliminary conclusions can be made about the parallel trajectories of Mexico, the United States, and Canada during the difficult middle decades of the nineteenth century? First, their respective civil wars and national constitutions responded to global trends and above all to *regional* dynamics that explain the simultaneous nature of the consolidation of the national state. In North America, the period from 1848 to 1867 was marked by intense realignments prompted by the Treaty of Guadalupe Hidalgo, epicenter of a lengthy political, economic, and social earthquake that coincided with the expansion of industrial capitalism and liberal Romanticism in Europe. Second, although this earthquake affected the region's three countries greatly, their reactions differed, shaped by the historical determinants and political traditions of each. The relative calm of the Canadian transition can be explained by the absence of slavery or an ecclesiastical authority as powerful as Mexico's, but that in turn requires an explanation of how the tense coexistence between francophone Catholics and Anglo-Saxon Protestants did not result in a war of religion or secession. Hence the decisive factor explaining the difference between Canada and its North American neighbors seems to have been the flexibility of a constitutional system that evolved in a gradual and pragmatic fashion, without a need for dramatic ruptures with the past. One may therefore modify what Ernest Renan said in 1882 regarding violence as "the origin of all political formations."[51] The Canadian case shows that civil war was not the only path possible for the national state and that the liberal mid-century revolutions of Mexico and the United States were rather a desperate method of imposing the new constitutional rules required by the dramatic continental transformation of 1848.

Notes

1. This chapter is a translation, with minor revisions, of "Guerra civil y Estado-nación en Norteamérica (1848–1867)," in Guillermo Palacios and Erika Pani, eds., *El poder y la sangre. Guerra, estado y nación en la década de 1860* (México: El Colegio de México, 2014), 43–62, translation by Andrew Paxman (CIDE—Aguascalientes). The author is grateful to the Colegio de México for its permission to republish this work.

2. See the introduction and conclusion to this volume for more on the transnational historiography of the American Civil War. Examples of recent studies include Alan Taylor, *American Revolutions: A Continental History, 1750–1804* (New York: Norton, 2016); Steven Hahn, *A Nation Without Borders: The United States and Its World in an Age of Civil Wars, 1830–1910* (New York: Penguin Random House, 2016); Don Doyle, *The Cause of All Nations: An International History of the American Civil War* (New York: Basic Books, 2015); Gregory P. Downs, *The Second American Revolution: The Civil War–Era Struggle over Cuba and the Rebirth of the American Republic* (Chapel Hill: University of North Carolina Press, 2019).

3. For Mexico, see José Antonio Aguilar-Rivera and Gabriel Negretto, "Rethinking the Legacy of the Liberal State in Latin America: The Cases of Argentina, 1853–1916, and Mexico, 1857–1910," *Journal of Latin American Studies* 32, no. 2 (2000), 361–97; José David Cortés Guerrero, "Desafuero eclesiástico, desamortización y tolerancia de cultos: una aproximación comparativa a las reformas liberales mexicana y colombiana de mediados del siglo XIX," *Fronteras de la historia* 9 (2004): 93–128; Riccardo Forte, "Los acuerdos de Ayutla (1854) y de San Nicolás (1852) y las constituciones liberales. Orígenes del poder coactivo del Estado en México y Argentina," *Historia Mexicana* 53, no. 4 (2004): 863–910; Florencia Mallon, *Peasant and Nation: The Making of Post-Colonial Mexico and Peru* (Berkeley: University of California Press, 1995); José Ragas, "Reformas liberales y sociedad en México y Perú, 1854–1872," in Sara Ortelli and Héctor Cuauhtémoc Hernández Silva, eds., *América en la época de Juárez. La consolidación del liberalismo. Procesos polí-*

ticos, sociales y económicos, 1854–1872 (México, UABJO/UAM, 2007), 287–320; Guy P. C. Thomson, "Liberalism and Nation-Building in Mexico and Spain During the Nineteenth Century," in James Dunkerley, ed., *Studies in the formation of the nation-state in Latin America* (London: University of London, 2002), 189–211. For the United States, see Carl Degler, *One Among Many: The Civil War in Comparative Perspective* (Gettysburg, Pa.: Gettysburg College, 1990); Peter Kolchin, *Unfree Labor: American Slavery and Russian Serfdom* (Cambridge: Harvard University Press, 1987); and Enrico Dal Lago, *Agrarian Elites: American Slaveholders and Southern Italian Landowners, 1815–1861* (Baton Rouge: Louisiana State University Press, 2005). The most ambitious and suggestive narrative effort is Thomas Bender, *A Nation Among Nations: America's Place in World History* (New York: Hill and Wang, 2006).

4. Mauricio Tenorio, *Historia y Celebración: México y sus Centenarios* (Mexico City: Tusquets, 2009), 226.

5. Charles A. Hale, *El liberalismo mexicano en la época de Mora* (Mexico City: Siglo XXI, 1972), 16–17; Louis P. Masur, *The Civil War: A Concise History* (New York: Oxford University Press, 2011), 11.

6. I draw, in particular, from Jack P. Greene, *The Constitutional Origins of the American Revolution* (New York: Cambridge University Press, 2011), and José María Portillo, *Crisis Atlántica: Autonomía e independencia en la crisis de la monarquía hispana* (Madrid: Marcial Pons, 2006).

7. On slavery and Catholicism within the U.S. and Mexican foundational pacts, see David Waldstreicher, *Slavery's Constitution: From Revolution to Ratification* (New York: Hill and Wang, 2009); William W. Freehling, *The Reintegration of American History: Slavery and the Civil War* (New York: Oxford University Press, 1994); and Brian Connaughton, *Clerical Ideology in a Revolutionary Age: The Guadalajara Church and the Idea of the Mexican Nation, 1788–1853* (Calgary: University of Calgary Press, 2003).

8. See, for example, Jonathan Hughes and Louis P. Cain, *American Economic History* (New York: HarperCollins, 1994), 83–190; Seth Rockman, "Jacksonian America," in Eric Foner and Lisa McGirr, eds., *American History Now* (Philadelphia: Temple University Press, 2011), 52–74; Eric Foner, *Give Me Liberty! An American History* (New York: Norton, 2009), 302–73; and Brian Schoen, *The Fragile Fabric of Union: Cotton, Federal Politics, and the Global Origins of the Civil War* (Baltimore: Johns Hopkins University Press, 2009).

9. Melvin I. Urofsky and Paul Finkelman, *A March of Liberty: A Constitutional History of the United States, Volume I: From the Founding to 1890* (New York: Oxford University Press, 2002), 271–82.

10. José Antonio Serrano and Josefina Z. Vázquez, "El nuevo orden, 1821–1848," in *Nueva historia general de México* (Mexico City: Colegio de México, 2010), 397–441; Enrique Cárdenas, *Cuando se originó el atraso económico de México. La economía mexicana en el largo siglo XIX, 1780–1920* (Madrid: Editorial Biblioteca Nueva, 2003), 59–101.

11. Manuel González Oropeza, "Pasado y futuro de la anulación de leyes según el Acta de Reformas (1847–1857)," in Cecilia Noriega and Alicia Salmerón, eds., *México: un siglo de historia constitucional, 1808–1917: Estudios y perspectivas* (Mexico City: Suprema Corte de Justicia de la Nación / Instituto Mora, 2009), 203–46.

12. Elliott West, "The Other War That Remade America," in William A. Frazier and Mark K. Christ, eds., *Ready, Booted, and Spurred: Arkansas in the U.S. Mexican War* (Little Rock: Butler Center for Arkansas Studies, 2009), 102–24.

13. Foner, *Give Me Liberty!*, 377–87, 450–58; Masur, *Civil War*, 9–15.

14. Eric Foner, *Free Soil, Free Labor, Free Men: The Ideology of the Republican Party before the Civil War* (New York: Oxford University Press, 1976).

15. David K. Burden, "Reform Before *La Reforma*: Liberals, Conservatives and the Debate Over Immigration, 1846–1855," *Mexican Studies/Estudios Mexicanos* 23, no. 2 (2007)," 283–316; Erica Pani, "De vuelta a la Gran Década Nacional: Reforma, Intervención e Imperio," in *Interpretaciones de la Reforma y del Segundo Imperio*, coord. Josefina Zoraida Vázquez (México: Grupo Editorial Patria, 2007), 41–68; Cárdenas, *Cuándo se originó el atraso*, 103–16; Hale, *El liberalismo mexicano*, 14–41.

16. Pablo Mijangos y González, *The Lawyer of the Church: Bishop Clemente de Jesús Munguía and the Clerical Response to the Mexican Liberal Reforma* (Lincoln: Nebraska University Press, 2015), 95–178.

17. Urofsky and Finkelman, *A March of Liberty*, 379–96; Masur, *The Civil War*, 11–17; Foner, *Give Me Liberty!*, 458–71.

18. Lira, "Administrar justicia sin Constitución," 115–40.

19. Covo, *Las ideas de la Reforma*; Pani, "Entre transformar y gobernar," 65–86.

20. Bender, *A Nation Among Nations*, Chapter 3.

21. McPherson, *Ordeal by Fire*, 117.

22. Lira, "La consolidación nacional," 188–92.

23. McPherson, *Ordeal by Fire*, 139–45; Foner, *Give Me Liberty!*, 476.

24. José María Vigil, *México a través de los siglos, vol. 5: La Reforma* (Mexico City: Editorial Cumbre, 1956), 280–81.

25. James M. McPherson, *Abraham Lincoln and the Second American Revolution* (New York: Oxford University Press, 1991).

26. The Laws of Reform were incorporated into the constitution in 1873.

27. Vigil, *México a través de los siglos*, 379–82.

28. Daniela Marino and María Cecilia Zuleta, "Una visión del campo: Tierra, propiedad y tendencias de la producción, 1850–1930," in Sandra Kuntz Ficker, ed., *Historia económica general de México: De la Colonia a nuestros días* (Mexico City: Colegio de Mexico, 2010), 438–48.

29. Urofsky and Finkelman, *March of Liberty*, 412–23; Foner, *Give Me Liberty!*, 500–5.

30. Urofsky and Finkelman, *March of Liberty*, 423–27.

31. McPherson, *Abraham Lincoln*, 16–18.

32. Urofsky and Finkelman, *March of Liberty*, 440–47.

33. Quoted in Jack N. Rakove, *The Annotated U.S. Constitution and Declaration of Independence* (Cambridge: Harvard University Press, 2009), 259, 269.

34. Foner, *Give Me Liberty!*, 500.

35. David Brading, "Liberal Patriotism and the Mexican Reforma," *Journal of Latin American Studies*, 20, no. 1 (1988): 37, 40. For the United States, see Melinda Lawson, *Patriot Fires: Forging a New American Nationalism in the Civil War North* (Lawrence: University Press of Kansas, 2002).

36. John G. Reid and Elizabeth Mancke, "From Global Processes to Continental Strategies: The Emergence of British North America to 1783," in Phillip Buckner, ed., *Canada and the British Empire* (Oxford: Oxford University Press, 2008), 37–41; John Herd Thompson and Stephen J. Randall, *Canada and the United States: Ambivalent Allies* (Athens: University of Georgia Press, 1994), 9–14; Robert Bothwell, *The Penguin History of Canada* (Toronto: Penguin Canada, 2006), 100–12; Jane Burbank and Frederick Cooper, *Empires in World History: Power and the Politics of Difference* (Princeton, N.J.: Princeton University Press, 2010), 240–45, 300–1.

37. The phrase "creole dream" (*sueño criollo*) is from José María Portillo.

38. Thompson and Randall, *Canada and the United States*, 15–23; Bothwell, *The Penguin History of Canada*, 124, 136–68.

39. Philip Buckner, "Introduction: Canada and the British Empire," in Buckner, ed., *Canada and the British Empire*, 6.

40. J. M. Bumsted, "Consolidation of British North America, 1783–1860," in Buckner, ed. *Canada and the British Empire*, 52–56; J. L. Finlay and D. N. Sprague, *The Structure of Canadian History* (Scarborough, ON: Prentice-Hall Canada, 1984), 111–26; Bothwell, *The Penguin History of Canada*, 162–83.

41. Bumsted, "Consolidation of British North America," 56–62; Finlay and Sprague, *Structure of Canadian History*, 129–42.

42. John A. Williams, "Canada and the Civil War," in Herold Hyman, ed., *Heard Round the World: The Impact Abroad of the Civil War* (New York: Alfred A. Knopf, 1969), 259–68; Finlay and Sprague, *Structure of Canadian History*, 145–75; Thompson and Randall, *Canada and the United States*, 32–33.

43. Williams, "Canada and the Civil War," 262–63; Finlay and Sprague, *Structure of Canadian History*, 175–79; Buckner, "The Creation of the Dominion of Canada," in Buckner, ed., *Canada and the British Empire*, 66–68.

44. Andrew Smith, "Toryism, Classical Liberalism, and Capitalism: The Politics of Taxation and the Struggle for Canadian Confederation," *Canadian Historical Review* 89, no. 1 (2008): 7.

45. Williams, "Canada and the Civil War," 269–83.

46. The raids upon Canada by U.S.-based Fenians aimed to pressure Great Britain into decreeing Irish independence, a strategy that resoundingly failed.

47. Bothwell, *Penguin History of Canada*, 209; Thompson and Randall, *Canada and the United States*, 37.

48. Williams, "Canada and the Civil War," 283–98; Bothwell, *Penguin History of Canada*, 210–13; Marian C. McKenna, "Introduction: A Legacy of Questions," in McKenna, ed., *The Canadian and American Constitutions in Comparative Perspective* (Calgary: University of Calgary Press, 1993), xv–xxviii.

49. For an introduction to the theory of "constitutional patriotism," see Gregorio Peces-Barba, "El patriotismo constitucional: Reflexiones en el vigésimo quinto aniversario de la Constitución española," *Anuario de Filosofía del Derecho* XX (2003): 39–61.

50. Mauricio Tenorio, *Historia y Celebración: México y sus Centenarios* (Mexico City: Tusquets, 2009), 221.

51. Renan, "What Is a Nation?," paper given at the Sorbonne, Paris, March 11, 1882.

4

1860s Capitalscapes, Governing Interiors, and the Illustration of North American Sovereignty

Robert Bonner

In most accounts of modern politics, sovereign authority is the product of intelligible language, with legitimate rulership emanating from compacts, constitutions, oaths, and other speech and text acts. Yet in operation, and as a matter of the historical record, sovereignty has often been more a matter of images than of words. Visualized acts of affiliation and acquiescence sanction the violent maintenance of hierarchy, obedience, and order needed by territorial states to govern vast populations. Graphic depictions of insiders and outsiders affirm the policing of geographical and conceptual borders and the legitimate deployment of lethal force against the regime's enemies. What might be termed a sovereign imaginary depends on emotive visual cues that work simultaneously to elevate, explain, and sacralize governance. Ensembles of crowns, heraldry, and other symbols of rightful rule originated with early modern monarchies and empires. With the launching of republics during an age of revolution, depictions of the "people" as the font of authority joined earlier motifs as essential ingredients of illustrated sovereignty. Scenes of a citizenry mobilized in highly charged settings thus became a common feature of mass-based political iconography.

Few historians have explored how sovereign imaginaries have operated during the past two centuries of modern representative government. This chapter uses this concept to relate the illustration of North American sovereignty during the 1860s, a crucial decade when North Americans pioneered what Charles Maier has lately termed "Leviathan 2.0."[1] Mass-circulated images distilled and shaped popular engagement with capital cities of countries experiencing those internal crises that essays in this volume address. Distinctive capitalscapes, as we shall see, brought into view three sites where the destinies of an entire continent were seemingly being worked out by rulers of huge federal states.[2]

As nodes of representative power and as the administrative centers of rapidly centralizing federal democracies, Washington, Mexico City, and Ottawa lent themselves to visualization during a decade that was saturated by patriotic imagery. Capital boulevards, public edifices, and monumental sculpture within these governing hubs showcased how armies, assemblages, and citizens were recasting hemispheric authority. What transpired in the interiors of governing spaces allowed for another aspect of this decade's sovereign imaginary to come into view. The visual display of deliberating representatives was especially pertinent to the ambitions of the Washington, D.C.–based Congress, the most powerful site of North American policy-making. The inner workings of capitalscapes depicted how those assembled to rule on behalf of "American," "Mexican," and "Canadian" peoples went about their work. This focus on parliamentary procedure, staged as a matter of federative give-and-take, served to offset and detract attention from the physical force on which the "self-rule" of territorial nation-states depended.

The distinctive visualizations of this moment can be clarified by contrasting the imagery of "Leviathan 2.0" with the chief iconic representation of the 1.0 version. Abraham Bosse's engraved introduction to Thomas Hobbes's *Leviathan* in 1651 represents one of the most notable depictions of sovereignty in all of modern politics (see Figure 1). Here, the conceptualization of legitimate rule came via the agglomeration of tiny individual subjects into a sword-wielding, staff-carrying monarch.[3] These subjects' lack of motive power (signaled by the inertness of these figures and their turning away from the viewer) brilliantly conveyed the Hobbesian conceit of how authority originated. As his text explained, state power was brought into being by those who purposefully sought deliverance from their brutish natural existence.

If no single classic image conveyed the various remakings of hemispheric sovereignty during the 1860s, the urge to conceptualize North American rulership via subtle and evocative visualizations was ubiquitous, forming part of the broader nineteenth-century penchant for collective self-observation and self-representation.[4] Capitalscape sovereignty of the 1860s rendered the "people" not in allegory but in actuality, with realistic scenes featuring individuals who, in keeping with the tenets of modern liberalism, simultaneously asserted themselves and advanced the best interests of their polity. Across the continent, rights-bearing individuals enacted sovereignty via engagement with realms of governance subject to the direct influence of individuals. Enlisting in an army of fellow citizens or participating, either as a male voter or a female patriot, in the selection of representative leaders were the two most important routes offered to democratic citizens in elaborating a "peoples-based" regime. As I have explored elsewhere, the themes of martial, democratic voluntarism permeated the American Civil War's vibrant "flag culture" in which a set of broad cultural practices

Figure 1. Abraham Bosse frontispiece for Thomas Hobbes's *Leviathan* (1651). Courtesy of Dartmouth College Libraries.

yoked themes of sacrificial violence (in which individuals willingly killed and died on behalf of a national cause) to the military mobilization undertaken by a central state.[5] Elements that imbued wartime flag culture with its emotive power can be discerned in the profusion of capitalscape imagery of these same years. In both phenomena, a functional relationship existed between how people witnessed their nation, how citizens understood a crisis that placed the nation at risk, and how a given federal polity expanded its governing capacity. Whether through transactional relationships between individual patriots, their community, and the semi-sacred flags of the battlefield, or via an immersion in the rich symbolism of urban nodes of governance, the Americas of the 1860s elaborated props of visualized political authority that retain their power to this day.

Of course, the capitalscapes of Washington, D.C. and Mexico City had lent themselves to powerful associations long before 1860. The symbolic potency of Mexico's chief urban center predated European imperialism itself; the American Union's Federal District had been a self-conscious vehicle of republican integration from the late eighteenth-century design of its main streets and public sites. Yet in the critical decade of hemispheric reorganization and civil war, emerging media forms invested each of these locales with new iconic possibilities. Chief among these was a profusion of wood engravings within mass-circulated illustrated weeklies. This same media apparatus allowed Ottawa and Richmond to emerge with sovereign capitalscapes of their own, and these two cities joined their older counterparts in an international montage sequence that cumulatively depicted the revolutionary emergence of three transcontinental federations. Audiences across the Atlantic world gained an appreciation for the stakes of military actions taken either in defense of or as an assault upon governing capital cities through the pages of magazines that, in regular succession, brought three vital cockpits of North American governance into a common field of vision.

The ritualistic quality of assuming control of a monumental capital city (either by force or, in the case of Ottawa, by careful urban and constitutional design) was ready-made for the mass-produced iconography of woodcut engraving. The decade's illustration of sovereignty also used the woodcut form to render visible the more mundane work of enacting popular rule via deliberate assemblies. Mass-circulated depictions of national delegates assembling within lavish confines secured by an aroused citizenry completed a circuit between citizenship and state power. The massive governing complexes that served as synecdoches for entire countries furnished images of dominance and command, to be sure. But within their interior spaces, there was a different mode of elaborating nationalist futures. By the end of the 1860s, a new aura had thus been established, not just around the imposing Capitol Hill but within its decorous Houses of Congress; in the inner sanctum of the Canadian legislative complex no less than in the majesty of Parliament Hill; and, in the case of the *Zócalo* complex, in the melding of a stunning plaza and Cathedral with a revivified *Palacio Nacional* whose caretakers were making good on their commitment to a decentralized constitutional order.

Four capital spectacles occurring between 1865 and 1867 demonstrated how North American sovereign imaginaries worked in dialogue with one another. The triumph of U.S. sovereignty in 1865 ended the existential threat to the polity and represented the most consequential development of mid-century global history. In terms of imagery, no scene more powerfully captured this victory than the ceremonial march of some 150,000 ordinary soldiers past the District of Columbia's chief government buildings on May 23 and 24 of 1865. After tramping up Maryland Avenue and past the newly completed Capitol Dome, this "Grand Review" coupled the efficacy of war (as signaled by the troops' iconic transit

down Pennsylvania Avenue past the White House) with the advent of peace (in
the immediate departure of most of these soldiers to their civilian lives hundreds,
if not thousands, of miles away).[6] The people's representatives left behind in the
Congress that loomed over the scene could be trusted to preside over a reunited
country, welcoming peace, via a system of federal representation worthy of a
mammoth transcontinental republic.

The most powerful renderings of this two-day march came via the cameras of
Matthew Brady and Alexander Gardner, whose vantage maximized the composi-
tional pairing of soldiers with a Dome that had become the chief icon of national
governance. The showy spectacle reached a global audience not by photorealism
alone but by its translation by skilled professional illustrators who adapted it to
the pages of *Harper's Weekly*, *Frank Leslie's Illustrated*, and the *London Illustrated
News* (see Figure 2). The cadre of mass media pioneers had made illustrated
magazines uniquely powerful imagemakers of the 1860s; in their prints, various
aspects of the Union's war to suppress the Confederate rebellion achieved maxi-

Figure 2. "Grand Review at Washington—Sheridan's Cavalry Passing through Pennsylvania Avenue, May 23, 1865—[Photographed by Gardner]," *Harper's Weekly*, June 10, 1865.
Courtesy of Dartmouth College Libraries.

mum exposure.[7] Efforts by the woodcut artists to make photographic work widely reproducible were supplemented by parallel ventures that translated hand-drawn sketches and diagrams into etchings; a unifying technology joined the observations into a common visual aesthetic. It was not a photograph but a sketch from life that allowed these weeklies to depict soldiers destined to participate in the "Grand Review" marching a month and a half earlier in triumph through the streets of Richmond. In the artifice of woodcut "realism," distinctions blurred between what was derived from a first-hand sketch, from a camera image, or simply from the imagination of an artist. The visual realm of this media form comprised interchangeable images of actual scenes captured from firsthand observations and deeply symbolic renderings achieved by such brilliant visual artists as Winslow Homer and Thomas Nast.[8]

Richmond's capitulation to Union forces in early April 1865 was a self-evidently important topic for those illustrated weeklies that had long emphasized that city's paramount military importance.[9] The consummation of the "war for the Union" required that Richmond not simply be taken as a military target but be brought back under the sovereign jurisdiction of the United States. A mass audience envisioned this process via a second iconic scene for consideration: the April 4, 1865, visit to the city of Abraham Lincoln, himself the living embodiment of America's "people's contest." Treated to a redemptive tour following an act of destruction, readers of the illustrated press could follow Lincoln's stroll through Richmond's still smoldering thoroughfares, his greeting of an African-American population that had endured life in a key node of the domestic slave trade, and his stop at the "Confederate White House," which, as the residence of Jefferson Davis, had long figured as the chief site of traitorous rebellion.[10] Accompanying Lincoln in this visit was David Dixon Porter who later reflected on what it had meant for the civilian leader to come "armed with the majesty of the law, to put his seal to the act which had been established by the bayonets of the Union soldiers." For Lincoln to signal reincorporation without the support of a massed soldiery had "a moral in it all," Porter noted. The welcoming of the U.S. President by locals themselves achieved "more effect than if he had come surrounded with great armies and heralded by the booming of cannon."[11]

In the summer of 1867, a third urban scene allowed a momentous shift in Mexican sovereignty to be illustrated, as troops escorted Benito Juárez to the *Palacio Nacional*, where he reinstated the constitutional order framed by Mexican liberals ten years earlier. Like the Grand Review in Washington and Lincoln's entry to Richmond, this occasion involved as much ceremony as military logistics, and it was carefully staged several weeks after Maximilian's execution and after the last *imperialista* forces had been driven from the city. Camera shutters clicked as troops traversed the same streets that three years earlier had witnessed a grand entry by a European-sanctioned, Hapsburg-led empire. The illustrated weeklies circulated scenes from the entrances of first Maximilian (in 1864) and then Juárez to the capital as bookended visualizations. They selected the signature image of the Juárez procession from a photograph taken, ironically enough, by former court photographer Francois Aubert. This image of the main square as a calm oasis featured middle-class strollers clustered beneath a massive republican flag and around a monument to a female figure of "Victory" specially raised for the occasion (see Figure 3).[12] The overriding visual message was the return of normalcy to a patriotic space that had witnessed the humiliating presence of American troops twenty years earlier and had more recently been the site of Maximilian's attempt to establish a seat of New World imperial glory. Stripping away the pomp that had marked the Habsburg's showy 1864 arrival seemed to be Juárez's intent. Readers of *Harper's Weekly* could consider the plaza scene as the culmination of what went before: a brief speech made by Juárez upon entering the city and his subsequent procession past "tablets bearing the names of

Figure 3. "Scene in the Grand Plaza of the City of Mexico on the Occasion of the Reception of President Juárez," *Harper's Weekly*, October 12, 1867. Courtesy of Dartmouth College Libraries.

the principal cities of the Republic, distinguished men, and also various engage-
ments in which the Liberal armies are said to have been victorious."[13]

The final episode in a quartet of capitalscape scenes coincided with an assembly on the banks of the Ottawa River, where representatives of four provinces
of British North America launched the Dominion of Canada in the fall of 1867.
The event was well matched with the location of the newly dubbed Parliament
Hill, whose perch on a cliff bridged two provinces while, by facing west, looked
toward the realm where Canadian nationality would be further elaborated. This
architectural complex, like the government it housed, was still under construction, as was the Canadian national project then being forged. Ottawa's visualization in the illustrated weeklies stood out for the absence of martial imagery. Signs
of the relationship between continental sovereignty and the force of arms was altogether absent. The contest shown to *Harper's Weekly* readers was a boat regatta,
a suitable means of blessing a political founding through an ordinary proceeding
of a stable civil society (see Figure 4). The transit of European-based sporting to
a New World setting signaled a form of nation-building that made the Canadian
experience the North American exception that proved the broader rule.[14]

The series of scenes appeared, roughly in the same chronological order in which
they transpired, before audiences who had grown to expect finely rendered en-

BOAT REGATTA AT OTTAWA—THE CONTESTANTS PASSING THE PARLIAMENT BUILDINGS.—[SKETCHED BY ALFRED JONES.]

Figure 4. "Boat Regatta at Ottawa: The Contestants Passing the Parliament Buildings.—
[Sketched by Alfred Jones]," *Harper's Weekly*, October 19, 1867. Courtesy of Dartmouth
College Libraries.

gravings of major events and faraway places. The key development in this oft-told story of Victorian mass media was the founding of the *Illustrated London News* in 1842. In the wake of this breakthrough, an international genre with a strong bourgeois sensibility took hold across Europe and North America and was then adopted by settler outposts as far away as the South Pacific.[15] Middle-class subscribers to what the *Harpers' Weekly* masthead dubbed a "Journal of Civilization" regularly received visual information about the latest fashions, the world of art, and global events. The steady fare of international illustrated reporting contained happenings deemed by editors to rise to the level of a historical event; the same held true for the evocative political cartoons that regularly engaged in stock diplomatic figures of "Uncle Sam" and "John Bull." As a vehicle for metropolitan-based taste-making, these journals represented a novel force of global integration.

Mid-nineteenth-century attentiveness to the iconography of capital cities had deeper roots than the period's woodcut globalism. Having said this, the mid-century decades did witness a growing appreciation for the symbolic importance of those governing sites where "conceptions of political order" could be "converted into geometry and stone," to borrow Jurgen Osterhammel's crisp formulation. The "symbolic terrain" of administrative centers acquired greatest potency when recalling the past, projecting the future, or becoming a stage for actors (most typically volunteer soldiers or elected leaders) to perform present shifts in national destinies. This was the era of new construction modeling old forms, whether one considers Charles Barry's iconic Westminster Palace complex (raised along the Thames between 1844 and 1860), the gathering of sovereign structures in Brussels, Belgium and St. Petersburg, Russia, or the fabrication of a "tropical Versailles" in Brazil's Rio de Janeiro.[16]

The sovereign locales of North America conjured up by the illustrated weeklies did not always align with actual urban geographies, a point evident in those masthead designs that served to popularize three out of four hemispheric capitalscapes. Though published in New York, *Frank Leslie's Illustrated News* featured the District of Columbia's signature domed complex on the top of its front page from its launching in 1855; the same iconography was carried over in 1857 to the German language-counterpart *Frank Leslie's Illustre Beitung*. The discrepancy of a Potomac scene atop a Manhattan paper persisted, in part because Washington in these years did not host its own illustrated weekly. Likewise, neither Mexico City nor Ottawa developed any such journals from this period, so that each of the three major North American capitals were objects of metropolitan visualization from afar.[17] Ottawa's Parliament Hill did grace the masthead of *Canadian Illustrated News*, a paper that over the course of its relatively short existence was edited and printed over a hundred miles away, in Montreal. Woodcuts of the Mexican *Zócalo* never achieved masthead status. When sovereign capitalscape imagery did appear in woodcut form, it was via non-Mexican publications designed and printed in Paris, London, and New York.

Intriguingly, masthead and sovereign locales achieved the closest match in the peculiar case of Richmond's *Southern Illustrated News*, which introduced its readers in its first series of issues to the most recognizable feature of that city's skyline.[18] Rather than focus on a building or port, the *Southern Illustrated News* placed the city's monumental statue of George Washington as the central icon of its first page. This massive stone and bronze creation had become one of the chief elements of Virginia's Capitol Square complex in the mid-1850s, as it was reared, with considerable fanfare, on a James River ridge beside the Jefferson-designed State House and the Governor's Mansion that had been constructed in 1813.[19] Confederate image-makers attempted to co-opt what Virginians had planned as a carefully orchestrated tribute to state pride. Mississippian Jefferson Davis laid claim to the legacy during his 1862 inaugural and then witnessed the selection of the same image for the Confederacy's official national seal.[20]

This towering equestrian image of Confederate sovereignty conveyed a Janus-faced message, drawing its power as much from present resonance with "cavalier" self-understandings as from its links to the American founding. A sculpted giant placed atop a horse seemingly primed for battle, this rendering of General Washington bestowed upon Confederates a fitting emblem of 1860s nationalist military mobilization (see Figure 5).[21] Omitted from most scenes of Confederate sovereignty was the grand State House of Capitol Square, the building that served both the Confederate Congress and the Virginia State Assembly.[22] A federative House and Senate sharing quarters with Virginia legislators were more than willing to cede the spotlight to those more celebrated generals whose portraits dominated the visual program of the *Southern Illustrated News*.[23] The publicity deficit experienced by civilian legislators was partly a conscious decision—the Confederate Congress spent a disproportionate amount of their time in secret session, where members shielded nationalist debates from public scrutiny. The Richmond appearing in the illustrated weeklies was, in any event, bereft of architectural symbols used to signal sovereignty via representative lawmaking, setting the Confederate case apart from comparable depictions of Washington, Mexico City, and Ottawa during these transformative years.[24]

The scant attention devoted to a Richmond governing center helps to make sense of Jefferson Davis's suggestion at war's end that his government could relinquish control of their capital by simply moving the struggle into a "new

AN ALABAMA REGIMENT MARCHING THROUGH CAPITOL SQUARE, RICHMOND, ON THEIR WAY TO JOIN THE REBEL FORCES UNDER BEAUREGARD

Figure 5. "An Alabama Regiment Marching through Capitol Square, Richmond, on Their Way to Join the Rebel Forces Under Beauregard," *Harper's Weekly*, October 19, 1861. Courtesy of Dartmouth College Libraries.

stage" fought out elsewhere. Loading trains with bureaucratic records and then taking flight in the days preceding Lincoln's visit, Davis bravely asserted that the Confederate cause would furnish an exception to the rule in which "the preservation of the capital" was "regarded as the evidence to mankind of separate national existence."[25] He was hardly the first to consider Richmond as a temporary home for the Confederate seat of government. Had Southern armies won on the battlefield, it seems likely that a peacetime Confederacy would have selected a new capital in Nashville, Montgomery, or New Orleans, or a brand new locale, perhaps near rail crossings of northern Alabama, Georgia, or Piedmont North Carolina.[26]

The limitations of Richmond as a sovereign capitalscape formed a contrast to the monumentalized spaces and structures across North America's other three governing hubs, whose permanence as a secure seat of governance became a vital objective for each polity. The most highly charged locale, at least in a visual sense, was Washington, D.C., a Potomac city made enormously vulnerable by its location between the two slave states of Virginia (with its proudly Confederates ties) and Maryland (with a white population of doubtful loyalty).[27] Observers of the wartime federal capital at the time and since have circled around the twin themes of Washington's susceptibility to Confederate assault and the city's steadfast efforts to deviate as little as possible from normal democratic governance. A visual shorthand for this second objective was the spectacular erection of a massive domed Capitol building completed and crowned by a statue of Freedom in 1865.[28] The symbolic transformation of the city and its chief symbol were achieved only through the presence of hundreds of thousands of soldiers, arranged in state organized regiments, whose prolonged residence jolted the city. Housed, nursed, and trained within a massive building complex supporting the governance of a spacious republic, these men brought the mores of New England, the Mid-Atlantic, and the Ohio Valley to what had been a sleepy slave-dominated town. The Northern governors and state dignitaries who arrived via rail connections from the Midwest and the Eastern Seaboard to look after the well-being of their constituents found a ready audience with Lincoln, who nurtured his relationship with state officials far more effectively than Davis had been able to do. By the time of the springtime 1865 Grand Review, the narrative of a nation becoming complete in form and through actual rhythms of wartime federative cooperation was a broadly shared conceit.

A steady stream of woodcuts in the illustrated news allowed readers to track how construction of this iron-supported dome progressed over the course of the United States' struggle for its existence. An engineering effort barely begun as Lincoln first took the oath of office would be fully formed, with a statue on top, by the time his second inaugural ceremony was choreographed in the very shadow of the edifice.[29] A subset of images showed how this same project might recast the interior spaces of the U.S. Congress. Depictions of Congress during the late antebellum years suggested a fractious, semi-governable multitude where popular government displayed its worst tendencies.[30] Visual coverage of what was planned for the new rotunda complex forecast a future of greater refinement, where the harangue of partisan and sectional advantage would be leavened by epic paintings and cathedral-like spaces. Such scenes might stage the saga of American history in ways that ordinary citizens might better appreciate a legacy too valuable to relinquish (see Figure 6).[31]

In its 1860 preview of the Rotunda, *Harper's* took up the architectural planning rather than the actual construction of this space. The erection of a dome projecting dominance outward did coincide with the considerable upgrade of interiors that seemed, in a visual sense, to assure the serenity of nationalist contemplation

INTERIOR OF THE NEW DOME OF THE CAPITOL AT WASHINGTON.—[From the Designs of T. U. Walter, Architect.]

Figure 6. "Interior of the New Dome of the Capitol at Washington.—[From the Designs of T. U. Walter, Architect]," *Harper's Weekly*, March 9, 1861. Courtesy of Dartmouth College Libraries.

within. Leading away from the massive Rotunda were lavish chambers that lent dignity to the work that Congressmen and Senators undertook to craft states-manlike compromises. Ennobling democratic practice was a potent combination of popular patriotism and firm leadership that became the essence of a national-ized program of liberal reform during these years.[32] Within such splendid new quarters, Congress undertook one of the most activist agendas of the pre–New Deal years. A highlight, captured in solemn woodcuts of the leading illustrated presses, was the enactment by Congress of an emancipationist rebirth via a self-consciously high-minded passage of the Thirteenth Amendment.[33] During the post-war years, the martial pageantry that had enlivened the streets of D.C. before the Grand Review rapidly dissipated. There was a corresponding uptick in scenes of grand legislative halls, which, as a result of Andrew Johnson's squandering of executive powers, emerged as the primary locus of American sovereignty. Revo-lutionary policy adopted by Congress was followed by an impeachment trial that brought forth a series of dramatic scenes in both the House of Representatives (where these 1868 proceedings began) and the Senate (which housed the trial that would acquit Johnson). Nine years later, illustrated magazines brought Con-gressional interiors into focus once more, as representatives struggled there to resolve the bitterly contested presidential election of 1876–77.

Portrayals of Richmond in the post-1865 years likewise turned away from the details of martial mobilization and toward interior sovereign scenes. During the early stages of Reconstruction, the illustrated weeklies began to peer, as they had not during the war, into the Richmond statehouse, which became a stage for ritu-als of loyalty oaths, mass meetings, and, most dramatically, the recasting of the body politic via the 1868 constitutional convention (see Figure 7).[34] As had been true before the war, sovereign polities at the state level framed their own forms of government via parliamentary give-and-take, followed by ratification by popular vote. The prominent inclusion of non-white figures in the halls of power cap-tured the radical departure that Congressional Reconstruction had spurred.[35]

The *Imperialistas* recast Mexico City's governing interiors intent on making deco-rum and order the identifying hallmarks of Maximilian's regime. Several recent scholars have affirmed the early 1860s as a critical time of Mexican urban design, as themes of mass democratic sovereignty were subordinated so as to burnish the ultimately ill-fated attempt to graft Hapsburg-derived forms onto a centralizing polity.[36] Republicans and *Imperialistas* alike realized how improvised modes of rule would have greatest effect if enacted in the country's central valley and with the occupancy of this ancient seat of governance. Simply put, ruling from the

Figure 7. "The State Convention at Richmond, Va, in Session," *Frank Leslie's Illustrated Magazine*, February 15, 1868. Courtesy of Dartmouth College Libraries.

grand central buildings of the *Zócalo* was critical to any regime's legitimacy in the international community. It was less clear to leaders of the *Reforma* that holding that capital—or any other permanent seat of government for that matter—was necessary to institute a confederal program framed while Juárez, in exile from Mexico City, conducted matters of state from the port city of Veracruz. Mexican liberalism of this period thus maintained a certain wariness about inherited governing forms and skewed toward federative proclivities already several decades in the making.[37]

The sovereign imagery of Mexico City during the 1860s mattered mostly to *imperialistas*, then, who attempted to blend conservatism in matters of state and faith with a constitutional centralism long associated with right-leaning Mexican politics. To the extent that theirs was a failed project, the iconic capitalscapes circulating in these years had more in common with the brief period during which Richmond was the key sovereign center than with the lasting achievements of Washington and Ottawa. The *Palacio Nacional* where Maximilian somewhat uncomfortably resided could hardly sustain its associations with nationalist assertion, which is partly why he developed a preference for nearby Chapultapec Palace as a platform for imperial marvels.[38] Governing interiors around the *Zócalo* complex did take on a distinctly courtly and palatial air that drew European forms into new settings. A carefully rendered full-page woodcut image produced in Paris visually situated the Maximilian-era *Palacio Nacional* in relation to the traditional forms of religious authority seen outside its window. Readers taking even a hasty glance could not fail to note the iconic Cathedral looming over the lavish wedding ceremony of the chief French general in 1865 (see Figure 8).[39]

Juárez's return to power in Mexico City between 1867 and his death five years later expunged the anti-republic taint from a city that Maximilian had made a theater for imperial rule. Deprogramming of courtly urban ventures meant a cessation of grand entrances, crowns, and ceremonial use of the massive Cathedral, three visualizations that comported with a notion that sovereignty emanated from the center and then spread over the rest of the nation. Political pageantry during Juárez's presidency did not cater to the illustrated press of faraway metropoles; accordingly, no woodcuts captured those showy rail trips that took him away from the capital into the "real" Mexico. The image of Juárez himself, not any governing structures, emerged as a key symbol of late 1860s *Mexicanidad*.

Figure 8. "Mexico. 26 juin.—Cérémonie du mariage de S.E. le maréchal Bazainé," *Le Monde Illustre*, August 12, 1865. Courtesy of Dartmouth College Libraries.

This in itself was a revolutionary development, signaling through thousands of *cartes de visites* the likeness of the Oaxaca-born Zapotec responsible for expelling European meddlers from their New World mishap.[40] Mexico City would return as a focus of sovereignty only during the Mexican *Belle Epoque* of the Diaz years, especially in the continued development of the *Paseo de la Reforma*, ironically a legacy of Maximilian's construction of a grand avenue between the *Zócalo* and his Chapultepec palace.[41]

Ottawa was no less a work in progress over the last third of the nineteenth century, but here there was a more fundamental progression as a governing center. The edifices of the Confederation Parliament, the most visible emblem of continental reorganization, took longer to complete than had been projected, and construction of other venues such as Rideau Hall combined expressions of sovereignty with a boom-town sensibility. As the considerable historical literature on the city makes clear, the siting of Ottawa, in a spot removed from the United States and on the border between Francophone Quebec and Anglophone Ontario,[42] helped to neutralize tensions between these two zones while laying the groundwork for a vast republic to be governed by a "city of the woods."[43] As such, the relation of sovereign node to burgeoning national project was unusually consequential.

Canada's administrative center incorporated few of the anti-European assertions of Washington and Juárez-era Mexico City. In the design of its four key buildings, there was a balance between local materials and a Gothic form evoking the new Westminster Parliament buildings.[44] Over time, this federal enclave acquired associations with the double division of Canadian governance in the wake of 1867 Confederation—involving both an ever-increasing quotient of autonomy for British North America and a steadily growing assemblage of provinces that would join, on equal terms, the original four members of the liberal Confederation. This latter aspect became a predominant theme of the city's self-presentation, so that it was more regularly called the "Washington of the North" than the "Westminster of the Wilderness." As Melissa Rombout has put it, its informing vision was "predicated . . . on shaping a choreographed processional site for nationhood." The geospatial dimension was important; in contrast to the United States and Mexico, the Canadian Confederation experienced dramatic territorial gains in these years. By 1905, the nation included five more provinces and two territorial domains within its jurisdiction than had existed at its founding.[45]

Staging a growing Confederation from Ottawa, the illustrated press featured images of how the massive complex was being completed. Yet the theme of "Parliament/Canada under Construction" never attained the drama of Washington's Dome erection while under direct threat from hostile Confederate invasion. The *Canadian Illustrated News* mixed exterior images with scenes from within, focusing less attention on the substance of policies crafted than on ceremonial occasions such as the opening of the legislative session each spring. Within spacious confines, a new governing elite established new norms for self-rule that the weekly press covered in considerable detail. As a self-conscious part of a monarchical empire, the founders of the Canadian Confederation approximated Maximilian's court in their appetite for ceremonies laden with symbolic import. A full-page depiction of the Senate at its 1870 opening was supplemented by a lengthy cataloguing of the spectacle, with attention to "the vice-regal throne," the "General Usher of the Black Rod," "the solemn Masters in Chancery around the Clerk's table," the "grave Senators, sitting in single rows on either side, with the privileged few in the centre," and, as a visiting rather than permanent presence, "His Royal Highness, Prince Arthur." Notably, this locus of Canadian sovereignty paired imagery of a European-derived governing elite with a large quotient of ordinary subjects/citizens, whose presence signaled their status as the pre-eminent legitimating force. The 1870 ceremonial scene prominently featured a "motley group of Commoners outside and beyond all" and an "assemblage of gay and elegantly-dressed ladies occupying the seats behind the Senators." In the gallery balconies overlooking this scene, there was what writers for the *Canadian Illustrated News* termed a "promiscuous crowd of respectable and respectfully-behaved people—ladies and gentlemen, young and old, representing all classes of the community" (see Figure 9).[46]

The iconic potential of three looming complexes in Canada, the United States, and Mexico demonstrates how sovereignty was not simply remade in the 1860s but re-envisioned. The artifice of mass-circulated woodcut engravings brought together common aspects of the sovereign imaginaries that existed across three distinctive national cases. Evidence explored here suggests that one important shared feature concerned the visual link made between the most effective forms of sovereignty and tranquil spaces where the governing ideal was grounding in consent and deliberation rather than command and martial violence. Like the Bosse image of Hobbes's *Leviathan*, sovereignty as seen via the capitalscapes of the 1860s helped to work through some of the latent tensions at the heart of legitimate rule. Across such imagery, the sovereign's potential to use force became more important than the actual deployment of brute power.

Illustrated weeklies consulted in Victorian parlors and gentlemen's reading rooms did not shy away from revealing the bloodiness of these years. Hundreds of thousands of genteel subscribers poured over the eight-page guides to the

Figure 9. "The Opening of Parliament," *Canadian Illustrated News*, March 12, 1870. Courtesy of University of Calgary Archives and Special Collections.

world on a weekly basis during the first half of the 1860s. Image-makers who appreciated the vibrancy of this market for news brought into focus the battles that made this epoch one of enormous carnage. We know from a range of private testimony that readers themselves responded viscerally to the framing emblems of sovereignty—flags, naval vessels, and government buildings perhaps most of all—and used these to help make sense of mangled bodies. During an era of "people's wars" the pictorial press played a critical role in acclimating broad publics to the patriotic imperatives that lay behind the empowerment of national states.[47]

After 1867, the illustrated press engaged in a visual compartmentalization that served to disassociate stately capitalscapes from unruly locales like Queretaro (where Maximilian was famously executed),[48] the Red River (during an episode crucial to the creation of Manitoba),[49] and those Southern and Great Plains locales where the Greater Reconstruction was worked out.[50] Representations of the lethal force exercised by North America's centralizing states focused on the margins of the nationalizing project rather than the iconic centers of powerful federations. One might identify the 1865 execution of the Lincoln assassins, in the shadow of the Domed Capitol, as an inflection point. While governing hubs imposed themselves on faraway populations with new force in the era of Leviathan 2.0, such endeavors did not figure in the most potent sovereign imaginaries then being circulated. Beyond the 1860s, the blunt iron that had secured national rulership across the continent tended to be visually cloaked by velvet interiors, as the epoch of North American upheavals gave way to a critical period of geo-political consolidation.

Notes

1. Charles S. Maier, *Leviathan 2.0: Inventing Modern Statehood* (Cambridge: Harvard University Press, 2014).

2. For my understanding of the problem in general, and the specifics of the late 1860s in particular, I am indebted to D. W. Meinig, *The Shaping of America. Vol. 2: Continental America, 1800–1867* (New Haven: Yale University Press, 1995).

3. The Bosse engraving and the sizeable literature it has inspired are discussed in Justin Champion, "Decoding the Leviathan: Doing the History of Ideas through Images, 1651–1714," in *Printed Images in Early Modern Britain: Essays in Interpretation*, Michael Hunter (Farnham: Ashgate, 2010), 255–78.

4. Jürgen Osterhammel, *The Transformation of the World: A Global History of the Nineteenth Century* (Princeton: Princeton University Press, 2014).

5. Robert Bonner, *Colors and Blood: Flag Passions of the Confederate South* (Princeton: Princeton University Press, 2002).

6. "Grand Review at Washington," *Harper's Weekly*, June 10, 1865; "Home from the Wars: Grand Review of the Returned Armies of the United States," *Frank Leslie's Illustrated Newspaper*, June 10, 1865; "Grand Review of the Army of the Potomac Before President Johnson at Washington," *Illustrated London News*, June 17, 1865.

7. "The Union Army Entering Richmond," "The City of Richmond," both from *Harper's Weekly*, April 22, 1865; "The Union Army Entering Richmond, *Frank Leslie's Illustrated Newspaper*, April 25, 1865.

8. Judith Bookbinder and Sheila Gallagher, eds., *First Hand Civil War Era Drawings from the Becker Collection* (Chicago: University of Chicago Press, 2009); Joshua Brown, *Beyond the Lines: Pictorial Reporting, Everyday Life, and the Crisis of Gilded Age America* (Oakland: University of California Press, 2006); John Nerone, "Newspapers and the Public Sphere," in *A History of the Book in America: The Industrial Book*, ed. Scott Casper (Chapel Hill: University of North Carolina Press, 2007), 241–42.

9. For example, Thomas Nast, "The Campaign in Virginia—'On to Richmond!'" *Harper's Weekly*, June 18, 1864.

10. "President Lincoln Riding Through Richmond," *Frank Leslie's Illustrated Newspaper*, April 22, 1865; "President Lincoln Visiting the Former Residence of Jefferson Davis," *Frank Leslie's Illustrated Newspaper*, April 29, 1865; "President Lincoln Entering Richmond, April 4, 1865," *Harper's Weekly*, February 24, 1866; Nelson Lankford, *Richmond Burning: The Last Days of the Confederate Capital* (New York: Penguin Books, 2003).

11. David Dixon Porter, *Incidents and Anecdotes of the Civil War* (New York: Appleton and Company, 1885); quoted by Michael Burlingame who terms this "the most remarkable day of Lincoln's presidency" in his *Abraham Lincoln*, Vol. 2.

12. "Scene in the Grand Plaza of the City of Mexico on the Occasion of the Reception of President Juárez," *Harper's Weekly*, October 12, 1867; reprinted in *Frank Leslie's Illustrated Newspaper*, October 26, 1867. The Getty Institute holds a print of the Aubert photograph used as a basis for the scene in "Views of Mexico during the French Intervention."

13. "Reception of President Juárez," *Harper's Weekly*, October 12, 1867; "Evenments du Mexique—Entrée a Mexico . . . ," *Le Monde Illustre*, July 30, 1864 (reproduced as "The Triumphal Entrance of the Emperor Maximilian and His Empress into the City of Mexico, June 12, 1864," in *Frank Leslie's Illustrated Newspaper*, September 3, 1864).

14. "Boat Regatta at Ottawa: The Contestants Passing the Parliament Buildings," *Harper's Weekly*, October 19, 1867. Earlier coverage of the site can be seen in "Proposed New Parliament Building at Ottawa," *Harper's Weekly*, September 1, 1860 and "Grand Canoe Race on the Ottawa River," *Frank Leslie's Illustrated Newspaper*, September 22, 1860. Ian McKay, "The Liberal Order Framework: A Prospectus for a Reconnaissance of Canadian History," *Canadian Historical Review* 81, no. 4 (2000): 616–78.

15. Chief elements of this story are laid out in Sinnema, *Dynamics of the Pictured Page: Representing the Nation in the Illustrated London News* (Brookfield: Ashgate, 1997), and Michèle Martin, "19th Century Illustrated Periodicals as International Means of Communication," *Revista Română de Jurnalism si Comunicare* 2, no. 1 (2007). See also Michèle Martin, *Images at War: Illustrated Periodicals and Constructed Nations* (Toronto: University of Toronto Press, 2006), and Janice Carlisle, *Picturing Reform in Victorian Britain* (Cambridge: Cambridge University Press, 2012).

16. Osterhammel, *The Transformation of the World*, 268–71. Donald Olsen has noted how in this period urban locales in general shifted from housing monuments to becoming monuments themselves. See *The City As a Work of Art: London, Paris, Vienna* (New Haven: Yale University Press, 1986). The achievement of novelty and tradition in Pugin's Westminster complex is evident in such *Illustrated London News* woodcuts as "Present State of the Clock Tower" (August 2, 1856), "The British Houses of Parliament" (April 11, 1857), and "Scene on the River at Westminster" (August 3, 1867).

17. John Mraz, *Looking for Mexico: Modern Visual Culture and National Identity* (Durham, N.C.: Duke University Press, 2009) dates the rise of Mexico City illustrated weeklies to the late nineteenth century.

18. The D.C. Capitol appeared on *Frank Leslie's* masthead beginning with its first issue of December 15, 1855; the incorporation of Parliament Hill is noted in Young, *The Glory of Ottawa: Canada's First Parliament Buildings* (Montreal: McGill University Press, 1995).

19. "Representation of the Equestrian Statue of Washington, at Richmond, Virginia," *Gleason's Pictorial Drawing-Room Companion*, April 16, 1853; "The Washington Monument at Richmond, Virginia," *Harper's Weekly*, February 20, 1858."

20. Bonner, *Colors and Blood*; idem, *Mastering America: Southern Slavery and the Crisis of American Nationhood* (New York: Cambridge University Press, 2009).

21. "An Alabama Regiment Marching through Capitol Square, Richmond, on their Way to Join the Rebel Forces Under Beauregard," *Harper's Weekly*, October 19, 1861.

22. Among the few views of the Richmond State House to emerge during war was "The Capitol at Richmond," *Harper's Weekly*, May 31, 1862 and these images from the

Illustrated London News: "The Capital of the Confederate States" (August 10, 1861); "The Civil War in America, General View of Richmond" (May 31, 1862); and the war-ending "Richmond Virginia, After Its Conquest" (May 20, 1865). Helpful in contextualizing the London-produced imagery is Kathleen Diffley, "Splendid Patriotism: How the *Illustrated London News* Pictured the Confederacy," *Comparative American Studies An International Journal* 5, no. 4 (2007): 385–407.

23. Ian Binnington, *Confederate Visions: Nationalism, Symbolism, and the Imagined South in the Civil War* (Charlottesville: University of Virginia Press, 2013).

24. Richard Bensel, *Yankee Leviathan: The Origins of Central State Authority in America, 1859–1877* (Cambridge: Cambridge University Press, 1991); Rable, *The Confederate Republic: A Revolution Against Politics* (Chapel Hill: University of North Carolina Press, 1994). Virginia state officials did not just govern the Commonwealth in these years but revised the state constitution, and shared responsibility with the military for the city's defense and governance.

25. Davis, "To the People of the Confederate States, April 4, 1865."

26. An early suggestion of Nashville to replace Richmond came in *DeBow's Review,* 30 (May and June, 1861), 682. Nearly two years later, a visiting English officer reported that objections to making Richmond the Confederacy's permanent capital were "raised by all classes of the people, from every one of the States, and strange to say, particularly from Virginia" and observed how the city "was not nearly central enough, and far too close to Yankeedom for safety." See [Garnet Wolseley], "A Month's Visit to the Confederate Headquarters," *Blackwood's Edinburgh Magazine* (January 1863): 10.

27. Kenneth J. Winkle, *Lincoln's Citadel: The Civil War in Washington, DC* (New York: Norton, 2013).

28. Guy Gigliotta, *Freedom's Cap: The United States Capitol and the Coming of the Civil War* (New York: Norton, 2013).

29. Among the most notable examples of a persistent iconographic presence are these full-page images: "Great War Meeting at Washington, District of Columbia," *Harper's Weekly*, August 23, 1862; "Convalescent Soldiers Passing through Washington to Join Their Regiments," *Harper's Weekly*, November 15, 1862; "Second Inauguration of Abraham Lincoln as President, in Front of the Capitol," *Frank Leslie's Illustrated Newspaper*, March 18, 1865; and "Second Inauguration of President Lincoln," *Illustrated London News*, April 30, 1865.

30. Anti-democratic satire is evident not only in the British "A Scene in the Hall of Representatives," *Illustrated London News*, April 6, 1861, but in "The Congressional Row," *Frank Leslie's Illustrated Newspaper*, February 20, 1858. Vivid examples of the lack of decorum within Congress can be found in Joanne Freeman, *The Field of Blood: Violence in Congress and the Coming of the Civil War* (New York: Farrar, Strauss, Giroux, 2018).

31. "Interior of the New Dome of the Capitol at Washington," *Harper's Weekly*, March 9, 1861.

32. Leslie Butler, *Critical Americans: Victorian Intellectuals and Transatlantic Liberal Reform* (Chapel Hill: University of North Carolina Press, 2007).

33. "Scene in the House of Representatives on January 31, 1865," *Frank Leslie's Illustrated Newspaper*, February 8, 1865; "Scene in the House on the Passage of the Proposition to Amend the Constitution," *Harper's Weekly*, February 18, 1865.

34. "Rebel Soldiers Taking the Oath of Allegiance in the Senate Chamber, at Richmond," *Harper's Weekly*, June 17, 1865; "The Mass Meeting Held at Richmond," *Harper's Weekly*, September 16, 1865; "The State Convention at Richmond, Va, in Session," *Frank Leslie's Illustrated Newspaper*, February 15, 1868.

35. This Richmond scene was echoed by other depictions of subnational expressions of legislative sovereignty, as can be seen in the following: "Opening of the First Session of the Provincial Parliament of Quebec Under Confederation Dec. 27th," *Frank Leslie's Illustrated Newspaper*, February 1, 1868; and "The New State Capitol, to be Erected at Albany," *Frank Leslie's Illustrated Newspaper*, February 8, 1868. Among other lavish state capitol buildings from the post–Civil War period were those erected in Atlanta, Georgia; Hartford, Connecticut; Austin, Texas; and Lansing, Michigan.

36. Erika Pani, "Republicans and Monarchists, 1848–1867," *A Companion to Mexican History and Culture* (Malden, Ma.: John Wiley and Sons, 2011), 273–87; idem, "Dreaming of a Mexican Empire: The Political Projects of the Imperialistas," *Hispanic American Historical Review* 82, no. 1 (2002): 1–31.

37. Brian Hammett, *Juárez* (London: Longman, 1996); Timothy E. Anna, *Forging Mexico, 1821–1835* (Lincoln: University of Nebraska Press, 1999).

38. "View of Three Public Buildings in the City of Mexico," *New York Illustrated News*, August 29, 1863; "The Emperor Maximilian's Palace," *Harper's Weekly*, September 9, 1865; David Pruonto, "Did the Second Mexican Empire under Maximilian of Habsburg (1864–1867) Have an 'Austrian Face'?" *Austrian Studies* 20 (2012): 96–111; European parallels can be seen through the analysis of David Baguely, *Napoleon III and His Regime: An Extravaganza* (Baton Rouge: Louisiana State University Press, 2000).

39. "Mexico 26 Juin: Ceremonie du Marriage de S.E. le Marechal Bazaine," *Le Monde Illustre*, August 12, 1865.

40. William H. Beezley, *Mexican National Identity: Memory, Innuendo, and Popular Culture* (Tucson: University of Arizona Press, 2008); Mraz, *Looking for Mexico*, 22. This is not to say that there were not previously metropolitan images of him, as seen in his front-page portrait for *Le Monde Illustre*, June 14, 1862.

41. Barbara A. Tenenbaum, "Streetwise History: The Paseo de la Reforma and the Porfirian State, 1876–1910," in *Rituals of Rule, Rituals of Resistance: Public Celebrations and Popular Culture in Mexico*, ed. William H. Beezley, Cheryl English Martin, William E. French (New York: Rowman and Littlefield, 1994), 127–50; idem, "Murals in Stone—The Paseo de la Reforma and Porfirian Mexico, 1783–1980," in *La ciudad y el campo en la Historia de México* (2 vols., México, Instituto de Investigaciones Históricas, UNAM, 1992), 369–79; Mauricio Tenorio-Trillo, *I Speak of the City: Mexico City at the Turn of the Twentieth Century* (Chicago: University of Chicago Press, 2013).

42. This terminology is an anachronism for the early 1860s, of course, because in 1841 the Province of Canada had collapsed Upper and Lower Canada into a single unit.

43. David B. Knight, *A Capital for Canada: Conflict and Compromise in the Nineteenth Century* (University of Chicago, department of geography research paper no. 182, 1977); evidence for neglect of visual information in the selection process is set forth in Richard J. Huyda, "Photography and the Choice of Canada's Capital," *History of Photography* 20, no. 2 (1996): 104–7.

44. Carolyn A. Young, *Glory of Ottawa: Canada's First Parliament Buildings* (Montreal: McGill-Queen's University Press, 1995).

45. Melissa Rombout, "Ottawa: On Display," in *Ottawa—Making a Capital*, ed. Brian S. Osborne and Geraint B. Osborne (Ottawa: University of Ottawa Press, 2001), 469. See also Rhoda Bellamy, "The Architecture of Government," in *Ottawa—Making a Capital* and Osborne and Osborne, "The Cast[e]ing of Heroic Landscapes of Power: Constructing Canada's Pantheon on Parliament Hill," *Material Culture Review / Revue de la culture matérielle* 60, no. 1 (2004). David L. A. Gordon, "From Noblesse Oblige to Nationalism: Elite Involvement in Planning Canada's Capital," *Journal of Urban History* 28, no. 1 (2001): 3–34.

46. "The Opening of Parliament," *Canadian Illustrated News*, March 12, 1870.

47. Andrea G. Pearson, "*Frank Leslie's Illustrated Newspaper* and *Harper's Weekly*: Innovation and Imitation in Nineteenth-Century American Pictorial Reporting," *The Journal of Popular Culture* 23, no. 4 (1990): 81–111; Jennifer E. Moore, "The Artist as Reporter: Drawing National Identity During the US Civil War," *Journalism History* 44, no. 1 (2018): 2–11.

48. "Execution of Maximilian" and "View of Queretaro," *Harper's Weekly*, August 10, 1867; "Remains of Maximilian," *Frank Leslie's Illustrated Newspaper*, October 5, 1867; "Maximilian," *Frank Leslie's Illustrated Newspaper*, October 26, 1867.

49. Lyle Dick, "Nationalism and Visual Media in Canada: The Case of Thomas Scott's Execution," *Manitoba History* 48 (2004): 2–18.

50. "Gathering the Dead after the Colfax Massacre," *Harper's Weekly*, May 10, 1873; "Colored Troops Attacking Indians Near Wilson's Creek Station," *Harper's Weekly*, September 7, 1867; "Engagement of Col. Forsyth's Command with Indians," *Harper's Weekly*, September 17, 1868.

II   Indigenous Polities

5

The Long War

Sustaining Indigenous Communities
and Contesting Sovereignties
in the Civil War South

Jane Dinwoodie

On a sweltering day in August 1862, in a remote mountain pass just behind the battlefields, a unit of Indigenous Confederate soldiers ambushed a group of Unionists. Amidst the skirmish, one Unionist dodged out; the Indian company's captain managed to grab him. For days after the battle, the company rejoiced in their "Yankee prisoner," even treating the capture as a wager, requiring that "each of them must take one to be even."[1] Within a year, they had fulfilled their promise: One soldier boasted that "we have decreased the Yankees" so much that "one would think that . . . [they] would be more than ready to give up."[2] Their enthusiasm betrayed the high stakes of their involvement. Like other Indigenous communities across the United States that had cast their lot with the Confederacy, the Indian Legion's very survival now depended on the fate of secession.

In the past decade, a new cadre of historians—including Ari Kelman, Adam Arenson, Andrew Graybill, and Virginia Scharff—have helped to incorporate stories like these into our understanding of the American Civil War. By broadening the geographies and chronologies of the conflict to include events west of the Mississippi River, they have called for a more expansive treatment of the Civil War as an imperial struggle in which a wider cast of characters, including Indigenous peoples, also vied for sovereignty.[3] At first glance, the story of the mountain ambush seems to neatly fit these new narrative arcs; yet on closer inspection, it actually challenges the conventional geographies and topographies of the conflict. The Indigenous soldiers did not hail from the known Indigenous theaters of the Civil War, like Indian Territory or the Great Plains. Instead, they were members of the Eastern Cherokees, a group of Indigenous Southerners who had escaped removal and continued to live in their traditional homes east of the Mississippi. They fought for the Confederacy in a unit known as the Thomas Legion. The mountains where the skirmish unfolded were not at the far edges of American empire, but in North Carolina, mere miles from the war's Southern heartlands.[4]

Stories of Indigenous struggles in the Southeast are largely absent from even these new Civil War histories. Several historians have traced the wartime experiences of Southeastern Indians removed to Indian Territory and their attempts to position themselves between the looming threats of Union and Confederacy.[5] These stories have done much to highlight the long legacies of removal and the southeastern origins of these groups but, ultimately, they reinforce this new historiography's suggestion that the Indigenous Civil War was something that unfolded in the West. Although groups like the Eastern Cherokees fought to maintain a permanent presence within the region, there has been little effort to seriously consider the Southeast as a third theater of the Indigenous Civil War. By and large, Indigenous wartime experiences east of the Mississippi remain consigned to the footnotes.[6]

This divide reflects a broader understanding of Southern history that treats Indian removal—a wave of state-sponsored forced migrations to Indian Territory that took place following the 1830 Indian Removal Act—as a pivot in Southern sovereignties, transforming the region from the Indigenous South into the familiar world of Cotton Kingdom and Confederacy. Southeastern Indigenous Civil War involvement has garnered little attention because historians assume that removal was the end of the Indigenous South.[7] Yet events such as the Thomas Legion's 1862 skirmish open a window into a very different struggle over mid-century sovereignties. In displacing over 65,000 of the region's Indigenous peoples and relocating the region's largest and best known Indigenous nations west of the Mississippi, removal undeniably had an enormous impact on the South and Indigenous life within it. Still, although removal transformed the region, it did not banish every Indigenous Southerner to the West or destroy every vestige of Indigenous community.[8] Instead, around twenty percent of the region's pre-removal population fought to escape federal power and remain in their homelands.[9] Some, like the Eastern Cherokees, splintered from the wider, removed Cherokee, Choctaw, Creek, Chickasaw, and Seminole nations to remain as distinct communities in their own right. Others, like the Lumbees, Catawbas, and Pamunkeys, were never targeted by federal removal processes in the first place.[10] During the Civil War, all struggled to protect their communities and remain within the region. These stories speak to many of the key themes of nineteenth-century history—sovereignty, empire, resistance, and expansion—yet they are virtually absent from most historians' understandings of the 1860s.

This essay foregrounds Indigenous Southerners' experiences of the American Civil War, exploring their implications for understandings of sovereignty in the American South. It particularly focuses on two groups—the Eastern Cherokees, with which this essay began, and the Bayou Lacombe Choctaws of Eastern Louisiana—whose responses to the conflict bookend a wider spectrum of Indigenous action in the region.[11] Their stories provide insight into an overlooked space of Indigenous conflict and, in turn, invite us to rethink our understandings of sovereignty across the mid-century continent.

The Long War Begins: Sustaining an Indigenous South, 1830–1860

In the early nineteenth century, the space that we know as the American South—an area stretching from the Chesapeake down to the Gulf of Mexico, and west to the Mississippi River—underwent a seismic transition.[12] White settlers and planters flooded lands that had previously housed sparsely populated settler outposts alongside Cherokee, Choctaw, and Creek settlements, transforming them into urban spaces and cotton plantations. These changes were massive but, for American policymakers, easy to explain as the product of Indian removal.[13]

For a generation of American expansionists, the success of removal in the South gave them the license to head farther west, believing themselves capable of crushing ever-larger Indigenous challenges, including that of the infamous Comanches.[14] However, for all their importance to these settlers' self-conception, these images actually tell us more about the ways that planters and policymakers wanted to see the South than about the way that it actually was. Removal undeniably shook the region and Indigenous Southerners struggled to navigate the disturbance. Many had little choice but to remove west, yet, from Virginia to Louisiana, thousands of Indigenous Southerners successfully resisted American attempts to control and relocate them. Individual responses to the threat of removal varied enormously, shaped by location, history, and personal circumstances. Some brokered agreements with local and federal officials to gain permission to remain in the United States; others distanced themselves from the reach of the settler colonial republic. Not every effort succeeded, yet thousands of people successfully avoided removal. By some estimates, as many as twenty percent of the region's original inhabitants remained, most in smaller, splintered, sub-national communities, ranging in size from tens to thousands of people.[15]

A group of around 1,200 people, the Eastern Cherokees were one of several communities that avoided removal by negotiating with federal and state officials.[16]

Deep in the mountains of North Carolina, this group of Cherokees drew on provisions for state citizenship granted to heads of families under federal treaties signed in 1817 and 1819, along with a series of private land purchases made with the help of white allies, to stake claims to exemption from mass deportation to Indian Territory along with the rest of the Cherokee Nation in the mid-1830s. They then combined this legal justification with a range of negotiations during removal efforts themselves, ultimately convincing federal officials and white neighbors that they had loyally served the United States and North Carolina and therefore ought to be permitted to remain.[17]

By contrast, the Bayou Lacombe Choctaws distanced themselves from the agents sent to remove them. This group of several hundred Choctaws splintered from the Choctaw Nation and escaped removal by fleeing from their homes in Mississippi into the swamps and forests surrounding the Bayou Lacombe in eastern Louisiana, not far from Lake Pontchartrain. These watery landscapes appealed because they were places where agents and settlers did not tread.[18] These areas were also traditional Choctaw hunting grounds, and, although they were close to New Orleans, in the 1830s they remained largely devoid of white settlement. Once established among the woods and weeds that lined the Bayou, the Lacombe Choctaw community survived by distancing itself from its black and white neighbors alike, running away from the small handful of people who visited the area into the 1850s.[19] Though they used very different means to remain, both the Cherokee and Choctaw groups splintered from their polities to stake claims to permanent communities east of the Mississippi, while the main Cherokee and Choctaw nations went west to Indian Territory.

By the mid-1840s, federal officials considered removal to be effectively complete in the South.[20] Yet as agents and officials left the region, neither the Bayou Lacombe Choctaws nor the Eastern Cherokees simply vanished into "the world the slaveholders made."[21] Instead, they fought to maintain their communities, lands, and cultures, upholding and adapting their previous strategies to do so. Unlike the bicultural, intermarried Cherokee and Choctaw elites, most of the Eastern Cherokees and the Bayou Lacombe Choctaws came from the least acculturated and most socially and politically liminal parts of their nations. Although they had chosen to strategically adopt some aspects of Euro-American life, such as settled agriculture and Christian worship, they also maintained many traditional ways of life and social organization before and after removal. For instance, both groups lived in traditional social units, spoke Indigenous languages, and had very low to nonexistent levels of black slaveholding.[22] Throughout the 1840s and 1850s, they faced ongoing challenges and new threats to their existence as local pressure encouraged Washington officials to take up new waves of removal. These challenges threatened both groups, but, by sticking to their strategies, both communities ensured that they remained in the South.[23]

In these decades, American policymakers in the nation's capital scarcely noted that these groups existed; if they did, they probably believed them to be small and insignificant. After all, settler colonial lawmakers had designed the legal apparatus of removal to permanently dismantle Indigenous sovereignties and large-scale polities within the South. *Cherokee Nation v. Georgia*, state extension laws, and removal treaties had promised to annul all Indigenous claims to power within the region.[24] On paper, groups such as the Eastern Cherokees existed only as potential citizens, and the Bayou Lacombe Choctaws as somewhere between squatters, vagrants, and fugitives.[25]

On the ground, however, things looked different. While removal undeniably changed the face of the Indigenous South, groups like the Eastern Cherokees and the Bayou Lacombe Choctaws demonstrate that removal did not erase Indigenous cultures and powers from the region altogether. Both groups remained: They sustained Cherokee and Choctaw communities, carved out distinctive Indigenous spaces, and upheld traditional lifeways. In doing so, they staked claims to Indigenous conceptions of power and sovereignty and, at the very least, served as a *de facto* challenge to the total reach of American sovereignties over the entire South. From the vantage point of these enduring communities, the decades following removal might be better characterized as a long war, in which groups like the Eastern Cherokees and the Bayou Lacombe Choctaws fought for survival, and to establish a permanent place for their descendants within the region. On the eve of the Civil War, these two communities endured in the South, mired in a decades-long struggle to remain within the region and to carve a permanent place within it. In 1860, the looming conflict threatened all that they had fought to sustain.

A New Front in an Old Fight: The Eastern Cherokees and the Thomas Legion

In December 1860, South Carolina seceded from the Union. The ensuing crisis jolted Indigenous communities throughout the South. For most groups, the acceleration of decades of sectional tension was no surprise; the urgent question was how to respond. For community elders, the threat of war was a faintly familiar experience. Indigenous Southerners were no strangers to choosing sides in Euro-American conflicts. Many had served in the American Revolution, while during the Creek war many Choctaws fought alongside Andrew Jackson's American troops. These tensions had extended into removal. After all, most groups that remained within the region by 1860 owed their survival to their ability to navigate conflicting federal, state, and local forces.[26]

In several key respects, however, the Civil War presented unique threats, especially to the communities' ongoing struggles for survival within the region. Secession placed Indigenous nations from California to Carolina "between two fires" of Union and Confederacy, but the situation was especially precarious in the South.[27] In the decades immediately following removal, Indigenous communities had worked to navigate changing rules about power and place in lands that planters and politicians claimed as the Cotton Kingdom. Yet as states seceded, and colonial jurisdiction passed from the United States to the Confederacy, Indigenous groups suddenly found that the game had changed once again, and they were now within the boundaries of a new nation with unknown rules, attitudes, and policies. The Eastern Cherokees had endured within the region by cooperating with American officials, staking claims to permanent presence that did not challenge Americans' own. In 1861, this left them in a legally "anomalous" position. Their legal right to remain within the region depended on their claims to citizenship, and their claims to persistence depended on this protection from renewed removals, yet American officials refused to recognize either.[28] There was no guarantee that communities' complex legal (or extra-legal) rights to remain would hold, especially if the Confederate or local state governments refused to honor earlier federal promises.

Faced with the threat of war, several communities responded by staking their allegiances to the newly formed Confederacy. The Eastern Cherokees were among the first and most prominent non-removed Indians to do so. Just days after North Carolina's secession, the community's representatives met in council and asserted their unanimous loyalty to the Confederacy. At leaders' request, the group's white agent William Holland Thomas publicly announced plans for a "Cherokee defense force" that would be "ready at a minute's warning . . . [to] track the enemy through all the mountains."[29] Specific motives spurred the community's actions. By asserting their loyalty to the Confederate cause, Eastern Cherokee leaders sought to build on their previous decades of negotiation and, especially, to preserve their uniquely precarious right to remain within the region. This decision was especially important for a group whose survival primarily depended on their relationship with North Carolina, rather than their ties to the federal government. Unlike in Indian Territory where both Union and Confederate allegiances signaled unclear fortunes, the Eastern Cherokees' Confederate loyalty followed relatively straightforwardly from their previous negotiations, especially since their homes now technically lay within Confederate borders.[30]

The community particularly sought to capitalize on the prospect of Confederate enlistment. Since the colonial era, "military service had explicit links to . . . inclusion as part of the American people." The revolution crystalized this association in the idea of the "citizen soldier," whose military service marked the performance of a citizen's duty that ought to be repaid with national membership.[31] As Civil War Americans began to renegotiate the very boundaries of what it meant to be a nation, a citizen, and a sovereign, the categories of citizenship and sovereignty became more flexible than ever before. Like other minority groups such as enslaved people, soldiers' wives, and foreign citizens, the Eastern Cherokees sought to take advantage of this uncertainty.[32] They aimed to renew their claims to state citizenship and their ties to North Carolina—their current legal basis for remaining in the region—by making their loyalty and military service to the Confederacy explicit, while also seeking to take advantage of their as yet undefined relationship to the Confederacy. It was no accident that Thomas's initial proposal for a Cherokee Legion stressed that the community would be eligible to serve because they were state (and hence Confederate) citizens under the Cherokee treaties of 1817 and 1819: something that the treaties had promised but North Carolina had previously refused to recognize.[33]

Despite leaders' enthusiasm for the proposals, the Cherokee community struggled to convince Confederate authorities to allow their enlistment. In September 1861, Thomas put forward a bill in the state's General Assembly proposing authorization "to muster into the service of the State, a battalion of Cherokee."[34] The proposal met immediate opposition. Local politicians baulked at the idea of Indigenous enlistment, even noting that they would rather be caught in a voting booth with a "free negro" than see Cherokees fight alongside Confederate troops.[35] By the time the bill reached the General Assembly, it was already doomed—after being "read the first time" it was instantly "rejected." [36] Yet just over a year into the war, everything changed. In the Cherokees' Appalachian homes, initial divisions over secession gradually escalated into a "most uncivil" guerrilla conflict that engulfed the region by late 1861.[37] These local problems mirrored national woes. By 1862, initial Confederate war enthusiasm frayed in the wake of military losses and growing hardships. As Americans settled themselves in for a long war, many one-year enlistments expired and were not renewed. Conscription, introduced that April, only worsened the problem.[38] Across the South, the army "haemorrhag[ed]" men, as entire companies "just went home and withdrew from the war entirely."[39]

This "truly Herculean" manpower crisis gave the Cherokees their chance.[40] In the summer of 1861, under the orders of Eastern Cherokee leaders, Thomas petitioned Jefferson Davis, offering the Cherokees' services. Davis dismissed the idea, but things soon looked different as enlistment figures continued to drop. In late September, Thomas received news that "the President decides that the Cherokee battalion may be mustered into the service of the Confederacy."[41] In April 1862, Confederate officials mustered the Thomas Legion of Indians and Highlanders into the armies of Tennessee under Thomas's command. The existing documentary record does not allow us to see each recruit's motivations, but most seem to have recognized the importance of the conflict to the community's fate. Over the course of the war, some four hundred men, or "nearly every able-bodied man in the tribe," enlisted to serve in the Legion's two Indian companies.[42] Major General Kirby Smith, Commander of the Armies of East Tennessee, charged them "with taking up deserters and absentees," and rounding up or "impress[ing]" "all soldiers you may find in your county or elsewhere belonging to the Confederate states service, who are absent without leave."[43] This decision mattered: The Eastern Cherokees were the only Indigenous group allowed to serve *en masse* as soldiers in North Carolina, and the only fully Cherokee units authorized to join a white Legion east of the Mississippi.[44] Despite the momentous nature of their relatives' enlistment, life in the early days of the Legion's service seems to have continued in its usual fashion for the women, children, and the elderly members of the community who remained at home. Cherokee legionnaires' letters asked relatives to send favorite delicacies and complained about rumors their own provisions had been depleted in their absence.[45]

Following their enlistment, the Cherokee soldiers set about their assigned duties of tracking guerrillas and deserters across the Smoky Mountains. Yet they did not simply blend into the ranks of gray-clad troops. Throughout their wartime service, the community actively leveraged their soldierly status and pro-Confederate credentials. Building on previous decades of struggle, the Cherokees sought to capitalize on their wartime service as part of a wider campaign to successfully perform the role of "civilization," which Euro-American policymakers expected as a prerequisite for the small number of Indigenous peoples that they had allowed to remain within the East.[46] Through their military service, the Cherokees cultivated an image of loyalty and benevolence toward North Carolina, the Confederacy, and their white neighbors. Some of these actions were carefully choreographed. In the wake of the Legion's recruitment, the community received visiting journalists and prominent locals on tours of their camps, allowing Cherokee legionnaires to perform calculated demonstrations of "civilized" and citizen-like behavior such as attending church services, reading aloud from the Bible, and performing military drills.[47] Cherokee soldiers also courted positive press by performing everyday military duties. In 1864, amidst a wave of Confederate defeats, Thomas Legion soldiers gained local praise after being captured by Union soldiers, but repeatedly refusing to switch sides.[48]

The performative aspects of military service reaped rewards. The Eastern Cherokees' strategic service had an enormous impact on their previously ambiguous relationship to both North Carolina and the national government. During the conflict, North Carolinian Confederate supporters and administrations responded positively to the communities' demonstrations of loyalty to the Confederacy. Across Appalachia, local pro-Confederate newspapers depicted the Thomas Legion's service as evidence of the Cherokees' steadfast commitment to the Confederacy, their good nature, and their positive relationship to North Carolina. In February 1863, the *Knoxville Register* claimed that the Legion "excel[ed] any troops in either the Northern or Southern armies" because they "always execute . . . an order with religious fidelity."[49] Their efforts continued until the end of the war. The Legion even reinforced their reputation as steadfast soldiers by being the last Confederate troops to surrender in North Carolina, on May 7, 1865.[50] This wartime service performed a vital function for the community's struggle, though it often came at great personal cost. Numerous men serving in the Thomas Legion returned home to Quallatown to discover that their children had taken ill or died while they were away.[51]

In the immediate aftermath of the conflict, these efforts translated into tangible, legally affirmed benefits for the community. Distracted by more pressing issues of national reconstruction, officials in Washington, D.C. effectively ignored the community in the months following surrender. Locally, however, they reaped legally enshrined rewards for their service.[52] In February 1866, during its first Reconstruction session, the North Carolina General Assembly passed a law formally recognizing the Eastern Band's residency, proclaiming that "the Cherokee Indians are now residents of the state of North Carolina" and as such "shall have the authority and permission to remain in the several counties of the state where they now reside," and that they would be "permitted to remain permanently therein . . . for as long as they may see proper to do so."[53] The legislature was typical of the Reconstruction-era South. It was filled with ex-Confederates who vetoed the Fourteenth Amendment, passed an immediate series of Black Codes, and renounced Republican authority.[54] While these men would have typically baulked at the idea of advancing the status of people they considered to be racial others, they were eager to honor loyal Confederate service.[55] As the state's only Indigenous Confederate veterans, the Eastern Cherokees were the single formal exception that the state made to its policy of Indian racial exclusion after the war.[56]

Although state lawmakers did not cast their promises in the explicit terms of sovereignty—or even of the formal promise of citizenship that the community had long sought—the law still had a positive effect on the Cherokees' claims to a distinct, permanent, and visibly Indigenous community in the Appalachians.[57] Although the Eastern Cherokees' formal relationship with the United States remained ambiguous until the 1870s, the act made their practical right to remain in North Carolina surer than ever, consolidating their pre-war claims to a type of power that did not explicitly challenge the United States. Though the community faced many hardships in the wake of the war, including a devastating smallpox epidemic, many likely breathed a sigh of relief that they had survived the conflict with the promise of renewed safety from removal, at least temporarily.[58]

Avoiding Colonial Conflict: The Bayou Lacombe Choctaws' Civil War

Several hundred miles to the south and west, in contrast to these overt displays of allegiance and military service, the Bayou Lacombe Choctaws distanced themselves from American contests. Deep in the swamps and bayous of Louisiana, they chose to navigate the uncertain 1860s by sticking to well-honed strategies of evading officials and retreating into isolated, inaccessible terrains.

On January 22, 1861, Louisiana delegates voted to leave the Union. Just weeks later, newly mustered Confederate troops thronged the state. Officials especially sought to protect New Orleans, whose cotton markets and continentally connected waterways made it one of the most strategically and symbolically important prizes for both sides.[59] Much like the Eastern Cherokees, the Bayou Lacombe Choctaws were probably aware of growing sectional tensions long before the war reached Louisiana thanks to their close connection to Adrien Rouquette, a Creole Catholic priest who had appointed himself unofficial (and unwanted) missionary to the Choctaw community in the 1850s. As war loomed, Rouquette watched closely and declared himself an avowed Union supporter.[60] Yet unlike the Eastern Cherokees and Indigenous polities west of the Mississippi, the Bayou Lacombe community initially took little action in response to the war. They did not approach Union or Confederate authorities in the area and made no effort to declare any allegiance to either side. By refusing to draw attention to their presence, the community presumably hoped to ride out the conflict in much the same way that they had navigated the previous half-century of removal threats: by simply being small, remote, and isolated enough for American officials to overlook them.[61]

Still, despite their best efforts, the community could not ignore the war forever. Since fleeing removal in the 1830s, the Bayou Lacombe Choctaws had lived at the edges of Lake Pontchartrain, just a few miles from New Orleans. In 1862, Union forces took control of the Crescent City.[62] On paper this ended the conflict and commenced Reconstruction in the area but, for the Choctaws, the war was just beginning. Despite Union victory, Lake Pontchartrain's Northshore areas remained under Confederate control, creating an ongoing conflict which soon spilled over onto the lake and the formerly isolated bayous, woodlands, and marshes around it. Previously silent areas now resounded with movement and gunfire. Over the coming months, the Choctaws faced not only regular boat patrols on the lake, but also the explosive fallout of the sinking and salvaging of a new Confederate submarine. Alongside these aquatic intrusions, smugglers and marauders penetrated the community's shoreside sanctuary, especially once Union forces halted official trade in the area.[63]

All of this had a disastrous effect on the Bayou Lacombe Choctaws. Previously distant from American intrusions, the community's homes and crops were soon "destroyed by jayhawkers and deserters, who applied the torch [to the areas around the lake] with fiendish liberality." Men, women, and children became caught in attacks and gunfights, and "came running to . . . [Rouquette's residence] with blood streaming from their wounds."[64] For the community, the lake became the backdrop for not only a terrifying wartime experience, but also a newly mounted contest to maintain their presence in the area. Blending old strategies and patterns with the unique demands of warzone life, many members of the group became highly mobile, staying on the move in order to remain out of American reach. "Forced to quit their village, their burned cabins, their devastated fields, their desecrated cemeteries," the little community moved out into the tangle of weeds and woods just behind the lake. As the conflict engulfed them, most Bayou Lacombe Choctaws chose to keep moving further away from it. Some "gathered around . . . [Rouquette's] chapel of Bayou Lacombe in the Nook," but many left "one family after another to establish themselves elsewhere" in the difficult terrains that surrounded the Lake and the Bayou, perhaps seeking to make themselves less detectable in tiny units. Many spent time actually living within the cypress swamps that surrounded the bayous and lakes.[65] To the Bayou Lacombe community, these places were important precisely because they were remote and vacant, even in a time of war and occupation. Under extreme threat of violence and destruction, they sought to sustain their own community within these gaps in effective American sovereignty.

In addition to their movement around the area's most inhospitable terrains, many Bayou Lacombe Choctaws continued to move across enemy lines. As hundreds of smugglers and marauders crossed Lake Pontchartrain, the community continued to move along its shores and hinterlands, while Adrien Rouquette also ran the federal blockade in his pirogue. These trips asserted the community's ongoing right to travel across the lake. They also served a practical purpose, as Rouquette darted his way to New Orleans to smuggle contraband goods back to the Choctaws under cover of darkness. Much like the Eastern Cherokees' alliance with Thomas, the Bayou Lacombe Choctaws cultivated this relationship because it held many strategic benefits for their community. This self-described "Daniel Boone in priestly garb" played a key role in allowing the community to retain its independence and survival, even in dire circumstances.[66] According to local legends, the ageing priest even fell victim to capture and arrest during one of these sojourns.[67]

The community's retreat into tough terrain had many benefits, but it was far from easy. These isolated places were far removed from the city and the fighting, but they were also unwelcoming and effectively uninhabitable. Following their retreat into the swamp, malaria afflicted the community.[68] The swamp offered little protection and a pathetically inadequate place to care for the sick. Rouquette drew on his connections with Union officials to supply quinine, but even this medicine could not inoculate the community and its most vulnerable members from all the dangers of swamp life.[69] Constant movement also disrupted the delicate subsistence patterns that the group had established over previous decades. Before the war the Choctaws had asserted their self-determination by adapting their diet around a series of crops that best suited their rugged lands, including corn, sweet potatoes, and pumpkins.[70] But as "their houses and fields were destroyed by jayhawkers and deserters," the group's very ability to survive within these hostile lands became imperiled, and "many who could not . . . obtain food . . . perished horribly."[71]

Following Lee's surrender at Appomattox, the fighting wound down around Lake Pontchartrain.[72] Peace revealed the war's toll on the community. The Bayou Lacombe Choctaws' original villages had been destroyed. Still more had perished from disease or had been lost to the community as they dispersed into ever more remote areas on their own.[73] Yet, though battered and bruised, the Bayou Lacombe Choctaws had seen out the war as a distinct, non-removed Indigenous community. They had done so by remaining relatively invisible to federal and local officials and their white neighbors. As a result, the community emerged from the war in a practically identical legal position to the one in which they began it: overlooked by federal officials, who regarded their terrains as undesirable and uninhabitable.[74] Unlike the Eastern Cherokees, the Civil War did not grant the Bayou Lacombe Choctaws any significant legal improvements to support either their sovereignty or their right to remain within the region. But they did not significantly lose out, either. By adapting their strategies to fit the unique wartime situation, the Bayou Lacombe community had managed to maintain fundamentally consistent claims to community and endurance in remote lands throughout the conflict. This outcome sharply contrasts with Indigenous experiences in the West, where involvement in the Civil War often entailed a series of punitive responses from the federal government, propelled by the dual ambitions of reconstruction and expansion.[75]

In the war's aftermath, many members of the community continued their fight for endurance. Most reunited, coalescing around inaccessible areas near the Gulf, the bayou, and the Lake. However, only around eighty of the Choctaws returned permanently to their old settlement.[76] Others decided to remain in small groups, distancing themselves from all settlers, even Rouquette. Writing in 1884, the elderly priest lamented that after the Choctaws were "dispersed and separated from me" during the war, a great number had not come back and "I have not been able since then to gather them into a village."[77] For these members of the community, the Civil War reaffirmed the lessons of removal: To remain unmolested, it was better to be effectively invisible, even to your former allies. Whether they dispersed or regrouped, for these Choctaws the hostile terrains surrounding Bayou Lacombe offered the key to their endurance throughout the war and beyond.

The Civil War Ends, the Long War Continues

At the end of 1865, both the Eastern Cherokees and Bayou Lacombe Choctaws surveyed the aftermath of the conflict. Rather than a clear-cut story of fighting Confederates in the East and an expanded struggle for empire in the West, their wartime experiences demonstrate that the conflict could take varied forms on both sides of the Mississippi. Indigenous groups survived in the South and used the conflict to reinforce their fight for power and presence within an increasingly settler colonial world. For Indigenous Southerners, the Civil War was an important battle in a decades-long war for survival as distinct communities east of the Mississippi.

If they had noticed them from their vantage points in Washington, D.C., Raleigh, or New Orleans, 1860s American policymakers would likely have dismissed these Indigenous Southerners and their claims to self-governance, community, and permanent persistence. However, the fact that postwar policymakers did not necessarily see or recognize these communities' endurance did not mean that they did not exist. The two groups' respective claims to power and permanent persistence within the region built on the foundations they had established prior to the war. By allying themselves with North Carolina and the Confederacy, the Eastern Cherokees built on their pre-war strategies, fighting to be recognized as a distinct community with a right to remain in the region, but also as a group whose claims could be seen as complimentary to, rather than worthy of conflict with, the United States and the Confederacy. For the community, the war had been an important opportunity to boost and reinforce their local loyalties, resulting in a promise of residency, if not something more concrete. Similarly, the Bayou Lacombe Choctaws explicitly recognized the shape of American sovereignty and settlement within the region yet, unlike the Eastern Cherokees, they then sought to place themselves explicitly beyond and outside the *de facto* limits of American reach. Before, during, and after the conflict, the community's survival and claims to distinction depended on their ability to position themselves in places that Americans did not desire and could not easily control.

The Eastern Cherokees' and Bayou Lacombe Choctaws' long fights for persistence were very different from the large-scale contests among competing Euro-American nation-states, which we associate with the 1860s. Similarly, unlike the other Indigenous sovereignty struggles that characterize the Civil War and Indian Wars in the West, these groups did not fight for a complete claim to power and regional dominance, nor did they seek the formal recognition of their power by American, Confederate, or foreign governments.[78]

Yet despite these differences, both of these groups' struggles matter to the bigger stories we tell about North American sovereignty at mid-century. Although they did not meet contemporary statesmen's definitions, both communities had secured claims to place and power that we ought to recognize as challenges to American proclamations to control the South. Through their actions, both groups maintained claims to community, land, and continued existence in the region, governing their own lives in ways either indirectly noticed by settler authorities, or simply out of their view altogether. Although both communities rejected American claims to grant and repeal their sovereignties, they positioned their claims to power and distinct, visibly Indigenous communities carefully within or beyond the limits of federal and local states, outwardly claiming a type of sovereignty that did not explicitly compete with American visions and that kept them out of officials' crosshairs. In sustaining communities in places where settlers and policymakers had sought to erase Indigenous presences, both groups refused to accept settler colonial assumptions that only American policymakers could give or remove Indigenous sovereignties.[79] Still, in placing themselves within the cracks of American power, they likely also knew that their survival depended on an official rhetoric of deference or the simple invisibility of their claims, rather than a formal recognition of their sovereignty, unlike other polities that exercised similar partial, sub-state power, such as formal federalized units of counties and states.[80] In this respect, we could argue that these two non-removed groups deliberately claimed public positions akin to those of maroon communities—physically located within the sphere of American claims, but challenging them by exercising control over their own lives and polities—or some of the many competing sovereign groups partially or incompletely absorbed into the sphere of other European empires elsewhere in the colonized world.[81]

By staking their communities and permanent polities within the gaps of American reach, Indigenous Southerners' claims to power little resembled the United States' conceptions of its own dominance, nor the Five Tribes' own pre-removal sovereignties in the South, which they had fought to have the Supreme Court recognize.[82] However, the complex and contested nature of these groups' claims actually reflect the wider nature of Indigenous sovereignties amidst a context of colonial rule. As former Navajo nation chief justice Robert Yazzie has argued, much debate around sovereignty has become "stale" because it assumes that when we talk about sovereignty, what we really mean is "state sovereignty": a way of seeing the world in which sovereignty is an exclusive property of (Euro-American) nation-states, hence inherently marginalizing Indigenous peoples and their claims.[83]

Although almost two centuries apart, this perspective is useful to understanding the Bayou Lacombe Choctaws' and Eastern Cherokees' 1860s struggles. The yardsticks that mid-century American policymakers devised to deny Indigenous power in the South—as enshrined in decisions like *Cherokee Nation v Georgia*—were not some universal or eternal understandings of sovereignty; they were themselves products of a specific colonial moment when the American colossus sought to diminish Indigenous power to reinforce its own.[84] As Chickasaw historian Amanda Cobb notes, American policymakers have often struggled to recognize minority sovereignties because "the American nation-state is so powerful, so hegemonic, that its cloak of sovereignty becomes almost invisible. The United States is so used to looking through the lens of its own powerful sovereignty... that

[it] too often cannot recognize that what is looked through is merely a lens."[85] In short, by sticking to the measures American policymakers used to define and create their own power, we become trapped in the visions of sovereignty that American policymakers saw and wanted to see. It becomes impossible to see the realities of power as they actually unfolded in the South, especially among small, non-removed Indigenous groups like the Bayou Lacombe Choctaws and Eastern Cherokees, whose claims to sovereignties—and whose challenges to total settler colonial sovereignty over the South—were often partial, contested, and unrecognized by American authorities. In the mid-nineteenth century, many of their claims to power lay not in ambitions to topple the United States, but instead in aspirations to live unmolested in the legal and physical gaps of its reach. In the cracks of American settlement, the Bayou Lacombe Choctaws and the Eastern Cherokees challenged Americans' claims to total hegemony over the region and rebuilt communities whose sovereignties would endure to the present day.

By re-centering this ongoing Indigenous struggle in our accounts of Civil War contests, we can rethink the ways that we understand sovereignty in the South and the wider continent during both the 1860s and the first half of the nineteenth century. Contrary to the stories statesmen told about their own power, American sovereignty did not blanket the South in the wake of Indian removal. Instead, this power was rife with gaps, as Indigenous communities fought to sustain a world of contested and persistent sovereignties that continued to coexist with the emerging Cotton Kingdom and rapid imperial extension. This jagged, incomplete, and piecemeal pattern of power speaks not only to the complexities of colonial sovereignties in general, but also to the plural and multiple varieties of power possible within nineteenth-century North America. By foregrounding the wartime experiences of these two groups, 1860s sovereignty struggles look a lot broader and more contested, and the line between American expansion and national incorporation looks much more ambiguous than many historians have imagined. By viewing the Civil War South through the lens of these two communities, we can begin to see another long war for sovereignty and a region of enduring Indigenous communities that refused to disappear, even in the face of expanding, clashing, and continentally consolidating nation states.

Notes

1. William Holland Thomas to Sarah Thomas, June 25, 1862, William Holland Thomas Papers (hereafter WHTP), Folder 4 (1860–64), David M. Rubenstein Rare Book and Manuscript Library, Duke University, Durham, N.C.

2. Tse:gh(i)sini to unknown, July 20, 1862, in John and Anna Kilpatrick, eds., *The Shadow of Sequoyah: Social Documents of the Cherokees, 1862–1964* (Norman: University of Oklahoma Press, 1965), 7.

3. See Adam Arenson and Andrew Graybill, *Civil War Wests: Testing the Limits of the United States* (Oakland: University of California Press, 2015); Ari Kelman, *A Misplaced Massacre: Struggling over the Memory of Sand Creek* (Cambridge: Harvard University Press 2013); Virginia Scharff, ed., *Empire and Liberty: The Civil War and the West* (Oakland: University of California Press, 2015); Steven Hahn, "Slave Emancipation, Indian Peoples, and the Projects of a New American Nation-State," *Journal of the Civil War Era* 3, no. 3 (2013): 307–30; Elliott West, "Reconstructing Race," *Western Historical Quarterly* 34, no. 1 (2003): 6–26; Elliott West, *The Last Indian War: The Nez Perce Story* (Oxford: Oxford University Press, 2009); Troy Smith, "Nations Colliding: The Civil War Comes to Indian Territory," *Civil War History* 59, no. 3 (2013): 279–319; Clarissa Confer, *The Cherokee Nation in the Civil War* (Norman: University of Oklahoma Press, 2007); Heather Cox Richardson, *West from Appomattox: The Reconstruction of America after the Civil War* (New Haven: Yale University Press, 2007); Stacey Smith, *Freedom's Frontier: California and the Struggle over Unfree Labor, Emancipation, and Reconstruction* (Chapel Hill: University of North Carolina Press, 2013). This scholarship builds on older literature. See Annie H. Abel, "The Indians in the Civil War," *American Historical Review* 15, no. 2 (1910): 281–96; Laurence M. Hauptman, *Between Two Fires: American Indians in the Civil War* (London: Free Press, 1995).

4. For background, see John Finger, *The Eastern Band of Cherokees, 1819–1900* (Knoxville: University of Tennessee Press, 1984); John R. Finger, "The North Carolina Cherokees, 1838–1866: Traditionalism, Progressivism, and the Affirmation of State Citizenship," *Journal of Cherokee Studies* 5, no. 1 (1980): 17–29; Vernon H. Crow, *Storm in the Mountains: Thomas' Confederate Legion of Cherokee Indians and Mountaineers* (Cherokee, N.C.: Press of the Museum of the Cherokee Indian, 1982). The Cherokees discussed in this essay are the ancestors of the modern Eastern Band of Cherokee Indians (EBCI) still based in North Carolina today and should not be confused with the main Cherokee Nation, by then removed to Indian Territory (modern-day Oklahoma) or with the other subsections of Cherokees who remained in the East during the early stages of Indian Removal, who were then forcibly deported to Indian Territory under military removal in 1838 (also sometimes called "Eastern Cherokees" or "Cherokees East").

5. See Jeff Fortney, "Lest We Remember: Civil War Memory and Commemoration among the Five Tribes," *American Indian Quarterly* 36, no. 4 (2012): 525–44; Jeff Fortney, "Serving the Choctaw Cause: Robert M. Jones, Sovereignty, and Pragmatic Diplomacy during the American Civil War," *American Nineteenth Century History* 17, no. 2 (2016): 215–33; Ari Kelman, "Deadly Currents: John Ross's decision of 1861 Sheds Light on Race and Sovereignty in the Cherokee Nation," *Chronicles of Oklahoma* 62, no. 1 (1995): 80–103.

6. See Megan Kate Nelson, "Indian America," in *A Companion to the U.S. Civil War*, ed. Aaron Sheehan-Dean (Malden: Wiley, 2014), 366–84. In an older Indigenous Civil War history, Laurence Hauptman includes a small section on the South, yet his focus is essentially military, out of step with recent historiographical interest into the social, political, and imperial dimensions of the conflict. See Hauptman, *Between Two Fires*, Part Two.

7. For this pivot, see Walter Johnson, *River of Dark Dreams: Slavery and Empire in the Cotton Kingdom* (Cambridge: Harvard University Press, 2013), 30; Edward Baptist, *The Half Has Never Been Told: Slavery and the Making of American Capitalism* (New York: Oxford University Press, 2014), 227. For the Indigenous South, see Christina Snyder, *Slavery in Indian Country: The Changing Face of Captivity in Early America* (Cambridge: Harvard University Press, 2010), 8. Other scholars have noted Southern historians' tendency to ignore post-removal Indigenous people. See John H. Peterson Jr., "The Indians in the Old South," in *Red, White, and Black: Symposium on Indians in the Old South: Southern Anthropological Society Proceedings 5*, ed. Charles M. Hudson (Athens: University of Georgia Press, 1971); Walter Williams, ed., *Southeastern Indians Since the Removal Era* (Athens: University of Georgia Press, 1979); J. Anthony Paredes, ed., *Indians of the Southeastern United States in the Late Twentieth Century* (Tuscaloosa: University of Alabama Press, 1992); Theda Perdue, "The Legacy of Indian Removal," *Journal of Southern History* 78, no. 1 (2012): 3–36.

8. While Southern histories have overlooked non-removed groups, regional Indigenous specialists have told many of their stories in tribal histories. See Finger, *Eastern Band*; Clara Sue Kidwell, *Choctaws and Missionaries in Mississippi, 1818–1918* (Norman: University of Oklahoma Press, 1995); Helen C. Rountree, *Pocahontas' People: The Powhatan Indians of Virginia through Four Centuries* (Norman: University of Oklahoma Press, 1990). Recently, several scholars have explored Indigenous experiences of segregation without exploring the Civil War explicitly. See Malinda Maynor Lowery, *Lumbee Indians in the Jim Crow South: Race, Identity, and the Making of a Nation* (Chapel Hill: University of North Carolina Press, 2010); Katherine M. B. Osburn, *Choctaw Resurgence in Mississippi: Race, Class, and Nation Building in the Jim Crow South, 1830–1877* (Lincoln: University of Nebraska Press, 2014); Melanie Benson Taylor, *Reconstructing the Native South: American Indian Literature and the Lost Cause* (Athens: University of Georgia Press, 2011); Theda Perdue, "Southern Indians and Jim Crow," in Stephanie Cole and Natalie J. Ring, eds., *The Folly of Jim Crow: Rethinking the Segregated South* (Arlington: Texas A & M University Press, 2012), 54–90; Mikaela M. Adams, *Who Belongs?: Race, Resources, and Tribal Citizenship in the Native South* (New York: Oxford University Press, 2016); Perdue, "The Legacy of Indian Removal."

9. Geary Hobson et al., eds., *The People Who Stayed: Southeastern Indians Writing After Removal* (Norman: University of Oklahoma Press, 2010), 6. A more comprehensive discussion of the number of people who remained is provided later in the notes.

10. Although federal officials did not formally target these groups for removal, many experienced parallel efforts to dispossess and erase them in this period. See Malinda Maynor Lowery, *The Lumbee Indians: An American Struggle* (Chapel Hill: University of North Carolina Press, 2018), esp. 64–67.

11. Where possible, I will tell this story through direct Indigenous voices from the primary record, like that of the Eastern Cherokee soldier cited in the Introduction. However, reflecting a wider issue with colonial archives, such first-hand accounts from members of these communities are limited. This is particularly a problem in the case of the Bayou Lacombe Choctaws: People who deliberately distanced themselves from state officials, white Americans, and settler-colonial society often leave little trace in the

traditional (state) archival record. Nonetheless, in this essay I will endeavor to capture important details about these communities' histories from a range of alternative sources, including ethnographical and anthropologists' accounts, while also creatively rereading traditional archives of federal and state records and contemporary white observers. As Ojibwe historian Michael Witgen notes, "The evidence capturing the Native perspective of this ongoing colonial encounter . . . is often readily available. This is not necessarily a matter of reading European texts against the grain. It is, rather, more simply a matter of reading texts written by Europeans without privileging the fantasies of discovery . . . [and] figuring out how to disentangle expectation from reality." Michael Witgen, *An Infinity of Nations: How the Native New World Shaped Early North America* (Philadelphia: University of Pennsylvania Press, 2011), 15.

12. Throughout this essay, my definition of the South focuses primarily on lands east of the Mississippi River and Louisiana, an area roughly aligned with the states of the Confederacy (though excluding Texas, Arkansas, and Western territories controlled or claimed by the Confederacy).

13. See H. G. Runnells, "Governor's Message," January 21, 1835, *The Mississippian*, January 23, 1835; Johnson, *River of Dark Dreams*, 30.

14. Brian DeLay, *War of a Thousand Deserts: Indian Raids and the US-Mexican War* (New Haven: Yale University Press, 2008), esp. Part Three; Pekka Hämäläinen, *The Comanche Empire* (New Haven: Yale University Press, 2008).

15. For an account of non-removal as a cross-regional process, see Jane Dinwoodie, "Beyond Removal: Indians, States, and Sovereignties in the American South, 1812–1860" (Doctoral Dissertation: Oxford University, 2017). For twenty percent figure: Hobson et al., *The People Who Stayed*, 6. It is extremely difficult to accurately quantify non-removal. At minimum, four key Five-Tribes splinter groups—large enough for federal officials to notice and record—contained at least 10,000–12,000 people. This figure is based on federal observations of 2,133+ Eastern Cherokees (Finger, *Eastern Band*, 50–53); 7,000+ Choctaws in Mississippi in 1844 (Gaines to T. Hartley Crawford, September 22, 1844, "Letters Received by the Office of Indian Affairs, 1824–1880," National Archives, Record Group 75, NARA Microfilm publication M234 [hereafter: NARA M234], roll 185, "Choctaw Emigration 1826–1845"); 500–1,000+ Seminoles in Florida in the late 1840s (Grant Foreman, *Indian Removal: The Emigration of the Five Civilized Tribes* [Norman: University of Oklahoma Press, 1932], 384–86); and about 400 Creeks in Alabama (J. Anthony Paredes, "Back From Disappearance: The Alabama Creek Indian Community," in *Southeastern Indians*, 126). However, these figures are certainly incomplete. They only include these major groups, overlooking many smaller non-removed groups that officials did not see (including the Bayou Lacombe Choctaws), and people who deliberately made themselves invisible to federal officials by evading or racially passing. Nor do the figures account for the fact that federal officials struggled (or refused) to count many Indigenous Southerners, and the thousands of Indigenous Southerners—such as the Catawbas, Lumbees, and Pamunkeys—who were not members of the Five Tribes.

16. For figures, see James Mooney, *Myths of the Cherokee: Extract from the Nineteenth Annual Report of the Bureau of American Ethnology*, reprinted (Mineola, N.Y.: Dover, 1995), 159; Finger, *Eastern Band*, 50–53.

17. For more on the community's ability to avoid removal, see Finger, *Eastern Band*; Duane H. King, "The Origin of the Eastern Cherokees as a Social and Political Entity," in *The Cherokee Indian Nation: A Troubled History*, ed. Duane H. King (Knoxville: University of Tennessee Press, 1979), 164–80; E. Stanly Godbold, Jr. and Mattie U. Russell, *Confederate Colonel and Cherokee Chief: The Life of William Holland Thomas* (Knoxville: University of Tennessee Press, 1990); Adams, *Who Belongs?*, 134–35.

18. Various scholars have observed a similar link between the limits of state and colonial sovereignty and spaces of refuge for fugitive groups. See, for example, Lauren Benton, *A Search for Sovereignty: Law and Geography in European Empires, 1400–1900* (Cambridge: Cambridge University Press, 2010), 279. See also James C. Scott, *The Art of Not Being Governed: An Anarchist History of Upland Southeast Asia* (New Haven: Yale University Press, 2009), 13.

19. The Bayou Lacombe Choctaws are sometimes called the *Butchu'wa* Choctaws. Various aspects of their history can be pieced together from several secondary and ethnographic sources, including David I. Bushnell, Jr., *The Choctaw of Bayou Lacomb, St Tammany Parish, Louisiana: Smithsonian Institution Bureau of American Ethnology Bulletin* 48 (Washington: Government Printing Office, 1909); Daniel H. Usner Jr., *American Indians in the Lower Mississippi Valley: Social and Economic Histories* (Lincoln: University of Nebraska Press, 1998), 122–24. Few historians have written explicitly about this community. Most scholarly coverage is in biographies of Adrien Rouquette (sometimes misspelled "Roquette"), missionary to the community. See Blaise C. D'Antoni, "Chahta-Ima and St Tammany's Choctaws," *The St Tammany Historical Society Gazette* 7 (Mandeville: St. Tammany Historical Society, 1986); Dagmar Renshaw LeBreton, *Chahta-Ima: The Life of Adrien-Emmanuel Rouquette* (Baton Rouge: Louisiana State University Press, 1947); Dominic Braud, "Pere Rouquette, Missionnaire Extraordinaire: Father Adrien Rouquette's Mission to the Choctaw," in *Cross, Crozier, and Crucible: A Volume Celebrating the Bicentennial of a Catholic Diocese in Louisiana*, ed. Glen Conrad (New Orleans: Archdiocese of New Orleans, 1993), 314–27. See also, Dinwoodie, "Beyond Removal," chap. 3. For population estimates and distance from neighbors: Dominique Rouquette, "The Choctaws," Unpublished MS, François Dominique Rouquette Papers, Box 1 (Journals and Translations, 1850), Manuscripts Collection 508, Louisiana Research Collection, Howard-Tilton Memorial Library, Tulane University, New Orleans, La. (hereafter: LRC-Tulane).

20. Foreman, *Indian Removal*, 177–90, 294–315, 381–86.

21. Eugene D. Genovese, *The World the Slaveholders Made: Two Essays in Interpretation* (Hanover: University Press of New England, 1969).

22. For Eastern Cherokees, see Finger, "The North Carolina Cherokees." For the Bayou Lacombe Choctaws, see D'Antoni, *Chahta-Ima*; Dominique Rouquette, "The Choctaws." It is likely that the Bayou Lacombe Choctaws came from the Six Towns Division of the (pre-removal) Choctaw Nation, which was the most politically liminal and socially traditional division. For more, see Kidwell, *Choctaws and Missionaries*, 3–4. For elites, see R. Halliburton Jr., "Chief Greenwood LeFlore and His Malmaison Plantation," in Samuel J. Wells and Roseanna Tubby, eds., *After Removal: The Choctaw in Mississippi* (Jackson: University Press of Mississippi, 1986).

23. Finger, *Eastern Band*, 41–81; LeBreton, *Chahta-Ima*, chap. 13; Kidwell, *Choctaws & Missionaries*, chap. 8.

24. For Choctaw legislation, see Kidwell, *Choctaws & Missionaries*, 128–45. For Cherokee legislation, see Tim Alan Garrison, *The Legal Ideology of Removal: The Southern Judiciary and the Sovereignty of Native Americans* (Athens: University of Georgia Press, 2002).

25. For "vagrants" and "squatting," see Agent Scott to Orlando Brown, February 10, 1850, NARA M234, Roll 187, "Choctaw Emigration: 1850–1859." For the Cherokees' legal status, see John R. Finger, "The North Carolina Cherokees, 1838–1866," 17–29; Ben Oshel Bridgers, "An Historical Analysis of the Legal Status of the North Carolina Cherokees," *North Carolina Law Review* 58, no. 6 (1980): 1075–1131.

26. Colin Calloway, *The American Revolution in Indian Country: Crisis and Diversity in Native American Communities* (New York: Cambridge University Press, 1995); Kathleen DuVal, *Independence Lost: Lives on the Edges of the American Revolution* (New York: Random House, 2015); Kathryn Holland Braund, *Tohopeka: Rethinking the Creek War and the War of 1812* (Tuscaloosa: University of Alabama Press, 2012); Greg O'Brien, ed., *Pre-removal Choctaw History: Exploring New Paths* (Norman: University of Oklahoma Press, 2008), chaps. 5–7.

27. Hauptman, *Between Two Fires*.

28. Finger, *Eastern Band*, 41.

29. Thomas to G. T. Jarrett, July 25, 1861, WHTP, Folder 7 (1860–64); Russell and Godbold, *Confederate Colonel*, 93–94. In previous decades, historians have tended to view William Holland Thomas as controlling the Cherokees' negotiations, before and after the war. For years, scholars romanticized his relationship with the Cherokees and uncritically repeated Thomas's own bombastic (and racially charged) claims to have been their "white chief." See, for example, Godbold and Russell, *Confederate Colonel and Cherokee Chief*, 21–22. However, in reality, it is much more likely that Yonaguska and the other claimants controlled and benefited from the relationship as much as Thomas did and entered into it on their own terms. They knew that his social capital as a businessman, his extensive family connections, his legal training, his relative wealth, and his whiteness offered them a route into spaces and audiences that would otherwise have been almost totally unavailable to them. This was as true in the 1860s as it had been in the 1830s.

30. Finger, *Eastern Band*, chap. 3; For Western Cherokee divisions, see Kent Blansett, "When the Stars Fell from the Sky: The Cherokee Nation and Autonomy in the Civil War," in Scharff, ed. *Empire and Liberty*, 87–105.

31. Christian G. Samito, *Becoming American Under Fire: Irish Americans, African Americans, and the Politics of Citizenship during the Civil War Era* (Ithaca, N.Y.: Cornell University Press, 2009), 40.

32. Stephanie McCurry, *Confederate Reckoning: Politics and Power in the Civil War South* (Cambridge: Harvard University Press, 2010); Steven Hahn, *A Nation Under Our Feet: Black Political Struggles in the Rural South from Slavery to the Great Migration* (Cambridge: Harvard University Press, 2003); Samito, *Becoming American Under Fire*; Susannah J. Ural, *Civil War Citizens: Race, Ethnicity, and Identity in America's Bloodi-*

est Conflict (New York: New York University Press, 2010); Paul Quigley, "Civil War Conscription and the International Boundaries of Citizenship," *Journal of the Civil War Era* 4, no. 3 (2014): 373–97.

33. Finger, "The North Carolina Cherokees," 22; Finger, *Eastern Band*, 83; Crow, *Storm in the Mountains*, 2; Russell and Godbold, *Confederate Colonel*, 96–97.

34. North Carolina General Assembly, *Journal of the Senate of the General Assembly of the State of North Carolina at Its Second Extra Session, 1861* (Raleigh: John Spelman, printer to the state, 1862), 217.

35. Russell and Godbold, *Confederate Colonel*, 96–97.

36. North Carolina General Assembly, *Journal*, 217, 262.

37. John Inscoe and Gordon McKinney, "Highland Households Divided: Family Deceptions, Diversions, and Divisions in Southern Appalachia's Inner Civil War," in John C. Inscoe and Robert C. Kenzer, eds., *Enemies of the Country: New Perspective on Unionists in the Civil War South* (Athens: University of Georgia Press, 2001), 68; Kenneth W. Noe and Shannon H. Wilson, eds., *The Civil War in Appalachia: Collected Essays* (Knoxville: University of Tennessee Press, 1997).

38. Albert B. Moore, *Conscription and Conflict in the Confederacy* (New York: Hilary House, 2nd ed., 1963); Joe A. Mobley, *Weary of War: Life on the Confederate Home Front* (Westport, Conn.: Praeger, 2008), 49–53.

39. W. Todd Groce, *Mountain Rebels: East Tennessee Confederates and the Civil War, 1860–1870* (Knoxville: University of Tennessee Press, 1999), 100, 108; John C. Inscoe and Gordon McKinney, *The Heart of Confederate Appalachia: Western North Carolina in the Civil War* (Chapel Hill: University of North Carolina Press, 2005), 115; Mobley, *Weary of War*, 56.

40. Moore, *Conscription and Conflict*, 11.

41. R. H. Chilton to Thomas, September 19, 1861, in *War of the Rebellion, Official Records of the Union and Confederate Armies* (Washington: Government Printing Office, 1881), Ser. 1, Vol. 51, no. 2, 304.

42. Crow, *Storm in the Mountains*, 156–64; Finger, *Eastern Band*, 84; Mooney, *Myths of the Cherokees*, 169.

43. Thomas to Sarah Thomas, June 26, 1863 and Brigadier General Vaughn to Thomas, November 29, 1863, WHTP, Folder 7 (1860–64).

44. Crow, *Storm in the Mountains*, xi. Other Indigenous soldiers served for the Confederacy in the East in subordinate positions, or as exclusively Indian formations. See Hauptman, *Between Two Fires*, 87–102. In North Carolina, Confederate officials also recruited Lumbee Indians as conscripted labor. A small number of Lumbees also signed up for military service as "free people of color" in North and South Carolina. See Lowery, *The Lumbee Indians*, 70–78; Hauptman, *Between Two Fires*, 65–87.

45. For delicacies (honey) see Tse:gh(i)sini to unknown, July 20, 1862. For stolen provisions (salt): Tso:na, Confederate Soldier to unknown, July 22, 1862, in Kilpatrick, eds., *The Shadow of Sequoyah*, 9–10.

46. Since the 1830s, a key part of the Cherokees' strategy to negotiate ongoing residence in North Carolina was to make public tours and displays of their "civilized" behavior as "proof" of their eligibility to remain. See Finger, *Eastern Band*, 69. For more

on "civilization" as a prerequisite for Indigenous belonging in the United States, and permitted exemptions to removal, see Stephen Kantrowitz, "Not Quite Constitutionalized: The Meaning of 'Civilization' and the Limits of Native American Citizenship," in Gregory P. Downs and Kate Masur, eds., *The World the Civil War Made* (Chapel Hill: University of North Carolina Press, 2015), 75–105; Karen L. Merrero, "Mobility, Community, and Nation in a Northern Indigenous Region," in Nicole Eustace and Frederika J. Teute, eds., *Warring for America: Cultural Contests in the Era of 1812* (Chapel Hill: University of North Carolina Press, 2017), 425–26.

47. *Knoxville Daily Bulletin*, May 2, 1862.

48. Finger, *Eastern Band*, 95–97; Crow, *Storm in the Mountains*, 58–59. The community disowned those who did desert.

49. *Knoxville Register*, February 21, 1863.

50. Finger, *Eastern Band*, 96–97; Crow, *Storm in the Mountains*, chap. 12.

51. "I:no:li issues clothing to soldiers and to Children of the War Dead (1865)," MS from "The Inoli Letters," in Kilpatrick, eds., *The Shadow of Sequoyah*, 12–15.

52. Despite their Confederate alliance, federal officials did not seek to punish the Eastern Cherokees. Thomas had to sign the oath of allegiance. See Finger, *Eastern Band*, 97–102.

53. North Carolina General Assembly, *Public Laws of the State of North Carolina, passed by the General Assembly at the Session of 1865–66, and 1861–'62–'63, and 1864, together with Important Ordinances Passed by the Convention of 1866* (Raleigh, N.C.: Robert W. Best, 1866), 120.

54. *NC Public Laws*, 99; Roberta S. Alexander, *North Carolina Faces the Freedmen: Race Relations during Presidential Reconstruction, 1865–1867* (Durham, N.C.: Duke University Press, 1985), 38; Gordon McKinney, *Southern Mountain Republicans, 1865–1900: Politics and the Appalachian Community* (Knoxville: University of Tennessee Press, 2nd ed., 1998), 44–50.

55. Finger, *Eastern Band*, 102–3.

56. Hauptman, *Between Two Fires*, 77.

57. Finger, *Eastern Band*, 102.

58. This sense of safety was relatively short-lived. In 1867, Thomas was committed to a mental institution, again jeopardizing the Eastern Cherokees' legal status, particularly as several court cases over his business affairs threatened their ownership of their lands held in Thomas's name. In 1874, the community took their case to court in an effort to maintain their lands. In 1875–76, this process ended with the federal recognition of the Eastern Cherokees and establishment of the Qualla Boundary, though the community faced further struggles to maintain control of their resources in the later nineteenth century. See Finger, *Eastern Band*, 102–25; Adams, *Who Belongs?*, 135–38.

59. John D. Winters, *The Civil War in Louisiana* (Baton Rouge: Louisiana State University Press, 1991).

60. LeBreton, *Chahta-Ima*, 219–20.

61. Rouquette's February letters suggest continuity: Adrien Rouquette to "Monsieur et bien cher confrère," Feb. 20, 1861, Adrien Emmanuel Rouquette Papers, Folder 5 (1847–1885), University of Notre Dame Archives, Notre Dame, Ind..

62. Chester Hearn, *The Capture of New Orleans, 1862* (Baton Rouge: Louisiana State University Press, 1995); Gerald Capers, *Occupied City: New Orleans under the Federals* (Lexington: University Press of Kentucky, 1965).

63. Robert W. Hastings, *The Lakes of Pontchartrain: Their History and Environments* (Jackson: University Press of Mississippi, 2009), 62–66.

64. "Choctaws in Louisiana," *Daily Picayune*, New Orleans, August 4, 1883.

65. Adrien Rouquette to John Dimitry, December 12, 1884, Folder 12, 230-26-12, Rouquette Doc 75. John Minor Wisdom Collection, 1710–1960, Louisiana Research Collection, LRC-Tulane, Braud, "Missionaire Extraordinaire," 324.

66. D'Antoni, *Chahta-Ima*, 76–77.

67. LeBreton, *Chahta-Ima*, 222–23.

68. D'Antoni, *Chahta-Ima*, 76. Nineteenth-century New Orleans was notorious for yellow fever and malaria: Jo Ann Carrigan, *The Saffron Scourge: A History of Yellow Fever in Louisiana, 1796–1905* (Lafayette: Center for Louisiana Studies, University of Southwestern Louisiana, 1994); Urmi Engineer Willoughby, *Yellow Fever, Race, and Ecology in Nineteenth-Century New Orleans* (Baton Rouge: Louisiana State University Press, 2017); Kathryn Olivarius, "Immunity, Capital, and Power in Antebellum New Orleans," *The American Historical Review* 124, no. 2 (2019), 425–55.

69. D'Antoni, *Chahta-Ima*, 76.

70. D'Antoni, *Chahta-Ima*, 76.

71. "The Choctaws in Louisiana," *Daily Picayune*, August 4, 1883.

72. Hastings, *Lakes of Pontchartrain*, 66–67.

73. D'Antoni, *Chahta-Ima*, 77–79.

74. Like Thomas, Adrien Rouquette had to pledge the oath of allegiance to the United States. Officials took no action against the community. D'Antoni, *Chahta-Ima*, 77.

75. See Nelson, "Indian America," 382–84.

76. Braud, "Missionnaire Extraordinaire," 325.

77. Rouquette to Dimitry, December 12, 1884.

78. Contests for Indigenous sovereignty in the West have been covered in an earlier note.

79. Many modern Indigenous communities also reject American claims to govern their sovereignty because these communities predate European arrivals in North America. See Cobb, "Understanding Tribal Sovereignty," 119. It is also crucial to note that Indigenous scholars have argued for the mutuality of (U.S.) citizenship and Indigenous sovereignty, rather than arguing that one necessarily cancels out the other. This argument has important implications for modern interpretations of the approach that the Eastern Cherokees took in the immediate wake of removal, reinforcing the argument that this strategic compromise did not necessarily invalidate their own claims to power and community. See K. Tsianina Lomawaima, "The Mutuality of *Citizenship* and *Sovereignty*: The Society of American Indians and the Battle to Inherit America," *American Indian Quarterly* 37, no. 3 (2013): 333–51. Additionally, numerous scholars have written about this kind of adaptive resistance throughout Native history, including Scott Richard Lyons, who terms these kinds of compromises "x-marks": Scott Richard Lyons, *X-Marks: Native Signatures of Assent* (Minneapolis: University of Minnesota Press, 2010), esp. 2–3.

80. Many non-removed Indigenous Southerners shared this type of *de facto* sovereignty. Lumbee attorney Arlinda Locklear has recently argued for Indigenous communities' abilities to hold these types of sovereignties unrecognized by—or, indeed, beyond the view of—the United States. See, for example, Lowery, *Lumbee Indians in the Jim Crow South*, 255.

81. For maroon communities and their claims to power, see Sylviane A. Diouf, *Slavery's Exiles: The Story of the American Maroons* (New York: New York University Press, 2014). See also Steven Hahn's argument comparing Northern free black communities to maroon communities: Steven Hahn, *The Political Worlds of Slavery and Freedom* (Cambridge: Harvard University Press, 2009], 26–44.

82. Garrison, *Legal Ideology of Removal.*

83. Robert Yazzie cited in Kevin Bruyneel, *The Third Space of Sovereignty: The Postcolonial Politics of US-Indigenous Relations* (Minneapolis: University of Minnesota Press, 2007), 23.

84. Thomas J. Biersteker and Cynthia Weber, eds., *State Sovereignty as Social Construct* (Cambridge: Cambridge University Press, 1996); Bruyneel, *Third Space of Sovereignty*, 10–11.

85. Amanda J. Cobb, "Understanding Tribal Sovereignty: Definitions, Conceptualizations, and Interpretations," *American Studies* 46, no. 3/4 (2005), 115.

6

Negotiating Sovereignty

*U.S. and Canadian Colonialisms
on the Northwest Plains, 1855–1877*

Ryan Hall

L ate in the summer of 2015, the authors and editors of this volume traveled to Banff, Alberta, for a three-day conference dedicated to discussing
the transformation of state sovereignty in mid-nineteenth-century North
America. Most of us flew into the plains metropolis of Calgary before undertak-
ing the scenic two-hour drive west to the mountains. The dramatic landscape of
southern Alberta provided a beautiful venue for our conference, but it also offered a useful lens for understanding the very transformation we came to discuss.
A little more than a century and a half ago, the Indigenous people known as the
Blackfoot dominated the northwest plains of what is now southern Alberta and
western Montana. Non-Native people—who today comprise this region's majority population—stuck to small enclaves, where they awaited occasional Blackfoot
fur trading parties. Today, the northwest plains look entirely different. The story
of this region's transformation begins with the aggressive expansion of state sovereignty in both the United States and Canada in the mid-nineteenth century, a
mutually reinforcing project that Blackfoot people twice sought to negotiate to
their own advantage.

Scholars and activists often refer to the region around Calgary and Banff as
"Treaty Seven territory": the lands of southern Alberta that Indigenous people
ceded to the Dominion of Canada in exchange for reserves (the Canadian equivalent of American reservations) in 1877. The seventh of the eleven "numbered
treaties" that Canadian officials conducted between 1871 and 1921, Treaty Seven
bore the signatures of fifty-one Indigenous representatives who gathered at
Blackfoot Crossing, a shallow stretch of the Bow River just east of what was then
Fort Calgary. Most of the signatories self-identified as Blackfoot, a closely related
alliance of the Kainai, Siksika, and Piikani nations. Stoney Nakoda and Tsuut'ina
representatives signed as well. Treaty Seven established two (later three) official
reserves for the Blackfoot in what became southern Alberta, along with reserves
for the Stoneys and Tsuut'inas, and opened the remainder of the region to set-

tlement, mining, and other economic activities. In return, the treaty ostensibly obligated Canada to provide material goods, services, and protection to Black-foot people. The seminal event in the Anglo-Canadian settlement of southern Alberta, Treaty Seven enabled the rapid expansion of railroads, ranching, and farming in the region during the 1880s and 1890s.[1]

Treaty Seven was a first on the Canadian side of the border, but Blackfoot people already had experience making treaties with the United States. In 1855, leaders from all three Blackfoot nations gathered about 250 miles to the south of Blackfoot Crossing to negotiate an accord with the U.S. government commonly known as "Lame Bull's Treaty," after its most prominent Piikani signatory. Signed in October of 1855 in what is now western Montana, Lame Bull's Treaty delin-eated Blackfoot territories south of the 49th parallel but, unlike Treaty Seven, did not create reservations. The treaty promised that the Blackfoot would receive ten years of annuity goods from U.S. officials in return for maintaining peace with their neighbors, allowing whites to traverse the region, and permitting the estab-lishment of a government agency. The first major treaty council on the northwest plains, Lame Bull's Treaty marked the opening of formal relations between the Blackfoot and the United States Government. Like Treaty Seven, it precipitated widespread white settlement in the region, which began shortly thereafter.[2]

The treaties of 1855 and 1877 laid the groundwork for U.S. and Canadian ex-pansion throughout the bulk of traditional Blackfoot territory, but for histori-ans, these documents raise more questions than answers, especially when ap-proached together. What connections did these treaties have to one another, and what set them apart? Although several American historians have written about the 1855 treaty, and a handful of Canadian scholars have studied the 1877 agreement, few have analyzed these agreements alongside one another. Doing so can lend new perspectives to Blackfoot history, while also providing insight into the similarities and differences between U.S. and Canadian expansion on the northwest plains. A comparative approach can also shed light on the role of the border itself. Both treaties defined territories adjoining the 49th parallel, which the Indigenous signatories of these treaties frequently crossed. Did the proximity of the international border affect white and Indigenous perspectives on these treaties? Finally, we need to understand how the Blackfoot themselves conceived of these agreements. Did Blackfoot leaders understand these treaties as constituting a transformation in sovereignty, and if so, what exactly did that sovereignty entail?

By comparing and analyzing Blackfoot treaty-making in 1855 and 1877, this essay will demonstrate key similarities and connections between the process of state expansion in the United States and Canada. Despite popular conceptions to the contrary, U.S. and Canadian officials brought remarkably similar approaches to expansion and to their dealings with Indigenous people. At the same time, Blackfoot people brought their own motivations and assumptions to the treaty councils. Rather than relinquishing their sovereignty, the Blackfoot saw both the 1855 and 1877 treaties as opportunities to maintain, and in some ways strengthen, their own sovereignty over their homelands, which to them entailed the autonomy to maintain their way of life without outside interference, not the supreme power of a centralized state. Seen together, these seemingly dissimilar agreements reveal much about the incomplete transformation of North American sovereignty in the mid-nineteenth century, and demonstrate the interconnectedness of U.S. and Canadian expansion.

Lame Bull's Treaty

Prior to 1855, the prospect of widespread Euro-American settlement on the northwest plains would have been almost unthinkable to the people who already lived there. These were the ancestral homelands of three closely related nations who knew themselves collectively as the Niitsitapi, or Real People, though English-speakers knew them as the Blackfoot.[3] During the first half of the nineteenth century, Blackfoot homelands stretched from the North Saskatchewan River south some 450 miles to the Missouri River, and from the foothills of the Rocky Mountains east as much as several hundred miles onto the Great Plains. Siksika people lived in the northernmost portions of this territory, between the Bow and North Saskatchewan Rivers, while the Kainais and Piikanis typically lived to their south, sometimes ranging as far as the Yellowstone River for hunting and horse raiding.[4] Blackfoot life had changed dramatically beginning in the early eighteenth century, as they acquired horses from their southern and western neighbors and European technologies such as guns and metal tools from the east.[5] The Blackfoot represented one of several plains Indigenous polities whose mastery of these new technologies allowed them to expand their military and economic influence dramatically during the late eighteenth and early nineteenth centuries.[6]

Blackfoot people's easy access to horses and metal technologies, as well as their advantageous position between American fur traders on the Missouri River and British fur traders on the North Saskatchewan River, allowed them to dominate neighboring Indigenous groups. The Stoney Nakoda, close relatives of the plains Assiniboines, occupied the mountains and foothills to the Blackfoot's west, around the present site of Banff. In the mountain valleys farther south and west dwelled Pend d'Oreille, Nez Perce, Kootenai, and Flathead Salish bands. The Tsuut'ina, or Sarcee, lived in the mixed prairies and forest to the Blackfoot's northwest, and maintained mostly peaceful ties with their more powerful neighbors. Cree, Assiniboine, and Gros Ventre bands occupied the plains and parklands to the Blackfoot's north and east, while Crows and Shoshones lived on the plains and river valleys to their south.[7] In 1818, British and American officials divided their own claims to this territory at the 49th parallel of latitude, but neither challenged Blackfoot dominance of the northwest plains. Militaristic, wealthy, and mobile, the Blackfoot occupied the last corner of the Great Plains to enter into formal treaty agreements with either the United States or Great Britain. Artist George Catlin exaggerated only slightly when he called the Blackfoot "perhaps the most powerful tribe of Indians on the continent" in 1832.[8]

Although confident in their position as the foremost power on the northwest plains, Blackfoot leaders nonetheless accepted U.S. treaty commissioners' invitation to convene for a treaty council in October 1855 at the confluence of the Judith and Missouri Rivers. Representatives from all three Blackfoot nations attended, most of whom led autonomous bands of around two to three hundred people. At the treaty grounds, these bands merged to form a grand Blackfoot encampment of 3,500 people, who erected their tipis among the cottonwood trees that draped the valley floor. The commissioners invited neighboring nations as well, including Nez Perce, Pend d'Oreille, Gros Ventre, Assiniboine, and Flathead people, all of whom erected their homes on the unsheltered plains above the valley. Altogether, more than ten thousand Indigenous people came together for the council, making it the largest single gathering of these diverse groups in the history of the northwest plains. On the morning of October 16, representatives from each of these groups assembled in semicircular rows in front of a square awning that had been erected at the behest of U.S. treaty commissioners Isaac Stevens and Alfred Cumming. Through a series of translators, Stevens and Cumming began describing their proposed treaty to the assembly at 1:00 on Tuesday, October 16, 1855.[9]

The proposed treaty, the commissioners explained, would have three primary components. First, it would establish peace between the assembled nations. The signatories would agree to cease all horse raiding and warfare amongst themselves. In order to prevent future conflicts over hunting rights, the treaty would create two "common hunting grounds" in the southernmost and westernmost corners of the treaty region, where all nations could hunt freely but where none could reside permanently. (These areas mapped closely onto already-existing neutral hunting territories.[10]) Second, the Indigenous signatories would allow whites to pass freely through their territory, to use its resources, and to reside there if they desired. Third, in return for these concessions, the U.S. government would provide ten years of annuity goods for the Blackfoot, along with agency buildings, demonstration farms, and other supposedly "civilizing" institutions. The treaty did not entail significant territorial concessions from Indigenous people. Because they were communicated through experienced and trusted translators such as mixed-ancestry vagabond James "Jemmy Jock" Bird and American fur trader Alexander Culbertson, the stated terms of the proposed treaty were probably clear to everyone who gathered along the riverbank.[11] But the attendees understood the purpose of the treaty, and its significance to the region's future, in very different ways.

From the perspective of United States officials, the 1855 treaty fit comfortably within the trajectory of federal Indian policy in the West. During the 1830s, U.S. Indian policy had followed the linked goals of Indian removal and the creation of a "permanent Indian frontier." State and federal officials forcibly relocated large eastern nations such as the Cherokees west of the Mississippi River, where they would supposedly remain in perpetuity while white Americans and their slaves colonized the lands they left behind. The flimsy logic behind removal—that the West would remain "Indian territory" indefinitely—soon crumbled under expansionist ambitions. Under the leadership of President James K. Polk, the United States negotiated the annexation of Oregon Territory in an 1846 treaty with the British, then forcibly seized the northern third of Mexico in 1848. Eager to populate these new lands with white settlers, federal policy shifted toward facilitating white, rather than Indian, emigration to the West. With nowhere left to remove Indians, federal officials instead focused on negotiating treaties that would restrict Indian people to reservations while opening the bulk of their lands to settlement. On the Great Plains, the military power of horse-rich nations made reservations less immediately practicable, so officials instead drew up agreements that would define Indigenous territories, decrease warfare, and protect overland migrants. The Fort Laramie Treaty of 1851 brought together signatories from the central plains, and the Fort Atkinson Treaty of 1853 did the same on the southern plains.[12] The 1855 Blackfoot treaty would complete federal officials' drive to secure safe passage throughout the Great Plains.

Commissioner Isaac Stevens embodied the Americans' aggressive approach to treaties. An ardent Democrat, former U.S. army major, and veteran of the U.S. invasion of Mexico City in 1847, Stevens believed wholeheartedly in the United States' destiny to expand. Stevens reminisced on the conquest of northern Mexico as but one step on America's "rapid march to greatness," in which Mexicans had "succumbed to a people having a future which they were resolved to achieve."[13] He applied similar logic to his dealings with Indian people. After securing appointments as Governor of Washington Territory and leader of the Northern Pacific Railroad Exploration and Survey in 1853, Stevens organized a series of treaties with the Indians of the Pacific Northwest that he believed would facilitate rapid American settlement. Fiercely energetic and ambitious, Stevens saw in treaties the power to extend American power, to undermine the British, and to transform Indian livelihoods. In councils, he forcefully advocated for assimilationist institutions such as demonstration farms and schools, which, coupled with agencies and annuities, would both bind Indians to the United States and weaken British interests like the Hudson's Bay Company. Discouraging Indians from crossing the border would also alleviate security concerns, especially regarding the possibility of cross-border raiding.[14] Stevens's treaty with the Blackfoot would accomplish regional security while also serving national interests.

Stevens's counterpart at the 1855 treaty, a venerable Piikani chief named Lame Bull, had far different considerations in mind. Experienced at diplomacy and negotiation, Lame Bull led a large band known as the Hard Top Knots and came of age at a time when the region's economy revolved around the fur trade. Likely a frequent visitor to British and American trading posts throughout his life, Lame Bull became an expert at negotiating exchanges, particularly of the Americans' favored trade item, the heavy woolen winter furs of bison known as robes. Widely respected for his skills as a warrior and known as a friendly and generous community member, Lame Bull came to power not through personal connections but through the communal acclimation of the Hard Top Knots themselves. At the time of the treaty council, Lame Bull was among the most respected of all the Blackfoot chiefs, and the commissioners therefore recognized him as "head chief" during the treaty council.[15] However, he had no power to compel other bands to his will because political power among the Blackfoot did not extend beyond the band level. Unlike the settler nations with whom they negotiated, the Blackfoot did not share a sovereign, centralized political authority. Only shared concerns and interests would motivate Blackfoot leaders to agree on signing the treaty.[16]

Growing competition over bison herds represented the primary consideration for Lame Bull and his fellow chiefs at the 1855 treaty council. During the early 1850s, bison populations in Blackfoot territory remained robust, and according to one official showed "no sensible decrease" despite the flourishing regional trade in robes and meat.[17] Fur trade returns reflected this resiliency, as records show that Blackfoot people continued to trade robes by the tens of thousands throughout the 1850s.[18] However, the strength of bison herds in Blackfoot country attracted competition from areas where bison populations were shrinking. To the Blackfoot's east, plains peoples such as the Crees, Lakotas, and Assiniboines, along with Métis market hunters, faced dwindling herds and pushed their hunting operations westward. To the west, a similar problem unfolded, as declining game populations in the mountains led Flathead, Pend d'Oreille, and Kootenai hunters to venture onto the plains in search of game. Outsiders' forays into Blackfoot territory led to an increase in violent conflicts, and finding a peaceful solution to these clashes weighed heavy on the minds of Lame Bull and his peers in October 1855.[19]

Treaty deliberations reflected the concerns of Indigenous people. Largely ignoring Stevens's grand pronouncements about a future of farms, schools, mills, and cattle herds, the chiefs instead focused their conversation exclusively on hunting rights. The proposed treaty would allow Flathead, Pend d'Oreille, Nez Perce, and Kootenai hunters to seek bison on the plains, but only in the "common hunting ground" between the Three Forks of the Missouri River and mountains. At the council, the Pend d'Oreille chief Alexander argued that the common hunting ground was "a very small place" that could not accommodate the needs of his people. In response, the Piikani chief Little Dog assured Alexander that the Piikanis would welcome him if he came north of the common hunting ground, and Alexander let the matter rest. At 3:00 P.M. on the second day of the council, the assembled chiefs and commissioners signed the treaty. U.S. officials then distributed promised goods, including food, blankets, and tools, and the diverse groups gradually dispersed.[20] In less than two days, they had reached an agreement that would change the region forever.

Lame Bull, Little Dog, Alexander, and the other chiefs who assembled for the 1855 treaty discussed it primarily as a peace treaty between the region's Indigenous peoples, not a transfer of power to U.S. officials. They had ample reason to emphasize intertribal diplomacy rather than state expansion or assimilation. Not only was treaty-making a longstanding practice among the region's nations, but such agreements had often been brokered by whites who could serve as semineutral third parties. For example, in 1819, Cree and Blackfoot leaders negotiated a peace at the Hudson's Bay Company's Edmonton House, and in 1831, the American Fur Company oversaw a temporary peace between the Piikanis and the Assiniboines at Fort Union.[21] In 1846, Jesuit missionaries witnessed a similar peace agreement between Flathead and Piikani leaders.[22] Indigenous women and fur trader husbands often played a central role as translators and trusted intermediaries. Fur trader Alexander Culbertson and his Kainai wife Medicine Snake

Woman helped Isaac Stevens assemble bands for the 1855 treaty council and translated preliminary meetings between Blackfoot leaders and U.S. officials.[23] Lame Bull's Treaty was unexceptional in the way it established peace between the Blackfoot and their neighbors.

Indigenous people had little reason to see Lame Bull's Treaty as representing a transformation in Blackfoot sovereignty, let alone its relinquishment. Although the treaty stipulated that Americans would have safe passage through the region, and permission to "live in" Blackfoot lands, it gave no indication of how many people might come, from where, and what might draw them there. Although they likely had some knowledge of momentous recent developments elsewhere in the West, they had little reason to expect that similar transformations were imminent on the northwest plains. Few Blackfoot people had ever traveled to eastern cities, and despite several generations of exchange, the region's fur trade continued to be conducted by small brigades or in isolated outposts such as Edmonton and Fort Benton. As one Blackfoot leader would ask in 1859, "If the white men are so numerous, why is it the same ones come back to the country year after year, with rarely an exception?" In his country, the Blackfoot were "a great and powerful people, but the whites [were] few and feeble."[24] Stevens's and Cummings's pronouncements about missions, schools, and farms carried little meaning to the Blackfoot because whites continued to have such a minuscule presence on the northwest plains. They foresaw an immediate future that resembled their present and imagined that the treaty would alleviate practical contemporary concerns.

The 1855 treaty reflected a fundamental disjuncture between the worldviews of its primary signatories. While the U.S. contingent believed the treaty would lay the groundwork for an expansion of state sovereignty over the northwest plains, Blackfoot leaders believed the treaty would help to protect the autonomy of their bands against outside threats. Stevens believed the region stood on the precipice of enormous changes, including the imminent extinction of the bison, the building of railroads, and widespread settlement by white farmers. Blackfoot leaders, most prominently Lame Bull, had little reason to expect that the treaty portended fundamental changes to life on the northwest plains. The treaty would establish peace with some Indigenous neighbors and would fortify the Blackfoot's privileged access to bison. To Stevens, a shift in sovereignty over the American West was already underway, but Blackfoot chiefs gave little indication that they sensed such a transformation in their own homelands. Blackfoot sovereignty would remain intact. Both Stevens and Lame Bull died relatively soon thereafter—the former felled by a Confederate ball at the Battle of Chantilly in 1862, the latter by a wounded bison bull in 1857—so neither would live to see the outcome of the treaty. Circumstances would soon unfold that defied the expectations of both.

Treaty Seven

The Blackfoot leaders and U.S. officials who negotiated and signed the 1855 treaty had different expectations for the future it would bring about, but none fully anticipated the violent chaos that would follow the treaty's ratification. In the two decades that preceded the signing of Treaty Seven with Canada in 1877, a series of crises visited the people of the northwest plains and adjoining mountains. As the violence and disorder of U.S. expansion swept across Blackfoot country, it shaped events on both sides of the border in crucial and unexpected ways.

The aftermath of Lame Bull's Treaty belied Blackfoot expectations about the agreement. In 1855, there had been little reason to anticipate an imminent increase in the number of whites on the northwest plains, and as a result, the treaty's allowances for U.S. citizens to pass through and reside in the region had little resonance for Blackfoot signers. This situation changed dramatically when news of the discovery of gold in Grasshopper Creek in southwest Montana attracted thousands of miners (many of whom came west escaping the U.S. Civil War) beginning in 1862. Boomtowns such as Bannack and Virginia City sprung up overnight. Ranchers and merchants followed the miners, many operating out of the fur trading outpost of Fort Benton, where they quarreled frequently with Blackfoot visitors. Meanwhile, the American Civil War delayed the government's promised deliveries of annuity goods to the Blackfoot and prevented their payment altogether in 1861 and 1863. Allegations of corruption and theft by under-qualified government agents circulated widely as well. These tensions exploded in early 1865 when Kainai warriors raided Fort Benton for horses and later killed eleven wood-cutters at a nearby prospective settlement named Ophir. The ensuing "war," a five-year series of small-scale raids and murders, ended decisively in 1870 when the U.S. Army's Second Cavalry slaughtered nearly two hundred peaceful Piikani people camped along the Marias River near the Canadian border.[25]

The conflicts of the 1860s led many Blackfoot people to retreat to lands north of the international border, which remained relatively free of white settlers and miners. But British territory proved a false sanctuary. In the winter of 1869-70, smallpox reduced the Blackfoot population by one-fourth. Meanwhile, restrictions on the alcohol trade in Montana led American whiskey traders to move their operations north of the border where they could sell alcohol to Native people without fear of reprisal from absent Canadian authorities. The so-called "Whoop-Up Trail" devastated the already demoralized Blackfoot. Scores died from alcohol-related causes, including exposure and internecine violence. The arrival of the North-West Mounted Police (NWMP) in 1874 disrupted the whiskey traders' activities, but not until after the trade had already done severe damage.[26] By the twentieth anniversary of Lame Bull's Treaty, the Blackfoot had been weakened both physically and mentally.

Still reeling from U.S. officials' abandonment of their treaty promises, Blackfoot people at first hesitated to turn to government officials for assistance despite their struggles. Kainai chief Medicine Calf, signer of the 1855 treaty, ruefully observed that "the Americans gave at first large bags of flour, sugar, and many blankets; the next year it was only half the quantity, and the following years it grew less and less, and now they give only a handful of flour."[27] Deepening their distrust, in both 1865 and 1868 the Blackfoot had negotiated new treaties with U.S. officials, but the U.S. Senate never ratified either agreement due to continued violence in the region and opposition by settlers.[28] After so many broken promises, many Blackfoot leaders wanted no part in making a treaty with Canadian officials. In 1871, Jean L'Heureux, a self-styled priest and longtime resident of the northwest plains, reported that the Blackfoot "dread troops and any conference business, since the treachery of the American government officials toward them."[29] Blackfoot leaders came by their cynicism honestly.

Deteriorating circumstances led Blackfoot chiefs to reconsider their stance on treaties. During the 1870s, Blackfoot people grew increasingly desperate to preserve their access to bison and to their traditional hunting grounds. As in 1855, they faced fierce competition from neighboring nations such as the Crees and Assiniboines, and in the intervening years this competition grew even more heated, especially north of the international border. More worrisome, during the 1870s, white and Métis hunters flooded Blackfoot territory, some even erecting semi-permanent camps near the NWMP posts of Fort Macleod and Fort Calgary. White farmers and ranchers also began to establish themselves in the region, staking claims to well-watered river valleys upon which bison relied. Blackfoot people worried that the trickle of settlers could become a deluge, as it had in Montana, and that the growth of settlements would lead to their country being "taken from them without any ceremony."[30] Blackfoot leaders needed to preserve access to bison while limiting the impact of white and Métis settlers.

By 1875 Blackfoot leaders began actively lobbying Canadian officials for a treaty, and a Siksika chief named Crowfoot became their most prominent advocate. A renowned warrior and respected leader of the Moccasin band,

Crowfoot maintained strong relations with the NWMP, especially Lieutenant-Colonel James Macleod.[31] In the autumn of 1875, Crowfoot gathered a council of chiefs that dictated a petition for the territory's governor, making clear that Blackfoot desired a treaty council, and in the meantime asked that the governor stop the "invasion" of Blackfoot hunting grounds by whites, Crees, and Métis.[32] Crowfoot told NWMP inspector Cecil Denny that the Blackfoot were "getting shut in" by invading hide hunters, raising the prospect that "the buffalo will all be killed, and we shall have nothing more to live on."[33] Blackfoot leaders sought an agreement that would reduce incursions onto their territory, thereby preserving their ability to hunt and to trade.[34] In some ways, Crowfoot's goals in 1877 were similar to Lame Bull's in 1855: By making some concessions to whites, they could offset dangerous over-competition over bison. A peace agreement would thus help preserve a measure of autonomy for Blackfoot bands and would stave off imminent disaster for his people.

Growing Blackfoot desperation coincided neatly with the national ambitions of Canada, a new country in the midst of its own massive territorial expansion. In 1867, the distinct British colonies of Quebec, Ontario, New Brunswick, and Nova Scotia united as the Dominion of Canada, a federated and self-governing polity within the British Empire. The new country expanded quickly, incorporating Manitoba in 1870, British Columbia in 1871, and Prince Edward Island in 1873. In 1870, the Dominion acquired the charter to Rupert's Land—the vast drainage basin of Hudson Bay encompassing most of what is now Alberta, Saskatchewan, and Manitoba—from the Hudson's Bay Company. Focus quickly shifted toward opening these new lands to settlement and resource exploitation through Indian treaties. Between 1871 and 1876, Canadian officials conducted six multilateral treaties with Indigenous peoples in the interior, beginning first in what is now Ontario, then moving west into what is now Manitoba, Saskatchewan, and Alberta. After completing Treaty Six with the Plain and Wood Crees in 1876, Canadian attentions shifted toward Blackfoot country.[35]

Enabling railroad expansion served as Canadian officials' most pressing reason for making a treaty with the Blackfoot and their neighbors. The 1871 incorporation of British Columbia into the Dominion explicitly obligated Canadians to build a transcontinental railroad within a decade. Such a project would link the new province economically with the East while also providing linkages to shipping routes with Asia. A transcontinental railroad would also enable the expansion of agriculture into the interior West by bringing farmers to the prairies and providing markets for their agricultural products. Altogether, the Numbered

Treaties—including Treaty Seven—were designed to enable rapid colonization of the Canadian West. Extinguishing Indian rights to western lands, buildings railroads, and expanding agricultural settlement would provide a foundation for the strength and survival of Canada. In the words of Sir John A. Macdonald, a railroad would transform Canada from a mere "geographic expression" into a unified and strong country. Like Isaac Stevens did two decades earlier, the Canadians linked their treaty with the Blackfoot to national ambitions.[36]

Concerns about the United States also figured prominently into Canadian expansionism. Following the U.S. Civil War, some American politicians advocated the annexation of part or all of Canada, exploiting loose ties between Canadians and the Confederacy as justification. The western prairies seemed particularly vulnerable to U.S. aggression, given the relative absence of Canadians there. By facilitating Canadian settlement and the establishment of state institutions in the West, treaties could provide a bulwark against potential American encroachment.[37] Treaties could also prevent the northward spread of America's Indian wars. Canadian officials worried that ongoing conflicts between the U.S. Army and nations like the Lakota and Nez Perce during the 1860s and 1870s would spill over the border, drawing in "Canadian" Indians such as the Blackfoot. These concerns grew stronger after Sitting Bull and several thousand Lakota followers fled to what is now Saskatchewan following the 1876 Battle of Little Big Horn.[38] By formalizing peaceful ties with Indian people and countering U.S. expansion, treaty-making could serve both national and geopolitical interests for Canadian officials.

With these motivations in mind, commissioners David Laird and James Macleod convened the treaty council at Blackfoot Crossing on September 19, 1877. One observer estimated that around 8,000 people gathered, including 6,000 Indians and around 2,000 white traders and mounted police.[39] The treaty that the commissioners proposed limited Blackfoot territories to two reserves: a shared reserve for the Siksikas, Kainais, and Tsuut'inas at Blackfoot Crossing, and a separate reserve near Brocket for the Piikanis. (The Kainais would later move to a separate reserve, near Fort Macleod in 1882, and the Tsuut'inas would receive a reserve near Calgary.) The Stoneys moved to a reserve "in the vicinity of Morleyville," between present-day Calgary and Banff. The Indian signatories would retain the right to hunt throughout their erstwhile territories, on lands that had not yet been claimed directly by the government nor by settlers with the permission of the Crown. The treaty guaranteed all tribal members a one-time payment of twelve dollars, with annual payments of five dollars thereafter,

and chiefs were guaranteed suits of clothing and a variety of tools and implements. The treaty also promised funds for schoolteachers, cattle, and farming
implements.[40]

Just as in 1855, negotiations for Treaty Seven focused almost exclusively on
what mattered most to the Indigenous signers, which was access to the region's
diminishing resources. Old Sun, a Siksika chief, asked the commissioners to ban
wolf poisons since they killed horses and bison as well. The Kainai chief Medicine Calf requested payment for the firewood collected by the NWMP since their
arrival in 1874. More important, Medicine Calf also pushed the commissioners
to ban Cree and Métis hunters from Treaty Seven territory entirely. Laird replied that newly implemented restrictions on killing bison calves and cows in
winter would prove sufficient and that he could never "exclude any class of the
Queen's subjects" from Canadian lands. After conferring amongst themselves,
representatives of each of the five nations signed Treaty Seven on September 22,
1877. (A band of Crees signed an adhesion to Treaty Six as well.) After distributing payments to the assembly, Laird and Macleod departed, as did most of the
Indigenous signatories.[41]

While the signers debated resource rights at length, neither Laird, Macleod,
nor the Indigenous signatories ever mentioned the treaty's massive territorial
concessions. Many have since claimed that deliberate obfuscation and faulty
translation limited the Indigenous signers' understanding of the treaty's land
provisions. Some Blackfoot oral traditions maintain that Treaty Seven was above
all a peace treaty, not a land surrender, and that the signers agreed to share, not
cede, their traditional lands.[42] Historian Hugh Dempsey has recently cast doubt
on this interpretation, but it seems clear that at the very least several factors limited Blackfoot signers' understanding of the treaty provisions.[43] Lead translator
Jerry Potts struggled to translate the treaty's complex terminology into Blackfoot. According to one observer, when Laird began the council, Potts "stood with
his mouth open. He had not understood the words as spoken, and if he had he
would have been utterly unable to convey the ideas they expressed."[44] The commissioners called on other translators to assist Potts, but confusion persisted. For
example, few Blackfoot people had any conception of the units of measurement
used to determine and describe the size of the reserves, especially the baseline
requirement of "one square mile" per family of five persons.[45] Debates over the
true meaning and intent of the treaty continue to the present day.

Whatever their understanding of Treaty Seven, events in the years following the council devastated Blackfoot people's ability to maintain their autonomy
on the northwest plains. Bison herds declined more rapidly than expected in

the years following the treaty, partly because Laird declined to enforce hunting restrictions against Cree and Métis hide hunters in the winter after the treaty's signing.[46] By 1883, the last herds of bison had disappeared from the prairies. Starving Blackfoot people became entirely dependent on the U.S. and Canadian governments for food. They also desperately needed medical care once tuberculosis and other illnesses wreaked havoc on their calorie-starved and weakened bodies. Scarce resources forced Blackfoot and other Indigenous people to stay near government agencies.[47] In the meantime, settlement of the northwest plains accelerated on both sides of the international border. In 1883, Americans completed the Northern Pacific Railway, linking Minnesota to the Puget Sound, and in 1885, Canadians completed the Canadian Pacific Railway, linking Ontario to the Pacific. The cattle industry expanded rapidly with easy access to bison-free grasslands and coastal markets. As Indigenous communities reached their physical, political, and economic nadir, the expansion of U.S. and Canadian sovereignty over the northwest plains seemed complete.

Convergences

The history of Blackfoot diplomacy with the United States and Canada between 1855 and 1877 provides a troubling window into the human costs of the transformation of North American sovereignty in the mid-nineteenth century. It also provides important insights for historians. Straddling the international border, the Blackfoot grappled directly with state expansion in both the United States and Canada during its most crucial period. Through the experience of the Blackfoot, we may observe that the transformations of these competing national sovereignties were deeply connected and shared more similarities than differences.

U.S. and Canadian state expansion were inextricably intertwined in Blackfoot country. In both the United States and Canada, the treaties followed on the heels of massive national territorial acquisitions. On the U.S. side, officials like Isaac Stevens sought to use treaties to consolidate the United States' hold on erstwhile British territories while also weakening the British Hudson's Bay Company's influence among Indigenous people. On the Canadian side, the United States factored even more strongly into motivations for making a treaty with the Blackfoot. Canadian officials used their Blackfoot treaty to strengthen their claim to the northwest plains against land-hungry Americans through the building of the transcontinental railroad, agricultural settlement, and the expansion of state institutions. In both cases, government officials sought to use the treaties to strengthen national and geopolitical interests.

Competing U.S. and Canadian claims to the northwest plains shaped Black-foot people's experience as well. Proximity to the international border shaped Blackfoot thinking at both treaty councils. In 1855, Lame Bull and his peers signed their treaty with the United States knowing that British territory provided an easy refuge. For example, because the 1855 treaty established peace with other nations south of the 49th parallel, some Blackfoot bands simply redirected their horse-raiding north of the border where no such restrictions existed, thereby maintaining access to horses while also honoring their treaty promises.[48] The border could also provide a safe haven in times of trouble, and many Blackfoot people retreated north of the international border when U.S.-Blackfoot relations grew violent during the 1860s.[49] In 1877, however, Blackfoot signers in Canada had no such refuge. Ironically, their bad experience in the United States helped push Blackfoot leaders to accept a treaty with Canada because by 1877 they no lon-ger had the option of crossing the border to safety. In both cases, circumstances on one side of the border shaped diplomacy on the other. National historical frameworks tend to dominate historians' approach to the study of treaty-making and Native-newcomer relations. The experience of the Blackfoot demonstrates the importance of transnational perspectives, especially with regard to mobile Indigenous people.

The history of these treaties also displays the similarities between U.S. and Canadian state expansion in the mid-nineteenth-century West, despite popular narratives to the contrary. Canadians and Americans tell very different stories about westward expansion. Popular and academic histories of the U.S. West tend to emphasize the violent and destabilizing impacts of state expansion. Historian Frederick Jackson Turner first depicted westward expansion as a process in which violence and disorder gave birth to democratic institutions, a model that has long since given way to a historiography that focuses on how direct and structural vio-lence have served to marginalize non-white peoples across the continent.[50] On the other hand, Canadian scholars have tended to emphasize ostensibly less de-structive elements of westward expansion, especially Native-newcomer collabo-ration during the era of the fur trade. Despite a recent turn toward more critical ethnohistorical approaches, Canada's westering past is still too often thought of in contrast to that of the United States—a West that was more "mild" than "wild," in which colonization unfolded in a largely bloodless and orderly fashion.[51]

The experience of the Blackfoot reveals these national distinctions to be more imaginary than real. Although the United States experienced more episodes of extreme violence, the basic mechanism of Indigenous displacement was the same. Both the United States and Canada relied on Indian treaties to expand their political and economic reach across the continent, with similarly devastating consequences for Indigenous people. The years following the 1855 and 1877 treaties were among the darkest in Blackfoot history. Thousands of settlers inundated Blackfoot territory, and government officials failed to mitigate the destruction and disorder these invasions caused. Furthermore, the treaties themselves shared key similarities. Both were multilateral agreements that established peace between the Blackfoot and neighboring nations while also making allowances for whites to traverse and settle traditional Blackfoot lands. Both documents embraced the ideology of assimilation and claimed to put the Blackfoot on the path to "civilization" through the establishment of schools, farms, and missionary instruction. Americans and Canadians went to the northwest plains with fundamentally similar goals and strategies in mind.

But a focus on the United States and Canada represents only half the story because Blackfoot people had their own ideas and motivations that brought them to the treaty councils. In both 1855 and 1877, Blackfoot leaders approached treaty-making with the goal of preserving their own sovereignty, not ceding it to others. In 1855, they believed that a treaty with the United States would provide them with secure access to bison and yearly payments from government officials, all in return for relatively minor concessions. The treaty did not call on them to surrender territory, and the provision allowing whites safe passage in the region meant little during an era when few whites ever visited the northwest plains. Lame Bull's Treaty would strengthen Blackfoot sovereignty, not weaken it. In 1877, many Blackfoot leaders had a similar outlook, albeit in more dire circumstances. They believed Treaty Seven would preserve access to rapidly dwindling bison herds and would ensure NWMP protection against American whiskey traders and white settlers. In return, the treaty would once again obligate them to share their lands with whites. Most Blackfoot people never saw the treaties as representing a transformation of sovereignty. To the Blackfoot signers, the treaty councils were negotiations about the extent of their own inherent sovereignty within their homelands.

Misunderstanding played a central role in both treaty councils. Blackfoot leaders' goals with both treaties differed markedly from that of the treaty commissioners, in part because they lacked vital information that would have explained the outsiders' thinking. In 1855, Lame Bull and his peers believed that the treaty would serve Blackfoot interests. He had little basis on which to understand fully the expansionary ambitions of the United States, nor to predict the voracious rapidity of American settler invasions that would follow. As a result, while he probably understood the terms clearly, he underestimated its potential dangers. The opposite held true in 1877. Hard experience in the intervening two decades had demonstrated the high stakes of treaty-making amidst the rapid settler colonization of the North American West. But the treaty commissioners failed to make the terms of the treaty entirely clear to Blackfoot signers. Crowfoot and his peers understood the stakes but not necessarily the specific terms of the treaty. Sadly, such misunderstandings—either willful or accidental—played a crucial role in the negotiation of North American sovereignty in the mid-nineteenth century.

The treaties of 1855 and 1877 cast long shadows over the northwest plains, and the debate and litigation over the true extent of U.S., Canadian, and Blackfoot sovereignty over this region continues to the present day. Acknowledging the historically contingent meanings of Indian treaties here and throughout the continent is a vital step toward understanding North American sovereignty. As we rethink how states expanded and asserted their power across North America, we should also consider how sovereignty was preserved and negotiated by the formidable peoples who have occupied the center of the continent for countless generations.

Notes

1. The best general histories of Treaty Seven are Hugh Dempsey, *Crowfoot: Chief of the Blackfeet* (Norman: University of Oklahoma Press, 1972), 93–107; Dempsey, *The Great Blackfoot Treaties* (Victoria, BC: Heritage House, 2015), 65–123; Treaty 7 Elders and Tribal Council with Sarah Carter, Walter Hildebrandt, and Dorothy First Rider, *The True Spirit and Original Intent of Treaty 7* (Montreal: McGill-Queen's University Press, 1996); Carter and Hildebrandt, "'A Better Life with Honour': Treaty 6 (1876) and Treaty 7 (1877) with Alberta First Nations," in *Alberta Formed, Alberta Transformed, Volume One*, ed. Michael Payne, Donald Wetherell, and Catherine Cavanaugh (Edmonton and Calgary: University of Alberta Press and University of Calgary Press, 2006), 237–70; John Taylor, "Two Views on the Meaning of Treaties Six and Seven," in *The Spirit of the Alberta Indian Treaties*, ed. Richard Price, 3rd ed. (Edmonton: University of Alberta Press, 1999), 9–46; and Sheila Robert, "The Negotiation and Implementation of Treaty 7, through 1880" (Master's thesis, University of Lethbridge, 2007).

2. See Ryan Hall, "The Divergent Wests of Isaac Stevens and Lame Bull: Finding Motive in the 1855 Blackfoot Treaty," *The Pacific Northwest Quarterly* 105, no. 3 (Summer 2014): 107–21; William Farr, "'When We Were first Paid': The Blackfoot Treaty, the Western Tribes, and the Creation of the Common Hunting Ground, 1855," *Great Plains Quarterly* 21, no. 2 (Spring 2001): 131–54; Dempsey, *The Great Blackfoot Treaties*, 31–53; John Ewers, *The Blackfeet: Raiders on the Northwestern Plains* (Norman: University of Oklahoma Press, 1958), 205–25.

3. This essay will use "Blackfoot" to refer to the three Blackfoot-speaking nations: Siksika (sometimes known as the Blackfoot proper), the Piikani (alternately referred

to as Piegan in the United States, and Peigan in Canada), and the Kainai (commonly referred to as Blood). The creation of the international border eventually divided the North and South Piikani into separate communities, but that division was far less significant in the mid-nineteenth century. For more on Blackfoot nomenclature, see Dempsey, "Blackfoot," in *Handbook of North American Indians*, vol. 13, *Plains*, ed. Raymond DeMallie (Washington: Smithsonian Institution, 2001), 622–27.

4. Dempsey, "Blackfoot," 604–5; Cynthia Chambers and Narcisse Blood, "Love Thy Neighbour: Repatriating Precarious Blackfoot Sites," *International Journal of Canadian Studies* 39–40 (2009): 253–79; Ted Binnema, "Allegiances and Interests: Niitsitapi (Blackfoot) Trade, Diplomacy, and Warfare, 1806–1831," *The Western Historical Quarterly* 37, no. 3 (Autumn 2006): 331.

5. Hall, "Blackfoot Country: The Indigenous Borderlands of the North American Fur Trade, 1782–1870" (PhD diss., Yale University, 2015), 21–67.

6. Pekka Hämäläinen, "The Rise and Fall of Plains Indian Horse Cultures," *The Journal of American History* 90, no. 3 (December 2003): 833–62.

7. For human geography, see DeMallie, ed., *Handbook of North American Indians*, vol. 13, *Plains*, ix; and Deward E. Walker, Jr., ed., *Handbook of North American Indians*, vol. 12, *Plateau* (Washington: Smithsonian Institution, 1998), ix.

8. George Catlin, *Illustrations of the Manners, Customs & Condition of the North American Indians. With Letters and Notes, Written During Eight Years of Travel and Adventure Among the Wildest . . . Tribes Now Existing* (London: Chatto & Windus, 1876), 51.

9. Isaac Stevens and Alfred Cumming to George Manypenny, October 22, 1855, p. 7, *Letters Received by the Office of Indian Affairs, 1824–1881* (National Archives Microfilm Publication M234, roll 30), Records of the Bureau of Indian Affairs, Record Group 75, National Archives, Washington, D.C.; Albert Partoll, ed., *The Blackfoot Indian Council: A Document of the Official Proceedings of the Treaty Between the Blackfoot National and Other Indians and the United States*, Sources of Northwest History, No. 3 (Missoula, Mont.: 1932), 3–4.

10. Farr, "When We Were First Paid," 132–39.

11. Treaty Between the United States and the Blackfoot and Other Tribes of Indians, October 17, 1855, pp. 3–9, roll 30, *Letters Received by the Office of Indian Affairs*. Unlike those of Treaty Seven, Blackfoot oral histories of Lame Bull's treaty do not emphasize miscommunication as a major challenge facing negotiators. See, for example, various interviews by Claude Schaeffer, 1950–1951, books 3–11, Claude E. Schaeffer Field Notebooks, M-1100-165-8, Glenbow Museum Archives, Calgary, Alberta.

12. For more on mid-nineteenth-century U.S. Indian policy, see Robert Utley, *The Indian Frontier of the American West, 1846–1890* (Albuquerque: University of New Mexico Press, 1984), 27–64; Elliott West, "Reconstructing Race," *The Western Historical Quarterly* 34, no. 1 (Spring 2003): 6–26.

13. Quote from Hall, "Divergent Wests," 111; Isaac Ingalls Stevens, *Campaigns of the Rio Grande and of Mexico: With Notices of the Recent Work of Major Ripley* (New York: D. Appleton, 1851), 107–8.

14. Kent Richards, *Isaac I. Stevens: Young Man in a Hurry* (Provo, Utah: Brigham Young University Press, 1979), 171–210; Hall, "Divergent Wests," 108. For discussion of concerns about Indigenous border-crossing in both the United States and Canada, see

Benjamin Hoy, "A Border without Guards: First Nations and the Enforcement of National Space," *Journal of the Canadian Historical Association* 25, no. 2 (2014): 89–115.

15. Ewers, *The Blackfeet*, 222–23.

16. For more on Blackfoot bands, see Binnema, "Old Swan, Big Man and the Siksika Bands, 1794–1815," *Canadian Historical Review* 77, no. 1 (March 1996): 1–32.

17. Edwin A. C. Hatch, Report of Blackfeet Agency, July 12, 1856, in *Annual Report of the Commissioner of Indian Affairs, 1856* (Washington: U.S. Government Printing Office, 1856), 76. See also Hugh Monroe, "Hugh Munro Reminiscence, 1855," p. 2, SC 551, Montana Historical Society Research Center, Helena.

18. James Bradley, "Bradley Manuscript—Book II: Miscellaneous Events at Fort Benton," in *Contributions to the Historical Society of Montana*, vol. 8 (Helena: Montana Historical and Miscellaneous Library, 1917), 156.

19. Hall, "Divergent Wests," 113–14.

20. Partoll, ed., *The Blackfoot Indian Peace Council*, 3–11, quote on 7.

21. Dempsey, *The Great Blackfoot Treaties*, 16–30. For examples, see Maximilian Wied, *The North American Journals of Prince Maximilian of Wied*, ed. Stephen Witte and Marsha Gallagher, vol. 2, *April–September 1833* (Norman: University of Oklahoma Press, 2008), 508; Francis Heron, April 5, 1819, *Edmonton House Post Journal*, 1818–19, B.60/a/17, Hudson's Bay Company Archives, Winnipeg, Manitoba (hereafter HBCA), 44–46; John Pruden, May 6, 1819, *Carlton House* (Saskatchewan) *Post Journal*, 1818–19, B.27/a/8, HBCA, 34.

22. Pierre-Jean de Smet, *Life, Letters and Travels of Father Pierre-Jean De Smet, S. J., 1801–1873*, vol. 2 (New York: F. P. Harper, 1905), 579.

23. Lesley Wischmann, *Frontier Diplomats: The Life and Times of Alexander Culbertson and Natawist-Siksina'* (Spokane, Wa.: Arthur H. Clark Co., 2000), 224–33.

24. Alfred Vaughan, Report of Blackfeet Agency, July 24, 1859, in *Annual Report of the Commissioner of Indian Affairs, 1859* (Washington: U.S. Government Printing Office, 1860), 119.

25. Hall, "Blackfoot Country," 191–231; Blanca Tovías, "Diplomacy and Contestation Before and After the 1870 Massacre of Amskapi Pikuni," *Ethnohistory* 60, no. 2 (Spring 2013), 269–340; Ewers, *The Blackfeet*, 226–53; Andrew Graybill, *The Red and the White: A Family Saga of the American West* (New York: Norton, 2013), 85–152.

26. Ewers, *The Blackfeet*, 254–96; Dempsey, *Firewater: The Impact of the Whisky Trade on the Blackfoot Nation* (Calgary: Fifth House Publishers, 2002), 39–207.

27. Alexander Morris, ed., *The Treaties of Canada with the Indians of Manitoba and the North-West Territories: Including the Negotiations on Which They Were Based, and Other Information Relating Thereto* (Toronto: Belfords, Clarke & Company, 1880), 270; Dempsey, *Crowfoot*, 99.

28. Dempsey, *The Great Blackfoot Treaties*, 47–53; Hall, "Blackfoot Country," 203–16.

29. Jean L'Heureux to J. W. Christie, 1871, p. 3, Richard C. Hardisty Fonds, M-5908-1502, Glenbow Museum Archives.

30. Dempsey, *The Great Blackfoot Treaties*, 73–78; Robert, "Negotiation and Implementation," 32–38, 52–55; quote from Constantine Scollen to the Governor of Manitoba, September 8, 1876, in Morris, ed., *The Treaties of Canada*, 249.

31. Dempsey, "ISAPO-MUXIKA," in *Dictionary of Canadian Biography*, vol. 11, University of Toronto/Université Laval, 2003, http://www.biographi.ca/en/bio/isapo_muxika_11E.html.

32. Petition reprinted in Treaty 7 Elders and Tribal Council, *True Spirit*, 276–77.

33. Frederick Scott to the Hon. R. W. Scott, December 30, 1876, in Canada Department of the Secretary of State, *Report of the Secretary of State for Canada for the Year Ending 31st December, 1876* (Ottawa: Maclean, Roger & Co., 1877), 22.

34. Scott to Scott, December 30, 1876, 23; Robert, "Negotiation and Implementation," 33–35.

35. J. R. Miller, *Compact, Contract, Covenant: Aboriginal Treaty-Making in Canada* (Toronto: University of Toronto Press, 2009), 129–85; Treaty 7 Elders and Tribal Council, *True Spirit*, 206–19.

36. Miller, *Compact, Contract, Covenant*, 148–49, quote on 156. See also James Belich, *Replenishing the Earth: The Settler Revolution and the Rise of the Anglo World, 1783–1939* (New York: Oxford University Press, 2009), 406–17.

37. Robert Bothwell, *Your Country, My Country: A Unified History of the United States and Canada* (New York: Oxford University Press, 2015), 117–18.

38. Robert, "Negotiation and Implementation," 47, 53–54; Treaty 7 Elders and Tribal Council, *True Spirit*, 212, 224–29.

39. William Scollen to parents, October 14, 1877, 2–3, Scollen Family Fonds, M-1108-2, Glenbow Museum Archives. The commissioners' official tally counted 4,392 Indians, not including Bobtail's Crees. Morris, ed., *The Treaties of Canada*, 250.

40. Robert, "Negotiation and Implementation," 59–63. The full text of the treaty can be found in Treaty 7 Elders and Tribal Council, *True Spirit*, 230–39.

41. Morris, ed., *The Treaties of Canada*, 251–62, 267–75, quote on 258.

42. Taylor, "Two Views," 40–45; Treaty 7 Elders and Tribal Council, *True Spirit*, 111–45.

43. Dempsey argues that the signers indeed understood the concept of land cessions, and that arguments to the contrary do the signers "a disservice." Dempsey, *Blackfoot Treaties*, 173–83, quote on 173.

44. Frank Oliver, "The Blackfeet Indian Treaty," *Maclean's Magazine* 44, no. 6 (March 15, 1931): 28.

45. Jane Richardson, Interview with White Headed Chief (Spumiapi), September 2, 1938, p. 114, in Lucien and Jane Hanks Fonds, M-8458-6, Glenbow Museum Archives; Treaty 7 Elders and Tribal Council, *True Spirit*, 142–43.

46. Laird to Mills, December 2, 1877, in Morris, ed., *The Treaties of Canada*, 259.

47. James Daschuk, *Clearing the Plains: Disease, Politics of Starvation, and the Loss of Aboriginal Life* (Regina, Sk.: University of Regina Press, 2013), 106–12.

48. Alfred Vaughan, Report of Blackfeet Agency, August 31, 1860, in *Annual Report of the Commissioner of Indian Affairs, 1860* (Washington: U.S. Government Printing Office, 1860), 85.

49. For example, see William Christie to Unknown Recipient, March 5, 1866, Edmonton Correspondence Book, 1864–68, B.60/b/2, HBCA, 399–401.

50. On the evolution of U.S. Western history, see Richard White, "Western History," in *The New American History*, ed. Eric Foner (Philadelphia: Temple University Press,

1997), 203–30; David Rich Lewis, ed., "The WHA at Fifty: Essays on the State of Western History Scholarship," Special Issue, *The Western Historical Quarterly* 42, no. 3 (Autumn 2011).

51. For discussion of Canadian western history, see Treaty 7 Elders and Tribal Council, *True Spirit*, 191–94; Daschuk, *Clearing the Plains*, ix–xv. Quote from George Colpitts, *Pemmican Empire: Food, Trade, and the Last Bison Hunts in the North American Plains, 1780–1882* (New York: Cambridge University Press, 2015), 18.

7

Indian Raids in Northern Mexico and the Construction of Mexican Sovereignty

Marcela Terrazas y Basante

T he Mexican nineteenth century—or rather the years between 1821, when the long War of Independence finally drew to a close, and the end of the century—constituted a lengthy period of efforts to build the national state and construct sovereignty. The case does not differ much from that of other Latin American countries, nor, however surprising this may seem, from that of the United States. Both experiences, the Mexican and the American, exemplified the desire of respective elites to assert the state's presence and effective control over territory and the flow of people and goods—in other words, territorialization—particularly in the borderlands. Throughout this period, it is possible to observe both the achievements and failures of the two young countries in this task.

Different groups nevertheless conceptualized sovereignty differently. Mexico had built its concept of sovereignty with sturdy roots in the colonial past, which in turn was based on the monarch's dominion over the earth. Upon its independence from Spain, sovereignty, which had been based on the territory, passed from the king to the new nation and the state representing it.[1] The population and its politicians therefore equated sovereignty with territory. For their part, frontier settlers in the United States conceived of territory in quite another way. They understood lands as places to be appropriated, exploited, and subjected to an economy of accumulation. A third actor in this scenario, Independent Indians[2]—particularly Apaches and Comanches—imagined territory as a permeable space with porous borders that permitted mobility, and as a source of resources to be appropriated.[3] While the three actors we will focus on in these pages—Indians, Americans, and Mexicans—regarded territory and what it meant for sovereignty in distinct ways, each also understood free transit through territory differently. Whereas the Indians defended and valued the right to travel unhindered as part of their desire to achieve sovereignty, the governments of Mexico City and Washington strove to establish control over the movement of

goods and persons within their jurisdictions. Mexicans were particularly sensitive to the entry of non-nationals, which they regarded as a violation of their sovereignty. It should be noted that in Mexico, the state was based on a geo-political
rather than an ethnic, ideological, or cultural definition, or one based on a social
pact; belonging to territory was the main sign of affiliation and identity. Thus,
territory, and matters related to it, acquired a particular meaning when it became
the basis of sovereignty and nationality.[4] This understanding of sovereignty explains why the outcome of the war between Mexico and the United States (1846–
48) dealt such a heavy blow to the sovereignty of the former, which was required
to hand over 619,000 square miles to the victor,[5] more than a fifth of current U.S.
territory.[6] The incorporation of this vast area did not mean, however, that federal
authorities in Washington, or even state authorities, had actual dominion over
it or over the settlers who swarmed into this land; the exercise of effective state
control over the regions acquired was, in fact, far from being a reality.

In Mexico, however, the problem of constructing sovereignty was not limited
to territorial loss, nor did it end with the signing of the Peace Treaty of Guadalupe Hidalgo on February 2, 1848. The establishment of a new international dividing line sparked population movements among Euro-Americans, numerous
Indian groups, and frontier Mexicans. The newly agreed to boundary led these
nations to engage in unprecedented interactions, while certain old practices also
became more pronounced in the years following the war. Indeed, for many years
before the war, the border region between Mexico and the United States had
been the scene of peaceful trade; but it was also a land of excesses, accompanied
by abuses and violations of the law.[7] Among these violations were filibustering,
looting raids into the neighboring country by settlers and criminals on either
side of the Rio Grande, taking or holding of captives by both Indians and frontiersmen,[8] raids by Americans and Mexicans to recover stolen cattle, expeditions
crossing the border to catch runaway slaves, and smuggling.[9] Cattle rustling was
also a very common activity involving Mexicans, Indians,[10] and Americans, a
violation that was far from peaceful or free of violence.[11]

This present article examines the phenomenon of Indian raids sparked by
cattle-trafficking, and their implications for the construction of the sovereignty
of Mexico.[12] It is a historical study of Indian expeditions to northern and central
Mexico and their effects on the border. It also examines responses to the raids by
both the settlers and their governments at the federal, state, and local level. The
aim of this work is to show the relevance of the actions of independent Indians
in the contraction and reconfiguration of populated zones of the Mexican north

and, as such, in the establishment of sovereignty within it.[13] It examines the perceived danger that Indian expeditions represented for Mexico and for the survival of its colonists, and reviews the ideas and actions initiated by the two governments, as well as the experiences of inhabitants of the Mexican North.[14] It also
concerns the response of governments to Indian raids. It considers the various
methods federal and local governments used to confront "the Indian Problem"
and explores how those methods were employed, along with their political ends.
In sum, it evaluates the link between indomitable Indians and sovereignty in the
construction of the National Government in Mexico. This essay begins with the
period just prior to the Mexican-American War and concludes in the 1880s.

Of all the calamities afflicting the Mexican government and the residents and
authorities of the border states, the expeditions of indomitable Indians were the
most feared. In both Mexico City and the border states, newspapers published
editorials on these raids, describing them as a serious challenge to inhabitants'
survival as well as to the authority of the general government in those regions.
On September 17, 1851, *El Monitor Republicano* published an article entitled "Indian barbarians," which explained that "border states are currently victims of
the depredations of the barbarians . . . because [the latter] are not satisfied with
invading the border and crossing the dividing line, stealing, killing and torching
small towns as they did in the past, but penetrate into the heart of the republic,
without encountering any obstacles and without the invaded populations being
able to defend themselves, since they lack all kinds of resources, as a necessary
consequence of the misery in which the entire republic finds itself."[15] Likewise,
an editorial dated October 11 of that same year, originally published in *El Constitucional*,[16] addressed the problem of Indian raids on the northern border, stating:
"every day we receive correspondence from the interior, we tremble when we
open the newspapers, due to the well-founded fear of seeing the sad accounts
of the misfortunes caused by the savages' raids."[17] Journalistic descriptions show
important features of the experiences of Mexican communities in the aftermath
of the 1847 war.[18] However, though Indian incursions had been recorded since
the colonial period, interactions between frontiersmen and Indians were not exclusively violent.[19] Cattle rustling and smuggling sometimes propagated lucrative
exchanges for both parties. So-called "Peace" Indians, such as Papagos (Tohono
O'odham), Seminoles, Kikapoos, Mascogos, Lipan Apaches, and Toncahues, who
settled in Mexican territory at least temporarily, could help neighbors and authorities to work against Apache and Comanche incursions. "Peace" Indians established in Coahuila State worked the earth and supported government efforts

against the Comanches and Apaches. In return, the authorities awarded them land[20] and endeavored to give them "tools, oxen, and other necessities for farming," such as funds to pay the principals of primary schools.[21]

In addition to obtaining the support of settled Indians, Mexicans living on the border launched numerous expeditions in pursuit of the nomads, though with poor results. Always dissatisfied with the insufficient aid of the federal government for their defense, Northerners organized themselves into groups, ranging in size from a dozen to more than a hundred men, to hunt down unsettled Indians. This is evidenced by the population data of Chihuahua, earmarked in the "Notice presented to the Municipal Presidency of Ojinaga Chihuahua to the Investigative Commission in the States of Sonora and Chihuahua" for the period between October 23, 1849 and August 8, 1874 (see the table later in this chapter). The report tells us, for example, that of the twenty-four campaigns carried out from this small village, seventeen failed completely. In the majority of cases, Indian groups escaped across the border into U.S. territory, a fact that thwarted the efforts of the frontiersmen to rescue captives, recoup stolen cattle, and punish the raiders. The municipal President of the Buenaventura Valley, in his report to the Investigative Commission wrote,

> The predation of the Indians that rustle cattle, murder Mexicans and set fire to our settlements from 1849 to the present originate from US territory. It is common and notorious knowledge that so many companies that have left these towns in pursuit of the Indians have been forced to return without punishing the Indians due to arriving at the border line, confirming this with the beasts that have been taken and are to be found in that territory in the area where they are divided up by the American government.[22]

In addition to such local efforts to respond to raids, it is essential to refer also to violent actions carried out by state authorities to confront the nomads. Such was the case of a campaign undertaken by the governor of Chihuahua, José Cordero, at the beginning of 1852, with the aim to combat Indian forays through the so-called "*guerra de contratas*," which consisted of paying individuals for each Indian scalp they produced.[23] The operation, promoted by Cordero without the knowledge of the federal government, caused serious problems between Washington and Mexico City. The U.S. Secretary of State complained to the Mexican minister when a group of these mercenaries, of U.S. nationality, committed atrocities and assassinated peaceful Indians settled in U.S. territory with the aim to collect the offered bounty.[24] This policy was not, however, common, and was not endorsed by the executive power in Mexico, which condemned the methods of the Chihuahuan authorities and gave instructions to punish those who had committed atrocities against the settled Indians.[25] What was common in northern Mexico were the forays of Apaches and Comanches, who attacked haciendas and settlements.[26] These caused damage, ranging from cattle theft and the practice of taking captives, to scalping, murder, and the destruction of outposts and settlements. John R. Bartlett, commissioned by his government to survey the boundary, wrote, "The dimension of the predations and murders committed by them [unsettled Indians] would be terrifying if summarised."[27] Similarly, George Ruxton, a young English traveler, and his companion, Josiah Webb, narrated their arrival at Jaral Chiquito, Durango, this way:

[They] found the humble settlement "entirely burned by the Indians, with the exception of one house which was still standing, the roof of which they had torn off, and from the upper walls had shot down with arrows all the inmates." Inside, Ruxton saw the skeleton of a dog and a confusion of human bones. "A dreary stillness reigned over the whole place, unbroken by any sound, save the croaking of a bullfrog in the spring, round which we encamped for a few hours.[28]

The account, written in autumn 1846—one of the few by a European to describe the devastation that extended across the vast region—illustrates the effect of the Indian forays, which left thousands dead, hundreds in captivity, and outposts and villages devastated or abandoned, as a consequence of what Brian DeLay has named "the war of a thousand deserts." DeLay suggests that between 1831 and 1848, approximately 2,649 Mexicans were killed and 852 were made captive by the Comanches alone. Meanwhile, the number of Indians who were victims of the Mexicans was noticeably lower: 702 Comanches and Kiowas were killed and 32 captured.[29] By comparison, in the five years after the end of the Mexican-American War, 635 Mexicans and 176 Indians were killed in only two of the six border states (Sonora and Chihuahua), so it can be inferred that there was a particularly high rate of violence in the decade following the war between Mexico and the United States. Certainly, the number of cattle stolen grew after the war, as illustrated in Table 1.[30]

Documents assembled by an investigative commission in Sonora and Chihuahua that was formed to gather reports, complaints, and claims of those who had suffered damage to their property or person, underscore the violence attendant upon these raids.[31] Table 2 summarizes reports received from Ojinaga, Chihuahua,[32] and Table 3 does the same for Cuchillo Parado.[33] The information

Table 1. Cattle Thefts in Which Indians Participated, 1848–83

	Number of cattle theft events	Number of cattle taken	Clashes between Indians and Mexicans	Total number of Indian incursions
Sonora	71	3,948	38	84
Chihuahua	111	36,616	77	135
Totals	182	40,564	115	219

Table 2. Reports from Ojinaga Chihuahua to the Investigative Commission of Sonora and Chihuahua, October 23, 1849 to August 8, 1874

Mexicans killed by Indians	36
Indians killed by Mexicans[a]	19
Mexicans wounded by Indians	10
Livestock theft from Mexican haciendas	31
Cattle	17
Horse	10
Mule	4
Freight theft	2
Luggage theft	2
Heads of livestock dead	512
Total number of Indian expeditions	35
Comanche expeditions reported	13
Gila Apache expeditions reported	22
Mexican expeditions pursuing Indians[b]	24
Failed expeditions	17
Recovery of livestock	5
Prisoners taken	2

[a] If indeed seventeen Apaches and only two Comanches, as reported, were killed by Mexicans. The identity of the dead should be viewed with caution as many times they were simply referred to in the sources as "savages."

[b] Often the outcome of the expedition was omitted. What is clearly noted is the large number of incursions (17 out of 24) that were frustrated by the Indians crossing the river.

Table 3. Reports of the Municipal President of Cuchillo Parado to the Investigative Commission of Sonora and Chihuahua (1849–74)

[Individuals] Killed by Indians	Date death was reported	[Individuals] Injured or captured (in the attack)	Consequences
Lucio Montes	August 11, 1849	José Ma. Hernández injured	Left a wife and two young sons
Hermenegilda Montes			Left mutilated and with a family
Lázaro Olguín	June 29, 1850		Left a wife whom he supported and a daughter
Manuel Alarcón	June 29, 1850		Left a wife whom he supported
Antonio Domínguez	June 29, 1850		Left a wife and his children
José Zamora	May 11, 1852		Left his wife and a daughter
Sebero [sic] Zamora	May 11, 1852		Left his wife
José Zuarez	June 10, 1853		Left no one
Bernardo Nav	October 11, 1854	Eutimio Nav and Vilvio Cautibo (captive, returned)	Left his wife and a daughter
Matías Nav	October 11, 1854	Regino Galeana. Did not return.	
Miguel Jaso	June 19, 1860	Olivo Cautibo (captive)	Left his wife and three daughters
Juan José Fdez.	June 19, 1860		Left a wife whom he supported
Francisco Gutiérres	August 21, 1862		Left his wife
Siriaco Baquera	August 21, 1862		Left his wife
Juan Peña	October 28, 1862		
Jorge Calderón	January 9, 1866		
Valentín Mata	January 9, 1866		
Patricio Núñez			Left his wife
Juan Aguirre	August 21, 1849		Left a wife whom he supported
Pascual N.	January 9, 1866		

was ultimately forwarded to the Mixed Claims Commission. The delegates interviewed, or from whom information was received by municipal, civil, or military authorities in the affected regions, functioned as witnesses for the claimants. It should be noted that both tables, which cover twenty-five years, offer data on only the small settlements of Ojinaga and Cuchillo Parado, Chihuahua, and as such they are just a small sample to give a sense of the situation in northern Mexico in the quarter century after the Mexican-U.S. War.

The desolation of these settings and the desperate situation of the residents of a wide zone of Mexico are reflected in these reports, just as it is seen in the numerous complaints made by their government to Washington. These incidents found their echoes in cases such as that of Don Guadalupe Grijalva, who resided near Guerrero city. He demanded compensation as Apaches from the Carpio hacienda in the United States robbed him in 1855 of twenty-seven mules, four prize studs, four tame studs, and two mares.[34] Camilo Grijalva presented a claim that the Apaches from Arizona killed his brother-in-law, Leandro Bokus, in 1874 on the El Aguaje ranch.[35] Antonio Arispe, native of Arizpe, Sonora, actually sued for compensation, claiming that in 1852, Apaches from Arizona (three leagues from Magdalena in the Alamo Plateau, en route to Cucupé) "made victims of" his brother, Jesús, with his wife, Narcisa Vadoya, and a two-year-old boy, and they also took five mules and four horses.[36] María del Rosario Grijalva is also a good sample case. She appeared before the Research Commission to testify that, years earlier, Apaches from Arizona had killed her husband, Ignacio Terán, at a place called "Los montones de piedra" (the stone mounds), three leagues from their village.[37] A large number of these cases had no resolution until years later. In 1873, the Commision Mixta de Reclamaciones was formed with the aim to determine which claims were to be considered and which were not, and what the amount of compensation would be.[38]

The Mexican government, as a consequence of such reports and other news of the situation in the northern provinces, maintained a pessimistic vision of the border issue. The suffering of both neighboring nationalities at these latitudes was interwoven with the penury of the national treasury. In 1848, the Ministry of Foreign Relations asked the plenipotentiary to attempt to secure an advance on the three million that Washington, as part of the compensation for the territories of New Mexico and California, was due to pay in 1849.[39] The efforts to improve the conditions for frontiersmen by stopping damage to their property and threats to their lives through the delivery of cash and weapons[40] and the establishment of military outposts were completely insufficient.[41] On the other hand, that which some Mexican politicians considered "the only positive outcome of the war," the obligation of the United States to "contain the incursions [of Indians] by use of force if necessary," was far from being a reality in 1848.[42]

Notwithstanding the fact that the press, local and central, was well aware of the difficulties on the frontier and the Mexican government received continuous reports suggesting that Washington had scant interest in meeting the terms of Article XI of the Treaty of Guadalupe Hidalgo (which established the obligation of the American government to stop Indian incursions in Mexico), the minister for Interior and Foreign Relations, Luis G. Cuevas, gave instructions toward the end of 1848 to prevent complaints from jeopardizing "even minimally . . . the good relations happily restored between the two Republics."[43] Without a doubt, the attitude of the Mexican government traced to the political and financial problems that it faced, and officials aimed to avoid any complications with its northern neighbor at the expense of the security of frontiersmen. The moderate administration confronted the hostility of the hard liberals, in addition to the sectors that made up the conservative party and other political factions that confronted them for having made peace. On the other hand, the difficulties of the Treasury had not been resolved by the partial payment Americans made upon signing the Treaty of Guadalupe Hidalgo. Although the galling situation of the Treasury lasted for a long while, the "acquiescence" of the Mexican government would not be sustained for long. The ministry embarked first on a persistent campaign to get Washington to carry out "[its] obligation stated in Article XI." Not a week went by when the Minister of Foreign Relations and his representative in Washington did not discuss this matter.[44]

It should be noted that in the first months after the war's conclusion, the tone of the dialogue between Mexican plenipotentiary Luis de la Rosa and U.S. Secretary of State John M. Clayton was amicable. There were gestures from the U.S. government toward its southern counterpart that showed their goodwill with respect to finding and rescuing Mexican captives. The State Department signaled its awareness of the grave problem facing border Mexicans as a consequence of Indian forays. Though officials assured Mexico that the Executive branch was making its best effort, they also pointed out that assigning resources for a force to stop Indian invasions was actually Congress's responsibility.[45]

It's fair to say that in the years that followed the war with Mexico, U.S. politicians seemed not to be in the mood for "nonsense" regarding Mexican complaints about savages. The topic of slavery, dormant since the Missouri Compromise, resurfaced with the "Mexican cession." The question posed was: Would slavery be allowed in the states that would be formed out of this newly acquired territory? Certainly, this problem absorbed so much of the energy of Congress that no one could have thought that Mexican border difficulties would occupy a great deal of legislators' time. The death of President Zachary Taylor in July 1850 was also decisive for the climate of the bilateral relationship, as was the attitude of the new Secretary of State, Daniel Webster, on the Indian question. Webster, in contrast with his predecessor, showed his feelings in the sporadic nature of his communication with De la Rosa, his reticence to discuss Article XI, and his scepticism about the fact that the invasions of Mexican territory were even being carried out by Indians from the United States (an argument supported by the fact that the Indians spent a season at the Laguna de Jaco every year).[46]

Meanwhile, in Mexico, the moderate government of Mariano Arista, an ex-War Secretary who was sensitive to the conditions facing the frontiersmen, became desperate to find a way to stop the predatory invasions. Inhabitants became so impatient and anguished that the minister for Foreign Relations suggested to the plenipotentiary to the U.S. government that it would be best to ask Washington to authorize Mexicans to cross the border in pursuit of Indian raiders. However, the Mexican representative felt that this request might not be prudent. Logically, he imagined that the Americans would prefer to prosecute their own. In requesting authorization from Washington for Mexican forces to cross the border, the Mexican authorities had to foresee that Washington would request the same privilege. Paradoxically, the Mexican government was so anxious to safeguard its territory that it put its own national sovereignty at risk. The Indian problem was to be "fixed" a year later with the Gadsden Treaty, which repealed the "bothersome Article" XI, to the good fortune of the United States, but this left the conflict intact for Mexico and its frontiersmen.

It is important to take into account that from the moment Article XI was introduced into the peace treaty, there was opposition. Senator Sam Houston from Texas said that the application of Article XI would cost more from a fiscal standpoint than all the vacant land acquired, and Senator Douglas from Illinois proposed that the part of the article that obliged the United States to compensate Mexicans who suffered damages as a result of raiding Indians should be eliminated, but his motion was defeated. Moreover, the Secretary of State, James Buchanan, gave reassurance that "the government possessed both [capacities]: the ability to stop the Indians from making incursions into Mexican territory, and the ability to execute all the other stipulations of the 11th Article."[47]

The fact is that during the years immediately following the signing of the Treaty of Guadalupe Hidalgo, Washington made a certain amount of effort to execute the article. The majority of the U.S. Army was assigned to the territory acquired from Mexico (8,000 out of 11,000 active personnel). General P. F.

Smith from the Military Department of Texas and Colonel E. V. Sumner of the Military Department of New Mexico received orders to protect Mexico and the United States from Indian predation, and military spending in New Mexico alone between 1848 and 1853 was $12,000,000. The Mexican government, for its part, insisted upon full compliance with the obligations the U.S. government had committed to.[48]

Despite zeal from Washington, these efforts did not bear fruit. Treaties made with the Apaches and Comanches were unhelpful, so much so that the United States acknowledged as much.[49] The same can be said of the determined Mexicans who sought to safeguard their border, both at military outposts and settled Indian communities in Coahuila. This last group became a source of friction between the two governments, when they were accused of crossing the border and causing problems.[50]

Five years after the peace accords, the "Indian question" had become a real national problem for Washington, which was now unwilling to recognize the commitment it had made and to acknowledge responsibility for compensating the victims of Indian forays. The problem was further complicated as speculators, both American and Mexican, claimed Indian land and pressured the U.S. Congress to insure their profits. When James Gadsden was named the U.S. representative in Mexico, one of the two most important of his orders was the annulment of Article XI. The treaty negotiated by him was enmeshed in an intricate speculative web related to the larger territorial transfer in which Gadsden was implicated, which included the aim to obtain land for a rail link to the Pacific, the complicated issue of a concession to build a trans-isthmus rail system for Tehuantepec, and, as has been seen, the interests of owners of "Indian claims." The muddled history of the repeal of Article XI has a further chapter: The Senate rejected the article that freed the United States from complying with the stipulation, as they had promised to help Mexico fight the Indians. Finally, the article was annulled with no aid concessions, but this fact was taken into account when considering the compensation Mexico received for the Treaty of La Mesilla, or the Gadsden Purchase.

The annulment of Article XI implied that the United States no longer had any particular responsibility to stem Indian incursions into Mexican territory, and it established the obligation of each government to do what was necessary to protect its inhabitants and punish its attackers. The following years saw a reduction in expeditions across the Lower Bravo, especially in Tamaulipas and Nuevo León, due to the rapid settlement of Texas, but expeditions continued at an intense rate in Chihuahua and Sonora. The old settlement of Janos, the place where

the Apaches arrived when they sought peace with Mexico, saw its final period
of activity at the end of 1856 and the beginning of 1857, when the last groups of
Apaches abandoned it and the Mexican authorities decided to relocate troops
to strengthen military units such as North and San Elizario. From then onward,
hostilities would continue without interruption until the 1880s, although attacks
became gradually weaker.[51] In the north, the Comanches, along with other Indian
groups in Arkansas and Texas, also fought to maintain their hunting grounds
as Anglo-American settlements advanced. As buffalo hunting possibilities grew
ever scarcer, the Comanches continued their invasions into Mexico, but in this
the objective was solely to acquire livestock as a substitute resource.[52]

In the 1860s, in both Mexico and the United States, attention at a national
government level was centered on internal political conflicts that would give way
to armed confrontation, and the "Indian wars" moved to second place on the
binational agenda for discussion.[53] At the end of the 1860s, governments became
preoccupied again with the security of their common border, and the mobility
of Indians and other groups of "renegades" made it imperative for states once
again to exert control over this territory so as to allow economic development
without setbacks.

This was true until around 1880, when Mexico consolidated its process of
territorialization in the north. Then the government made common cause with
the Americans against the Indians, as shown by the fact that, in 1882, Mexican
authorities consented to cooperate with their U.S. counterparts and signed a
reciprocal agreement allowing the passage of troops to pursue Indians and to
defeat them.[54]

Final Considerations

During the nineteenth century, the United States and Mexico, which had achieved
independence shortly before from their European metropolises, sought to build
and consolidate the nation-state model and strengthen their sovereignty. Both
countries shared the view that for this purpose control over the movement of
goods and persons within their jurisdiction was essential. The point was to territorialize their constituency through state presence and effective control of
the flow of people and goods, especially in the borderlands. This idea clashed
with that of certain Indian nations in the region—particularly Apaches and Comanches—for whom transhumance, including free movement throughout the
territory without regard for international boundaries, was a resource regarded
as irrevocable.

After the end of the war that pitted the United States against Mexico (1846–48), Mexico granted the victor an area equivalent to just over half its territory.[55] This constituted a major blow to its sovereignty, given that from the start of the colonial period, Mexico had identified sovereignty with territory. The Mexican government's imperative was therefore to restore control in the border regions it still preserved. A great deal of work would take place over several decades before the federal government achieved its aim because the demarcation of a new dividing line meant more than the mere establishment of a northern border that had delimited the country. Beyond the fact that borders were officially established years after the signing of a peace agreement,[56] the border that was agreed upon between the two countries constituted an imaginary line drawn on paper by the negotiators of the treaty that was quite different from an actual border. This was a broad, shifting space, with fuzzy limits, that sought to delimit the jurisdiction of two countries. The new "line" resulting from the peace treaty triggered demographic changes and population movements involving Americans, indomitable Indians, settled Indians, and Mexicans.

The population movements occurred when the Americans set their sights on the provinces of Mexico that they had newly acquired: New Mexico and California.[57] The advance of settlers impacted the regions where Indian nations of the prairies had settled, and some Indian groups reacted to this encroachment by venturing into northern and even central Mexico and settling in this territory for long periods. It is hardly surprising that new dynamics of interaction should have arisen between all those involved—Indian and non-Indian. These dynamics were much more violent than those observed during the colonial period, given the economic opportunities afforded by smuggling as well as the thriving cattle industry that was developing in the United States. The growing demand for cattle for the livestock industry as well as the need for horses, mules, and cattle among settlers bound for California, was precisely what led to the theft and trafficking of livestock, accompanied by a considerable amount of violence. Illegal trading, coupled with the stealing and trafficking of cattle, benefited several Indian nations, as well as Americans and Mexicans, who often acted together. The links between frontiersmen were tainted by violence or mediated by what a noted Mexican scholar has called *cooperative violence*, although peaceful relations were also formed.[58] Whether violent or peaceful, ties between the residents of the borderlands were characterized by growing reciprocal interaction.

Once the new frontier was established, the left bank of the Rio Grande was swiftly populated.[59] In contrast, the population of the right bank of the river, the Mexican side, either contracted, as in the case of Sonora, or failed to increase.

Thus the vast, barren stretch of territory that had previously abutted the United States along its southern border ceased to be just a land of Indians, and prosperous towns soon emerged. The demographic changes and population movements in this new frontier helped drive Indians toward the new north of Mexico. Indian populations declined as a result of epidemics and shrinking herds of bison, which also forced them to withdraw to the border regions of Mexico.

Possibly one of the most significant consequences triggered by the demarcation of the new border was the rise of Indian raids into Mexican territory to steal cattle to sell to Texan farmers, Euro-Americans bound for California, the United States Army, and even military persons and landowners in Mexico. These raids, which had begun in the colonial period, acquired different characteristics after the Mexican-American War, increasing in frequency and violence. Consequently, the establishment of the newly agreed border did not put an end to Indian raids into north and north-central Mexico; on the contrary, the forays intensified.

Why did the raids and violence increase? The answer is by no means simple; it has to do not only with the establishment of a new border but also with numerous factors discussed throughout this essay. The advance of European American settlers coupled with the progressive disappearance of the bison drove Indians into Mexican territory, where they engaged in cattle rustling in a context of expanding livestock enterprises with a capitalist approach. This emerging livestock industry created an extraordinary demand for cattle that Indians were able to satisfy; demand also increased as a result of the requirements of the men and women heading for California. Moreover, the settlers' advance into the former provinces of Mexico led to contact between Euro-Americans and the unsettled Indians, which gave rise to an exchange of weapons, provided by the former, for the latter's surpluses of cattle and horses. The Apaches and Comanches were thereby able to acquire more weapons than the Mexicans and to engage in more ruthless and ferocious forays into Mexican territory. The number of stories in the Mexican press and primary documents of village destruction, crimes, seizing of women and children as captives, and theft of horses, cattle and mules, is enormous. Although the Indian raids also affected American states, the Mexican border states bore the brunt of the war against the Indians both because of the number of dead, wounded, and captive and because of the amount of livestock stolen from their herds.

Although the Indians had stolen and smuggled livestock since the colonial period, they had once largely focused on livestock trafficking. This activity led them to form alliances with cattle rustlers, whom they informed about livestock resources in the region. When the Indians came to directly participate in the theft of livestock and horses, they did so with the goal of selling them to the Americans or keeping them for their own use, taking advantage of the knowledge they had acquired in the earlier period. This latter practice was accompanied by a hefty dose of cruelty and violence, as part of the goal was to take captives and steal other effects. Independent Indians, it should be said, were blamed for all the cattle rustling in the northern Mexican states. This was, in fact, a miscalculation; many Americans and Mexicans took part, sometimes even forming alliances with the Indians. Indian participation was undoubtedly the most energetic and efficient, while American participation had more to do with the purchase of stolen herds. Yet many sectors were involved in the looting and trafficking of cattle, apart from the Indians: residents on either side of the border, and both American and Mexican civil and military authorities. The involvement of all of these groups increased as the livestock business prospered, first in the United States and subsequently in Mexico.[60] They all found this activity to be a means of obtaining resources at a time when the livestock industry had reached its apogee.

In short, violence was not the only feature of the interaction between Indians, Mexicans, and Americans, but it was certainly a predominant one. For this reason and as a result of the human and material losses suffered, one can understand the terror among settlers in northern Mexico of the "barbarians," as they called them, and therefore the contraction of population on the northern Mexican border. The Mexican government regarded Indian raids as a threat to the nation's sovereignty; it thought they seriously compromised their dominance in the border region and feared that because the Americans endorsed the Indians' raids by providing them with weapons, they might form an alliance that could result in the loss of more territory.

The government's apprehension was the result of its poor command of and presence in the north of the country. Settling these areas was essential, yet the vicious circle was not easy to break because people did not wish to settle in a region besieged by Indian attacks. The construction of sovereignty in Mexico was still underway. This situation continued until Mexico consolidated its territorialization in the 1880s. It was then that it formed an alliance with the government in Washington against the Indians, agreeing to collaborate to defeat them.

At this point, it is worth asking about the reaction of the Mexican federal, state, and local governments and the population to the raids by the independent Indians. From the account presented here, one can infer that state governments, assuming the powers of the federal authority, took policy toward indomitable Indians during the three post-war decades into their own hands; it was the state governments that made pacts with the Indians. A review of the documentation and newspapers of the time, however, shows that, in practice, the towns them-selves undertook their defense with their limited personal resources, usually led by a resident or the mayor. The results were extremely limited; the expeditions to pursue Comanches and Apaches to retrieve cattle and captives came up against the superior weaponry of the indomitable Indians, their extraordinary horse-manship, the ability to cross the border to evade pursuers, and the tolerance by the U.S. military and civilian authorities of Indian expeditions; it is reported that the booty obtained was even sold in certain U.S. forts not far from the border.

This does not mean that the federal government had not taken action or made an effort to direct policy toward the Indians. The project to set up military colonies along the border was designed for this purpose and was the result of the authorities' concern with leading the defense, and their desire to be present, territorialize, and exercise sovereignty. Yet many of these efforts proved unsuc-cessful because of lack of resources, the distance between the center and the far north, and because they encountered resistance from state governments. The only level at which the federal executive branch played a more active, although not a more successful, role was in the field of diplomacy. The correspondence between the governments of Washington and Mexico City is full of complaints about Indian raids.

Thus, Indian raids into Mexican territory were considered a threat to the sov-ereignty of the nation. The issue of indomitable Indians and their expeditions was crucial for the Mexican government in the context of its efforts to consolidate control over the north of the country. The problem was not limited to finding ways to force indomitable Indians into submission; it had to do with the need to establish national sovereignty in a key region: the northern border. Hence its im-portance in the construction of border areas, sovereignty, and the nation state.

Notes

1. Jorge Schiavon, Daniela Spenser, and Mario Vázquez Olivera, eds., Introduction to *En busca de una nación soberana. Relaciones internacionales de México, siglos XIX y XX* (Mexico: SRE/CIDE, 2006). Manuel Ángel Castillo, Mónica Toussaint Ribot, and Mario Vázquez Olivera, *Espacios diversos, historia en común. México, Guatemala y Belice, la construcción de una frontera* (Mexico: Secretaría de Relaciones Exteriores, 2006).

2. The terms "warlike," "barbarians," or "savages" ("belicosos," "barbarous," or "sal-vajes") are those that the local, state, and federal Mexican authorities most often used when referring to the Indians of the North, whom first Spain then Mexico could not subdue. In all the documentation from the period they are named in this way. We have preferred to use "nomadic" or used the terms "indomitable," "independent" (indios

libres), warfaring (indios de Guerra), or "rebellious," considering that these terms express the nature of the link between the Indians and the non-Indians.

3. Ignacio Almada Bay, Juan Carlos Lorta Sainz, David Contreras Tánori, and Amparo A. Reyes Gutiérrez, "Casos de despueble de asentamientos atribuidos a apaches en Sonora, 1852–1883: Un acercamiento a los efectos de las incursiones apaches en la población de vecinos," in *Violencia interétnica en la frontera norte novohispano y Mexicana. Siglos XVII–XIX*, ed. José Marcos Medina Bustos and Esther Padilla Calderón (Hermosillo, Sonora, Mexico: El Colegio de Sonora, El Colegio de Michoacán, Universidad Autónoma de Baja California, 2015), 237.

4. Manuel Ángel Castillo et al., *Espacios Diversos*, 14.

5. The territory ceded by Mexico now encompasses California, Nevada, Utah, most of New Mexico, Arizona, and parts of Wyoming and Colorado. Much of New Mexico, Colorado, and Wyoming had been claimed by Texans as part of the Republic of Texas during the preceding decade. See David Potter, *The Impending Crisis, 1848–1861* (New York: Harper and Row, 1976), 1 and n1. One should recall that the independence of Texas (1836) and its annexation to the American federation (1845) had not been recognized by Mexico. Including Texas, however its boundaries were construed, Mexico's territorial cession exceeded two million square kilometers, or 800,000 square miles.

6. The continental area of the United States is 3,022,000 square miles. The addition was comparable only to the area acquired through the purchase of Louisiana in 1803, which represented the acquisition of 828,302 square miles. See Potter, *Impending Crisis*, 1.

7. Lance R. Blyth, *Chiricahua and Janos: Communities of Violence in the Southwestern Borderlands, 1680–1880* (Lincoln: University of Nebraska Press, 2012), ix.

8. Cramaussel speaks of Indians, especially children, taken in the campaign, who remained in Chihuahua society. Chantal Cramaussel, "La violencia en el estado de Chihuahua," in Bustos and Calderón, *Violencia interétnica*, 216.

9. On contraband, see Walther L. Bernecker, "Contrabando. Ilegalidad y corrupción en el México decimonónico," in *Espacio, tiempo y forma*, Series V, Historia Contemporánea, t. 6 (1993), 393–418.

10. The documents and newspapers that have been reviewed, both local and from Mexico City, only mention Apaches and Comanches, without distinguishing which group they belonged to. Chantal Cramaussel agrees with this observation. See Cramaussel, "La violencia en el estado de Chihuahua," 204.

11. Ignacio Almada Bay et al. state that there are sources that speak of the presence of Apaches in what is now the state of Sonora dating back to 1684. Almada Bay et al., "Casos de despueble de asentamientos," 227–73.

12. We use the term "raids" in the same way as Ignacio Almada Bay et al., on the basis of the documents and newspapers of the time. Almada Bay et al., "Casos de despueble de asentamientos," 230.

13. It is important to stress that the other relevant actors in this scenario were the so-called "peaceful" Indians, with whom the frontiersmen on both sides of the Bravo formed links entirely different from those established with the unconquered groups. However, they are only of interest to us tangentially here.

14. Ramos emphasizes the importance of investigating the relationships between Indians and border societies locally. See Raúl Ramos, "Finding the Balance: Béxar in Mexican/Indian Relations," in Samuel Truett and Elliot Young, eds., *Continental Crossroads: Remapping U.S.-Mexico Borderlands History* (Durham: Duke University Press, 2004), 36. Mexican scholars such as Chantal Cramaussel, Ignacio Almada Bay, Jesús Hernández Jaimes, and Cuauhtémoc Velasco are working on this research.

15. "Indios bárbaros," *El Monitor Republicano*, September 17, 1851, 3, retrieved from Hemeroteca Nacional Digital de México (http://www.hndm.unam.mx/index.php/es/). Newspaper translations here and below by author.

16. *El Constitucional* was the official newspaper of the Mexican government.

17. "Indios bárbaros," *El Monitor Republicano*, September 21, 1851.

18. A version of this section was discussed in "Efectos del nuevo lindero. Indios, mexicanos y norteamericanos ante la frontera establecida al término de la guerra entre México y Estados Unidos," *Norteamérica* 11, no. 1 (June 2016): 75-98.

19. In "Finding the Balance," Raúl Ramos discredits the stereotype that the Mexicans and the Indians were always fighting. He demonstrates how the Texans in Béjar developed more elaborate strategies for peace and cooperation, which continued in contrast with the policies toward Indians developed in the colonial period and those later established in the United States. See Truett and Young, *Continental Crossroads*, 20.

20. The Indians received ten acres of land per family on the condition that they would protect the region from attacks from other Indians. Paul Neff Garber, *The Gadsden Treaty* (Gloucester, Mass.: Peter Smith, 1959), 33.

21. Santiago Vidaurri, Secretary General of the Government of Nuevo León and Coahuila and Captain and Commander of an auxiliary company charged with preventing Indian incursions, wrote about the efforts of leaders who had "desired the possible civilization of said tribes" ("deseado la posible civilización de dichas tribus") to assign an instructed person to take charge of the education of young Indians. In the same way, he had arranged the construction of a chapel and planned to ask the diocese for a priest to administer the sacraments to the Indians, preach the gospel, and instruct them "in the healthy principles of our sacred religion so that they can, with time become part of the joys of the great Mexican family, and lend their services to the nation, like good sons" ("en los sanos principios de nuestra sagrada religión para que así puedan con el tiempo entrar en los goces de la gran familia mexicana, y prestar sus servicios a la nación, como sus buenos hijos").

22. "Files containing reports from a range of authorities attesting to the barbarians' attacks and invasions of armed North American citizens in the border region of our republic, in the years 1849–1875," Investigative Commission in the States of Sonora and Chihuahua, in Archivo Histórico de la Secretaría de Relaciones Exteriores de México (hereafter AHSREM), Box 2, 20-9-1/14, folders 57 to 59. Quotation from G. C. Caravantez, Municipal President of Buenaventura, to the Investigative Commission, January 19, 1875.

23. In 1863, the government of Coahuila approved poisoning watering holes frequented by Indians. See Ana Lilia Nieto, *Defensa y política en la frontera norte de México, 1848–1856* (México: El Colegio de la Frontera Norte, 2012), 57.

24. The Mexican minister asked for instructions from his government (El ministro mexicano pidió instrucciones al respecto a su gobierno). De la Rosa to the Interior and Exterior Affairs Minister, Washington, March 20, 1850, in AHSREM, Artículo XI del Tratado de Guadalupe Hidalgo . . . , despacho s. núm.

25. [S. A.] a Lacunza, Mexico City, April 13, 1850, in AHSREM, Artículo XI del Tratado de Guadalupe Hidalgo . . . , despacho s. no. [COPY]; De la Rosa to the Minister for Foreign Relations, Washington, April 22, 1850, in AHSREM, Artículo XI del Tratado de Guadalupe Hidalgo . . . , despacho no. 40 [COPY].

26. The Indians are usually identified in the documents as simply Apaches, or as Gila Apaches and Comanches (rarely do they mention their Kiowa allies).

27. J. R. Bartlett, *Personal Narrative of Explorations and Incidents in Texas, New Mexico and Chihuahua connected with the United States and Mexican Boundary commissions, during the years, 1850, '51, '52, and '53*, Vol. 1 (2 vols., New York: D. Appleton and Co., 1854), 5. As quoted in Garber, *Gadsden Treaty*, 29.

28. George Ruxton, *Adventures in Mexico and the Rocky Mountains* (1848 Reprint; Glorieta, Texas: Rio Grande Press, 1973), 127–29. DeLay, *War of a Thousand Deserts*, quotation on xvi.

29. DeLay, *War of a Thousand Deserts*, 318.

30. The term "Indian incursions" in this table is defined as sudden attacks on haciendas or Mexican villages by Apaches or Comanches. Information obtained in México, Ministerio de Relaciones Exteriores, Sección de América, Núm. 3, Año de 1874. Comisión pesquisidora mexicana en las fronteras de Chihuahua y Sonora. La información compila los datos de los Cuaderno de pruebas. Comisión Investigadora en los Estados de Sonora y Chihuahua. Expediente que contiene los informes de diversas autoridades que comprueban las depredaciones de los bárbaros e invasiones de Ciudadanos Norte-Americanos a mano armada a la frontera de nuestra República, en Año de 1849–1875. Comisión investigadora en los estados de Sonora y Chihuahua, en Archivo Histórico de la Secretaría de Relaciones Exteriores de México, 20-9-1/14.

31. The Investigative Commission was created by the Mexican government in response to the Rodd Commission, which has been established months before by the U.S. government. The U.S. commission was tasked to investigate complaints about the theft of horses and cattle from Texan ranchers, who blamed Mexicans for their losses. As a result, the Rodd Commission demanded $44,572,425 USD from the Mexican authorities as reparation for the damages suffered by the Texans.

The Investigative Commission, in its way, undertook its own inquiry. It pushed for, in accordance with Congressional law, the extension of its investigation into Mexican and American claims since 1848, the year of the Guadalupe Hidalgo treaty. With this end it invited neighbors to Mexico and Texas to present their complaints before the commission. The delegates interviewed or received reports from municipal authorities about the areas affected, and both civil and military authorities bearing witness for the claimants. The result of this meticulous work from the commission was a collection of reports that responded to the U.S. government and the creation of a voluminous report, in 1875, which was principally concerned with Indian incursions and the theft of cattle on the border between the two countries. See Martaelena Negrete Salas,

"La frontera texana y el abigeato 1848–1872," *Historia Mexicana* 31, no. 1 (121) (July–September 1981).

32. The subtitle of these reports reads "News which comprises[:] 1st the no. of dead killed by the savages from 1848 to the present in this municipal section, with expression [expreción (*sic*) in the original Spanish] of the date or an approximation of that in which the death was reported, 2nd the number of injured or captivated [cautivadas (*sic*) in the original Spanish] with express mention of the family left behind or supported." The reports from various municipalities presented to the Investigative Commission of Sonora and Chihuahua, part of the Investigative Commission of the Northern Frontier, covers the period from February 1848—the date when the Guadalupe-Hidalgo treaty established in Article XI the obligation of the North American government to stop Indian incursions in Mexico—to the second half of 1874, when the commission would conclude the compilation of reports to present to the binational organ: the Mixed Complaints Commission.

33. The president of the municipal section of Cuchillo Parado to C. Secretary of the Investigative Commission in the states of Sonora and Chihuahua. Cuchillo Parado, November 14, 1874, in Comisión Investigadora en los Estados de Sonora y . . . , en AHSREM, CAJA 2, 20-9-1/14. This table reproduces the report except that an uninformative column has been omitted and some information has been slightly reformatted for clarity and continuity.

34. AHSERM [Reclamaciones], 29-5-32.

35. AHSREM [Reclamaciones], 14-7-452.

36. AHSREM [Reclamaciones], 29-5-185.

37. AHSERM [Reclamaciones], 29-5-32.

38. Investigative Commission of the Northern Frontier. Martelena Negrete Salas, "La frontera Texana y el abigeato 1848–1872," *Historia Mexicana* 31, no. 1 (July–September 1981); *Informe de la Comisión Pesquisidora de la Frontera Norte al Ejecutivo de la Unión, en cumplimiento del artículo 30 de la ley del 30 de septiembre de 1872* (Monterrey, *mayo 15 de 1873*), México, Imprenta del Gobierno, 1877. Negrete, "La frontera," 79. For our part, we carried out a meticulous review of the seven boxes of documents pertaining to the Investigative Commission, safeguarded in the Archivo Histórico Diplomático Genaro Estrada de la Secretaría de Relaciones Exteriores.

39. Otero to De la Rosa, Mexico City, November 3, 1848, in AHSREM, Artículo XI del Tratado de Guadalupe Hidalgo . . . , [Instrucción] Reservada, no. 4.

40. In 1848, even before the implementation of the military settlement plan, the War Minister sent 2,686 men to the North and asked the treasury for the largest possible quantity of resources in order for the settlers to fight the Indians. They bought guns, long-distance rifles, and ammunition. See Nieto, *Defensa y política*, 108.

41. The settlements were military bases that formed a defensive line, whose cavalry would pursue "warlike" Indians and where the soldiers would also be settlers. This model introduced the idea of forming population nuclei that prevented the advance of the "indomitables"; it followed the presidio model, established through the paths that linked the mining centers of Zacatecas with the center of the viceroyalty.

If their aim were to contain Indian incursions, they did not achieve it. Nieto, *Defensa y política*, 105–7. It should be added that resources destined for the purchase of weapons for the colonies came from the indemnity paid by the United States to Mexico after the war. In fact, these supplies were obtained by a Mexican official in Washington, who had been instructed to obtain weaponry and 800 hundredweights of powder at a lower cost as they had adopted the automatic rifle for the North American army. Luis De la Rosa to the Minister for Interior and Foreign Relations, Washington, February 27, 1849 in AEMEUA, tomo 200, s.f., nota 24.

42. Otero to De la Rosa, Mexico City, November 3, 1848, in AHSREM, Artículo XI del Tratado de Guadalupe Hidalgo . . . , Instrucción no. 37.

43. Cuevas to de la Rosa, Mexico City, November 27, 1848, in AHSREM, Reclamaciones.

44. De la Rosa remembers having convinced the Secretary of State to have several meetings with the aim of sorting out the complaints pending without the necessity of a lengthy official correspondence. In the only meeting held, the Mexican spoke principally of the failure of the Americans to uphold Article 11, relating to Indian incursions in Mexican territory. De la Rosa emphasized the Mexican government's wish that the Americans carry out what was stipulated in the 11th article. De la Rosa to the Foreign Affairs Minister, Washington, October 20, 1849, in AEMEUA, tomo 200, s.f., nota 122.

45. See George W. Crawford, War Secretary [Copy made March 21, 1849], in AHSREM, Artículo XI del Tratado de Guadalupe Hidalgo . . . , despacho sin número, [Copy]; San Antonio, Texas, March 24, 1849; El Secretario de Guerra al de Estado, Washington, April 7, 1849, in AHSREM, Artículo XI del Tratado de Guadalupe Hidalgo . . . , despacho sin número [Copy].

46. Nieto, *Defensa y política*, 173 ss.

47. Garber, *Gadsden Treaty*, 27.

48. De la Rosa to the Minister for Foreign Affairs, Washington, October 20, 1849, in AEMEUA, tomo 200, s.f., nota 122.

49. In the same way, the Mexican official Luis De la Rosa made the Minister for Foreign Affairs see, from the notes and documents that accompanied his correspondence, that "almost nothing has been done until now by the US government that has had an effect to stop the savage Indians" ("Casi nada ha hecho hasta ahora el gobierno de Estados Unidos que sea eficaz para reprimir a los indios salvages"). De la Rosa to the Minister for Foreign Affairs, Washington, March 20, 1850, in AEMEUA, tomo 200, s.f., nota 26.

50. Garber, *Gadsden Treaty*, 33.

51. William B. Griffen, *Apaches at War and Peace: The Janos Presidio, 1750–1858* (Norman: University of Oklahoma Press, 1998), 249–58.

52. Pekka Hämäläinen, *The Comanche Empire* (New Haven: Yale University Press, 2008), 304–7.

53. Both the dialogue maintained with the Department of State by the representative of Benito Juárez's government, Matías Romero, and the accounts to the Investigative Commission allow us to see that although Indian expeditions to Sonora and Chihuahua continued, neither government was interested in the issue.

54. Shelley Bowen Hatfield, *Chasing Shadows: Indians Along the United States—Mexico Border, 1876–1911* (Albuquerque: University of New Mexico Press, 1998), 2.

55. Remember that for Mexico the signing of the peace treaty meant not only the transfer of its provinces of California and New Mexico, but also the recognition of the

loss of Texas and the renunciation of the territory between the Nueces River and the Rio
Grande or the Rio Bravo.

56. The new boundary was set according to the line agreed to by the boundary treaty
negotiated in 1853 between James Gadsden representing Washington and the Mexican
government.

57. The California case was notable because of the avalanche of people—many of
them adventurers and fortune hunters—attracted by the "gold rush."

58. Gonzalez Quiroga described it as one in which people of different nations—Indians, Mexicans, and Americans—joined forces to act in concert against a common enemy
or in favor of a common cause. Miguel Ángel Gonzálaz-Quiroga, "Conflict and Cooperation in the Making of Texas-Mexico Border Society, 1840–1880," in *Bridging National
Borders in North America: Transnational and Comparative Histories*, eds. Benjamin H.
Johnson and Andrew R. Graybill (Durham, NC: Duke University Press, 2010), 33–58.

59. We have already noted the unprecedented case of California, although it should
be pointed out that the case of New Mexico was not as quick. Texas deserves special
mention, as it was an American state that was already populated at the time of the war.

60. By the last decades of the century, Sonora and Chihuahua, with a higher population density as a result of the advent of the railroad and modernization of the country in
general, engaged in the livestock business and therefore needed cattle.

III

The Complications
of the Market

8

State, Market, and Popular Sovereignty in Agrarian North America

The United States, 1850–1920

Christopher Clark

The period from 1845 to 1870 established the territorial borders within which national sovereignty has since been exercised in North America. The United States, by annexing Texas, conquering huge areas of Mexican (formerly Spanish) territory, and completing the Gadsden Purchase of 1853, fixed a new, lasting border with Mexico. Meanwhile, the United States and British North America had also settled their border disputes and largely agreed on permanent boundaries between them. The outbreak of the American Civil War in 1861 led European powers to watch carefully for opportunities to benefit: France invaded Mexico and subsequently imposed an emperor to rule as a French puppet. But the defeat of the Confederacy in 1865 both reunified the United States and put paid to the possibility that power on the continent might become more fragmented. Mexicans booted the French out and, in 1867, executed the Emperor Maximilian. Great Britain, recalculating its options now that it was clear that the United States would not remain divided, passed the British North America Act of 1867, establishing the Dominion of Canada as a framework for consolidating its disparate provinces into a confederation. The purchase of Alaska from Russia the same year completed the United States' continental acquisitions. Native Americans in the Great Plains and Far West found themselves increasingly pressed by hunters and herders, settlers, railroads, and military actions. These changes marked the point at which North American settler societies shifted emphasis from accumulating sovereign territory to determining how this land would be divided up, owned, and run—in short, how sovereignty would be exercised in practice. Territory formerly just marked out on maps came to be explored, exploited, settled, and integrated into national polities, economies, and cultures.[1]

For current and former parts of the British Empire in North America, the late nineteenth century was, of course, noteworthy for rapid industrialization and urbanization in some areas. But territorial consolidation also unleashed a spectacular agrarian expansion, part of the widespread "settler revolution" that, in James Belich's words, carried the "rise of the Angloworld" to various corners of the globe during the "long nineteenth century."[2] The expansion of farming, ranching, and associated agrarian pursuits paralleled that of industry, and was, in many ways, just as dramatic. As late as 1923, Thorstein Veblen could write of the United States that "the taking over and settlement of the farming lands is the most impressive material achievement of the . . . people," to which "the rest of the industrial system has, in the main . . . [been] . . . subsidiary or auxiliary."[3] In the United States, farms, plantations, and ranches increased in number from around two million in 1860 to nearly seven million by 1935. During the 1880s, agriculture's share of total employment fell below half for the first time, but actual employment in farming continued to rise until the 1910s. Growth in Canada, though more modest, was also impressive: The number of farms more than doubled between 1871 and 1921, to two-thirds of a million, while farm acreage quadrupled.[4]

Agriculture's prominence poses questions about the interpretive frameworks we use to explore the "remaking of sovereignty." The extension of national territory and the consolidation of political control by federal and state or provincial governments and institutions over lands once in indigenous hands were of course of prime significance. But it is important also to take account of the elements of individual and family independence and "self-rule" embodied in the concept of sovereignty and that inhered in a system of private, freehold landownership.[5] Agricultural history and the history of the West often used to be treated as subfields, separate from mainstream narratives and to a degree subsidiary to them. However, recent scholarly trends have sought to reintegrate them into wider interpretations of national development and to introduce a sharper sense of the political economy of settlement and its consequences. In this process, historians have particularly emphasized the roles of state power and market influences. But to these two strands we need to add consideration of the freehold property system and the ideologies that accompanied it.

The consolidation of state power and its exercise clearly had profound influence in shaping agricultural settlement. As two historians have recently argued, "nowhere else . . . did people experience the power and control of the modern centralized state as early or directly as did people in the countryside."[6] Federal authority in the United States expanded during and after the Civil War, as it did with the emergence of Dominion government in Canada after 1867. These governments encouraged agricultural settlement under the 1862 Homestead Act and the Dominion Lands Act of 1872 that mimicked it. They promoted transcontinental railroads to bind national territory together. The political and governmental expansion that produced a new "Yankee Leviathan" in the United States was sustained by the growth and proliferation of large private organizations in transportation, manufacturing, finance, and other areas. In Canada, the establishment of federal politics and the Confederation's extension across the continent made land policy, railroads, and state building central to forging a national consciousness.[7]

Equally important was the role of commercial and financial capitalism in linking growing agrarian hinterlands to international commodity, labor, and capital flows. Canada's development as a staples exporter, and myriad U.S. efforts to forge a national market in agricultural products, either turned farmers into agricultural capitalists or doomed them to failure. Scholars from William Cronon to Jonathan Levy have shown that the power and scope of markets, which commoditized not only farm products but also the financial instruments devised to handle them, profoundly shaped farmers' lives and the conduct of agriculture. Grain elevators, mercantile exchanges, insurance, credit and mortgage arrangements emerged to coordinate and profit from the production and exchange of farm products, while increasingly powerful railroad corporations also strongly influenced farming's fortunes.[8]

These emphases on government and market power have been invaluable in helping explain the integration of new territory into national and international patterns of politics and trade. However, they treat state and market institutions and practices primarily as impositions on rural societies, and rural people as subject to or victims of forces beyond their control: price fluctuations, the relentless demands of the farm mortgage, or the policies of governments controlled by metropolitan elites. To fully understand the exercise of sovereignty, we should also attend to how people subject to its extension were themselves able to engage with political and economic processes.[9]

One key will be to focus on the relationships settlers had with the land: their status as owners, tenants, or as landless people in an expanding farm economy. As William Appleman Williams suggested more than half a century ago, the continent's occupation and displacement or destruction of indigenous societies resulted not only from government policies or capitalist development, but also expressed the culture and aspirations of settlers themselves.[10] These aspirations were particularly orientated toward land, its possession, and the ideal of a society where property-owning farmers would achieve a measure of independence. State or national sovereignty would be exercised in conjunction (and sometimes in tension) with the "self-government" of individuals and households occupying their own land.

In the United States, these aspirations had taken prominent form in the land reform and Free Soil movements of the antebellum period.[11] In Canada, too, they embodied settlers' hopes that farm-ownership could spare them from urban poverty, aristocratic oppression, or plantation agriculture's exploitation. In both places, hopes for agrarian independence animated the extension of national sovereignty. The massive expansion of agriculture in the post–Civil War / post-Confederation decades constituted a distinctive phase in which rural settlements, work, and culture grew as a social formation alongside those associated with cities and industries—a formation rooted in the ideology of freehold land-ownership. Concepts of a freeholder society shaped the terms in which settlers understood their relationships to the land they occupied.

The United States provides a particularly fruitful case study of agriculturalists' sovereignty. Freehold ownership was, of course, not new, but the prospect that its wide availability could create a society of, by, and for farmers gained strength in the antebellum decades as land reform and Free Soil movements emerged to help reshape American politics. Robert Dale Owen echoed many Americans' thoughts when he told the Indiana constitutional convention in 1850, "A large majority of our people are small proprietors of land; the best, and happiest, and most independent class in the world."[12] Omar Morse, a young laborer on a Brockport, New York, farm, acted on familiar impulses when he declared in 1847 that "no white man less than sixteen feet between the eyes could ever make a slave of me," quit his employer, and spent the next two decades trying to establish himself in one Midwestern state after another as a farmer on his own land.[13] Abraham Lincoln argued in an 1859 speech that agriculture was the "best field for labor and cultivated thought," and that "the art of deriving a comfortable subsistence from the smallest area of soil" was the best protection against social or political oppression. He congratulated Wisconsin farmers for being "alike independent of crowned-kings, money-kings, and land-kings."[14] Elsewhere, Lincoln spelled out the wider implications of freehold farming. Would his Midwestern audience willingly swap places with either Canadians or South Carolinians? Self-evidently, the answer was "No" because "*Equality* . . . beats *inequality*, . . . whether of the British aristocratic sort, or . . . the domestic slavery sort."[15] In a North America fragmented by geopolitical divisions, Lincoln asserted the advantages of living free from either slavery or colonialism.

The American Civil War and the destruction of slavery within a few years transformed that picture. Now the United States could present itself as the uncontested model of the freehold ideal and the concepts of private sovereignty it embodied. There were sharp inconsistencies, of course, as we shall see. The postbellum South, in particular, perpetuated patterns of inequality and oppression largely based on race, and that used the institutions of a formally free system substantially to reinstitute the burdens of slavery. But the ideology of freehold farming nurtured by movements for land reform, free soil, and free labor, assumed a thoroughly normative status.

Understood in its broadest sense as a set of values and beliefs, not only as a political grouping, the movement for Free Soil and for free homesteads constituted a revolutionary force. Drawing on the popular aspiration for property ownership, and rejecting as "aristocratic" both slavery and colonialism, this movement, with farming folk at its core, prosecuted and won the Civil War, reshaped North America, and made a considerable portion of the continent a field for its social vision.[16] Stephen A. Douglas appropriated the concept of "popular sovereignty" for the effort to prevent western territories from being *closed* to slavery in 1854, but the subsequent sectional fragmentation of the Democrats and consolidation of Republican hegemony in the North reattached it to the *antislavery* cause.[17] Once the Civil War began, Unionists contemplated extending "free soil" across the South. Massachusetts infantry officer William Smith Clark wrote from Virginia in 1862 that "this must be the land of freedom. . . . If the southerners will not repent then they must be exterminated and their goodly land possessed by the chosen people." "Public lands," Clark noted on another occasion, "will be plenty."[18]

Though not primarily in the South but across the vast range of "Western" territory, public lands did become readily available under the Homestead Act of 1862, the most potent and visible expression of the freehold ideal, whose passage was made possible by the withdrawal of its southern opponents from Congress. "You, young mechanic," declared Pennsylvania congressman William D. "Pig Iron" Kelley, "have a right to go to . . . any . . . State in which there are public lands, and, under the Homestead law, settle on . . . the best land you can find . . . , and 'walk in glory behind the plough' on your own broad acres."[19] The Act provided 160-acre parcels of free public land to qualified settlers under certain terms. The *Baltimore Sun* reported in 1871 that 90,000 homesteaders had taken up land since the Act was passed, claiming that this was "70,000 more landowners than there are in Great Britain."[20] Measures intended to facilitate successful cultivation, the formation of the U.S. Department of Agriculture and the passage of the Morrill Land-Grant Act, both also in 1862, were as significant as the provision of land itself. Exponents of the agricultural colleges the Morrill Act encouraged were clear about the implications of placing education and science at the service of independent farmers. The trustees of the Massachusetts Agricultural College, one of the first land-grant foundations, noted in 1866 that "we live under a republican and not an aristocratic government; . . . inequality in property, in education, and therefore in political rights and power" should be avoided. The college curriculum would suit a society where a family's land "is equally divided among all the children and so the accumulation of great estates is prevented." The College, they concluded, would promote farming "adapt[ed] to our political institutions."[21] In the Midwest especially, homestead laws and land-grant colleges together fostered this marriage of farming and education.

Like their Revolutionary-era predecessors, commentators of the Civil War period celebrated freehold landownership as an emblem of political and personal virtue, but they also added that it was the mark of a superior civilization. "The zeal of absolute ownership," wrote political economist Arthur Latham Perry, "has been observed to produce almost magical effects, as well upon character as upon lands. . . . The masses of men are educated and developed by nothing so much as by the ownership of land." "The possession of small freeholds educates and gives energy to the masses," and the nation's strength would be best secured "on a broad basis of independent yeomanry to lean back upon." Of all possible land systems, Perry wrote, "fee-simple is the best mode."[22] Many Northerners believed that their re-conquest of the South, the destruction of chattel slavery, and efforts to dismantle the plantation system signaled that they were approaching the heights of human achievement.

The successful campaign to rid the United States of slavery was congruent with other changes during the mid-nineteenth century that pointed North America toward free soil and free labor, expressing the connotations of self-rule and autonomy inherent in both national and personal dimensions of "sovereignty." Other unfree or coercive labor systems and practices had also been abolished, or were falling into disuse. Many states abolished imprisonment for debt. Formal apprenticeships largely died out in white society (though were revived in some states to control minors of color). On the land itself, freehold tenure held sway. State constitutions, such as Minnesota's in 1858 and that of Arkansas in 1874, specifically upheld the system of allodial (freehold) tenures and repudiated remnant feudal forms of ownership, while New York's Hudson Valley manorial system was undergoing a long legal death following state constitutional reforms in 1846.

Settlers, whether they were purchasers from speculators or railroads, or beneficiaries of free public lands, sought the privileges of freehold ownership. Yet as James C. Scott has noted, freehold property regimes channeled particular vectors of state power.[23] Survey systems, land allocation and registration, and the legally enforceable mechanisms of purchase, sale, mortgage, and inheritance, lay literally at the foundations of states: the Northwest Ordinance of 1787, for example, had specified terms for landownership and inheritance in its first article, ahead of those concerned with forming and conducting governments. Freehold tenure conferred a direct relationship between owner and land unmediated by any formal dependency; even so, the means of preserving and transmitting ownership status were deeply rooted in the state. Taxation, eminent domain, and legal defenses against efforts to seize ownership all embodied the role of state institutions in a private property system.

Settlers who acquired land saw themselves as obtaining a degree of personal independence that other forms of tenure or livelihood could not provide, and attached significance to the instruments and symbols of this personal dimension of sovereignty. Studying early European explorations of the New World, Patricia Seed noted the "ceremonies of possession" by which representatives of European monarchies had claimed sovereignty over land and peoples, whose significance was not just symbolic but a basis for legal claims to occupy new territory against the interests of indigenous inhabitants.[24] To these "top-down" "ceremonies" asserting the rights of rulers over new territory, we might counterpose the many thousands of small, private rituals that marked modest families' acquisition of their parcels of freehold land. Early nineteenth-century figures such as Daniel Webster had venerated the freehold system; the Civil War era only enhanced its evocative power. To the writer and lecturer Bayard Taylor, even the language of a title deed, with its litany of continuity and possession ("to have and to hold the same to the said _____ _____ his heirs and assigns to his and their use and behoof forever") conjured up a "reverential spirit." Such expressions suggested that the freehold had attained not merely a normative, but effectively a sacred status.[25] If such systems entangled citizens in webs of state influence, they also empowered citizens to assert themselves within the political system and to put pressure on it. Individuals' rights and political influence inflected the exercise of national sovereignty.

The different aspects of sovereignty were mutually reinforcing. Settler freeholders in the United States simultaneously extended national power and their independent spheres of autonomy. Native Americans who faced the expansion of the freehold system during the mid-nineteenth century, encountered (as had often been so in the past, also) not simply the power of the State that pressed upon them, but the power of a State acting at the behest of its ordinary citizens. In California, as Stephen Aron has noted, the rapid expansion of mining and agricultural settlements during the 1850s effectively destroyed many indigenous groups.[26] During the Civil War itself, settlers and town promoters pushed into the Great Plains and the Mountain West, establishing new settlements and jurisdictions in advance of the so-called "frontier," and placing heavy pressure on Native Americans.[27] As historians now recognize, the Civil War unleashed a violent assault on many indigenous societies, prompted not by a centralizing State (which was preoccupied with other things), but by grassroots movements that demanded state and federal assistance to clear obstructions from their path. Alvin P. Josephy has noted of Civil War military action that once regular Federal troops had been recalled from the West in 1861 to fight further East, most units formed to address settlers' conflicts with Indians were local or regional militias unsympathetic to native claims, often predisposed to visit violence upon indigenous people.[28] These settler pressures on Indian lands largely preceded the cattle drives, railroad building, and buffalo hunting that spread so rapidly on the Plains after the war ended. Yet they introduced to the West patterns of settler-induced incursions, conflict, and demands for military assistance that marked territorial expansion between 1865 and the century's end: patterns that characterized the final Indian Wars, the occupation of the Black Hills, and the extension of railroads and farm settlements throughout the Great Plains.[29] Extensions of state power and injections of capital often followed channels already carved by settlers and their influence.

Even though market capitalism extended its domain across the agricultural economy, rural society itself changed less radically than did the transportation, handling, and financing of farms' output: the Civil War–era framework of freehold landownership and "free labor" persisted. Alongside national or international influences, local conditions and farm households' autonomous decisions also continued to hold sway. Farmers controlled crop mixes, sometimes broadening their range rather than specializing in monocrop production.[30] They established networks of cooperation to help them acquire and use new technology.[31] European settlers, especially, subordinated the pursuit of individual interests to measures that would build and sustain their communities.[32] Just as before the War, new settlers in farming regions paid close attention to the conditions they encountered, and to what they often referred to as "the health of the country."[33] Farm journals and organizations promoted "agricultural improvement," but debates over livestock rearing and crop cultivation saw farmers and their families seeking to adopt "improvements" suited to their own needs and circumstances. Members of Granges and other organizations saw them as agencies for their own education and as reinforcing their identities as independent farmers, as well as means for seeking favorable political action. As Charles Postel has argued, these movements, culminating in the Populism of the 1890s, projected a concept of Progress that assumed a future America with farming and farmers at its center.[34]

Just as they had summoned military power to their aid in occupying land and removing indigenous inhabitants, settlers continued to call upon government to assist them. Gregory P. Downs has noted the patronal relationships embodied in rural claims upon state legislatures. Ariel Ron has argued that the creation of the U.S. Department of Agriculture exemplified rural peoples' ability to obtain government's support—a process he calls "summoning the state." Government sponsorship of agricultural science and education was built on evaluations of local conditions and standards. Soil science, the epitome of efforts to diagnose farmers' needs, necessarily entailed intensive attention to matters of place, embodied in exhaustive and detailed reports on soil conditions and cultivation.[35] Government involvement was not simply an extension of state power but a subtle, usually invited, interaction with people who farmed the land. Practices reported by farm journals and agricultural experiment stations (before and after the 1887 Hatch Act established the latter on a federal basis) were observed in local circumstances and adapted to regional conditions. Although there would later be criticism of college-trained "experts" telling experienced farmers how to do their work, the basis for experiment stations', agricultural colleges' and extension services' activities lay in this careful observation of localities.[36] Even in the vast areas of the United States where the rectilinear land survey system appeared to impose rigidity, the projection of a freehold agricultural vision did not produce uniform patterns of settlement or development. Differing physical conditions and social and cultural roots ensured diverse paths of settlement. California and the Pacific Northwest emerged with different crop regimes and growth patterns than one another or than those of the Midwest or Great Plains.[37]

Behind the land reform and Free Soil movements that had produced the Homestead Act was the hope that rural societies would be based on modest-sized farms whose dominance would foster social equality. Pervading the later nineteenth-century decades was the anxiety that this ideal was being subverted by the emergence of large estates. California's large grain and livestock farms, many based on Spanish or Mexican land grants confirmed under American law, achieved a scale rare in the East or Midwest. These fueled Henry George's outrage at the inequalities and land monopolies that he condemned in *Progress and Poverty* and other works of the 1870s.[38] Signs of domination by large-scale landholdings also appeared in the prairies, Great Plains, and Southwest. Large "bonanza farms" created in the wheat belt appeared to threaten the death-knell for small farms and the triumph of mechanized, capitalist agriculture. By the 1880s, numerous commentators joined Henry George in warning of the dangers posed by large estates to small farms and the freehold vision.[39] In *Land and Labor in the United States* (1883), William Moody expressed alarm at "monster estates . . . swallowing up the small holdings of the people, and undermining and destroying the small farm interests of the country." Small farmers, instead of being owners of their own land, subject to "no master," would become mere laborers, Moody warned, and he anticipated national destruction and revolution in consequence of the "gigantic growth of the large farm interest."[40] In the South, sharecropping and tenancy had become the chief successors to slavery, but in the Midwest, too, tenancy appeared to be on the rise and the topic of farm tenancy was widely debated. Omar Morse, the fugitive from New York State wage slavery, never firmly established himself as an independent farmer, buying several small farms in succession but repeatedly losing them and reverting to tenancy as he struggled to meet mortgage payments to stave off foreclosure.[41]

However, most agricultural expansion was accomplished on small or moderate-sized, household-based farms. Many great estates and bonanza farms were relatively short-lived. Indeed, railroads such as the Atchison, Topeka, and Santa Fe discouraged large accumulations of land by single owners, instead promoting settlement by household-based farmers on modest acreage so as to cultivate communities that would sustain their business.[42] Even California developed small-scale cultivation in viniculture, fruit growing, and truck farming, permitting some settlers (including, eventually, Japanese immigrants) to obtain land.[43] The state's politicians were eager to present themselves as champions of modest farms. The 1879 California constitutional convention debated the merits of large and small landholdings. Critics of "land monopolies" who proposed limits to the size of holdings faced resistance from delegates who denied that monopolies existed and claimed that legal curbs on holdings would retard settlement. Democrats charged Republicans with supporting corporate interests on the land question. Republicans retorted that they had sponsored the Homestead Act and the subsequent adjustments intended to ensure that its purposes were carried out.[44] Large agricultural units often proved problematic to finance or run, and were broken up into smaller farms, either owned or rented. When James Bryce wrote about monopolies in *The American Commonwealth* in the late 1880s, he could observe with some accuracy that "[o]f the tendency to aggregation there are happily no signs so far as relates to agriculture."[45] The congressional Industrial Relations Commission reported in 1916 that though farmers facing retirement or financial difficulty might consolidate their land with that of neighbors or relatives, corporations and large estate owners were at the same time selling off or breaking up large holdings into smaller farms because large acreages were uneconomic to manage.[46]

Freehold ideology held its own for two generations after the end of the American Civil War. One effect, of course, was to help impose the logic of freehold property-ownership on people who were not necessarily willing to accept it. It was the basis for the most disruptive legal and institutional (as distinct from violent and military) interventions in the lives of Native Americans, the efforts to force them to assimilate into settler society by themselves becoming independent farmers. As Radical Republican colleagues pressed for black voting rights in the South in the late 1860s, Massachusetts reformers campaigned to enfranchise the state's Indians. The Massachusetts Indian Enfranchisement Act of 1869, which accomplished this, also replaced communal landholding with fee-simple tenure, enabling tribal lands to be divided up and sold.[47] This foreshadowed subsequent federal action. During the 1870s and 1880s, reformers and philanthropists determined to extend private property ownership as a facet of civilization made such efforts central to federal policy, backed by railroads and settlers, and by lumber and mining interests eager to acquire Indian land.[48] Though some Indian groups themselves petitioned for the breakup of their land into individually owned "allotments," they did so primarily as a defensive tactic. Most resisted the change. The Indian Rights Association warned in 1882 that a "protected individual title to land" would be "the entering-wedge by which tribal organization is to be rent asunder."[49]

The federal General Allotment Act of 1887, sponsored by Massachusetts senator Henry L. Dawes, aimed to achieve just that, and would rival military action and the destruction of the bison in spelling disaster for Plains Indians. Resettling Indians on individual farms would, according to the aptly named Thomas Jefferson Morgan, Commissioner of Indian Affairs in Benjamin Harrison's administration, be the means by which "tribal relations should be broken up, socialism destroyed, and the family and the autonomy of the individual substituted."[50] The severalty policy identified "unused" Indian land that could be released for sale to whites so, in addition to imposing an alien way of life on Native Americans, it provided a legal mechanism for settlers and speculators to obtain large quantities of land to which they would otherwise have had no access. In the United States between 1881 and 1900, more than seventy-seven million acres were transferred to non-Indian ownership.

Prominent among those persuading Native Americans to accept the allotment policy were officials with Free Soil credentials, such as General Oliver Otis
Howard, who saw themselves as progressive and humanitarian. Allotment would
advance "civilization"—of which freehold landownership was a key index. Indians did not own all of the United States, Howard told one group: "All God's
children had an interest in it," and so (citing the system of land survey and division in his native New England) "we must fix metes and bounds."[51] Meanwhile,
the idealization of modest freehold farms and the critiques of large estates that
had animated Henry George and his allies were turned against Native Americans, too. Some of the southeastern Indians who had been removed to Indian
Territory in the 1830s accumulated substantial landholdings that by the 1880s
were under attack as "aristocratic" signs of an incipient "land monopoly." Many
were broken up for distribution to white settlers in the last great land rush of the
nineteenth century.

Confidence in freehold ideals and their "civilizational" effects led to further
efforts to extend them, sometimes despite evidence that limits to the freehold
land system were being reached. Pushing cultivation into western Nebraska and
adjacent states in the 1870s and 1880s, settlers occupied the higher, drier regions
of the Plains.[52] Fears that their efforts would be stymied by drought were initially
assuaged by the assurance that "civilization" itself would improve nature—in the
belief that "rain follows the plow" or, more substantially, that planting trees for
fuel and building materials could overcome the region's aridity. With agricultural
depression came a retreat from the High Plains by the early 1890s and the col-
lapse of the western farm-mortgage market.[53] The later revival of agricultural
prices, however, also revived efforts at settlement. Land agents, railroads, and agriculturalists promoted elaborate, well-publicized theories of "dry farming" that
enticed many thousands of families to take up land in the western Dakotas and
eastern Montana over the following two decades to establish wheat farming. Experience at first seemed to validate their confidence that new farming methods
could beat aridity, but events subsequently proved this illusory. Cultivating "virgin" land for grain was initially successful, partly because nutrients long accumulated in the soil were available to use, but these nutrients were soon exhausted.
Moreover, the peak of settlement in this region, from about 1908 to 1917, coincided with a period of unusually high rainfall. The return of drought destroyed
confidence in dry farming and set in motion another retreat of settlement.[54] Most
settlers in the northern plains were household-based farmers taking up standard
160-acre homestead claims. The difficulties they faced raising grain and keeping
livestock on such acreage in this dry region led to pressure for Congress to pass

the Enlarged Homestead Act of 1909 that increased the acreage to 320. Yet these larger units still proved inadequate for the grazing needs of livestock, and the consolidation of landholdings in Montana and North Dakota during the twentieth century resulted not from a "monopolizing" tendency but from the gradual, reluctant acceptance that modest-sized holdings were too small to support farming in the region's climate and topography.

But proponents of irrigation to overcome the West's aridity did draw on the small-freehold tradition to make their case. Measures such as the Desert Land Act of 1877 adjusted homestead rules to encourage agricultural expansion. Publicists such as William Ellsworth Smythe advocated a process of internal colonization by small farmers to turn arid regions into productive settlements. In *The Conquest of Arid America*, his 1900 manifesto for irrigated farming, Smythe asserted that aridity and the practicalities of irrigation would limit the size of farms and so favor small producers. California, whose great estates had once made it "a rich man's paradise and a poor man's hell," could become, Smythe claimed, a place for the "common man" in which large holdings and even standard quarter-section homesteads would be displaced by smaller farms. He pointed to the replacement of monocrop regimes by diversification, and argued that the chance to live with "neighbors and society" in concentrated rural settlements was replacing the "loneliness and heart-hunger" of the isolated farmstead. "A large farm under irrigation is a misfortune; a great farm, a calamity," Smythe wrote. "Only the small farm pays." Moreover, he concluded with an ideological flourish, "this small farm blesses its proprietor with industrial independence and crowns him with equality."[55]

International connections linked North American interest in small farms and landed independence to reform currents elsewhere. Henry George's proposed "single tax" on land as a panacea for social inequalities, and his attachment to "diffused proprietorship" attracted a widespread following.[56] In the 1880s, George's campaign meshed with that of American supporters of land reform in Ireland, and with the more than 1,500 branches of the American Land League organized by the Irish land-leaguer Michael Davitt. Among exponents of the land league movement, Patrick Ford, editor of the widely read New York *Irish World*, urged resistance to land monopolies, bonanza farms, and tenancy, arguing that Irish peasants and American farmers had essential interests in common.[57] North America was only part of a widespread movement for settlements that prominently featured household-based farming, in South America, South and East Africa, Australasia, and Russia, and political arguments for freehold landownership.[58] The circulation of lecturers, campaigners, and publications about land issues played a substantial role in radical and reform politics, registering as much impact as the international labor movement, or nationalist or anti-colonial causes. Henry George was linked to the antebellum land reform movement through Shaker elder Frederick W. Evans, brother of George Henry Evans of the National Reform Association. Michael Davitt not only worked to build American, Canadian, and Australasian support for Irish land reform, but also—like George—campaigned for tenants' rights in Scotland and elsewhere.[59] There was a kind of Populist International of politicians, activists, writers, and supporters, for whom land questions were central to wider political campaigns. These sought not only protections for tenants against landlords but legal changes that would expand the scope of the freehold system by enabling cultivators to acquire the land they worked.

Yet despite the confidence of its exponents, and its international attractiveness, the freehold vision for North America faced contradictions that would ultimately undermine it. Some were ideological, or the results of assumptions not necessarily inherent in the freehold system. As many scholars have noted, Free Soilers' and Radical Republicans' efforts to settle former slaves on their own land in the American South during Reconstruction faced massive racial, political, and institutional obstacles. Though freedpeople had some success in obtaining homesteads in the Carolinas and parts of Florida, by the mid-1870s only about 5 percent of black families in the South as a whole owned land. There was subsequent growth: 19 percent of black farmers in the Lower South and as many as 44 percent in the Upper South owned some real property by 1910, though this still represented only a small proportion of the African American population.[60] Any increase resulted mainly from black families' own determined efforts to acquire property despite white hostility and popular indifference. Meanwhile, even as black Americans were struggling to obtain land, many Native Americans were resisting the efforts to turn them into farmers through the allotment system—successfully enough that they finally forced the abandonment of the allotment policy in 1934 and an ability to retain remnants of the very different concepts of personal and tribal sovereignty that private, freehold property ownership had undermined.

Other contradictions were deeply rooted in the property system and in structural constraints that prevented the freehold vision's full realization. The first constraint concerned labor. The overthrow of slavery had presented a paradox. In an important essay fifty years ago, Evsey C. Domar argued that serfdom or slavery had flourished historically when land was abundant, labor scarce, and landholders needed either to tie laborers to the land or to own and control their work-forces.[61] Yet the end of American slavery came just at the moment when, with the extension of its national territory, the U.S.'s land:labor ratio was increasing and conditions for continuing slavery should have been favorable. The triumph of free-labor agriculture in these circumstances created tensions underlying the massive extension of farming after the Civil War. It took place in conditions of labor shortage and hence uncertainty. As Eric Rauchway has written, expansion represented not the imposition of a "developmental state," but the projection into the West of a "free labor/extensive" model of growth.[62]

The rapid expansion of freehold farm making, by exaggerating rather than di-minishing the land:labor ratio, made viable commercial agriculture problematic. Advocates of homesteads offered few solutions to the conundrum of how newly settled land would be worked productively. Farmers celebrated their ownership of land; political economists recognized that farmers' productiveness rested on access to labor. In the final chapter of the first volume of *Das Kapital*, published in 1867, Karl Marx criticized schemes for settling farmers on freely available land. Though his immediate target was the 1836 proposal of Edward Gibbon Wakefield that Britain should offer land grants to assure the rapid settlement of Australia, Marx's remarks applied equally well to North America in the era of the Home-stead Act. Free land constituted an "anti-capitalist cancer," he wrote, turning people away from the need to labor in order to pursue a fantasy of independent landed proprietorship. Labor remained sufficiently scarce on the postbellum U.S. frontier that legislators searched for ways of supplying it. A scheme proposed to Congress in 1878 would have created an Enlisted Labor Association to sign up 100,000 volunteers for five years' work on government-run "military and agri-cultural" reservations.[63] As Harriet Friedmann and others have noted, in the ab-sence of slavery or large pools of surplus labor, household-based farms remained the most viable kind of agricultural unit on the extensive lands of North America, Australasia, and Argentina. Production in household-based agriculture required systematic self-exploitation of and by family members. Difficulty in obtaining or controlling labor helped undermine the large estates and "bonanza farms" that small-farm advocates feared.[64] But although it helped preserve the independent freehold farm system, this labor shortage hampered its success. Agrarian inde-pendence did not assure prosperity.

The inheritance system posed further difficulties. More than for its alienabil-ity, freehold land was celebrated for the principles of partible inheritance, seen as a safeguard against inequality. However, owners of modest homesteads faced the problem of continuing their farms and replicating the advantages of ownership if property was to be divided among children. Sioux and other Native American resistors to the seizure of "surplus" lands under the allotment system argued in vain that under partible inheritance their need for land would be greater than that for members of their own generation alone.

Three consequences, the subjects of much debate, flowed from this question. Some writers advocated an intensification of effort on the smaller farms that would result from intergenerational division. Partible inheritance would both restrain property accumulation and "monopoly" and work positively to encourage increased output and a concentration of rural settlements and activities. There was also recognition that partible inheritance would cause members of each generation to find employment away from the land. This, too, could be a virtue if it did not result in wholesale emigration or the abandonment of farmland. But the third recognition was rooted in the conventional perspective on the history of national expansion: that freeholds with intergenerational partibility were viable only because "new" land was available for farm making, and that sovereign national territory would continue to be available for the multiplication of sovereign independent landholdings.

By the 1890s, this assumption was being questioned. The shapers of the Homestead Act had contemplated the continent's vast scale and envisaged great opportunities for the settlers who would farm it. Their successors were increasingly conscious of limits to expansion. The perception that the continent was filling up and that the "frontier" dividing open from settled land was "closing" shaped the U.S. Census Bureau's report on the results of the 1890 census and in turn led the historian Frederick Jackson Turner to formulate his famous "frontier thesis," that the closing off of opportunities hitherto afforded by access to fresh land would mark a new phase in national development.[65] Anxiety about limits to settlement fed wider apprehensions about industrialization, urbanization, and class conflict, and helped fuel aspirations for overseas expansion that lay behind America's acquisition of Hawaii and its prosecution of the 1898 war against the remains of the Spanish Empire.[66]

These structural circumstances, of labor shortage and of apparent constraints on the supply of land shaped the experiences of late nineteenth-century farmers. Agrarian movements, from the Grange to the variety of Farmers' Alliances, Farmer-Labor Parties, and Socialist organizations that emerged in different parts of the rural United States were all responses to economic constraints and uncertainties. Efforts to seek political relief from the business cycle, and the ups and downs of farm prices; difficulties paying mortgages; relationships with grain elevators and other "middlemen"; anger at railroad rates and dependence on large corporations for shipment of goods; efforts to influence tariff policies; and, above all, raging disputes over currency and the money supply all took shape during the phase from the 1860s to the 1890s when land:labor ratios were at their highest and ability to control other than family labor was at its weakest.

Farmers' movements have most often been understood as responses to the incursions of market institutions, and to the power and influence of finance and its mechanisms that appeared as outside intrusions upon independent farm life. Farmers' efforts to deal with these, by setting up cooperative institutions or by summoning the power of government to regulate affairs, sought to reassert a form of independence that seemed to have been lost. One writer in the 1890s distinguished the "pioneer age" of sixty years before, with its "equal rights for all, and special privileges for none," from the present "money age," with its "monopolists and millionaires" and "conditions . . . [of] privilege, monopoly, and inequality."[67] But apparent intrusions were only part of the equation. The systemic weaknesses of family-based farming in the absence of available labor also contributed to the crisis. "The mortgage worked the hardest" according to a famous song, but it is no moral judgment on rural people to remark that this was partly because the labor available to farm families was finite, and not usually generous. The family worked hard, too, but as the song implied, its members were obliged to sleep at night. The fact that many claims to land under the Homestead Act were never "proved up" by their claimants reflected the challenge of establishing farms under the system it established.[68]

The easing of the agricultural depression after the mid-1890s and the upward trend in farm prices culminating in the First World War-era boom took some of the pressure off farm families and, in national politics at least, reduced the potency of the protests that had animated the Populist movement. But local and regional farmer parties and protest movements remained active in many parts of the United States as fundamental structural conditions remained unaltered. The solution to farmers' predicament would eventually lie in mechanization, seed hybridization, and other capital intensive measures that would turn successful farms into large businesses, promote the consolidation of landholdings, and drive large proportions of the rural population off the land. The key would be labor saving technologies and methods that circumvented the labor shortages endemic to a household-based agricultural system. Though the second half of the nineteenth century saw many steps in this direction, the culmination of these developments lay in the future, particularly from the 1930s onward. Before they became effective, other efforts to provide labor for farm households remained significant.

There was growth in the permanent wage labor force available in agriculture, as immigration from overseas and internal migration augmented rural populations. But despite commentaries noting the increase of wage work in farming, most famously in a study by V. I. Lenin shortly before World War One claiming that American agricultural labor had been proletarianized, evidence suggests that this diagnosis was exaggerated; fewer than one-quarter of those employed in American farming in 1910 were hired hands.[69] Farmers, as well as drawing on their own and family-members' labor, frequently resorted to makeshift arrangements to obtain assistance. They continued patterns of neighborhood cooperation and exchange. They sometimes employed new emigrants who were seeking work to support themselves while setting up their own farms. State and private agencies supplied labor: training schools for Native American children; orphanages and adoption societies; and the now notorious ships and trains that carried abandoned children to new "homes" on American farms; all were deployed to meet the labor needs of farm households.[70] Finally, seasonal workers who migrated from place to place following the crop cycle, forming a floating agricultural proletariat, provided much supplementary labor. Often landless, and sometimes stigmatized as "hoboes" or "drifters," these migrant workers enabled the freehold farm system to work at the cost of remaining largely invisible within it.[71] The freehold ideal, having offered "sovereignty" over the land and substantial equality to those owning property, could not sustain the social inclusion envisaged by its original proponents.

Between the Civil War and World War One thinking about the role of land in a free labor society evolved to produce a subtle shift of emphasis in the public discourse about farming. Advocates of a Homestead Act had stressed access to land itself as a key to policy. By the early twentieth century emphasis was shifting to the families that owned farms. Although the term "family farm" had long been in use, only during the late nineteenth and early twentieth centuries did it acquire its modern meaning, connecting the farming system with the idealization of "family" that has been attached to it ever since. Among the early shifts in usage that established a sentimental association between "family" and "farm" were discussions of the displacement and allotment of land to Native Americans. An Indian agent writing in 1877 claimed that preparations to move Pawnee Indians from Nebraska to freehold allotments in "Indian Territory" would give "an opportunity to all progressive Indians in the tribe of selecting and laying out family farms for cultivation, in accordance and harmony with the government system of land partition." He was not employing a normative concept here, but making an ideological point: "family farms for cultivation" were to be distinguished from the collective arrangements associated with tribal organization. "Family farms" would be the new homes of "progressive" Pawnees taking their steps toward "civilization" and abandoning their tribal past. Within another generation or so, the concept of "family farm" would be widely applied to agriculture in general, and then used by farmers' organizations and lobby groups to justify measures to preserve farmers' interests.[72]

In the mid-nineteenth century, Americans had moved from acquiring territory to exercising ownership and control over it. During the early twentieth century, they came to present farming as a preeminent bulwark of a sacrosanct social institution. This shift reflected both the attributes and the weaknesses of a freehold agricultural system. A generation ago, William Appleman Williams noted the significant part farmer-settlers played in the extension of American sovereignty.[73] As we have seen, farm populations in late nineteenth-century North America were not simply subjects of state power or market forces. They helped shape these, and attempted to put them to use for their own ends, within the constraints imposed by the ideals they were pursuing.

Notes

1. Rachel St. John, *Line in the Sand: A History of the Western U.S.-Mexico Border* (Princeton: Princeton University Press, 2011).

2. James Belich, *Replenishing the Earth: The Settler Revolution and the Rise of the Angloworld, 1783–1939* (Oxford: University of Oxford Press, 2009).

3. Thorstein Veblen, "The Independent Farmer," in *The Freeman* (June 13, 1923): 321–22.

4. R. M. McInnis, "Output and Productivity in Canadian Agriculture, 1870–71 to 1926–27," in *Long-Term Factors in American Economic Growth*, ed. Stanley L. Engerman and Robert E. Gallman (Chicago: University of Chicago Press, 1986), 751, table 14.4.

5. On the diverse colonial origins of North American property systems, see Allan Greer, *Property and Dispossession: Natives, Empires, and Land in Early Modern North America* (Cambridge: Cambridge University Press, 2017).

6. See Richard Franklin Bensel, *Yankee Leviathan: The Origins of Central State Authority in America, 1859–1877* (Cambridge: Cambridge University Press, 1990); quotation from Catherine McNichol Stock and Robert D. Johnson, eds., *The Countryside in the Age of the Modern State: Political Histories of Rural America* (Ithaca: Cornell University Press, 2001), 5.

7. W. L. Morton, *The Critical Years 1857–1873: The Union of British North America* (Toronto: McClelland & Stewart, 1964); P. B. Waite, *Canada, 1874–1896: Arduous Destiny* (Toronto: McClelland and Stewart, 1971); Andrew Smith, *British Businessmen and Canadian Confederation: Constitution Making in the Era of Globalization* (Montreal: McGill-Queen's University Press, 2008).

8. William Cronon, *Nature's Metropolis: Chicago and the Great West* (New York: Norton, 1991); Jonathan Ira Levy, "Contemplating Delivery: Futures Trading and the Problem of Commodity Exchange in the United States, 1875–1905," *American Historical Review* 111, no. 2 (April 2006): 307–35; Levy, "The Mortgage Worked the Hardest: The Fate of Landed Independence in Nineteenth-Century America," in *Capitalism Takes Command: The Social Transformation of Nineteenth-Century America*, ed. Michael Zakim and Gary J. Kornblith (Chicago: University of Chicago Press, 2012), 39–68; Levy, *Freaks of Fortune: The Emerging World of Capitalism and Risk in America* (Cambridge: Harvard University Press, 2012), chap. 5. For Canada see, for example, Peter A. Russell, *How Agriculture Made Canada: Farming in the Nineteenth Century* (Montreal: McGill-Queens, 2012).

9. See Kenneth M. Sylvester, *The Limits of Rural Capitalism: Family, Culture, and Markets in Montcalm, Manitoba, 1870–1940* (Toronto: University of Toronto Press, 2001); Colin C. Williams, *A Commodified World? Mapping the Limits of Capitalism* (London: Zed Books, 2005).

10. William Appleman Williams, *Roots of the Modern American Empire: A Study of the Growth and Shaping of Social Consciousness in a Marketplace Society* (New York: Random House, 1969).

11. Eric Foner, *Free Soil, Free Labor, Free Men: The Ideology of the Republican Party before the Civil War* (New York: Oxford University Press, 1970).

12. *Report of the Debates and Proceedings of the Convention for the Revision of the Constitution of the State of Indiana, 1850* (Indianapolis: A. H. Brown, 1850), I: 463.

13. "The Autobiography of Omar H. Morse," in James M. Marshall, *Land Fever: Dispossession and the Frontier Myth* (Lexington: University of Kentucky Press, 1986), 42.

14. "Address before the Wisconsin State Agricultural Society, Milwaukee, Wisconsin, September 30, 1859," in *The Collected Works of Abraham Lincoln*, ed. Roy P. Basler (New Brunswick: Rutgers University Press, 1953), III: 481.

15. "Fragment on Free Labor," in *The Collected Works of Abraham Lincoln*, III: 462.

16. See James L. Huston, *The British Gentry, the Southern Planter, and the Northern Family Farmer: Agriculture and Sectional Antagonism in North America* (Baton Rouge: Louisiana State University Press, 2015); and Adam Wesley Dean, *An Agrarian Republic: Farming, Antislavery Politics, and Nature Parks in the Civil War Era* (Chapel Hill: University of North Carolina Press, 2015).

17. Christopher Childers, "Interpreting Popular Sovereignty: A Historiographical Essay," *Civil War History* 57, no. 1 (March 2011): 48–70.

18. William S. Clark to Atherton Clark, Jan 5, 1862, May 29, 1862, William Smith Clark Papers, Box 4, folder 4, Special Collections and Archives, W. E. B. Du Bois Library, University of Massachusetts, Amherst.

19. *Speeches of Hon. William D. Kelley: Replies of the Hon. William D. Kelley to George Northrop, Esq., in the Joint Debate in the Fourth Congressional District* (Philadelphia: Collins, 1864), 6.

20. *Baltimore Sun*, September 30, 1871. For a recent evaluation of the effects and importance of the Homestead Act, see Richard Edwards, Jacob K. Friefeld, and Rebecca S. Wingo, *Homesteading the Plains: Toward a New History* (Lincoln: University of Nebraska Press, 2017).

21. *Annual Report of the Massachusetts Agricultural College*, Mass. Senate Doc. no. 39 ([Boston]: n.p., 1866), 4, 19.

22. Arthur Latham Perry, *Elements of Political Economy*, sixth edition (New York: C. Scribner, 1871), 179–80, 182.

23. James C. Scott, *Seeing Like a State: How Certain Schemes to Improve the Human Condition Have Failed* (New Haven: Yale University Press, 1998).

24. Patricia Seed, *Ceremonies of Possession in Europe's Conquest of the New World, 1492–1640* (Cambridge: University of Cambridge Press, 1995).

25. Taylor quoted by J. M. Hubbard, "The Ownership of Land," *Nineteenth Annual Report of the Secretary of the Connecticut State Board of Agriculture* (Hartford: Case, Lockwood, and Brainard Co., 1885), 192–213.

26. Stephen Aron, *The American West: A Very Short Introduction* (New York: Oxford University Press, 2014).

27. Eugene P. Moehring, "The Civil War and Town Founding in the Intermountain West," *Western Historical Quarterly* 28, no. 3 (1997): 316–41.

28. Alvin P. Josephy, *The Civil War in the American West* (New York: Vintage, 1991).

29. Jeffrey Ostler, *The Plains Sioux and U.S. Colonialism from Lewis and Clark to Wounded Knee* (Cambridge: Cambridge University Press, 2004); Ostler, *The Lakotas and the Black Hills: The Struggle for Sacred Ground* (New York: Viking, 2010).

30. Mary Eschelbach Gregson, "Rural Response to Increased Demand: Crop Choice in the Midwest, 1860–1880," *Journal of Economic History* 53 (June 1993): 332–45.

31. Alan L. Olmstead and Paul W. Rhode, "Beyond the Threshold: An Analysis of the Character and Behavior of Early Reaper Adopters," *Journal of Economic History* 55, no. 1 (1995): 27–57, discusses local cooperation.

32. Jon Gjerde, *The Minds of the West: Ethnocultural Evolution in the Rural Middle West, 1830–1917* (Chapel Hill: University of North Carolina Press, 1997); Edwards, et. al., *Homesteading the Plains*, 172–79 notes, in particular, the tendency of farm families from Central Europe to cluster in distinct settlements.

33. Conevery Bolton Valencius, *The Health of the Country: How American Settlers Understood Themselves and Their Land* (New York: Basic Books, 2002).

34. Charles Postel, *The Populist Vision* (New York: Oxford University Press, 2007).

35. Gregory P. Downs, *Declarations of Dependence: The Long Reconstruction of Popular Politics in the South, 1861–1908* (Chapel Hill: University of North Carolina Press, 2011); Ariel Ron, "Summoning the State: Northern Farmers and the Transformation of American Politics in the Mid-Nineteenth Century," *Journal of American History* 103 (September 2016): 347–74.

36. Roy V. Scott, *The Reluctant Farmer: The Rise of Agricultural Extension to 1914* (Urbana: University of Illinois Press, 1971) discussed farmers' skepticism; for another view, see Nancy K. Berlage, *Farmers Helping Farmers: The Rise of the Home and Farm Bureaus, 1914–1935* (Baton Rouge: Louisiana State University Press, 2016).

37. D. W. Meinig, *The Shaping of America: A Geographical Perspective on 500 Years of History, Vol. 3: Transcontinental America, 1850–1915* (New Haven: Yale University Press, 1998), 47–55.

38. Henry George, *Progress and Poverty: An Inquiry into the Cause of Industrial Depressions and of Increase of Want with Increase of Wealth* (New York: Appleton, 1879).

39. See, for example, "The Bonanza Farms of the West," *Atlantic Monthly* 45, no. 267 (January 1880): 42.

40. William Godwin Moody, *Land and Labor in the United States* (New York: Charles Scribner's Sons, 1883).

41. Marshall, *Land Fever*, 50–80.

42. "Kansas Farmers and Illinois Dairymen," *Atlantic Monthly* 44, no. 266 (December 1879): 723.

43. Valerie Matsumoto, *Farming the Home Place: A Japanese American Community in California, 1919–1982* (Ithaca: Cornell University Press, 1993).

44. *Debates and Proceedings of the Constitutional Convention of the State of California*, 3 vols. (Sacramento: State Printing Office, 1880–81).

45. James Bryce, *The American Commonwealth* (London: Macmillan, 1888), 3: 669; Bryce noted exceptions, particularly in the Far West.

46. *Report of the Commission on Industrial Relations* vol. 10, 64 Cong. 1 Sess., Senate Document No. 415 (1916).

47. Ann Marie Plane and Gregory Button, "The Massachusetts Indian Enfranchise-ment Act: Ethnic Contest in Historical Context, 1849–1869," *Ethnohistory* 40, no. 4 (1993): 587–618.

48. Rose Stremlau, "'To Domesticate and Civilize Wild Indians': Allotment and the Campaign to Reform Indian Families, 1875–1887," *Journal of Family History* 30, no. 3 (July 2005): 265–86.

49. Francis Paul Prucha, ed., *Americanizing the American Indians: Writings by the "Friends of the Indian," 1880–1900* (Cambridge: Harvard University Press, 1973), 43.

50. Prucha, ed., *Americanizing the American Indians*, 74–76.

51. O. O. Howard, *My Life and Experiences Among Our Hostile Indians* (Hartford: A. D. Worthington, 1907), 208.

52. Edwards, et al., *Homesteading the Plains*, 67–72, 96–102.

53. Levy, *Freaks of Fortune*, chap. 5.

54. Zeynep K. Hansen and Gary D. Libecap, "The Allocation of Property Rights to Land: U.S. Land Policy and Farm Failure in the Northern Great Plains," *Explorations in Economic History* 41, no. 2 (2004): 103–29; see also Kate Brown, "Gridded Lives: Why Kazakhstan and Montana are Nearly the Same Place," *American Historical Review* 106, no. 1 (February 2001): 17–48.

55. William Ellsworth Smythe, *The Conquest of Arid America* (New York: Harper and Brothers, 1900), 43, 118, 148–49.

56. George, *Progress and Poverty*; John L. Thomas, *Alternative America: Henry George, Edward Bellamy, Henry Demarest Lloyd and the Adversary Tradition* (Cambridge: Har-vard University Press, 1983), 14, 49–50, 63–64; Fred Nicklason, "Henry George: Social Gospeller," *American Quarterly* 22, no. 3 (Autumn 1970): 652–53.

57. On the Land League, see Eric Foner, *Politics and Ideology in the Age of the Civil War* (New York: Oxford University Press, 1980), 150–200; on its international dimen-sions, see Ely M. Janis, "The Land League in the United States and Ireland: Nationalism, Gender, and Ethnicity in the Gilded Age" (Ph.D. diss., Boston College, 2008).

58. See Belich, *Replenishing the Earth*.

59. Laurence Marley, *Michael Davitt: Freelance Radical and Frondeur* (Dublin: Four Courts Press, 2007), chap. 6.

60. Eric Foner, *Reconstruction: America's Unfinished Revolution* (New York: HarperCollins, 1988), 375, 404; Loren Schweninger, *Black Property Owners in the South, 1790–1915* (Urbana: University of Illinois Press, 1990), 176. Steven Hahn, *A Nation Under Our Feet: Black Political Struggles in the Rural South from Slavery to the Great Migration* (Cambridge: Harvard University Press, 2003), 245, discusses localities where black landownership grew in the postbellum decades.

61. Evsey C. Domar, "The Causes of Slavery and Serfdom: A Hypothesis," *Journal of Economic History* 30, no. 1 (1970): 18–32.

62. Eric Rauchway, *Blessed Among Nations: How the World Made America* (New York: Hill and Wang, 2006).

63. *Philadelphia Inquirer*, September 28, 1878.

64. Harriet Friedmann, "World Market, State, and Family Farm: Social Bases of Household Production in the Era of Wage Labour," *Comparative Studies in Society and History* 20, no. 4 (1978): 545–86.

65. Frederick Jackson Turner, "The Significance of the Frontier in American History," paper presented to the American Historical Association, Chicago, July 12, 1893. For a modern critique of the legacy of this ideological moment, see Greg Grandin, *The End of the Myth: From the Frontier to the Border Wall in the Mind of America* (New York: Metropolitan Books, 2019).

66. Jackson Lears, *Rebirth of a Nation: The Making of Modern America, 1877–1920* (New York: HarperCollins, 2009), chaps. 6 and 7. See also Daniel Immerwahr, *How to Hide an Empire: A History of the Greater United States* (New York: Farrar, Straus, and Giroux, 2019).

67. Edward W. Barber, *The Vermontville Colony: Its Genesis and History, with Personal Sketches of the Colonists* (Lansing, Mich.: R. Smith, [1897]), 2.

68. Edwards, et.al., *Homesteading the Plains* demonstrates, however, that the proportion of uncompleted Homestead claims, at about one-third of the total, was considerably lower than the figure of three-fifths frequently cited in modern accounts.

69. Gavin Wright, "American Agriculture and the Labor Market: What Happened to Proletarianization?" *Agricultural History* 62, no. 3 (1988): 182–209.

70. See, for example, Dianne Creagh, "The Baby Trains: Catholic Foster Care and Western Migration, 1873–1929," *Journal of Social History* 46, no. 1 (2012): 197–218.

71. Cindy Hahamovitch, *The Fruits of Their Labor: Atlantic Coast Farmworkers and the Making of Migrant Poverty, 1870–1945* (Chapel Hill: University of North Carolina Press, 1997).

72. Barclay White, "Report of Barclay White, for the Pawnee Agency Under the Joint Care of Baltimore and Illinois Yearly Meetings," *Friends' Intelligencer* (November 3, 1877): 577; Berlage, *Farmers Helping Farmers*, chap. 6.

73. Williams, *Roots of the Modern American Empire*.

9 Reconstructing North America

The Borderlands of Juan Cortina and Louis Riel in an Age of National Consolidation

Benjamin H. Johnson

Viewed from a continental perspective, the consolidation of national sovereignty in mid-nineteenth-century North America was a matter of three comparatively strong central governments, with some basis in popular sovereignty, conquering or incorporating other powers claiming sovereignty. Seen from above, as if looking down on a modern map or computer screen, one would see these three powers emerge—sequentially, the United States, Mexico, and Canada—and spread whatever colors the mapmaker chose to denote them across the continent's map. A more complicated representation might show a darkening of each color within national boundaries to represent the greater uniformity of sovereign power, as national law and authority became more uniform in the domain of their sovereignty.

Sovereignty has always been a matter of competing and contested claims. To nationalize the continent, these three states had to avoid the centrifugal forces of disunion within their boundaries (a loose confederation for Mexico, secession by New England or nullification by southern U.S. states, the persistent challenges of holding the loyalty of French Catholics in a polity controlled by English Protestants in British North America) and sometimes breakaway provinces and regions (Yucatán and Tabasco in Mexico, the Kingdom of Deseret and the Confederacy in the United States). And, of course, in a sense all three states were empires, conquering and subordinating the continent's native polities as well as occasionally fighting one another.

Canada, Mexico, and the United States were different countries born out of distinct (if interconnected) circumstances. All three were premised on the idea that legitimate sovereignty derived from the consent or support of the governed. Even Canada, which is not a republic and which Andrew Smith points out in this volume chose to remain a part of empire, emerged in the 1860s as a single state and legal system with provisions for self-government rather than the widely disparate relations that the British crown had previously conducted with the different regions and peoples. Yet despite their differences, all three governments posed similar challenges for peoples living beyond their effective reach. One of the benefits of examining national histories from border areas, the approach taken in this essay, is to draw attention to the parallel histories of seemingly different states and seemingly isolated areas and communities. Despite their distinct genealogies, reigning ideologies, and legal systems, all three of these states were intent on extinguishing competing sovereignties in the territory that they claimed as their own. Indeed, unlike the empires from which they emerged, for these nation states territoriality took on a heightened importance. For them, sovereignty meant the trinity of state, territory, and identity. As Abraham Lincoln told his Congress in 1862, in the midst of the U.S. Civil War,

> A nation may be said to consist of its territory, its people, and its laws. The territory is the only part which is of certain durability. "One generation passeth away, and another generation cometh, but the earth abideth forever." . . . That portion of the earth's surface which is owned and inhabited by the people of the United States, is well adapted to be the home of one national family, and it is not well adapted for two, or more. Its vast extent, and its variety of climate and productions, are of advantage . . . for one people, whatever they might have been in former ages.[1]

As Charles Maier and Saskia Sassen argue in different ways, this North American emphasis on the territorial aspects of sovereignty mirrors a wider development across much of the globe, in which an "enhanced concept of territory" appealed to empires and newly consolidated nation-states.[2]

By the mid-nineteenth century, these states and their insistence on destroying other claims to sovereignty within their territory posed stark challenges to peoples who used to live beyond their effective reach. On the one hand, some of these peoples engaged in military resistance, epitomized by the Indian wars of the American plains; the similar pressures by Canada on the Lakota, Métis, and others; and the difficult conquest of Apaches and Yaqui in Arizona and Sonora. Others sought incorporation on equitable terms, with Tejanos and Nuevo Mexicanos going so far as to enlist in the Union Army during the U.S. Civil War, and *caudillos* in the Mexican Northeast jostling for continued regional autonomy within a Mexican national project.

This essay focuses on two borderland regions that gave rise to regional leaders who both fought *and* embraced central governments, from the eve of the U.S. Civil War to 1885. Manitoba's Louis Riel and South Texas's Juan Cortina exhibit striking parallels: Both bore arms against the central states claiming their homeland, both justified their actions in terms of the very republican notions that undergirded those nations' claims to sovereignty, both expressed some willingness to acknowledge the legitimacy of the nations they fought against, and both held public offices in their native lands and in the United States. And both met unhappy ends for doing so: Cortina languished in jail for nearly twenty years until shortly before his 1894 death, and Riel was hanged for treason in 1885.

Riel and Cortina embraced much of the ideology of republicanism in their insistence that borderland communities display the political virtues and coherence that gave them the right to form ties with different nations as they themselves saw fit.[3] The discussions of legitimate authority and political and economic freedoms that roiled the North Atlantic world in the nineteenth century deeply shaped the communities on the peripheries of the emerging national governments of North America from which the two men emerged. This under-explored intellectual history means that the nationalization of North America represented not only a military victory of three nations over other polities, but also the eclipse of more consensual and multilateral understandings of national belonging.

Riel and Cortina remain compelling figures long after their deaths in part because their relations with the states of Mexico, Canada, and the United States reflect some of the enduring paradoxes of nation-building in North America. What political or moral valence should we attach to the nationalization of North America? Is this history a triumph or a tragedy? Neither or both? The close ties between nation-states and the rise of history as a modern academic discipline in the late nineteenth century, to say nothing of ethnocentrism, ensured that early accounts of Métis and border Mexicans dismissed people like Riel and Cortina as marginal curiosities, mere bandits, or (in Riel's case in particular) as lunatics. Younger, more inclusive nationalist accounts continued to celebrate the nationalization of the continent as a great step forward for freedom. And with good reason: in the U.S. context, Lincoln's insistence that Americans were "one people, whatever they might have been in former ages" justified not only the Union triumph on the battlefield, but also the extension of civil and political rights to the four million enslaved people liberated by that triumph. One might well tell a similar story about Juárez's defeat of Maximilian. Nations have indeed been emancipatory for their citizens.

On the other hand, these nations and the republican notions of sovereignty that served as their ideological basis were disasters for borderland peoples. This is a major argument of both the "New Western History" that emerged in the late 1980s and the more recent flowering of Native American history, whose portrayal of the United States as a settler colonialist state is the dark flip side of the celebration of the virtues of the United States as the epitome of republican (and later, democratic) governance. The insistence that the residents of a nation constituted "one people" was also the basis for the systematic destruction of native sovereignties and cultures that all three of North America's nation-states have engaged in, to an appallingly greater extent than did the colonial empires from which they emerged.[4] The nationalization of North America has brought us emancipation, the very idea of civil rights, and also tragic conquest and destruction. Lincoln's statement resonates in one way if we think of the emancipation of four million enslaved people, and in a very different, if equally strong, way if we think of Sand Creek or the Dakota War, just as the triumph of the Juaristas brought nothing good for Mexico's Indian peoples, and the exercise of Canadian sovereignty was a disaster for native peoples. Riel and Cortina take us right to the heart of this paradox: The nationalization of the continent was both triumph and tragedy.

Borderland Rebels

Although both men would one day cause tumult and divisiveness in national capitals, they were born far from the corridors of power. Juan Nepumuceno Cortina was born in 1824 in Camargo, Tamaulipas, into a prominent ranching family. His mother was one of the heirs to one of the largest land grants in the Mexican northeast, located just to the north of the Rio Bravo in what became Texas when the United States defeated Mexico in 1848. His father served as mayor of Camargo. Cortina fought with Mexican forces in their unsuccessful efforts to fend off the invading U.S. Army in 1846. Soon after the war, he moved north of the river, working for the U.S. quartermaster as a teamster and thereafter assembling his own cattle herd. In the 1850s his brother was elected tax assessor and collector for Cameron County, which included the important town of Brownsville.[5] Riel was born twenty years later, in 1844, in the young Red River settlement in the domain of the Hudson's Bay Company, near what is now Winnipeg. His family enjoyed a similar regional prominence: Louis Riel, Sr., was a political and business leader of the colony who played key roles in mobilizations against the company's regulations. The Riel family was of mixed lineage, like most of the residents of Red

River: Riel's mother's parents were some of the first European settlers in Red River, while his paternal grandparents were a French-Ojibwe family. Like his father, Riel for a time studied for the priesthood, in Quebec. He left behind his religious education, studied law for a time, worked for a while in St. Paul, Minnesota, and returned to Red River in 1868.

Conflicts over land tenure and ethnicity catapulted both men into fame. Cortina grew increasingly upset at what he regarded as Anglo American usurpation of Spanish and Mexican land grants, including his mother's. In an 1859 visit to Brownsville, he saw an Anglo deputy sheriff beating a man who had worked on his family's ranches. Cortina shot the sheriff. After fleeing to Mexico for several months, he led a paramilitary force in the capture of Brownsville, where he evened scores with newly arrived Anglos and released several ethnic Mexicans from the town jail. Here he issued proclamations defending the safety, property, and autonomy of Hispanics under Anglo-American rule.

Cortina's foes mobilized Texas Rangers, units of the Mexican Army, and parts of the United States Army (under the command of Robert E. Lee, freshly arrived from suppressing John Brown's raid on Harper's Ferry). The resulting war lasted for nearly two years, laying waste to a region half the size of Connecticut. Forced into Mexico, Cortina remained a key player, running guns to Union partisans in Texas and fighting on the side of the Juárez government in the War of the French Intervention. For a time he was a claimant to the governorship of Tamaulipas, where he continued to be the scourge of south Texas Anglo ranching barons, until Porfirio Díaz removed him from power and subjected him to arrest beginning in 1877. He remained a prisoner until shortly before his 1894 death.[6]

Cortina became a folk hero and a fixture of the history of Mexican Americans and the U.S.-Mexico border but never achieved the kind of continental and trans-Atlantic fame of Louis Riel. Riel led a similar rebellion in 1869, preventing the Canadian Confederation's appointed governor from entering the Red River district. Like Cortina, he epitomized the fears of his community that its economic independence, political power, and cultural integrity would be destroyed by an Anglo central government. At first, Riel's uprising looked to be much more successful, resulting in the creation of the province of Manitoba, with written protection for the French language and Métis landholding and political rights. Twice elected to Canadian parliament but prevented from taking his seat, Riel, like Cortina, fled to the nation to the south, where, also like Cortina, he became an officeholder (deputy sheriff) and ultimately a citizen. But the compromise in Manitoba came undone, and Métis who had moved west into Saskatchewan invited Riel back into Canada in 1884. He became the figurehead of the North-West

Rebellion the next year, was arrested upon its defeat, and was tried and executed for treason in November of 1885. Riel fought the law, and the law won.[7]

Both men mobilized and spoke on behalf of distinctive regional and ethnic communities. Both condemned Anglo avarice—Cortina described Anglos as "flocks of vampires," a phrase that may still accurately describe Texas's political class. And indeed, the later struggles of Mexican Americans, Métis, and French Canadians account for the strong historical memories of Riel and Cortina. Yet what is striking about the language of their proclamations is not so much the invocation of distinct peoplehood and oppression because of their racial difference, but rather their invocation of republican political virtues and notions of sovereignty as derived from a social contract. Canada and the United States had no right to rule them without their consent.

In the first proclamation that he issued after taking Brownsville, Cortina invoked the "sacred right of self-preservation" and described a "popular meeting with a view of discussing a means by which to put an end to our misfortunes." In the second, he similarly began by discussing the importance of deliberation, consensus, and "public opinion" in instances of violent resistance. He went to some lengths to describe the region's ethnic Mexican community as demonstrating the republican virtues of productive labor and love of liberty. "The Mexicans who inhabit this wide region," he declared, "some because they were born therein, others because since the treaty [of] Guadalupe Hidalgo, they have been attracted to its soil by the soft influence of wise laws and the advantages of a free government . . . are honorably and exclusively dedicated to the exercise of industry, guided" by the belief "that only in the reign of peace can he enjoy without inquietude the fruit of his labor."[8] Moreover, as literary scholar Alberto Varon argues, Cortina presented himself as the embodiment of republican manhood, neither cowering before his enemies nor abusing his power in the exercise of indiscriminate violence.[9]

Cortina went to florid lengths to argue that the virtues of self-government, impartially administered law, and respect for property rights and free labor were the exclusive property of no single nation or people. Indeed, against the ethnic chauvinism of his foes, he suggested that governments derived their legitimacy from respect for whoever practiced these virtues. "Ever diligent and industrious, and desirous of enjoying the longed-for boon of liberty within the classic country of its origin," he said of Mexican Americans, "we were induced to naturalize ourselves in it and form a part of the [nation], flattered by the bright and peaceful prospect of living therein and inculcating in the bosoms of our children a feeling of gratitude towards a country beneath whose aegis we would have wrought their felicity and contributed with our conduct to give evidence to the whole world that all the aspirations of the Mexicans are confined to one only, that of being freemen; and that having secured this ourselves, those of the old country, notwithstanding their misfortunes, might have nothing to regret save the loss of a section of territory."[10]

Louis Riel's proclamations invoked a very similar language of republicanism. "The Declaration of the People of Rupert's Land and the North West," issued in December of 1869 to justify the establishment of a provisional government in defiance of Ottawa's wishes, sounds at first like a tract of political theory: "Whereas it is admitted by all men as a fundamental principle that the public authority commands the obedience and respect of its subjects. It is also admitted that a people, when it has no government, is free to adopt one form of Government in preference to another to give or to refuse allegiance to that which is proposed." Because Canada had not secured the consent of the Métis community, and had dispatched a military force, Riel and his compatriots argued that "we have but acted conformably to that sacred right [the same phrase as Cortina] which commands every citizen to offer energetic opposition to prevent his country being enslaved." Legitimate sovereignty, both men suggested, lay in republican self-government.[11]

Where did Riel, Cortina, and their leading lieutenants get their republican ideology? How and why did leaders of communities far removed from national print cultures and centers of education, and with low rates of literacy, craft such detailed and eloquent statements of republicanism so clearly in conversation with the larger orbits of the English, French, and Spanish worlds? These questions are especially acute in Cortina's case: The fact that he was illiterate and the florid language of the proclamations made it easy for hostile contemporaries and even many later historians to dismiss him as a windbag or a passive vessel for the more educated.[12]

Yet in fact both men were heirs to long local traditions of republicanism, adapted to serve the needs of their communities. Starting before Riel's birth, Red River Métis had pushed for elected representation on the Council of Assiniboia, which was created by the Hudson's Bay Company to administer the law in its domains.[13] Red River Métis practiced their own form of self-government in the management of the enormous buffalo hunts in which they engaged. By the 1820s, they mounted two hunts a year, a large one at the start of summer and a smaller in fall. By the time of Riel's birth, these expeditions employed as many as 1,200 of the community's distinctive Red River Carts, and could last two months. The complicated logistics of coordinating the movement of this many people, organizing their efforts, processing the animals, and dividing the proceeds led to the development of well-articulated structures and principles of self-government outside the control of the Council or Company. There was an elected hunt leader and lieutenants, but their power lay not in written law or the machinery of state, but in their social power as representatives of the larger body of the settlement. These leaders also represented the Métis on the hunts to the outside world, especially to indigenous neighbors such as the Ojibwe and Dakota, with whom hunting parties often came into contact.[14]

Moreover, although the Red River settlement remained on the periphery of English and French print cultures alike, its residents had access to the formal debates about sovereignty raging in the Atlantic world in the age of independence. Father George Belcourt, an extraordinary Catholic missionary to the settlement, "taught Métis leaders the basic elements of liberalism with its call for the freedom of political expression and commercial intercourse." Fluent in Ojibwe as well as English and French, Belcourt had come to be a key civic advisor by the time of Riel's birth.[15] Whereas clerics such as Belcourt essentially became a part of Red River Métis society, some Red River Métis looked outward to engage Atlantic political culture in more metropolitan institutions; the bishop of Red River's St. Boniface Parish actively recruited young Métis for the priesthood, for which Riel, like his father before him, studied for a time. His seven years at the Petit Séminaire of the Collège du Montréal surely exposed him to the Catholic scholastic tradition and its Thomistic emphasis on society rather than monarchs or states as the basis of legitimate political authority. Red River Métis lived far from the centers of wealth and power but were well acquainted with the pressing questions of sovereignty roiling the larger western world.[16]

Juan Cortina and his circles were located even more centrally in debates about sovereignty. It is easy to think of Texas, the northeastern province of New Spain and later Mexico, as an intellectual backwater: It had no universities and the first printing press arrived there only in 1817. Yet the Franciscan convent of Monterrey, Nuevo León, about one hundred miles south of the Rio Grande, provided the region's elite men with an opportunity to study law, philosophy, and political theory. The men who led the movement for Mexican independence in the northeast—a region where the struggle came earlier and stronger than in most of what became Mexico—availed themselves of this opportunity, particularly crediting Franciscan Father Bellido for introducing them to critiques of monarchy even as the Spanish Bourbons sought to purge such notions from their realms. These rebels invoked the good of a community more often than the individual rights that were more important to Anglo-American republicanism. They circulated their ideas by *pronuncamientos*, or manifestos, posted in public places and intended to be read aloud and heard by the community to which they appealed. The public recitation and hearing of these pronouncements, by large groups assembled in such places as the plazas that lay at the heart of Spanish-Mexican towns, was the counterpart to the more individualistic print culture of the north Atlantic world and to the council gatherings on the Métis bison hunts.[17]

This political tradition marked Juan Cortina's pronouncements. For a supposedly illiterate man, Cortina cared an awful lot about how he presented his actions and what the borderland public thought of them. In the aftermath of his Brownsville raid, he worked closely with Miguel Peña, a revolutionary and former Mexican Army officer who published a paper in Brownsville; with Jesús Ballí, one of his most socially prominent and best-educated lieutenants, and with his own brother, José María, a former tax collector widely thought of as a cerebral counterpart to his hot-headed younger sibling. The two proclamations he released explicitly invoked public opinion, followed the general mold of early revolutionary proclamations, and were published in both English and Spanish. After having been driven into Mexico, Cortina continued to publish a series of such proclamations throughout the tumultuous 1860s, justifying his actions in the war of the French Intervention as serving the republican cause embodied in the liberal constitution of 1857. Pledging his support for Juárez and his embattled government in 1864, Cortina condemned "the invader" who installed an illegitimate government "emanating from the will of their bayonets." In 1870, he helped orchestrate the publication of a lengthy biographical pamphlet ostensibly published by "various citizens of Tamaulipas," first in Mexico City and then in Brownsville. Here he went to great lengths to rebut charges made against him by a French author writing about Emperor Maximilian's ill-fated regime. The pamphlet concluded by describing him as "a true republican soldier" who "has not shrunk from danger, when he has seen his soil profaned by the invader's foot."[18] Like Riel, Cortina went to great lengths to present himself as acting in accord with the ideas of republicanism.

Changing Flags

Taking into account these long traditions of republicanism allows us to understand the willingness of Riel, Cortina, and many of their foot soldiers to change national loyalties and citizenship. This practice is often attributed to mere opportunism by nineteenth-century observers and recent scholars alike, but as Eric Schlereth observes, many early nineteenth-century North Americans believed that the right to voluntary expatriation was a fundamental aspect of liberty. In this line of thought, articulated in eighteenth-century legal treatises by Emer de Vatel and Jean-Jacques Burlamaqui, the rights of individuals to affiliate themselves with nations to advance their own interests took primacy over the claims of nations to perpetual obedience. The United States Supreme Court recognized some rights to repatriation in 1804 and 1822, and Mexico did from its Independence. Canada wrote such a right into law in 1881, though it obviously refused to apply it to Riel. For his part, the Métis rebel made a series of desperate pleas to the U.S. consul in Winnipeg for diplomatic intervention on behalf of his rights as a citizen. The Grover Cleveland administration ignored these pleas, for which it was condemned in the U.S. Senate and press after Riel's execution. As Wilbur Bryant, a Nebraska attorney and judge argued forcefully,

> It boots little that Louis Riel was Catholic or Protestant; that he was of French or Germanic, or of Indian, or of Irish, or of Swedish extraction; that he was patriot, fanatic, imposter or madman. For such purpose, it matters not whether he be considered a John Brown, a Count Cagliostro, an Anacharsis Clootz, a Don Quixote, a George Francis Train, or a William Tell. One proposition is beyond cavil: He was, at his death, an American citizen. That undisputed fact stamped upon him a dignity which neither race, religion, character or condition could obliterate. *Civis Americanus fuit.* Forget all beside.[19]

Cortina was more open about the voluntary nature of his claims to citizenship. For all of his condemnation of Texas and U.S. authorities, he insisted on his people's claims to U.S. citizenship, and indeed mocked his foes for turning to the Mexican army to assist in suppressing his revolt. He explained that, "separated as we are, by accident alone, from the other citizens of the city, and not having renounced our rights as North American citizens, we disapprove and energetically protest against the act of having caused a force of the national guards from Mexico to cross unto this side to engraft themselves in a question so foreign to their country that there is no excusing such weakness on the part of those who implored their aid."[20] Such flexibilities exasperated Cortina's foes, as in the case of the army officer who reported that Cortina acted "at one time claiming to be an American, and at another a Mexican citizen."[21]

Cortina demonstrated that this commitment to some form of American nationalism was more then rhetorical several years later, when he and many fellow Texas Mexicans fought on behalf of the Union during the Civil War. Nearly one thousand Hispanic South Texans enlisted in the Union Army, many of them

serving in the Second Texas Cavalry, which saw action as far away as Mississippi. The Confederate draft ensured that even more Tejanos would fight for the
stars and bars. In April of 1861, prominent Cortina Lieutenant Antonio Ochoa
led the Union forces in a bloody clash in the border county of Zapata, where
his forces disavowed the allegiance to the Confederacy pledged by the county's
judge, Isidro Vela, who had ensured that not a single Union vote was cast in the
secession referendum. Vela defeated Ochoa's uprising for the time being, but, for
the next five years, Cortina and allied Tejano unionists fought the forces of the
Confederacy in South Texas by interdicting cotton shipments, killing prominent
Confederates such as Vela, and smuggling weapons to Union armies.[22]

Many observers have depicted this support of the union in anti-political terms,
as a reflection of local factionalism and straightforward self-interest rather than
of any ideology or political beliefs.[23] But self-interest and ideology are generally
tied, no less for the planters of the South or the farmers of the North than for
borderland ranchers. The clear class difference between Zapata County's Tejano
unionists and confederates colored both their political interests and their ideology. The unionists' invocation of "Old Abe, rail splitter" suggests that they saw a
kinship with the free labor ideology of the North, and the repeated complaints
of slaveholders and pro-slavery Texans about border Mexicans' racial egalitari-
anism suggest that anti-slavery ideology also had a purchase in these communities. As an Anglo visitor to Rio Grande City wrote in 1858, "This admiration
for Negroes somewhat disgusted me with the Mexicans." A pro-Confederate
Brownsville paper made a similar point in the midst of the Civil War with its
condemnation of the "lower order" of Mexican Texans as "not only abolitionists
but amalgamationists."[24]

Not all of Cortina's followers held unabashed enthusiasm for the Union, of
course. Some had great difficulty in seeing the United States as a bearer of republican virtues, whatever their doubts about the Confederacy. Teodoro Zamora,
one of Cortina's chief lieutenants, refused a commission in the Union's First Texas
Cavalry. He wrote to Abraham Lincoln, chastising him for "trying to buy the influence of Cortina and his accomplices, offering them commissions, in order to
render his supporters your supporters." But the "justice that God gave to all civilized nations" prevented Zamora from accepting the Union Army's offer.[25]

Free Trade and Borderland Republicanism

Their advocacy of free trade constituted another way in which Riel and Cortina, like other republicans, resisted the exclusive claims of central governments

to exercise sovereignty. Their critiques of mercantilist restrictions on commerce bore striking resemblance to one another, and were both deeply rooted in the republican political traditions of their regions.

The contemporary politics of trade and protectionism are so driven by the desire of capital to escape national regulation in the name of larger social good that they make it difficult to see the very different debates surrounding these issues in the late eighteenth and nineteenth centuries. The rise of republican self-government as the basis of legitimate self-government in the western world enabled agrarian and early industrial capitalism in numerous ways, including by its validation of national territoriality. As Charles Maier and Saskia Sassen have emphasized, unlike the more mobile capital and more easily relocated production techniques and technologies of our own day, an emphasis on exclusive national sovereignty worked quite well for emerging capitalism.[26] Yet republican ideology justified not only the nation-state as a political community designed to protect liberty, but also endowed individuals and (especially in Spanish republicanism) communities with the right to engage in advantageous trade, manufacture, and agriculture. There was, in other words, a realm of commerce that transcended the claims of governments. This ideology reflected the grievances of borderland communities that often felt themselves oppressed by distant and aloof governments.

Cortina and his followers were heirs to several generations of anti-mercantilist arguments offered by Spanish and Mexican republicans. Mercantilism, in which states aimed to control trade so as to foster metropolitan economic growth and to amass the largest possible stocks of precious metals, structured Spanish trade policy. The crown prohibited many local manufactures, and required all trade with the outside world to be conducted through the port of Veracruz, inconveniently located some 500 miles from the lower Rio Grande valley. Such measures chafed the residents of Spanish America. Attacks on mercantilism were major features of the anti-Spanish agitation that eventually led to the independence movements of the 1810s. In 1799, for example, the third known Spanish-language imprint published in the United States appeared in Philadelphia. It was a ninety-page tract entitled *Reflexiones sobre el comercio de España con sus colonias en America* ("Reflections on Spain's Commerce with Its Colonies in America"). The unnamed author relentlessly criticized Spanish trade policies. Invoking Scottish political economist Adam Smith, he argued that mercantilism had brought about "an absolute want of everything." Residents of places such as northern New Spain could not purchase, or could purchase only "at a most exorbitant price," such goods as "woolens, shoes, brandies, wines, and others of the same kind." Unless, of course, they violated the law and traded with more accessible American and British merchants, acts which could only "accustom themselves to depreciate the laws." Later, critics of Spanish rule who supported and instigated revolts in the 1810s similarly focused their ire on trade restrictions. These criticisms were not incidental, or merely technical matters of economic policy, but rather indicted the Spanish Crown for having betrayed its obligations to foster the welfare of Spanish Americans. What one author called "mercantile tyranny" proved that any monopoly, "*of whatever kind it may be,* carries along with it the principles of destruction, while under the influence of liberty, every thing prospers." The stifling of free trade was one way in which the crown had lost its legitimate authority.[27]

Attacks on monopolies, trading bans, and import restrictions in the name of the sovereignty of the people were not confined to the Hispanic world. "Next to a fort, arsenal, naval vessel, and military array," wrote U.S. abolitionist William Lloyd Garrison in 1847, "I hate a Custom House . . . as a matter of principle. I go for free trade and free intercommunication the world over, and deny the right of any body of men to erect geographical or national barriers in opposition to these natural, essential and sacred rights."[28] Although Garrison's declaration, made in a private letter, never reached the ears of the Red River Métis, they and their allies had made similar pronouncements for more than a generation before the Riel Rebellion. Starting in the 1830s, influential Métis traders began a campaign of withering attacks on the legitimacy of the Hudson's Bay Company monopoly. They not only argued that as natives, Métis ought to be exempt from the royal grant of monopoly privileges to the Company, but invoked wider republican critiques of monopoly and free trade. In 1846, an outright revolt against the company over its fur monopoly and control over consumer goods was narrowly averted, in larger part due to Father George Belcourt's urging the disaffected to submit their grievances to the British governor and crown.[29]

Their spokesman in England, the Red River–born William Isbister, advanced relentless critiques of monopoly in *A Few Words on the Hudson's Bay Company*, published in London. He opened the pamphlet with a dismissal of the company as "the only survivor of the numerous exclusive bodies which at one time depressed almost every branch of British commerce," made his case for the legal weakness of the company's claims, and attached petitions from European, Métis, and native Red River residents. The company's monopoly and arrest of those who sought other markets for furs and pemmican, wrote these petitioners, meant that "the natives, who are the original owners of the soil, have their energies and hopes completely paralysed and are doomed." Not only did the monopoly ensure that hard work was not rewarded, but it defied the common British practice of free trade that was "so powerfully maintained in all other possessions of our august Sovereign," as the more than one thousand native petitioners argued. The result was that the Métis and other inhabitants lived under a "kind of slavery."[30]

Economic dynamics ensured that republican notions of free trade held particular appeal for the residents of northeastern New Spain (which, of course, became the Mexican Northeast in 1821, a disputed borderland with the Texas Republic in 1836, and then the US-Mexico border with Texas annexation in 1845). Maritime and overland ties to the key commercial entrepôt of New Orleans put the burgeoning U.S. market within easy reach starting in the late eighteen century. The lower prices and higher quality of American manufactured goods and textiles was one side of the coin, while the prospect of selling cattle hides and cotton was the other. Little wonder that in 1822, when the first governor of the Mexican province of Texas, an old revolutionary, first addressed Texas's population, he declared to them that "you are free," which meant among other things that "you are going to freely engage with other nations."[31] Northeastern Mexican leaders, despite the obvious acrimony generated by the Texas Revolution and U.S.-Mexico War, consistently pushed for permissive trade regulations to allow them access to Texas and U.S. markets. Secessionist efforts such as the proposed Republic of the Sierra Madre emphasized restrictions on trade as reasons for breaking away from Mexico. In the midst of the U.S.-Mexico War, for example, discontented northern Mexicans briefly published a newspaper from Matamoros called *La República del Rio Grande y Amigo del Pueblo*. The paper's first issue urged its readers to support the secession of the Northeast and to resurrect the ill-fated Republic of the Rio Grande. "Abandon the Mexican vulture, that preys upon your vitals," it urged, "the fitting symbol of a government that has no deeper commiseration for your sufferings, than the voracious bird upon her crest feels for the serpent that writhes in his beak." The second issue consisted of a sustained attack on the Mexican tariff and a familiar invocation of the benefits that free trade with the United States would bring to residents of the Mexican northeast.[32] A few years later, when a similar group of northerners proposed a similar breakaway "Republic of the Sierra Madre," five of the twelve provisions of their plan concerned liberalizing a trade and tariff regime.[33]

Such sentiments continued after the war, though without the outright rejection of Mexican sovereignty sometimes associated with earlier efforts. Northern leaders pushed for a *zona libre*, or free zone, along the border, to allow the border strip to remain free of the tariffs that the Mexican government, like most states, relied on for its tax revenue. They enjoyed some success in convincing officials of the central government that such an allowance would better uphold national sovereignty than the doomed task of enforcing high customs duties (30 to 40 percent) along a porous border. The border area of Tamaulipas was first granted *zona libre* status in 1849, just ten years before Cortina's revolt, allowing goods destined for local consumption to be imported duty-free. The Mexican government extended similar measures to the entirety of its northern border until 1905.[34]

The economic circumstances of the Red River colony similarly made arguments over free trade central matters of the colony's politics. The Hudson's Bay Company depended on deliveries to York Factory on distant Hudson's Bay for the manufactured goods that it exchanged for furs. South of the border, the absorption of the Midwest into the United States, particularly the establishment of Fort Snelling in what became St. Paul in 1825, brought a larger and better-developed market into close proximity to the Red River settlements. As in the Mexican Northeast, residents chafed at the economic impositions of the sovereign that ruled them. American traders established posts along the 49th parallel, inviting Métis and natives to sell the furs that the Hudson's Bay Company claimed as its own. The establishment of a trading post at Pembina in 1845, located just two miles south of the border, intensified this dynamic, beckoning Métis and others to shift their operations just slightly south on the Red River. In Pembina, where many Métis soon lived, goods such as tobacco, whiskey, and sugar could be bought for less and furs, hides, and tongues sold for more.[35]

The company met this challenge by doing what it could to offer better terms of trade. Company officials also implemented more currency restrictions and "increased import duties, detentions, and searches." Matters again came to a head in 1849, when Pierre Guillame Sayer was charged with trading furs in Pembina. A crowd of three hundred armed Métis surrounded the courthouse in Fort Garry (now Winnipeg). Although the jury found Sayer guilty, the judge declined to fine or incarcerate him. Shouting "Le commerce est libre! Le commerce est libre!" among other slogans, the Métis crowd, whose organizers included Louis Riel's father, celebrated what they rightly considered to be a victory over the Hudson's Bay Company. As O. O. van Otter concludes, "[T]he Métis obviously had learned to use the rhetoric of liberalism—the arguments for representative institutions and free trade—as well as the power of its tools—the petitions laden with signatures. Their leaders, who articulated the needs and wishes of their people and enjoyed their support, understood the dominant mindset of the period."[36]

This long history of conflict over the economic controls of the Hudson's Bay Company, so closely tied to the republican ideals that circulated in Red River, found its way into the public pronouncements of the Red River Rebellion. The

"List of Rights" issued by Riel and his compatriots continued this tradition of free trade republicanism in its calls for Canada to establish "steam connection between Winnipeg and Lake Superior" and "tighter" rail links between Winnipeg and St. Paul. In calling for recognition of the right of self-rule for their own distinct political community, they were just as insistent on linking the Red River district to the rest of Canada and to the United States. The rebels also insisted that import duties on all goods besides alcohol be frozen for three years, at which point they assumed that greater integration with the rest of Canada would make for a working market. Like the Mexicans of the Northeast, the Métis rebels insisted that legitimate sovereignty respect the rights of trade as well as of formal political representation.[37]

Conclusion

The "Cortina War" and the Northwest Rebellion were bitter defeats for the border-straddling communities that gave rise to Louis Riel and Juan Cortina. Both Métis and ethnic Mexicans saw their longstanding aspirations for autonomy and self-determination replaced by violent incorporation into national communities. Later stages of the imposition of Canadian and U.S. sovereignty in Cortina and Riel's homelands saw property regimes and legal systems further marginalize ethnic Mexicans and Métis in both economic and political terms. Little wonder, then, that subsequent generations of borderlanders, discontent with these societies, saw Riel and Cortina as implacable foes of Canadian and American rule. Yet the tragedy lay not only in what befell these communities in a material sense, but also in the foreclosure of the possibility of equitable belonging that had once beckoned Juan Cortina, Louis Riel, and their countless followers.

Notes

1. Abraham Lincoln, "Annual Message to Congress [December 1, 1862]," in *Lincoln: Speeches and Writings, 1859–1865* (New York: Library of America, 1989), 403.

2. Charles Maier, "Consigning the Twentieth Century to History: Alternative Narratives for the Modern Era," *American Historical Review* 105 (June 2000): 816, 818; Saskia Sassen, "Territory and Territoriality in the Global Economy," *International Sociology* 15, no. 2 (June 2000): 372–94; Sassen, *Territory, Authority, Rights: From Medieval to Global Assemblages* (Princeton: Princeton University Press, 2006). Maier defines this notion of territoriality "as a bounded geographical space that provides a basis for material resources, political power, and common allegiance" ("Consigning the Twentieth Century," 823).

3. Historians have had a notoriously difficult time defining "republicanism" with much specificity, especially enough to distinguish it from the related but sometimes

conflicting ideas of liberalism and democracy. I use "republicanism" in this essay in a minimalist sense, to invoke the idea that legitimate governments are constituted by discrete communities that possess the civic virtues that enable rational self-rule (rather than by the force of a tyrant or the weight of tradition). Republicanism shares notions of individual autonomy and rights with the more individualistic and atomistic tradition of liberalism; in some contexts and for some authors, a republic differs from a democracy, while for others they are close cousins or democracy even the rightful heir to republicanism. As with all concepts used by historical actors and historians across broad expanses of time and place (western classical antiquity; early modern city-states in Europe; revolutionary France, Haiti, and the United States; Latin America in the early nineteenth century; numerous parts of the Atlantic world in the mid and late nineteenth centuries; and historians of the Anglophone, Hispanophone, and Francophone worlds since the 1960s), republicanism has meant somewhat different things to different people. For a history of its shifting uses and meanings (or lack thereof) in the context of United States history, see Dan Rodgers's classic essay "Republicanism: The Career of a Concept" in the *Journal of American History* 79, no. 1 (June 1992): 11–38; for an analysis of Latin American politics and political cultural that fruitfully blurs the boundaries between liberalism, republicanism, and democracy, see James Sanders, *The Vanguard of the Atlantic World: Creating Modernity, Nation, and Democracy in Nineteenth-Century Latin America* (Durham: Duke University Press, 2014); for recent long dureé histories of these three related ideas, see Helena Rosenblatt, *The Lost History of Liberalism: From Ancient Rome to the Twenty-First Century* (Princeton: Princeton University Press, 2018), and James Miller, *Can Democracy Work? A Short History of a Radical Idea, from Ancient Athens to Our World* (New York: Farrar, Straus and Giroux, 2018).

4. See, among many others, Patricia Nelson Limerick, *Legacy of Conquest: The Unbroken Past of the American West* (New York: Norton, 1987); James Brooks, *Captives and Cousins: Slavery, Kinship, and Community in the Southwest Borderlands* (Chapel Hill: University of North Carolina Press, 2002); Ari Kelman, *A Misplaced Massacre: Struggling over the Memory of Sand Creek* (Cambridge: Harvard University Press, 2013).

5. Jerry Thompson, *Cortina: Defending the Mexican Name in Texas* (College Station: Texas A & M, 2007), 8–10; Charles Goldfinch, "Juan N. Cortina 1824–1892: A Re-Appraisal," in *Juan N. Cortina: Two Interpretations* (New York: Arno, 1974), 17, 30, 33–34, 39.

6. The most thorough account of Juan Cortina's career is Thompson, *Cortina: Defending the Mexican Name in Texas*, though as its subtitle suggests, it focuses more on Cortina's impact in Texas than on his role in Mexican politics. Andrew Graybill first drew my attention to the parallels between Cortina and Riel. See Graybill, *Policing the Plains: Rangers, Mounties, and the North American Frontier, 1875–1910* (Lincoln: University of Nebraska Press, 2007), 71–81.

7. See, among many others, D. N. Sprague, *Canada and the Métis, 1869–1885* (Waterloo, ON: Wilfrid Laurier University Press, 1988); Thomas Flanagan, *Louis "David" Riel: Prophet of the New World* (Toronto: University of Toronto Press, 1978); George F. G. Stanley, *Louis Riel* (New York: McGraw-Hill, 1963); Joseph Howard Kinsey, *Strange Empire, A Narrative of the Northwest* (New York: William Morrow, 1952).

8. *Difficulties on the Southwestern Frontier* (36th Congress, 1st session, House of Representatives, Executive Document 52, 1860), 79, 80.

9. Alberto Varon, "Pronouncing Citizenship: Juan Nepomuceno Cortina's War to Be Read," in *The Latino Nineteenth Century: Archival Encounters in American Literary History*, ed. Rodrigo Lazo and Jesse Alemán (New York: New York University Press, 2016), 192, 206.

10. "Juan Nepomuceno Cortina to the inhabitants of the State of Texas, and especially to those of the city of Brownsville," House Executive Document, 36th Cong,. 1st sess., H. Exec. Doc., no. 52, ser. 1050 (Washington, D.C., 1860): 71–72.

11. "Declaration of the People of Rupert's Land and the North West," as reprinted in Raymond Huel, ed., *The Collected Writings of Louis Riel / Les Escrits Complets de Louis Riel: Volume 1* (University of Alberta Press, 1985): 42–44, quotes from 42. My depictions of Riel's ideology differ from those of some scholars. Michael Witgen characterizes the Red River and North-West rebellions primarily as adaptations of native and particularly Anishinaabeg political traditions, downplaying the extent to which their proclamations clearly trafficked in western ideas of republicanism, and ignoring altogether Riel's distancing of himself from other Métis claims rooted much more clearly in indigeneity. On the other hand, Thomas Flanagan portrays Riel as a Catholic arch-conservative, even theocrat, downplaying these clearly republican notions. Riel is a complicated figure with a long and tumultuous career, who left us extensive poetry, proclamations intended for public consumption, private letters and pleas, and records of a messianic phase. There are, perhaps, contradictions and tensions in these writings, although some of the strands—particularly republicanism and Catholicism—would likely weave together more neatly if we were to import Raul Coronado's idea of a Catholic republicanism and public sphere into French North America. See Michael Witgen, *An Infinity of Nations: How the Native New World Shaped Early North America* (Philadelphia: University of Pennsylvania Press, 2012), 360; Gerhard Ens, "Prologue to the Red River Resistance: Pre-liminal Politics and the Triumph of Riel," *Journal of the Canadian Historical Association* 5, no. 1 (1994): 111–23, especially 114–16; Flanagan, "Political Theory of the Red River Resistance," 164; Raul Coronado, *A World Not to Come: A History of Latino Writing and Print Culture* (Cambridge: Harvard University Press, 2013), esp. 213–60.

12. On other treatments of Cortina, see Thompson, *Cortina*, 250; for a recent example of dismissive treatment, see Felipe Fernéndez-Armesto, *Our America: A Hispanic History of the United States* (New York: Norton, 2014), 169.

13. Marcel Giraud, *The Métis in the Canadian West* (Edmonton: University of Alberta Press, 1986), 223–24.

14. Gerhard Ens, *Homeland to Hinterland: The Changing World of the Red River Metis in the Nineteenth Century* (Toronto: University of Toronto Press, 1996), 39–40.

15. A. A. den Otter, *Civilizing the Wilderness: Culture and Nature in Pre-Confederation Canada and Rupert's Land* (Edmonton: University of Alberta Press, 2012), 152–53.

16. For the Thomistic strain in scholasticism, see Coronado, *A World Not to Come*, especially 225–27; for the uses of this tradition in the context of struggles for independence in Spanish America, see 229.

17. Coronado, *A World Not to Come*, 33, 44–46, 175, 209, 217, 220, 298.

18. Thompson, *Cortina*, 31, 45, 47, 66; Goldfinch, *Juan N. Cortina*, 39.

19. Eric Schlereth, "Privileges of Locomotion: Expatriation and the Politics of Southwestern Border Crossing," *Journal of American History* 100, no. 4 (2014): 995–1020, especially 999, 1006; Jeremy Mumford, "Why Was Louis Riel, a United States Citizen, Hanged as a Canadian Traitor in 1885?," *Canadian Historical Review* 88, no. 2 (2007): 238–62, esp. 255; Lauren L. Basson, "Savage Half-Breed, French Canadian or White US Citizen? Louis Riel and US Perceptions of Nation and Civilisation," *National Identities* 7, no. 4 (December 2005): 369–88, 383–84; Wilbur F. Bryant, *The Blood of Abel* (Hastings, Nebraska: The Post-Gazette Company, 1887), 74.

20. *Difficulties on the Southwestern Frontier*, 72.

21. Omar S. Valerio Jiménez, *River of Hope: Forging Identity and Nation in the Rio Grande Borderlands* (Durham: Duke University Press), 229.

22. Jerry Thompson, *Vaqueros in Blue and Gray* (College Station: Texas A & M, 2000), 81, 87, 94, 97, 102; 118; 143; Valerio Jiménez, *River of Hope*, 249–50.

23. See the discussion of Confederate dismissal of Tejano Unionist sentiment in Valerio-Jiménez, *River of Hope*, 249; Clarence Clarendon's characterization of Cortina and other border Mexican unionists in Clarendon, "Mexican Unionists: A Forgotten Incident of the War Between the States," *New Mexico Historical Review* 39, no. 1 (1964): 32–39, especially 33; and Jerry Thompson's general lack of interest in exploring the ideology of Mexican pro-unionists in *Vaqueros in Blue and Gray*, passim.

24. Quoted in Valerio-Jimenez, *River of Hope*, 252, 257.

25. Alice Baumgartner, "Teodoro Zamora's Commission," *New York Times* Disunion Blog, January 6, 2014, http://opinionator.blogs.nytimes.com/2014/01/06/teodoro -zamoras-commission/ (accessed June 23, 2015). My thanks to Baumgartner for sharing her transcription of Teodoro Zamora's letterbook, from the Archivo Genaro Estrada, from which the quotes (her transcription and translation from the original Spanish) are taken.

26. See especially Maier, "Consigning the Twentieth Century to History," 821–24.

27. Quotations in *Observations on the Commerce of Spain with Her Colonies in Time of War* (Philadelphia: James Carey, 1800), 30–31, 20 (emphasis in original). Also see Coronado, *A World Not to Come*, 128–29; 153, 172. Coronado argues that the unnamed author was surely Spanish diplomat Casa Irujo.

28. Wm. Lloyd Garrison to Louisa Loring, Boston, July 30, 1847, folder 36, Ellis Gray Loring Family Papers, 1830–1919, Schlesinger Library, Harvard, A-115. Quote courtesy of Kate Masur.

29. Giraud, *Métis in the Canadian West*, 2:219–20, 234; den Otter, *Civilizing the Wilderness*, 138.

30. Andrew Isbister, *A Few Words on the Hudson's Bay Company* (London: C. Gilpin, 1846), 1, 7, 10.

31. Quoted in Coronado, *A World Not to Come*, 277–78.

32. Justin H. Smith, "La Republica de Rio Grande," *American Historical Review* 25 (July 1920): 666.

33. Plan del Campo de la Loba, September 3, 1851, reproduced in Román Iglesias González, *Planes politicos, proclamas, manifiestos y otros documentos de la Independen-*

cia al México modern, 1812–1940 (Universidad Nacional Autónoma de México, Instituto de Estudios Históricos, no. 74, 1998), 284–85.

34. Octavio Herrera Pérez, "El regimen de excepción fiscal y la formación histórica de la frontera norte de México," in Manuel Ceballos Ramírez, ed., *Encuentro en la frontera: mexicanos y norteamericanos en un espacio común* (Tijuana: Colegio de la Frontera, 2001), 199, 204; Sonia García Ochoa, "Baja California: Historia de la Zona Libre," *El Sol de Tijuana*, July 27, 2009; Samuel E. Bell and James M. Smallwood, "Zona Libre: Trade and Diplomacy on the Mexican Border, 1858–1905," *Arizona and the West* 24, no. 2 (1982): 119–52.

35. Giraud, *Métis in the Canadian West*, 212–14.

36. Den Otter, *Civilizing the Wilderness*, 151, 158–59.

37. Den Otter, *Civilizing the Wilderness*, 148–50, 156–57; Ens, "Prologue to the Red River Resistance," 116; see provision 20 in the "List of Rights" issued December 8, 1869, as reproduced at http://www3.sympatico.ca/rd.fournier/inter.canada/doc/metis1.htm.

10   City Sovereignty in the Era of the American Civil War

Mary P. Ryan

To the citizens of San Francisco, California, the issue that divided the eastern United States along the Mason-Dixon line was not always the preeminent political concern. One prominent San Francisco politician put it this way: "What do we in California have to do with slavery. Really nothing." Local journalists sometimes spoke of "the national struggles" as an annoying distraction from more pressing municipal matters. George Foster Kelley, a resident of Santa Rosa, California, had a different quarrel related to the issue of sovereignty. In 1863, he took it all the way to Washington. As Kelley spun the tale, a five-dollar bribe to the doorkeeper at the White House secured him a private audience with Abraham Lincoln. Disavowing any "personal or sectional interest," he informed the President that a "deadly struggle between Democracy and Despotism" was underway in the state of California. The issue was neither slavery nor preservation of the Union, but another dispute about federal policy, what he called the "malfunctioning of the preemption act of 1841." Kelley's grievance concerned the granting of title to a portion of the land ceded to the United States by Mexico after the war of 1846–48. Kelley had been unable to secure such title. He laid blame for this unhappy outcome on the local rather than the federal government, what he called "the Land Stealing Department of San Francisco."[1]

Kelley's unhappiness, a mere archival curiosity perhaps, suggests that the struggle over Western land could sometimes obscure the sectional drama unfolding in the East. From 1846 until well after the Civil War, the shores of San Francisco Bay were the site of a contest over sovereignty that was in some ways more complicated than the assertion of states' rights by the slave South. Citizens of Mexico and of the United States—George Kelley was just one of many—had to navigate multiple levels of government in order to exercise what they claimed as their inalienable rights to landed property. Neither the President of the United States, nor any other federal or state authority for that matter, proved to be a dependable and ultimate arbiter of land titles.

While San Franciscans were neither unaware of nor untouched by the sectional warfare back east, their distinctive local perspective on the events of the

1860s deserves attention. Their story helps us slip free of what geographer John Agnew has called the "Territorial Trap," whereby history is seen to transpire only in relation to institutional boundaries, usually those of the nation, where power descends from a single center of government, most often the capital of the centralized state. This chapter proceeds in another direction. Following political geographers like Neil Brenner, it assumes that sovereignty is usually multifarious, played out on competing scales of authority including the municipal, the state, the federal, and the global. Of these various sites of sovereignty, the municipal is perhaps the least recognized by historians. Yet what is called the "local state" demands scrutiny, especially at a moment in history when most of the world's population lives in cities, and when globalization, neoliberalism, and massive migration appear to be eroding the power of the nation state. This "rescaling" or "rezoning" of sovereignty is not exclusive to the contemporary period but had intriguing precedents along the shifting border between Mexico and the United States in the nineteenth century. Sovereignty over the lands around the San Francisco estuary was particularly ambiguous and unstable in the era of the American Civil War.[2]

The historiography of the American Civil War often reduces the multiple layers and shifting contours of sovereignty to the opposition between the Union and States' Rights, the two positioned along the geographical poles of North and South. This political geography, however reflective of the most traumatic event in the nation's history and the source of America's painfully stubborn racial divide, simplifies the very complicated and fluid patterns of sovereignty characteristic of the antebellum United States. To forge a federation of states out of the English colonies required Herculean effort from the nation's founders, who devised and balanced multiple levels and locations of political authority. James Madison described the results of the political calculations and debates at the Constitutional Convention as a "compound republic" that first divided sovereignty and then sliced it up into functional units. As he put it in Federalist 51, "In the compound republic of America, the power surrendered by the people, is first divided between two distinct governments, and then the portion allotted to each, subdivided among separate and distinct departments."[3] Recounting how this fragile scaffolding of sovereignty collapsed under the weight of slavery is the major concern of nineteenth-century American historiography.

This essay takes that history into an important back channel. First of all, it courses west following an important tributary to the ultimate national conflict, the disputes over the territory acquired from Mexico in 1848. Focusing in on the far shores of the continent where the City of San Francisco was founded, it will introduce another complicating factor into the history of sovereignty in America, that considerable token of governmental authority delegated to neither the states nor the federal government but to municipalities. The citizens and politicians of the City of San Francisco demonstrated how this third plane of sovereignty was a separate but related site of conflict in the decades defined as "the Era of the Civil War." At this level of sovereignty, the most contentious issue was not slavery but property, not labor but land. The many twists and turns in this side-story of the Civil War era can be ordered into four acts. This drama's first act covers the years before California was admitted to the Union, in 1850, and will depict how the Spanish and Mexican settlers of the San Francisco Bay area selectively implemented, adapted, and ignored the land policies of (first) the Spanish Crown and (second) the Republic of Mexico. Act II, commencing in 1851, tells of the period when the U.S. federal government took on direct oversight of land titles in the Western Territories. The United States Land Commission investigated hundreds of Mexican land grants, considering each case in a careful and judicious fashion, a process substantially completed by 1856. It is in Act III that the story of sovereignty goes awry. Beginning in 1857, the city of San Francisco contested the decisions of the Land Commission; dissents, appeals, reversals, and indecisions overwhelmed the municipal council and the state and federal judiciaries, in a massive imbroglio continuing until well after the Civil War. Act IV returns to local ground to take stock of the palpable material consequences of this long quarrel over sovereignty and how it shaped the landscape of one American city.

Act I, 1846–1850: The Local Sovereign:
Mexican *Ayuntamiento* and American Town

Locating this investigation near San Francisco Bay puts the notion of sovereignty to an especially strenuous test. As late as the 1830s, the settlements in the region operated almost like stateless societies. The Spanish never established a secure outpost of empire in the more northern reaches of Alta California. When the leaders of the Spanish expedition of 1776 deserted the flimsy Presidio of San Francisco, the small band of soldiers and settlers who remained quickly scattered to more salubrious sites and more productive ranch land. Without interference or authorization from external authorities, the first families created a kind of polity by simply living together in adjacent physical places. Some of the early settlers who gave their names to the streets and neighborhoods of San Francisco, such as José Jesús Noé, Francisco De Haro, and José Cornelio Bernal, made homes around the ruins of the old Franciscan Mission and gave their impromptu village the name, *Establecimiento de Dolores*. Although no state or constitution authorized this settlement,

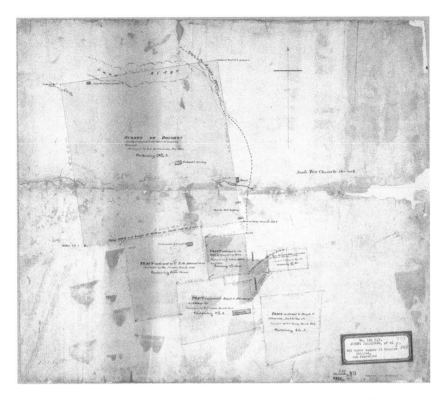

Figure 1. *Survey of 400 varas square in Mission Dolores: San Francisco, Calif.* Land Case Map D-913A. Courtesy of the Bancroft Library, University of California, Berkeley.

the founding families shaped Dolores in rough conformity to the Mexican towns of their birth, places like the town of Pitic in the Mexican province of Sonoma, laid out around a plaza some two hundred years before (see Figure 1).[4]

Scholars of other places in Latin America have used the term *vecindad* (roughly, "neighborhood-ness") to designate the informal way of establishing citizenship and of making cities, even shaping nations. The term nicely captures the informal, local process giving shape to rudimentary urban spaces on the San Francisco Peninsula.[5] When an international port grew up around a quiet inlet of the Bay a few miles north and east of Dolores, it was the result of the same local, ad hoc method of taking up land. The founders of this second settlement, however, brought a more diverse experience of place-making to the shores of the Pacific. The first to take up residence in the area of present-day downtown San Francisco included an enterprising dairy farmer, Juana Briones, her friend the

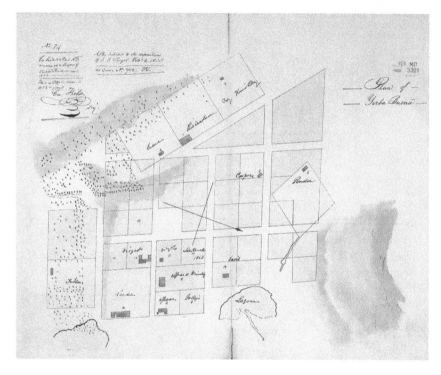

Figure 2. Jean Jacques Vioget, *Plan of Yerba Buena* [1839?]. Maps of private land grant cases of California. Courtesy of the Bancroft Library, University of California, Berkeley.

runaway British sailor Guillermo Ridley, and San Francisco's first map maker, Juan Vioget, from French Switzerland. What these urban pioneers had in common was their dependence on seafaring commerce. Be they innkeepers, sailors, or ship captains, they chose to settle near the most advantageous harbor, a place called Yerba Buena Cove (see Figure 2).

For the next half-century, the local *vecinos* were virtual sovereigns of the territory within the Golden Gate. When Mexico won independence from Spain in 1821, however, the denizens of Dolores and Yerba Buena were formally incorporated into the Republic of Mexico, which had its own complex scale of sovereignty. In keeping with the liberal Spanish constitution of 1812, the new Republic of Mexico created a federal system that divided sovereignty between the nation-state and separate provinces, and then diluted authority further by delegating considerable power to municipalities. Sovereignty in the province of Alta California was thereby partitioned into the separate offices of the governor, the regional legislature (the *deputacíon*) and the local municipality (the *ayuntamiento)*, with its mayor (the *alcalde)* and town councilmen (the *regidores*). In 1835, the governor of the far Northern province, José Figueroa, got around to decreeing that the port of Yerba Buena be marked off as a *pueblo* with a formal government, the *ayuntamiento*. Ranchers and farmers came from around the Bay to elect local officials, the *alcalde* and two *regidores*. The officers of the *ayuntamiento* met irregularly over the next decade, either at the Presidio or at Mission Dolores. A chief order of business was to divide the land once overseen by the Franciscans in trust for the local Indians into loosely bounded parcels of varying sizes, the private property of individual Mexican families.[6]

While the Mexican Republic established elaborate procedures for distributing land, the local government exercised control over the actual process. Individual citizens petitioned the *alcalde*, or a justice of the peace, for a grant of land (called an *informe*); if approved by the local authority and documented by an *expediente* (formal document) and a diseño (a rather impressionistic graphic representation of property lines, as shown in Figure 3), the grant was forwarded to the governor of Alta California for approval. The settlers who were granted land on the San Francisco Peninsula were likely to know the *alcalde* or the governor as a neighboring rancher, or even a relative. This slow deliberate process carved up the land around San Francisco Bay area into a piebald expanse of private property, while retaining reserves for communal purposes such as common pasturage and waterfront. By the 1840s the *vecinos* of Dolores and Yerba Buena had become Mexican citizens, some presiding over large ranchos around the Bay, parcels as large as 100,000 acres, others holding titles to small *solars* (house lots) near the abandoned workshops of Mission San Francisco de Asís. Most all of them had arrived in Alta California as humble migrants from the Mexican provinces of Sonora and Sinaloa. By the 1840s, a second generation of colonists was pasturing large herds of cattle on the nearby ranches, trading hides and tallow in Yerba Buena, and socializing in the village of Dolores.

The leading San Franciscans had by now grown weary of the distant and erratic Mexican authority, and some expressed an interest in affiliating with the nation of either Great Britain or the United States.[7] When a ship of the United States Navy sailed through the Golden Gate in July of 1846, it consequently met little resistance. The official transfer of land from the Mexican Republic to the United States in 1848 was perhaps the most straightforward and orderly act in the long ensuing quarrel over sovereignty. It was worked out according to international law as implemented by the Treaty of Guadalupe Hidalgo. Both parties agreed that the "law of nations" or the "laws of war" protected the land rights of

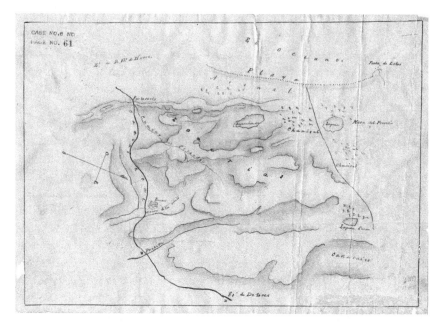

Figure 3. [*Diseño del Rancho San Miguel: San Francisco, Calif.*] [1857]. Maps of private land grant cases of California. Courtesy of the Bancroft Library, University of California, Berkeley.

the conquered peoples. In addition to guaranteeing the land grants Mexico had issued to individuals, the treaty left any established municipal government and its associated public property undisturbed. The U.S. citizens who began to stream into the former Mexican territory were obliged to operate within the rules of the *ayuntamiento*, including its procedures for distributing land. Once the Americans had raised the stars and stripes, they elected one of their number, Washington Bartlett, *alcalde* and began practicing local self-government under the very loose oversight of the U.S. military. The *ayuntamiento* began distributing land at a slow pace, as some Mexican citizens exchanged their lots for small amounts of cash, from twenty-five pesos to six dollars, and on occasion for a bottle of brandy.[8]

Eight days after the Treaty of Guadalupe Hidalgo was signed, gold was discovered in the foothills of the Sierra Nevada. Tens of thousands of people, mostly young men, rushed for the goldfields, creating havoc in Yerba Buena *pueblo*, which the American *alcalde* hastily renamed San Francisco. An immense new trade in ship-borne goods changed the nascent city, as did the emergence of land speculators. San Francisco's first real estate boom commenced. The owners of large outlying ranches, including former officials of the Mexican *ayuntamiento*, such as *alcaldes* Francisco De Haro and José Jesús Noé, purchased lots near the booming port at Yerba Buena. The Yankees called Noé's lot along the plaza a real estate office. Naturalized Mexican citizens such as Guillermo Richardson, Juan Vioget, and a West Indian merchant named Guillermo Leidesdorff all bought up prime land near the dock of the bay. A tidal wave of land and lot seekers came ashore in the rush for gold. One Henry Fitch, who arrived in October 1849, and who may be taken to represent a whole class of newcomers, declared unequivocally, "The sale of Real Estate [is] my principle employment."[9]

The most politically astute of these urban frontiersmen arrogated "sovereign" authority unto themselves. They gathered in the old Mexican plaza to draft a series of town charters and to organize a state constitutional convention. To the extent that the instant city was governed at all, such governance was the work of a succession of self-appointed and competing town councils, given little direction from Washington or anywhere else. The new Californians promptly auctioned off hundreds of lots in the old Mexican plaza.[10] The *ayuntamiento* of 1849 was particularly loose with the public domain. Scores of lots were sold by *alcaldes* George Hyde and Thaddeus Leavenworth, and by a justice of the peace, G. Q. Colson. It was not hard to sympathize with the practical dilemma faced by Leavenworth and Hyde, the first a former Episcopal minister and the second a Mormon émigré. With the town council gone to the gold fields, and in the absence of standard currency or banks, the municipal officials paid basic expenses with deeds to land in the public domain (typically, lots of fifty square *varas*, or less than half an acre). Leavenworth reputedly paid the rent on his office in this way, with the currency of the boom town, small parcels of real estate. In 1849, at the peak of the rush to the goldfields, *Alcalde* Leavenworth executed the sale of fifty-one lots and, like his successor *Alcalde* Hyde, soon was hounded from office by irate citizens and competing land speculators.[11]

A higher authority soon voided these profligate *alcalde* sales. Horace Hawes, appointed to serve in the Mexican office of Prefect of the Legislative Assembly of the Territorial Government of California, bluntly informed the San Francisco town council that "the sales made by the *Ayuntamiento* to any one of their own body, since the first of August last, are disapproved." Hawes had inherited his office from the *Diputación del Partido de San Francisco*.[12] Like the *ayuntamiento*, the *diputación* represented a legitimate scale of sovereignty within the Mexican constitution, and in keeping with international law it was to continue to exercise authority during the transfer of power from the Mexican to the U.S. government. Acting according to the concept of sovereignty as he might have learned it in his native state of New York, Hawes proceeded to assume his superiority over the local magistrates in San Francisco. The municipal officials, however, did not agree with his interpretation of constitutional law. Instead, they commissioned the city attorney, A. C. Peachy, to contest Hawes's judgment that the sale of public lands was illegal. Fortified with Peachy's argument, the Council defied Hawes and the authority of the territorial government. Declaring the Prefect's decree a "high handed act of usurpation," they countercharged that Hawes had himself illegally purchased lots from the impeached Justice of the Peace Colson, and they proceeded to schedule another sale of land.[13] Alarmed that "we have not a dollar in the public treasury," the next *alcalde,* John Geary, exchanged 262 water lots for a "fee and town sale."[14]

The units of San Francisco real estate became political footballs, tossed between the city and territorial officials. In April 1850, Peter Burnett, the ad hoc governor of California (still a territory, five months away from being granted statehood) supported Hawes's suspension of San Francisco land sales. But then he had second thoughts. "A much larger amount of municipal funds could be raised," he reasoned, "if said lands were sold to the highest bidder." Burnett fired Hawes and approved the resumption of a public auction of the land and water lots around San Francisco harbor. In authorizing the municipal sale of parts of the public domain, the Governor aimed simultaneously to shore up the city's finances and to advance the economic growth of California. He warned that "the uncertainty in which many of the titles are involved has had the effect of late to prevent capitalists from investing money in real estate in the city and forcing many to invest in other places."[15]

The confused state of sovereignty caused alarm among politicians as well as capitalists. It was hard to find a site of decisive legal authority amid all the competing sovereignty scales—the *ayuntamiento,* the *diputación,* the U.S. military, the office of the territorial government, and town councils whose members often ran off to the gold fields. Nonetheless, even before California was formally admitted into the Union on September 9, 1850, the desirable land around the harbor had all been recast as a grid of private property and sold to the highest bidders. Once state government had been established, municipal leaders drafted a new city charter and resumed the sale of the remaining public lands. Even before California was admitted to the union, the city announced "250 fifty vara Town Lots to be sold at Public Auction on Friday the 10th instant." The new city council commissioned an engineer named M. C. Eddy to provide a proper survey of the municipal land. He divided all the space within the boundaries established by the charter of 1851 into 1,400 lots (see Figure 4). An inventory of land sales between 1842 and 1850 counted a total of 2,646 lots sold.[16]

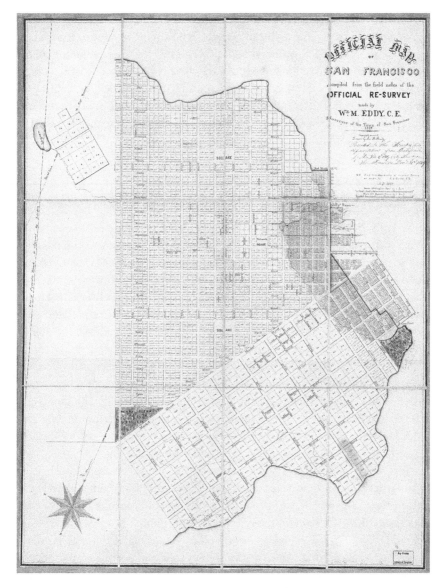

Figure 4. *Official Map of San Francisco compiled from the field notes of the official re-survey made by Wm. M. Eddy, surveyor of the town of San Francisco*, 1849. Courtesy of the Library of Congress, Geography and Map Division, Washington, D.C.

All these real estate transactions demonstrated, among other things, that wily individuals could capitalize on the uncertainties of sovereignty during the transition from Mexican to U.S. governance. If power rested anywhere amid the chaos of the Gold Rush, it was on the ground at the time and in the place where savvy pioneers could take advantage of local political opportunities. But ominous questions were being raised. Were any of the titles to real estate in San Francisco valid under U.S. law? And, could either astute capitalists or responsible political leaders tolerate such diffuse and ambiguous sovereignty?

Act II: Federal Intervention

The selling of San Francisco had proceeded at a furious pace for half a decade but without the sanction of the federal government of the United States. Preoccupied with rising tensions between the slave and free states, neither Congress nor the President rushed to formulate a policy regarding the lands acquired from Mexico. This period of neglect allowed land-hungry newcomers to cover the San Francisco Peninsula with a ragged patchwork of conflicting titles. Finally in August 1851, federal authorities created the United States Land Commission and added a questionable innovation to the practices of international law: The Mexican citizens of Alta California were required to appear before federally appointed judges to prove that they held legitimate title to the land they occupied, often for two generations. In September of that year, three commissioners, all Whigs, from the states of Vermont, New Hampshire, and Alabama, arrived in San Francisco to investigate Northern California land titles. Accompanying them was William Casey Jones, the Commission's agent, who was charged with the formidable task of assembling documentation of the Mexican land grants.[17]

The Commission called scores of witnesses and subjected them to exhausting interrogation and cross-examination, in one case demanding answers to 172 questions. The majority of those subject to the commission's scrutiny were Spanish-speaking *Californios*, many of them with limited education. Even the second *alcalde* of Yerba Buena, José Jesús Noé, was intimidated by the process. His lawyer recalled asking Noé in 1852 "if he was afraid his title would not be confirmed—he answered that at the first he was afraid, for that when he first got his papers they were incomplete." Less prominent witnesses must have been even more anxious. Maria Sota, who signed her deposition with a mark, testified that she had dutifully improved her land in compliance with Mexican policy, but was unable to protect her home from squatters "since the hoisting of the America flag" and "the revolutionary state of the country." Her neighbor, Can-

dalario Bernal, was befuddled by the commission's questions and pleaded igno-
rance of English.[18]

The members of the Commission regularly accepted the testimony of Spanish speaking witnesses when written documentation was sparse. At the same
time, they conducted an exhaustive search for written records to support Mexican grants. Agent Jones assiduously tracked down "the great mass of old papers
which were stored in the back room" of the *alcalde*'s office in Yerba Buena. He
journeyed to the archives of the Alta California capital at Monterey in search
of *expedientes* and *informes* and searched far back into Mexican and Spanish
history for relevant precedents. Several commissioners had some knowledge of
Mexican law, and those who did not enlisted local expertise. Guillermo Hartnell,
who had spent decades trading European goods at the missions and ranchos,
was particularly skillful at mediating among *Californios* and *Americanos*. Some
thought that Hartnell, like so many of the naturalized Mexicans of Alta California, had gone native. In appearance "white," speaking Spanish, married to a
Mexican, and known to wear a blue serape and to ride on a Mexican saddle, he
presented an identity confusing on many levels to recent immigrants from the
United States.[19]

American lawyers often played a hand in securing Mexican land titles. The
firm of Halleck, Peachy, and Billings aggressively solicited *Californio* clients.
They courted business in a form letter, under the date April 21, 1851, that warned
Mexican citizens to act quickly or "las tierras deberán pasar al dominio del Go-
biérno de los Estados Unidos." At the bottom of the page, the American lawyers
listed twenty-five satisfied clients and testifiers to the firm's integrity, most with
Spanish surnames and a few with hybrid names, such as Guillermo Howard of
San Francisco. The firm took on clients from around San Francisco Bay and
carefully collected evidence on their behalf. The file for Presentación Ridley, of
Yerba Buena, contained municipal records from the original *expediente* signed
by Governor Alvarado, through evidence of subsequent sales confirmed by *Alcalde* Francisco De Haro, to an order of the *ayuntamiento* of 1845 ejecting poach-
ers from her property. The Bernal file was even heftier. It included documents
signed by two governors of Alta California—Figueroa and Alvarado—and
excerpts from the Mexican laws of colonization. The legal skill and obsessive
document hunting of lawyers like Halleck, Peachy, and Billings have to be accounted among the reasons that most Mexican titles were confirmed by the U.S.
Land Commission. Fully three-fourths of Mexican citizens, be they owners of
large ranches, homesteads in Dolores, or warehouses in Yerba Buena, had their
titles approved.[20]

Grants to individual Mexicans, however, accounted for only a fraction of the lands at issue. At the end of the Mexican-American War, vast acreage on the San Francisco Peninsula remained open; often it was used as communal pasturage, some of it having been appropriated by Indian *rancherias*, most of it uninviting to settlers—covered in sand dunes, chaparral, and sage. According to the American constitution, this land, acquired from Mexico but not deeded to individuals or to corporate entities, was the possession of the federal government (an exception to the constitutional delegation of land matters to the states). The leading landowners and their allies in the municipal government of San Francisco had other ideas and were not about to let this bounty pass out of local control. On February 11, 1854, the city came before the Commission claiming title to a huge chunk of real estate. This was the last item on the docket of the U.S. Land Commission for the Northern District of California; it generated hundreds of pages of depositions. Known as the Pueblo Case, it represented both the most substantial tract of disputed real estate considered by the Commission and the most anomalous land title.

Consistent with international law, the appellants in the case argued that upon a transfer of sovereignty from one nation to another, any pre-existing municipality enjoyed continued control over any public land within its borders. The city limits of San Francisco as set by state charter extended only a few miles beyond Yerba Buena Cove. Such a small tract of real estate would not satisfy the tax-starved municipal government. The city decided on a colossal land grab, declaring its territory to include, "So much of the peninsula where on the said City is located as will contain an area equal to four leagues square, said parcel or tract being bounded on the North and East by the water of the Bay of San Francisco on the West by the Pacific Ocean and the South by a due East and West line including the Area aforesaid" (see Figure 5).[21]

The city advanced this claim to over 250,000 acres by an awkward and ironic legal maneuver. It deployed Spanish and Mexican law in order to justify the claim. If it could be proven that the City of San Francisco was an extension of a legitimate Mexican pueblo, then the municipality held title to all the unoccupied land extending out from its center to such limits as would encompass four square leagues.[22] On the surface, the question before the Commission was fairly simple: Did Mexican law and the practice of the *Californios* establish a legitimate municipality under the name San Francisco? If so, what were its geographical boundaries? But translating the land policies of one nation into those of another, particularly when the sovereignty of each was fractured into different levels and domains of authority, was not a simple matter. A regiment of lawyers proceeded

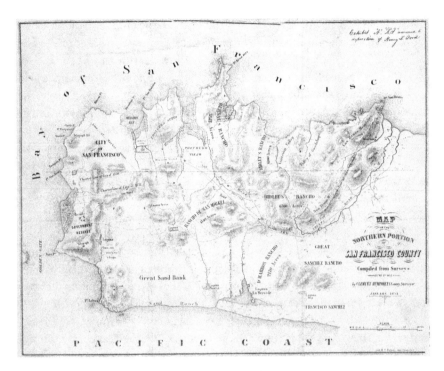

Figure 5. Clement Humphreys, *Map of the Northern Portion of San Francisco County: Compiled from Surveys, June 1st 1852* [1853]. Land Case Map E-922. Maps of private land grant cases of California. Courtesy of the Bancroft Library, University of California, Berkeley.

to assemble evidence in support of the city's position. They came before the U.S. Land Commission with piles of documents that reached back to the sixteenth-century Law of the Indies. Peachy sent his partner Billings to the Alta California archives in Mexico to unearth records of the actual meetings of the *ayuntamiento* held at Mission Dolores. Billings came back with what he thought was primo facie evidence that San Francisco was a pueblo. Accordingly Peachy argued that "[t]he Common Council has traced its origins to the *Ayuntamiento* alternatively called 'San Francisco de Asís' after the Mission, 'El Puerto de San Francisco' and 'Establecimiento de Dolores,' or 'Paraje de Yerba Buena.'"[23]

While the town council accepted Peachy's conflation of "San Francisco," "Dolores," and "Yerba Buena," the Land Commission was less credulous. They heard counter evidence from longtime residents of Yerba Buena, including Guillermo Richardson, the major candidate for the honor of founding an international port on San Francisco Bay, at his dock at Yerba Buena Cove. To the question, "Was any place ever known as the pueblo or town of San Francisco in California before the month of July A.D. 1846?" Richardson responded with an emphatic, "Not any." He recalled that annual elections of an *ayuntamiento* were sometimes held at Dolores, but not anywhere near the town of his residence, Yerba Buena. The name "San Francisco" was attached to the bay or its far-flung surrounding settlements and ranchos, not to any discreet, clearly bounded plot of land or settlement. Richardson's sense of geography was closer to the way the *vecinos* of Alta California had defined political space. Asked to identify a plan of Yerba Buena "adopted by the Mexican Government" Richardson replied that "[t]here was [a] plan made in 1839 but not by the government or the authorities. It was made by order of the people of the town and under a survey made by Captain Vioget."[24]

The Land Commissioners might have had Richardson's firsthand account in mind when they ruled that while the City of San Francisco had originated in a pueblo, it was centered in Yerba Buena, and its borders did not extend beyond the limits established in the San Francisco Charter of 1851 (along Larkin Street to the west and Mission Creek to the south). They might also have had nationalist reasons for awarding the outlying lands to the United States rather than to San Francisco. They were Whigs, after all, federalist in ideology and with a long-standing concern for the economic development of America as a nation-state. The sectional crisis of the 1850s had destabilized the second-party system, leaving the Whigs, like Free Soilers and some Democrats, looking to the territory ceded by Mexico as a counterweight to the slave-holding South. These Union partisans also had a major material stake in the land acquired from Mexico. If it was determined that the disputed land did not constitute a Mexican pueblo of four full leagues, the bounty of the region surrounding the booming port of San Francisco would have fallen under the sovereignty of the Federal Government, its to conserve, to distribute to private buyers, or to dispense as incentives for economic development, for example, as grants to private railroad corporations.

The ruling of the Land Commissioners drew a line literally in the sand, cutting off San Francisco's access to revenue from the sale of the dusty, arid hinterland on its southern and western borders. That line also was drawn in dollar signs. According to the United States Preemption Act of 1841, federal land could be put up for sale at the modest price of $1.25 an acre, far less than the going rate within the boundaries of the 1851 charter of San Francisco. A whole new set of land lusters lined up along the city limits. Municipal politicians greedy for tax revenue from further sales of public land allied with those who held disputed titles issued by the city and faced off against newcomers (called squatters or, more politely, "actual settlers") who coveted preemption claims to outlying land. These new-comers included everyone from small time farmers to stockholders in large en-terprises, those who could afford to buy up federal land in the 160-acre portions specified by the Preemption Act. The contested border became a legal battle line between local, state, and federal governments, all, again, claiming sovereignty.

Act III: *The City of San Francisco v. the United States*

The municipal leaders of San Francisco did not quietly submit to a ruling from a federal commission. They promptly appealed the Land Commission's decision and prepared an arsenal of arguments to take into battle against the federal sov-ereigns, first before the highest court of the State of California and then on up the judicial ladder to the United States District, Circuit, and ultimately Supreme Courts. The first appeal of the Land Commission decision bore the blunt case name *The City of San Francisco v. the United States*. Arguing for the city, attorney John Dwinelle came to court armed like a historian of New Spain and the Re-public of Mexico. His brief was virtually a documentary history, with forty-five addenda later published under the title *The Colonial History of the City of San Francisco*. Dwinelle cited chapter and verse from medieval monarchs, the Law of the Indies, the Bourbon plan of colonization, the constitution of the Mexican Republic, and arcane Mexican documents such as the plan of the town of Pitic in Sonora, all to prove that pueblos were fundamental to Hispanic political or-ganization and routinely entrusted with vast reserves of public land—as much as fifteen square leagues in the case of Mexico City.[25]

Converting San Francisco into such an expansive pueblo required prodigious and selective readings of Hispanic law and of California precedents. To retrieve the maximum stretch of land from the clutches of the federal authority would require adroit deployment of geometry as well as history. Neither the scattered ranches of the *Californios* nor the rudimentary and ad hoc pueblos of Dolores and Yerba Buena conformed to the urban plans of sixteenth-century Spain or of nineteenth-century Mexico. To begin with, the San Francisco settlement did not extend out in an orderly fashion from one central plaza. There were at least three possible candidates for the center of the disputed pueblo of San Francisco: at the Presidio, at Mission Dolores, and at Yerba Buena. Extending the Pueblo out four leagues square from any one of these sites would place the city limits in the Bay or the Pacific Ocean. Those who argued San Francisco's case necessarily took an imaginative approach to geography. While Dwinelle "declined entering into the geometrical and arithmetical detail of Spanish regulations," he conceded that the

"the peninsula of San Francisco is of such conformations that the tide water of the Ocean and Bay present natural obstacles in every direction except towards the south. The four leagues of the Pueblo must therefore be determined by taking all the land embraced in the peninsula north of such a parallel of latitude, as, with its tide-water limits, shall include four square leagues."[26]

More than history and geography were on the line in the dispute between the City and the Land Commission. Underlying the dispute was a fundamental issue of municipal political economy. To the municipal officials, those four leagues represented private lots whose assessed value would yield the tax revenue needed to fund such basic infrastructure as grading the region's steep hills and fashioning the silt, sand, and mud of Yerba Buena Cove into a functioning international harbor. Therefore, Dwinelle skipped those sections of Spanish and Mexican law that reserved large swathes of pueblo land for communal purposes. He made no reference to the 200 *varas* of shoreline that Mexico had reserved for public use on San Francisco Bay and ignored the Bourbon reforms and policies of California Governor José Figueroa, who had hoped to reserve land for the local Indians. Dwinelle focused instead on the campaign of the Mexican Republic after 1821 to encourage private ownership in land, citing such examples as the grants to Noé in Dolores, Bernal in the southern ranchos, and Vioget in Yerba Buena. To further his argument, Dwinelle imaginatively translated various terms relating to the Spanish and Mexican conceptions of municipal government. The *ayuntamiento* was a town council, he asserted; Spanish categories of public land, such as *ejidos* and *propios*, were "vacant suburbs"; and the plan of Pitic was "a perfect paraphrase of . . . an Anglo-American City Charter."[27] The lawyers for San Francisco had artfully combined principles of urban land distribution drawn from two different nations: the practices of municipal sovereignty in the United States and the customary dimensions of the Mexican pueblo. Combining these different land policies of the two nations entitled the city government to convert a great stretch of the San Francisco Peninsula into a source of municipal revenue, through either the direct sale of land or the collection of property taxes.

The first confrontation between the city and the federal government ended in a draw. Both sides appealed the initial decision of the Land Commissioners; the United States denied the existence of a pueblo, and the city claimed a full four leagues of surrounding land. This was in 1857, when the government in Washington was preoccupied with the sectional crisis and let their appeal lapse. The lawyers for the City of San Francisco presumed that they had won the Pueblo case by default and did not bother to pursue their claim for the next eight years. That was not the end of the matter, however. Squatters on the outlying lands, both small farmers and speculators from back east, took one another to court to secure individual titles to the still disputed territory. In 1860, two disgruntled claimants to the same parcel on the margins of the city argued their case before the California Supreme Court. This litigation, *Hart v. Burnett*, became the next critical test of municipal sovereignty.

The panel of three judges who heard the case conceded that "the immense interests involved" required a "laborious and careful examination" of the land practices of Spain, Mexico, and the United States. John Dwinelle came to court once again to uphold the "right which the law conferred upon . . . municipal organizations" to hold land in trust for its citizens and, if need be, to sell it for revenue. The arguments from the bench were exhaustive and the final decision ran to almost one hundred pages. Justice J. Baldwin, writing for the majority and joined by a new member of the three-judge tribunal named Stephen J. Field, rehearsed the evidence presented by Dwinelle in *The City of San Francisco v. the United States*—from minute questions of geography to broad issues of Mexican and United States Law. In its final opinion, the California Supreme Court upheld the right of the city, subject to affirmation by the state government, to control all the pueblo land. The court noted that an ordinance to this effect had already been enacted by the City of San Francisco and confirmed by the state legislature. It "was a legal and proper exercise of this sovereign power."[28]

The city won this round—a round fought before sympathetic California judges. San Francisco, deemed a pueblo, might sell or otherwise control lands as far south as Rancho Buri Buri (now the border of San Mateo and San Francisco Counties). The decision in *Hart v. Burnett* was a triumph for states' rights. On this score, two of the three judges of the Circuit Court, Baldwin and Fields, were adamant: "The pueblo lands of San Francisco were public and municipal, subject to the control of the state sovereignty, but not to that of the federal government." One sharply worded aside in the *Hart v. Burnett* decision suggests that the jurists were aware of a larger national and sectional context for their decision. The Justices observed that to transfer state land rights to the national government would be "disastrous to the United States" and "very soon it would utterly corrupt our Federal administration, and destroy our Federal organization."[29]

The decision was announced in April 1860, when the nation was about to divide along a North-South border. To challenge state sovereignty, even in far distant California, at that moment would have been politically perilous. Four years later, however, the tide of war had shifted in favor of the Union and proponents of states' rights were in retreat. Those who coveted land claimed by the city of San Francisco renewed their challenge to the decision in *Hart v. Burnett*.

The initiative came from the United States Congress, which in 1864 enacted a law to "to expedite the settlement of titles to land in California" and thereby revived the federal appeal of the Pueblo Case, sending it on to the United States Circuit Court. Arguing against the California city, attorney John Williams reinterpreted the political geography of New Spain and Mexico yet again. He contended that according to both the Spanish constitution of 1812 and the laws of the Republic of Mexico, sovereignty rested in the *Diputación* of the Northern District of Alta California, not with any single *ayuntamiento* located anywhere on the San Francisco Peninsula. Because there was no single center of municipal government from which a pueblo could extend out four leagues (again, neither at the Presidio, the Mission, or Yerba Buena), most of the land around the Bay belonged to the federal government.[30]

Williams did not persuade the United States Circuit Court. The judges marshaled precedents set by the U.S. Supreme Court to defend the interests of cities and the states in which they were located. Citing *The City of New Orleans v. the United States,* they ruled that when sovereignty passed from one nation to another (as it had between France and the United States in 1803), the state and not the federal government retained control over public lands. The argument relied on the interpretation of the Pueblo Case originally supplied by the lawyers for the city, Peachy and Dwinelle. Justice Stephen Field ruled once again in favor of municipal San Francisco. His Honor now sounded impatient: "The decision not being subject to appeal, the controversy between the city and the Government is closed, and the claims of the city stand precisely as if the United States owned the land and by an Act of Congress had ceded it, subject to certain reservations to the city in trust for its inhabitants."[31]

Yet life, and wiggle room, remained in the Pueblo Case. In *Townshend et al v. Greeley* (U.S. Supreme Court, 1866) the litigants both claimed title to one of the many lots that had repeatedly changed hands while the Pueblo Case was wending its way through the courts. The justices declined to engage in any further wrangling over Spanish and Mexican precedents and focused instead on the question of legal jurisdiction. Invoking the Judiciary Act of 1789, they maintained that the Supreme Court could only overrule the highest court of a state in the matter of an international treaty if a statute or lower court decision was "repugnant to the constitution" or in the case of conspicuous errors in the decision of the lower courts. The Supreme Court found no such grounds for overruling *Hart v. Burnett.* The ownership and control of the San Francisco Peninsula remained a state and not a federal matter. At the same time, the Court did not grant autonomy to the municipality, but rather ruled that the city was "subject to the control of the state sovereignty," a position consistent with the ruling of Chief Justice John Marshall's opinion in the Dartmouth Case of 1819. The ruling in *Townsend v. Greeley* granted California ultimate authority over the San Francisco Peninsula. Justice Field carefully calibrated the division of authority among the municipality, the state, and the federal government and put the Pueblo Case to rest in late December 1866, after almost twenty years of confused or suspended sovereignty over increasingly valuable real estate.[32]

The struggle for sovereignty was playing out in the West differently than in the Southern states, which were about to be reconstructed under the military authority of the federal government. The two sectional quarrels were not unrelated, however. Western land was a significant factor in the buildup to the Civil War. In the 1830s, President Jackson had seen the value of the Pacific port and had tried to purchase California from Mexico, and in 1846 President Polk went to war to secure that prize. When Polk appealed to Congress for an appropriation to fund treaty negotiations with Mexico in 1846, David Wilmot proposed that slavery be banned in the Western territories acquired in the process. The bitter congressional debate that followed shattered the long-standing compromise over slavery. As sectional antagonism increased in the 1850s, congressional leaders looked anxiously to the Mexico cession, concerned that their admission to the Union as new states would unsettle the precarious balance between the slave South and the free North. Meanwhile, the antislavery movement raised the standard of "free labor" and "free land" in the West as a rhetorical weapon against Southern slavery. Simultaneously, San Francisco politician Daniel Broderick made his way to the United States Senate carrying the standard of free (white) labor and the banner of "Squatter Sovereignty." In Illinois in 1856 Broderick's ally Stephen Douglas used that slogan in a debate with Abraham Lincoln. Four years later Lincoln would capture the presidency; Douglas's efforts to reconcile the sections would prove futile; West, Midwest, and East came together on the road toward civil war.

The timing of the sectional crisis looked somewhat different from the California perspective. To Peter Burnett, a Southerner who served briefly as the governor of the California territory, the coming of the Civil War was already predetermined at midcentury. Already in 1849, Burnett observed that the stability of the federal union, divided between fifteen slave and fifteen free states, was threatened by westward expansion. Fearful of toppling that fragile balance in the federal legislature, the Senate delayed admitting to the Union any of the western territories acquired from Mexico. Burnett concluded that it was "to the institution of slavery that we owe the non-establishment of government in this country." By June of 1850 Burnett had lost patience with what he called "the General Government," and joined in a call to California residents to "assemble in their sovereign capacity" and elect delegates to the state constitutional convention meeting in Monterrey. That body voted, with little fanfare, to exclude slavery from the new state. To Burnett, the path to civil war was nigh inevitable once California was admitted to the Union as a free state. The ultimate confrontation was delayed by the Compromise of 1850, thanks in large part to the legislative acumen of Stephen Douglas who carefully wedged the admission of the free state of California into the sequence of congressional acts that temporarily satisfied all the sections, North, South, and West. As for Peter Burnett, he looked even further westward, toward Asia and the Pacific where San Francisco would enjoy an "onward march to greatness."[33]

The bloody tide of the Civil War that followed also swept the Republican national agenda westward toward the Pacific shore. The Homestead Act opened yet cheaper public land in the West; a transcontinental railroad linked markets from coast to coast; the Morrill Act spread public higher education out to the frontier. In sum, the history of sovereignty between 1846 and 1866 tells a story not just of the divide between the North and the South, the Confederacy and the Union. During the same tumultuous decades, citizens and politicians, working through multiple levels of sovereignty, constructed a land bridge between the Atlantic and Pacific.

Act IV: Who Ruled the Land and Shaped the City?

The warfare over the lands along the Pacific had subsided by the end of the Civil War. The Pueblo case was retired by the Supreme Court in 1866 and all but forgotten. The last paragraph of the decision in *Townsend et al. v. Greeley* reads as follows: "From this decree the United States and the City of San Francisco appealed . . . but during the present term of this court both parties have, by stipulation, withdrawn their objection, and their respective appeals have been dismissed." Three years earlier, in 1863, the *San Francisco Alta* had already reported that its readers greeted the latest ruling in the Pueblo Case with "entire indifference" because its resolution "would not now enrich the city by giving it great domain, nor protect honest settlers from extensive or fraudulent claims." The editor estimated that only 1,000 acres of disputed Mexican lands remained to be converted into private property. He was happy to put the question of the Pueblo lands to rest and found it "almost incredible" that the case "should at last have escaped from the lawyers."[34]

In truth, the ownership of the land around San Francisco Bay had escaped the lawyers some time before. Establishing sovereignty under the law did not determine the finite distribution of the lots and ranches. All the while that lawyers and jurists were arguing the Pueblo Case, local politicians and real estate speculators had been carving up the Peninsula into parcels to be sold, mortgaged, foreclosed on, and sold again. On their own turf, the locals were agile players in the game of sovereignty. Small time "squatters" made formidable adversaries for the municipal officials who claimed sovereignty over those four leagues of putative pueblo. They seldom summoned legal precedents or documentary evidence to support their claims; rather, they asserted an inalienable right as American citizens to cheap land in the West. John B. Polley, who identified himself as a "citizen of the United Stated and residing at the Mission of Dolores in the said State of California," felt entitled to displace the De Haro family because he was "in actual possession [of the property] and engaged in the cultivation and improvement of the same for his own benefit." As to the rights of Mexican citizens, they were forfeited to American chauvinism: "The large grants of land in that state made by the Mexican Government to individuals," read Polley's declaration, "are incompatible with the spirit of our Republican institutions and deeply injurious to the growth and prosperity of the State and especially so when such grants are located within or near the limits of a large commercial city like San Francisco." Similarly, a squatter named William Thompson poached on the Bernal Ranch and argued before the Land Commission that "I was a settler there at a very early time and think I am entitled." Other newly arrived Americans took land by way of "shot gun sales." One plot near the Mission cost two deaths and five casualties. On Mission Street, near De Haro's disputed land grant, a sheriff was shot trying to protect another disputed title.[35]

As the city expanded farther outward from Yerba Buena Cove, the battle for pueblo land grew fiercer and more sophisticated. The grasp of the real estate market quickly reached as far as Rancho San Miguel, where José Jesús Noé was enjoying his new prosperity in a home said to cost $30,000. Noé sold his land to a merchant from New Jersey named John Horner who paid $200,000 for the property and rechristened the "rancho" Horner's "tract." "Big Squatters" like Horner had the capital to take possession of large parcels beyond the charter line, usually in the amount of the 160 acres designated by the U.S preemption law. Philadelphia was the home office of the California Land Distribution and Home Association, for example, whose aim was to acquire "desirable land in this state" and to distribute it "in subdivision among its members by allotment." The company assured residents of San Francisco or "elsewhere" that an investment of $2.50 a month would yield an annual income of $130 to $750. Such promoters welcomed modest investments, and advised "Persons of either sex" that "married women can, under the laws of this State, hold stock or land entirely under their own control."[36]

Another purveyor of pueblo land put his name on a large plot north of Noé's ranch and west of the 1851 border on Larkin Street. When the Land Commission invalidated a grant from Governor Micheltoreno to French shipping merchant José Limantour, the city promptly rechristened it the "Subdivision of the Western Addition" and put it up for sale. The ensuing auctions proceeded at the dizzying pace of the capitalist urban frontier. Newspapers announced the "Extensive Sale of Real Estate" to which "the attention of speculators and settlers is particularly called." The conversion of the Limantour grant into American real estate had required the exercise of municipal sovereignty. It was local politicians who took the initiative and assumed the authority to "quiet the claims" for city land west of the 1851 boundary. In 1855, without waiting for the ruling of the Land Commission or of any other state or federal authority, the Board of Supervisors of the City and County of San Francisco passed an ordinance that marked off the Pueblo lands in the northwestern quadrant of the Peninsula as part of the city's tax base. Section 2 of the ordinance, named after Mayor James Van Ness, reads as follows: "The city of San Francisco hereby relinquishes and grants all the rights and claims of the city to the land within the corporate limits to the parties in the actual possession thereof." In essence, the Van Ness Ordinance made a blanket donation of land to the squatters, be they small farmers or east coast stockholders. In return, the recipients of this municipal bounty had to agree to pay their back taxes. The city authorities were aware that a legal shadow still hung over the Western Addition, and they attached this proviso to the Van Ness Ordinance: "Nothing contained in this ordinance shall be construed to prevent the city from continuing to prosecute, to a final determination, her claim now pending before the United States Land commission, for Pueblo land."[37]

The record of titles for Block No. 276 in the Western Addition gives rich evidence of how such sophistical municipal politics shaped the land around San Francisco Bay. The record begins with a 160-acre preemption claim, dated 1850, secured by one Merrit Welton. In 1851, the acreage was divided in half and sold for $500 and a mortgage, a pittance compared to the cost of lots near Yerba Buena Cove. Divided again within the year, this section of American public land became a fractured checkerboard of disputed titles. By 1856, most of it had been carved into residential lots of 50 square *varas*, but sales lagged as the gold rush subsided. In 1857, international financial panic battered the real estate market of

San Francisco with depressed prices, defaulted mortgages, sheriff's sales for unpaid taxes, continued disputes about titles to the Pueblo lands. The cycle of boom and bust in the real estate market of San Francisco was underway.[38]

Financial instability combined with legal ambiguity to create political turmoil in the streets and the municipal offices of San Francisco. During the debates about the Western Addition, a councilman named Beideman reportedly "struck a fellow alderman in the face." Another member of the municipal legislature, a man named Sweeney, complained of an ethnic assault in the form of sarcastic comments about his accent. The battle over real estate on the outskirts of the city also inspired an urban social movement of sorts. The People's Party, a.k.a. the Tax- Payers' Union, issued broadsides and called public meetings to advocate the sale of disputed tracts to pay off the municipal deficit.[39] While the Union and Confederate armies were locked in battle, real estate capitalism marched farther west and south in San Francisco, reaching all the way to the county line. This last frontier of the city was called simply "the Outside Lands." A letter to the *Alta*, dated 1861, laid claim to the territory with a familiar salvo: "the title is clear," the lands "belong to the city. They are the last fragment of its patrimony. They are worth millions of dollars—worth more than the whole amount of our funded debt." The municipal government obligingly assumed sovereignty over more territory at the margins of settlement. As early as 1862, the Board of Supervisors moved to confer title on "actual settlers" of the Outside Lands "for a trifling fee." In 1866, the state government finally endorsed the city's scheme for the development of the Outside Lands, enacted as the Clement Ordinance. Once again, local authorities tried to elide the fact that title to the pueblo land was still being debated in federal courts. "Not wishing to be disrespectful to the Supreme Court," the spokesman for the San Francisco Board of Supervisors observed that the decisions of the federal judiciary "on this point had been multifarious."[40]

The legal status of the Outside Lands might have been in doubt, but that had not stopped San Franciscans from turning them into real estate. Plans for the Western Addition and the Outside Lands were debated in the press, in the offices of municipal officials, and at public meetings of the Taxpayers' Union. In 1862, supporters of the prototype of the Clement Ordinance met in a "grand public meeting" and sent a petition with over 8,000 signatures to the state legislature. When that body endorsed the Clement Ordinance in 1866, the city surveyor quickly drew a map of the San Francisco Peninsula that concretized the legislation. It was a relentless grid of small lots, whose owners were obliged to pay taxes to the city (see Figure 6). When the Supreme Court finally ruled on the Pueblo case a few months later, its decision was largely moot. The land around the Bay

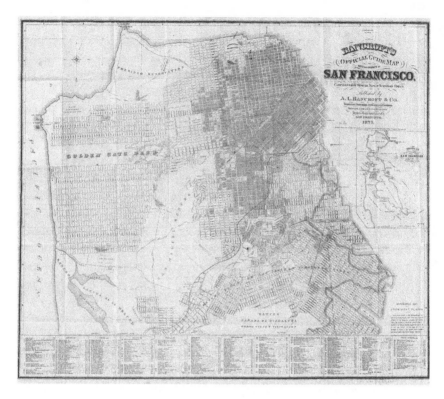

Figure 6. A. L. Bancroft, *Bancroft's Official Guide Map of City and County of San Francisco* . . . 1873. Courtesy of the David Rumsey Map Collection, www.davidrumsey.com.

had already been sold and resold many times under the ambiguous authority (but muscular influence) of the municipal government.[41]

The federal government did ultimately put its official stamp on the San Francisco landscape. Just as the Clement ordinance was going into effect, a Senator from Sacramento, John Conness, put through legislation that officially conveyed the pueblo lands to the city and ordered that titles be awarded to the current occupants. In other words, the actions of the municipal politicians were being rubber-stamped by Congress. The San Francisco press thought Congress's act "superfluous." The editor of the *Alta* speculated that "The Senators and Representatives, absorbed in the more exiting and doubtless interesting work of reconstructing the nation and repairing the ravages of war, did not pay a great deal of attention to the bill." In the meantime, local citizens and local government had had their way with the land. They had shaped it into an urban landscape, a loose grid of private lots interspersed with a few public squares and a single large park.

Conclusion

If we measure the difference that sovereignty made by its impact on the places where people lived, worked, played, and claimed ownership, then the local authorities of San Francisco had a foundational and enduring power. Be they represented by *alcaldes*/mayors or the *regidores*/councilmen, local citizens created the grid of streets that remains largely unchanged to this day, and they did so without explicit a priori authorization from state or national authorities. The matrix of streets, lots, an occasional square, and one large park laid out in the decade of the American Civil War has endured through turbulent cycles of boom and bust. The case of nineteenth-century San Francisco displays the ineluctable advantage enjoyed by those who are on the ground in the places where fundamental decisions about property rights are worked out in a messy political process.

That process was the work of a large and varied cast of historical agents who built a city along San Francisco Bay. Although an act of Congress in 1866, and a decision from the Supreme Court in the same year, put a federal seal on the urban landscape, it owes its general aspect as well as its particularities largely to the Mexican *pobladores* who founded the settlement, to the scrappy squatters on the outside lands, and to the wily politicians on the town council and the county Board of Supervisors. The twists and tangles of political authority in San Francisco multiplied the points of access to power and sometimes could serve to expand democratic participation and level inequalities of wealth. Clearly, small squatters on the ground as well as large land corporations back east—along with ambitious San Francisco Supervisors and Solomonic Supreme Court Justices—maneuvered complicatedly through the "multifarious" chambers of sovereignty. Yet those with greater financial resources and more efficacious connections undoubtedly exercised more leverage at every level of sovereignty. Take the case of Thomas Hayes, who made one of the first preemption claims for the pueblo lands. His personal papers reveal that he championed the Van Ness Ordinance locally, but also discussed it with his associates in Washington, and at the same time wrote to Paris and London to solicit capital for his San Francisco investments. ("Hayes Valley" is now one of the more trendy commercial districts of the Silicon City.)[42]

Sometimes access to the different sites of sovereignty compounded the opportunities for graft. The federal appeal of the decision in *Hart v. Burnett* was

mounted in 1864 by an assistant district attorney said to be employed by the
"Outside land faction."[43] Many of the principle actors in this saga of sovereignty,
Peter Burnett, Horace Hawes, David Broderick, and those pugnacious councilmen Beideman and Sweeney, to name just a few, had financial stakes in the
pueblo lands. Sovereignty operated in a nation of men as well as laws. One man,
in particular, stands out as a kind of Zelig figure in the long saga of the Pueblo
lands. The young lawyer named Stephen J. Field arrived in California from Connecticut before the Gold Rush, and soon made a smart bargain, acquiring, for
virtually nothing, sixteen lots near Sacramento in the heart of the gold country.
Field quickly mastered the political art of land speculation. He drew up the deeds
for a town on land near an old Mexican plaza, conveniently including his sixteen
lots. Field was promptly elected *alcalde* of a pueblo called Marysville. He rose
rapidly up the hierarchy of California sovereignty and at each step protected the
real estate interests of San Francisco. The year 1859 finds Judge Field serving on
the state Supreme Court just in time to rule on behalf of the city of San Francisco
in its suit against the U.S. government. Then, in 1863, within days of upholding
the city's argument in *Hart v. Burnett*, Stephen Field ascended to the U.S. Supreme Court. At a moment when the outcome of the Civil War was still uncertain, Lincoln chose Field, a Union Democrat, in hopes of maintaining sectional
and partisan balance on the high court. In 1864, and again in 1866, Field ruled
in favor of the city when the custody of the Pueblo land came before the federal
judiciary. For Field, the gradations of sovereignty were stepping stones in a long
political career. In 1877, he presided over another land case, once again ruling in
favor of San Francisco and against the federal government. The *Alta* wrote in appreciation that "Judge Field has shown himself a true friend of San Francisco and
it is a matter of congratulations that he should have been here to try the case."[44]

The multiplicity and fluidity of sovereignty permitted a large number of ambitious men and a few women to acquire private property in fee simple and to
take personal profit from the land that was the habitat of Indian hunters and
gatherers for tens of generations. The different scales of government, of Spain,
Mexico, and the United States, came together to form the integral political matrix that eventually converted land into American real estate. The *Establecimiento
de Delores*, the *Diputación del Partido de San Francisco*, the San Francisco Board
of Supervisors, the United States Land Commission, the State of California, and
the Supreme Court of the United States all had a hand in preparing the lands of
the West for rapid capitalist development. In the first city of the North American
Pacific, it was the local state that initially and repeatedly played a crucial role in
this process. In so doing, cities like San Francisco gave shape to a major sector

of modern economies, the production of urban space. They should, therefore, be included among the key political players on the sectional, the national, and increasingly the global stage.

Notes

1. Leonard Richards, *The California Gold Rush and the Coming of the Civil War* (New York: Vintage, 2007); Roger Lotchin, *San Francisco, 1846–1856: From Hamlet to City* (Champaign-Urbana: University of Illinois Press, 1997), 240; George Foster Kelley, "Land Frauds of California," Pamphlet Collection, 1864, Bancroft Library, University of California, Berkeley (hereafter UCB).

2. Neil Brenner, *New State Spaces: Urban Governance and the Rescaling of Statehood* (Oxford: Oxford University Press, 2004); John Agnew, "The Territorial Trap: The Geographical Assumptions of International Relations Theory," *Review of International Political Economy* 1, no. 1 (1994): 53–80; Jean Cohen, *Globalization and Sovereignty: Rethinking Legality, Legitimacy, and Constitutionalism* (Cambridge: Cambridge University Press, 2012); Brian Balogh, *A Government Out of Sight: The Mystery of National Authority in Nineteenth-Century America* (Cambridge: Cambridge University Press, 2009); Eric H. Monkkonen, *The Local State: Public Money and American Cities* (Stanford: Stanford University Press, 1998); Katherine M. Johnson, "The Glorified Municipality: State Formation and the Urban Process in North America," *Political Geography* 27, no. 4 (2008): 400–17; Aihwa Ong, *Neoliberalism as Exception: Mutations in Citizenship and Sovereignty* (Durham, N.C.: Duke University Press, 2006).

3. As quoted in Peter S. Onuf and Nicholas Greenwood Onuf, *Federal Union, Modern World: The Law of Nations in an Age of Revolutions, 1776–1814* (Madison, Wisc.: Madison House, 1993), 54.

4. Jordana Dym, *From Sovereign Villages to National State: City, State, and Federation in Central America, 1759–1839* (Albuquerque: University of New Mexico Press, 2006); Tamar Herzog, *Defining Nations: Immigrants and Citizens in Early Modern Spain and Spanish America* (New Haven: Yale University Press, 2003); Cynthia Radding, "The Colonial Pact," in *North American Borderlands*, ed. Brian DeLay (New York: Routledge, 2013), 43–58.

5. Cynthia Radding, *Landscapes of Power and Identity: Comparatives Histories in the Sonoran Dessert and Forest of Amazonia form Colony to Republic* (Durham, N.C.: Duke University Press, 2005).

6. Brian Hammett, "Ibero-America as a Multiplicity of States," in *Connections after Colonialism: Europe and Latin America in the 1820s*, ed. Mathew Brown and Gabriel Paquette (Tuscaloosa: University of Alabama Press, 2013), 29–45; Antonio Annino y Marcela Ternavasio (coords.), *El Laboratorio Consitutcional Iberoamericano: 1807/1808–1830* (Colección: Estudios AHILA, 2012).

7. Iris H. W. Engstrand, "The Legal Heritage of Spanish California," *Southern California Quarterly* 75, no. 3–4 (1993): 205–36; Bernard Moses, "The Establishment of Municipal Government in San Francisco," *Johns Hopkins University Studies in Historical and Political Sciences*, ser. 7 (1889): 75–153.

8. "Early Documents of California," December 1831, 1837, Bancroft Library, UCB.

9. Land Case 427 ND, 39–40, 320, "Records of the United States Land Commission," Bancroft Library, UCB.

10. Land Case 427 ND, 13–19.

11. *Minutes of the Proceedings of the Legislative Assembly of the District of San Francisco, March 12, 1849 to June 1849 and a Record of the Proceedings of the Ayuntamiento or Town Council of San Francisco from August 6, 1849 until May 3, 1850* (San Francisco: Towne and Bacon, 1860), Pamphlet Collection, Bancroft Library, UCB.

12. "Records of the Legislative Assembly," in *San Francisco, History, Incidents, Etc.: A Collection of Pamphlets* (San Francisco, 1853), 283–341.

13. *Minutes of the Proceedings of the Legislative Assembly*, Appendix 4, 221–40.

14. Alfred Wheeler, *Land Titles in San Francisco and the Laws Affecting the Same with a Synopsis of All Grants and Sales of Land within the Limits Claimed by the City* (San Francisco: Alta California Printing Office, 1852), appendix I; Frank Soulé et al., *Annals of San Francisco* (1855 reprint, Palo Alto, Ca.: Lewis Osborne, 1966), 229–31.

15. "Peter H. Burnett Governor Overrules Hawes," Photostat, MS 521, California Historical Society, San Francisco.

16. *Minutes of the Proceedings of the Legislative Assembly*, April 2, 1849.

17. *Organization, Acts and Regulations of the U.S. Land Commissioners for California* (San Francisco: Monson, Whitton, and Co., 1852), Land Pamphlets, Bancroft Library, UCB.

18. Land Cases 6 ND, 175; Halleck Peachy and Billings Papers, box 1, folder 260, Bancroft Library, UCB; Land Cases, 5 ND, 209–12.

19. Land Cases 5 ND, 214.

20. Halleck, Peachy, and Billings Collection, box 3, folders 250–75, 280–94; box 1.

21. John W. Dwinelle, *The Colonial History of the City of San Francisco* (San Francisco: Towne and Bacon, 1863), quotations on 2; Karen Clay and Werner Troesken, "Ranchos and the Politics of Land Claims," in *Land of Sunshine: An Environmental. History of Metropolitan Los Angeles*, ed. William Deverell and Greg Hise (Pittsburgh: University of Pittsburgh, 2005); Paul Gates, *Land and Law in California: Essays on Land Policies* (Ames: Iowa State University Press, 1991); William G. Robbins, *Colony and Empire: The Capitalist Transformation of the American West* (Lawrence: University Press of Kansas, 1994).

22. Land Case 424 ND.

23. Halleck, Peachy, and Billings Collection, box 3, folder 304.

24. Testimony of William Richardson, Land Case 424 ND 59, 60.

25. Dwinelle, *Colonial History*, 1–21, 35, 56–61, Addenda.

26. Dwinelle, *Colonial History*, 23.

27. Dwinelle, *Colonial History*, 1–21, 35, 56–61, Addenda. Quotations on 12, 35.

28. *Hart v. Burnett*, 15 Cal. 530 (1860) accessed WestlawNext, 530, 553–54; *Testimony Showing the Time of Possession, etc. of the Beideman Tract, and the Decision of the Supreme Court, of California, thereon* (San Francisco: Towne and Bacon, 1861), Pamphlet Collection, Bancroft Library, UCB.

29. *Hart v. Burnett*, 562.

30. Land Case 427 ND, 732, 793–821.

31. *Daily Alta California*, April 30, 1861, March 16, 1862, January 14, 1863; *The Question of the Title to the Outside Lands. Settler (in proper) vs. the City of San Francisco, Argument for Plaintiff* (San Francisco: Alta California Book and Job Printing Office, 1866), 3; Land Case 427 ND; "Map of the Outside Lands of the City and County of San Francisco showing Reservations Selected for Public Purposes under the Provision of Order," (San Francisco: Britton and Rey, 1868), Bancroft Library, UCB; Land Case 417 ND, 772.

32. *Townsend et al. v. Greeley*, 72 U.S. 326, accessed through Westlaw.

33. Peter Burnett, *Recollections and Opinions of an Old Pioneer* (New York: D. Appleton and Company, 1880).

34. *Daily Alta California*, October 25, 1863, December 25, 1866.

35. Land Case 6 ND, 22, 25; Land Case 166 ND, Heirs of De Haro, 67–69, 78; W. W. Robinson, *Land in California* (Berkeley, 1948); *Daily Alta California*, December 19, 1862.

36. "Prospectus of the California Land Distribution and Home Association," Pamphlet Collection, Bancroft Library, UCB; Mae Silver, "Rancho San Miguel" (San Francisco: Mouse Type Inc. and Stanyan Printing, 1992).

37. "An Act concerning the City of San Francisco and To Ratify and Confirm Ordinances of the Common Council" [March 11, 1858], *The Clement Ordinance for Settling the title to the Outside Lands of the City and County of San Francisco approved October 12 1866* (San Francisco: Towne and Bacon, 1866); "Map of the Outside Lands of the City and County of San Francisco Showing Reservations Selected for Public Purposes under the Provision of Order."

38. Abstract of Deeds, Western Addition, Bancroft Library, UCB; *Daily Alta California*, July 5, 1851.

39. "California Taxpayer's Union," Pamphlet Collection, Bancroft Library UCB; *Daily Alta California*, January 19, 1856.

40. *Daily Alta California*, April 30, 1861, March 16, 1862, January 14, 1863; *Question of the Title to the Outside Lands*, 3.

41. *Daily Alta California*, March 15 and 16, 1862.

42. Thomas Hayes to F. B. Austin, Esq., August 22, 1857, Thomas Hayes Miscellany, California Historical Society, San Francisco, Ca.

43. Land Case 427 ND, 876–77, 972.

44. Paul Kens, *Justice Stephen Field: Shaping Liberty from the Gold Rush to the Gilded Age* (Lawrence: University Press of Kansas, 1997). Field lived long enough to vote on two momentous Supreme Court decisions: He upheld corporate personhood in *Santa Clara v. the Southern Pacific* (1886) and racial segregation in *Plessy v. Ferguson* (1896).

Conclusion

Continental History and the Problem of Time and Place

Frank Towers

Whereas the introduction to this volume focused on the question of sovereignty and the nation-state, our conclusion takes stock of another important theme of this volume, writing North American history outside of a national framework. Riding the crest of a wave of studies on transnational and global comparative studies of the nineteenth century, historians working in this field would do well to pause briefly to take stock of its achievements, limitations, and future research questions.

In terms of achievements, historians working outside the national framework have opened entirely new geographic areas of study such as Atlantic history, borderlands, and the Pacific. These areas have not only been the subject of important scholarship but have also become categories for university courses, professional journals, book series, and academic hiring. Standing above them all is world history, a subject area that moved from the margins of mid-twentieth-century historical scholarship to the forefront of twenty-first-century teaching and research.[1]

And yet, just as globalization has met with fierce resistance in present-day politics, the global/transnational turn in historical studies has come in for criticism. Although separated by very significant differences (most importantly the appeal to ethnic nationalist falsehoods by rightwing anti-globalist political movements) these patterns share some common themes. In contemporary politics, critics of globalization stand on the ground of the grounded—that is, the long-term residents of a particular place, usually in communities left behind by the "circulations," "flows," and "innovations" that have enriched the metropolitan centers of global capitalism. For their part, academic critics of the transnational turn have noted how this discourse has flourished in the academies of the two major imperial powers of the nineteenth and twentieth century—Great Britain and the United States—but has been viewed more skeptically in places with less triumphant narratives of national power and imperial dominance.

Critics of transnational approaches often have experience working on histories of places at the margins of empire, and are wary of intellectual projects that look like the older colonialist imaginaries of the past. Take, for example, this assessment from three historians of Canada: "The rubric of transnational has perhaps had the greatest purchase in contexts with long-acknowledged and well-resourced national historiographies . . . It is one that is registered differently in national contexts with less seamless national histories to interrogate." Similarly, David Hanlon, a historian of Micronesia, argues that "Transnational histories allow for little to no consideration of the details and particulars that are so crucial to Island histories and Island history making." Meanwhile, the transnational turn has made some Latin Americanists "fearful both of the loss of culture-specific knowledge and of the potential homogenization of the historical discipline."[2]

More generally, when historians talk of regional "worlds," be they British, Pacific, Atlantic, Indian Ocean, or Mediterranean, they need to ask whose world it was. The significance of connections across vast spaces very much depends on whose point of view the historian investigates. For example, David Chang's recent study of Hawaiian exploration of the Pacific shows how the meaning of transnational ties varied wildly according to the location of the participant.[3]

These critiques have an institutional dimension as well as an intellectual one. Along with anti-imperial skepticism of calls to think outside of the national framework, the development of national historiographies came later to historians working in the British settler-states and Latin America, making calls to move beyond those projects seem premature and less rewarding within particular national academies. Even worse, historians writing in languages other than English have great difficulty getting noticed by the U.S. and U.K. academies, even when they write on the history of those countries. Indicative of the enduring power of professional history's origins as a state-sponsored enterprise, "much more than in social sciences disciplines, history continues to be written in national languages for national audiences." Finally, better funding for research travel and language training in American and British universities compared to other countries has made it easier for U.S.- and U.K.-based historians to carry out ambitious multinational archival projects.[4]

These conditions in which transnational historiography has emerged inform U.S. immigration historian Mae Ngai's warning that "owing to our privileged position in the world and within the global academy, we run the risk of turning transnational history into another variant of imperial history." "'North American' history," she writes, "cannot be that which remains centered in the United States, with Canada and Mexico appended thereto."[5] This volume has tried to tell the history of 1860s North America by giving as much equal weight as possible to Canada, Mexico, and indigenous polities but the United States nonetheless looms over all of these histories as the colossus that came to dominate the continent, the Western Hemisphere, and eventually the entire world. Recognizing this imbalance of power in the continent's political past does not mean that historians have to repeat U.S., or British imperial, domination in their own research, but neither should they ignore the realities of state power in trying to think across national borders.

Imbalances in state power were especially important for determining the outcomes of the many wars, both civil and interstate, that broke out across the globe in the mid-1800s. In addition to the conflicts in North America, revolutions and civil wars occurred in the following countries: the Balkan possessions of the Ottoman Empire, Chile, China, Colombia, at least eleven European states in the Revolutions of 1848, Iran, India, Italy (1860s), Japan, Pahang (Malaysia), Spain (both an internal civil war and wars with former and current colonies in the Dominican Republic and Cuba), and Venezuela. Meanwhile, European powers waged wars to colonize sub-Saharan Africa, New Zealand, and East Asia. Finally, the period witnessed three major interstate wars beginning in 1854 with the British, French, and Ottomans fighting Russia in the Crimea; then, from 1864 to 1870, Argentina, Brazil, and Uruguay waging a brutal war against Paraguay; and ending in 1870–71 with Germany's victorious struggle against France. [6]

Some of the wars were relatively bloodless, as was the case in the Revolutions of 1848, whereas others, such as the Indian Rebellion, the Paraguayan War, and the U.S. Civil War, killed hundreds of thousands of people. In China's Taipeng Civil War, the bloodiest of such conflicts in human history, casualty estimates range from a low just over 20 million to a high closer to 90 million.[7] Combined, these military conflicts stood as the world's most convulsive period of warfare prior to the twentieth century.

Transnational and comparative analysis has the potential to move from simply observing the simultaneity of these state-making wars to investigating them as a process that transcended particular national stories. Such a research agenda might ask whether there was a common global crisis in the mid-nineteenth century—something approximating the later era of world wars from the 1910s to the 1940s—or, if the period manifested correlations between political crises in different regions, but no interconnected cause. Historians have also explored the nature of expanded state power in the 1860s. Did it advance the cause of liberty and equality advocated by many of the period's nationalists? Or, was the general tenor of the era one of anti-democratic consolidation of power at the top?

Finding satisfactory answers to those questions inevitably raises more questions about what period historians are studying when they write about the mid-nineteenth century and their choice of geographic emphasis. In other words, the age-old methodological frames of time and place can help guide further research into the problem of state making in the 1860s. As noted in the introduction to this volume, historians who interpret events in North America as a victory for democratic forces tend to contrast the continent's liberal nationalists with their anti-democratic foes either within their polities or in imperial monarchies of Europe. Alternatively, historians who cast doubt on gains for liberty and equality in the 1860s pay more attention to victims of state-making projects in North America and look to the western reaches of the continent rather than its Atlantic connections.

Applied globally, the same basic pattern holds. Historians who emphasize the relationship between the colonized peoples and imperial powers of the West see the era as the triumph for entrenched power and a necessary step on the road to the new imperialism. Similarly, their chronological frame often extends to the late nineteenth century and the First World War. Finally, technology and economics matter more in these studies than do ideology and mass politics. Speaking about the global history of emancipation, Peter Kolchin argues that how one assesses the process "can depend in part on when one is making it: from the vantage point of 1870 the antebellum world seemed turned upside down, whereas someone looking back from 1910 might conclude that many of the resulting changes had been ephemeral and short-lived."[8]

Making the case for conservative victory in the mid-nineteenth century's wars, Charles Maier points to the significance of new technologies and the importance of strong states in mobilizing them. He portrays the nation-state as a top-down creation "built on the ashes of revolution, the reform of institutions not from 'below'—not by the effort of peasant or national populists to bring about the millennium—but by the programs of modernization and rationalization carried out both by farseeing conservative statesmen and middle classes."[9]

Echoing Maier but more interested in nationalism than the state in its own right, Jörn Leonhard argues that the U.S. Civil War and the Wars of German Unification "pointed to a transformation in the meaning of war and a changing character of modern warfare: this was essentially characterized by a new combination of technological progress, based upon increased firepower and railway transport, and mass mobilization in the name of an abstract ideal of nationality and the nation-state." Leonhard sees nationalism as a dangerous force in this process: "War was no longer regarded as a conflict over territory or dynastic interests, but it was fought for the ultimate existence of nations and peoples. This necessitated the stigmatization of the enemy and the overcoming of the traditional separation between a state's armies and its people."[10] The mid-1800s, viewed from this perspective, was a period of "hegemonic unification" "in which one regional power seized the initiative, brought its military strength into play, and puts its stamp on the newly emergent nation state."[11]

Such pessimistic assessments echo earlier work on the origins of the second quarter of the twentieth century's dictatorships. Not coincidentally, states like Germany and Japan get more attention in these histories as do global capitalists and exploitive commodity chains. For example, looking at the history of cotton, Sven Beckert describes the post-emancipation "global Reconstruction" that followed the American Civil War as a change in the form of labor exploitation but one that kept power in the hands of the merchants, manufacturers, and landlords who had held the upper hand in the age of slavery.[12]

In contrast, historians who foreground the political ideas of these conflicts, namely nationalism and liberalism, see the middle decades of the nineteenth-century as "unfinished revolutions" that tried but failed to bring about the egalitarian vision of the nation state that came to the forefront in the West after the Second World War.[13] It was the later defeat of liberal nationalist movements, not their victory, that led to new colonizing adventures in Africa and Asia in the late 1800s and the Great War of 1914.[14]

For Eric Hobsbawm, an early advocate of this thesis, popular movements for nationalism and democracy were forces in opposition not only to the landed aristocracy but also the means for breaching liberalism's efforts to shield the masses off from the social advance of the bourgeoisie. Democracy and nationalism "were the same," argued Hobsbawm, "in so far as nationalist movements in this period became mass movements, and certainly at this point pretty well all radical leaders supposed them to be identical." In this perspective, nationalist wars to make self-governing states are best understood as popular reactions to the very kind of top-down hegemonic control that more recent global histories have identified as the prime movers of the period. The victories of revolutionaries across the globe made the 1860s "a decade of reform, of political liberalisation, even of some concession to what was called the 'forces of democracy.'"[15]

In this broad narrative, the economic depression of 1873 punctured the forward movement of liberal progress. Meanwhile, many of the principles advocated by liberal nationalists, such as the rule of law, the equality of all citizens, and power of the state to improve the lives of all of its subjects, remained alive in public memory and reform politics at the turn of the century and came back in stronger form during the Great Depression and Second World War. For North America, it is this latter perspective on the mid-nineteenth-century period of state making that resonates in public memories of John A. Macdonald, Abraham Lincoln, and Benito Juárez that treat them as visionaries of the twentieth-century pluralist nation-state. This perspective on the 1860s finds expression in Don Doyle's international history of the U.S. Civil War, which shows how Europeans understood the war as "a decisive showdown between the forces of *popular* versus *hereditary* sovereignty, *democracy* versus *aristocracy*, *free* versus *slave* labor, all rolled into one grand epic battle taking place in the distant American arena."[16]

Doyle's deeply researched study fits with other scholarship on the connections between the Americas and Europe in this period. In fact, when viewed primarily as an Atlantic World phenomenon, the "multi-faceted, interconnected set of crises" of the mid-1800s clearly shared a common transnational alignment of forces contending over slavery, republican self-government, and the integrity of national borders.[17] Liberal nationalism as a force for freedom and equality was clearest in the Atlantic context where its advocates confronted slaveholding reactionaries up and down the Western Hemisphere.[18]

A well developed historiography of comparative emancipation debates many points but generally agrees that the U.S. government's abolition of slavery in 1865, over the opposition of the most determined proslavery force in the Atlantic system, was part of a transnational antislavery struggle that involved both free, mostly white, reformers as well as enslaved revolutionaries on plantations throughout the Americas, and that U.S. slavery's "sudden destruction sent a deep tremor through those slave societies that remained intact."[19]

Although the general picture of emancipation is one of expanding liberty, as Kolchin, quoted earlier in this Conclusion, notes, the temporal and geographic frames for studying this history influence how it is interpreted. For example, in her comparison of emancipation in sugar-growing regions of the United States and Cuba, Rebecca Scott takes the story into the early twentieth century when the U.S. "federal government had endorsed Louisiana's forcible exclusion of people of color from shared public spaces and from the voting booth, [but] in Cuba the sphere deemed public continued to be defined very broadly, and within it equal rights and nationalist unity were widely acknowledged." This pessimistic view of gains for freedpeople in the United States depends very much on extending the story through the rise of segregation and disfranchisement in the era of Jim Crow.[20]

Like Scott, who paid close attention to African-descended military service in both national armies, Vitor Izecksohn also views the involvement of the enslaved in nation-making wars as a critical part of their broader push for equal citizenship. However, Izecksohn compares the U.S. Civil War with Brazil's army in the Paraguayan War, and he ends his study in the late 1860s, prior to the defeat of Reconstruction in the United States and more than a decade before final emancipation in Brazil. From this different time/place framework, Izecksohn concludes that "participation in the U.S. Civil War helped to consolidate emancipation in the Southern states. Freed slaves serving in Brazil's Imperial army, however, returned to a depressed and unchanged society, where the values and practices of slavery still mattered." Both arguments are persuasive but their divergent conclusions show the importance of deciding what period the 1860s belonged to and, for historians of North America, what parts of the world mattered most for understanding "what changed and what didn't, and how we should evaluate those changes."[21]

Although the complications of time and place add to the challenges facing historians as they explore a continental history of mid-nineteenth-century North America, they also show the potential for such studies to reach seemingly distant chronological and geographic histories. To make those connections, historians will be aided by keeping in mind how important it was to the winners of state-making contests in the 1860s to write the history of those triumphs as distinctly national achievements that revealed enduring truths about the distinctive virtues of each particular polity. That framing of the period not only inspired future praise of these regimes but also shaped the perspectives of their critics who turned claims for unique national accomplishments into attacks on unique national failures. The essays in this volume attempt to think outside of these interpretive pathways. They owe a great debt to the work that has come before them in thinking across the boundaries of time and place, and they are in no way a last word on the history of the continent. Instead, they mark a provisional step forward in the task of studying the remaking of North American sovereignty in the mid-nineteenth century through a continental framework.

Notes

1. This scholarship is too vast to catalog here. For examples of periodicals, see *The Journal of World History*, *Journal of Global History*, *Journal of Borderlands Studies*, *Atlantic Studies*, and *The Journal of Pacific History*. Useful reviews of these developments include Bernard Bailyn, *Atlantic History: Concepts and Contours* (Cambridge: Harvard University Press, 2005); Ian Tyrrell, "Reflections on the Transnational Turn in United States History: Theory and Practice," *Journal of Global History* 4, no. 3 (November 2009): 453–74; Phillip D. Morgan and Jack P. Greene, "Introduction: The Present State of Atlantic History," in Phillip D. Morgan and Jack P. Greene, eds., *Atlantic History: A Critical Reappraisal* (New York: Oxford University Press, 2009).

2. Karen Dubinsky, Adele Perry, and Henry Yu, eds., *Within and Without the Nation: Canadian History as Transnational History* (Toronto: University of Toronto Press, 2015), 12; David Hanlon, "Losing Oceania to the Pacific and the World," *The Contemporary Pacific* 29, no. 2 (2017): 286–318, 302 (quotation); Matthew Brown, "The Global History of Latin America," *Journal of Global History* 10, no. 3 (2015): 365–86, 365 (quotation).

3. David Chang, *The World and All the Things Upon It* (Minneapolis: University of Minnesota Press, 2016). The author thanks Dr. Chang for his insights into the problem of "worlds."

4. Georg G. Iggers, O. Edward Wang, and Supriya Mukherjee, *A Global History of Modern Historiography*, 2nd ed. (New York: Routledge, 2017), 312. For an informative study of the problems facing U.S. historians located outside of the United States, see Nicolas Barreyre, Michael Heale, Stephen Tuck, and Cécile Vidal, *Historians Across Borders: Writing American History in a Global Age* (Ithaca: Cornell University Press, 2014).

5. Mae M. Ngai, "Promises and Perils of Transnational History," *Perspectives on History* (December 2012), https://www.historians.org/publications-and-directories/ perspectives-on-history/december-2012/the-future-of-the-discipline/promises-and -perils-of-transnational-history.

6. A list of these conflicts is in Charles Maier, *Leviathan 2.0: Inventing Modern Statehood* (Cambridge: Harvard University Press, 2012), 98–99.

7. For China casualty estimates, see Stephen R. Platt, *Autumn in the Heavenly Kingdom: China, the West, and the Epic Story of the Taipeng Civil War* (New York: Vintage Books, 2012), xxii, 358.

8. Peter Kolchin, "Reexamining Southern Emancipation in Comparative Perspective," *Journal of Southern History* 81, no. 1 (February 2015), 7–40, 38–39 (quotation).

9. Maier, *Leviathan 2.0*, 7.

10. Jörn Leonhard, "Nation-States and Wars: European and Transatlantic Perspectives," in *What Is a Nation?: Europe 1789–1914*, ed. Timothy Baycroft and Mark Hewitson (New York: Oxford University Press, 2014), 238.

11. Jürgen Osterhammel, *The Transformation of the World: A Global History of the Nineteenth Century*, trans. Peter Camiller (Princeton, N.J.: Princeton University Press, 2014), 409.

12. Barrington Moore, Jr., *Social Origins of Dictatorship and Democracy: Lord and Peasant in the Making of the Modern World* (Boston: Beacon Books, 1966); Sven Beckert, *Empire of Cotton: A Global History* (New York: Vintage Books, 2014), 280. For the acceleration of segregationist urban planning as the product of mid-1800s Western imperial projects in Asia, see Carl H. Nightingale, *Segregation: A Global History of Divided Cities* (Chicago: University of Chicago Press, 2012), 137.

13. The phrase "unfinished revolutions" refers to the landmark study of the resolution of the U.S. Civil War by Eric Foner, *Reconstruction: America's Unfinished Revolution, 1863–1877* (New York: Harper and Row, 1988).

14. E. J. Hobsbawm, *The Age of Capital, 1848–1875* (1975, rpt.; London: Abacus, 1995).

15. Hobsbawm, *Age of Capital*, 90, 12.

16. Don H. Doyle, *The Cause of All Nations: An International History of the American Civil War* (New York: Basic Books, 2015), 17. Also see the sources cited in the introduc-

tion and Timothy Mason Roberts, *Distant Revolutions: 1848 and the Challenge to American Exceptionalism* (Charlottesville: University of Virginia Press, 2009); W. Caleb McDaniel, *The Problem of Democracy in the Age of Slavery: Garrisonian Abolitionists & Transatlantic Reform* (Baton Rouge: Louisiana State University Press, 2013); Enrico Dal Lago, *William Lloyd Garrison and Giuseppe Mazzini: Abolition, Democracy, and Radical Reform* (Baton Rouge: Louisiana State University Press, 2013); Enrico Dal Lago, *The Age of Lincoln and Cavour: Comparative Perspectives on 19th-Century American and Italian Nation-Building* (New York: Palgrave Macmillan, 2015).

17. Don H. Doyle, "Introduction: The Atlantic World and the Crisis of the 1860s," in *American Civil Wars: The United States, Latin America, Europe and the Crisis of the 1860s*, ed. Don H. Doyle (Chapel Hill: University of North Carolina Press, 2017), 2.

18. For a recent counterpoint, see Gregory P. Downs, *The Second American Revolution: The Civil War-Era Struggle over Cuba and the Rebirth of the American Republic* (Chapel Hill: University of North Carolina Press, 2019).

19. Seymour Drescher, *Abolition: A History of Slavery and Antislavery* (New York: Cambridge University Press, 2009), 332. The literature on comparative and transnational histories of emancipation is too large to catalog here. In addition to Drescher, widely cited recent studies include David Brion Davis, *Inhuman Bondage: The Rise and Fall of Slavery in the New World* (New York: Oxford University Press, 2006); Stanley Engerman, *Slavery, Emancipation, & Freedom: Comparative Perspectives* (Baton Rouge: Louisiana State University Press, 2007); Robin Blackburn, *The American Crucible: Slavery, Emancipation and Human Rights* (New York: Verso, 2011).

20. Rebecca J. Scott, *Degrees of Freedom: Louisiana and Cuba After Slavery* (Cambridge: Harvard University Press, 2005), 256.

21. Vitor Izecksohn, *Slavery and War in the Americas: Race, Citizenship, and State Building in the United States and Brazil, 1861–1870* (Charlottesville: University of Virginia Press, 2014), 162; Kolchin, "Emancipation in Comparative Perspective," 39.

Acknowledgments

It is hard to believe that it has been eight years since the original conversations that led to this book, but here we are. Although William Allen Blair is not included in the volume, it would not have happened without his early support and insight. In 2012, Bill Blair and Frank Towers discussed ways to build on recent interest in transnational histories of the American Civil War. That discussion led to a conference of the same name as this book, held from July 30 through August 1, 2015 in Banff, Alberta, Canada. As Ferree Professor of Middle American History at Pennsylvania State University, for many years the editor of *Civil War History*, and then founder and editor of the *Journal of the Civil War Era* and director of the Richards Center for the Study of the Civil War Era, Bill has been at the forefront of expanding the field of American Civil War studies and was very excited about the idea of pulling together scholars from different national historical traditions to think about the 1860s as one common story. He also convinced the Richards Center to provide crucial funding for the Banff conference and then shepherded some of the papers into print in a special issue of the *JCWE*. Everyone involved in this project owes him a debt.

Bill Blair is one of the many people and institutions whose collaboration made this book possible. The Banff conference and the ideas that inform this book owe a great deal to the conference organizing committee members: Lyndsay Campbell, Gregory P. Downs, Patrick Kelly, Amelia Kiddle, Paul Quigley, Brian Schoen, Jay Sexton, and Andrew Slap. In the spring of 2015, Matthew Isham and Barby A. Singer at the Richards Center for the Civil War Era stepped in to help manage the logistical challenges of an international conference. Other key contributors included Erika Pani who got involved early and made connections with other academics in Mexico that enhanced the conference and this volume. Similar early commitments by Thomas Bender and Pekka Hämäläinen helped the conference gain momentum. Susan Ferber at Oxford University Press lent her support to this endeavor, attended the meeting, and gave numerous attendees, including graduate students, invaluable advice on bringing their research projects to publication. R. Douglas Francis at the University of Calgary, who co-organized earlier, influential meetings on the British world, guided us to scholarship on Canadian Confederation.

In addition to the Richards Center for the Study of the Civil War Era, the Banff conference benefited from generous funding from Canada's Social Sciences and Humanities Research Council, the Virginia Center for Civil War Studies (VCCWS), and, at the University of Calgary, the Centre for Military, Security and Strategic Studies (CMSS), the Latin American Research Centre (LARC), the Department of History, and the Faculty of Arts. In this search for funding, we especially thank Paul Quigley, director of the VCCWS; David Bercuson, CMSS's longtime director; and Hendrik Kraay, who was simultaneously running LARC and serving as head of the Department of History.

Moving from the conference to this edited volume would not have happened without Andy Slap, series editor at Fordham University Press. Andy agreed to support this volume before we had any chapters to show him and then worked diligently to help us as the volume took shape. He and the anonymous reviewers at Fordham University Press provided invaluable feedback to the volume's authors. We also appreciate the help of Will Cerbone and Eric Newman at Fordham, as well as Nancy Rapoport, who copyedited the volume.

On behalf of everyone involved with the meeting at Banff, the editors want to acknowledge the contribution of Tony Kaye and express their sorrow at his untimely death in 2017. Tony's paper for that meeting, "Understandings of Sovereignty among Slave Rebels and Abolitionists, 1829–1848," looked across the Americas to uncover a theory of sovereignty expressed in the culture of rumor used by slave rebels. It was a fascinating study that typified Tony's innovative understanding of the history of slavery. He gave a great deal to the profession and is missed by his peers.

Finally, the editors want to acknowledge a very long-term intellectual debt to their graduate mentors to whom the book is dedicated. For Jewel, Christine Heyrman made early America so fascinating that an aimless college sophomore ended up a history major bound for graduate school. Both she and Rachel Klein modeled what a successful career in the profession could look like and provided non-stop support to help her on her way. For Frank, Joyce Appleby taught him how to think about intellectual history, and Mike Johnson introduced him to the United States South and the Civil War era. Although Joyce passed away in 2016, her impact on the profession lives on among her many graduate students. Finally, we learned a great deal from Steven Hahn, who served on both of our Ph.D. committees. Steve's ability to bring out the big picture in histories that draw together the lowly and the mighty, as well as the local and the global, has been a model for both of us. We were very gratified to work with him on this project.

Contributors

Robert Bonner is Kathe Tappe Vernon Professor in the Dartmouth history department and author of *Mastering America: Southern Slaveholders and the Crisis of American Nationhood.*

Christopher Clark is Professor of History at the University of Connecticut. His books include *Social Change in America: From the Revolution through the Civil War.*

Jane Dinwoodie is a Postdoctoral Research Fellow in American History at the University of Cambridge. She is currently writing a book about Indian Removal and the thousands of people who avoided it.

Steven Hahn is Professor of History at New York University. A Pulitzer and Bancroft Prize recipient, his most recent book is *A Nation Without Borders: The United States and Its World in an Age of Civil Wars, 1830–1910* (2016).

Ryan Hall is Assistant Professor of Native American Studies and History at Colgate University and author of the forthcoming *Beneath the Backbone of the World: Blackfoot People and the North American Borderlands, 1720–1877* with the University of North Carolina Press.

Benjamin H. Johnson is Associate Professor of History and Environmental Sustainability at Loyola University Chicago. He is the author or editor of seven books, including *Revolution in Texas: How a Forgotten Rebellion and Its Bloody Suppression Turned Mexicans into Americans.*

Pablo Mijangos y González is Associate Professor of History at the Centro de Investigación y Docencia Económicas (CIDE) in Mexico City. He is the author of *The Lawyer of the Church: Bishop Clemente de Jesús Munguía and the Clerical Response to the Mexican Liberal Reforma* with Nebraska University Press (2015).

Mary P. Ryan is Emeritus Professor of History at Johns Hopkins University and the University of California, Berkeley. Her most recent book is *Taking the Land to Make the City: A Bicoastal History of North America* (2019).

Andrew Smith is a Senior Lecturer at the University of Liverpool and author of *British Businessmen and Canadian Confederation: Constitution Making in an Era of Anglo-Globalization.* Recently, he has published on the co-evolution of political institutions and organizational cultures in other regions of the British Empire, such as Hong Kong, India, and the Caribbean.

Jewel L. Spangler is Associate Professor of History at the University of Calgary in Alberta, Canada. She is the author of *Virginians Reborn: Anglican Monopoly, Evangelical Dissent and the Rise of the Baptists in the Late Eighteenth Century* and is currently at work on a cultural history of the United States before the War of 1812.

Marcela Terrazas y Basante, Ph.D., is a researcher at the Instituto de Investigaciones Históricas at the Universidad Nacional Autónoma de México (UNAM). Her most recent publications include *Diplomacia, negocios y política. Ensayos sobre la relación entre México y el Reino Unido en el siglo XIX*, which she coordinated and coedited with Will Fowler (2018), and "Violence, Collaboration, and Population Movements: The New United States–Mexico Border, 1848–1853," in *Mexico, 1848–1853. Los Años Olvidados*, edited by Pedro Santoni and Will Fowler (2018).

Frank Towers is Associate Professor of History at the University of Calgary in Alberta, Canada. His research focuses on the U.S. Civil War era and the themes of cities, politics, and historiography. His books include *The Urban South and the Coming of the Civil War.*

Index

abolition: colonialism and, 29–30; land ownership and, 181, 182
absolute powers, 4–5
Adams, John Quincy, 32
Agnew, John, 15, 221
agriculture: in Canada, 178–80; capitalism
and, 14, 179, 185–87; Dominion Lands
Act and, 178–79; economy and, 14, 178,
179–80, 185–86, 193–94; education and,
181–82, 185; Enlarged Homestead Act and,
188–89; expansion and scale of, 185–87;
Homestead Act and, 69, 178–79, 181–82,
193; inheritance and, 191–92; labor and,
14, 66, 186, 191, 194–95; land ownership
and, 179–92; Lincoln on, 180; Morrill
Land-Grant Act and, 181–82; politics
and, 14; science and, 185; settlement and,
178–79, 184–85, 188–89; slavery and, 64,
180–81; socioeconomic class and, 185–86;
sovereignty and, 178–95; water and irrigation for, 188–89
"An Alabama Regiment Marching through
Capitol Square, Richmond" (*Harper's
Weekly*), 89–90, *90*
Alaska, 1, 52, 177
alcalde authority, 225–28, 246
alcohol, 141
Alta California, 222–25, 233
American Civil War (1861–1865), 1, 7–8, 12,
177, 178, 256; American South in, 30–31,
239–40; beginning of, 45–46, 66, 67–69;
Canada and, 45–46, 50, 143; city sovereignty
in era of, 220–47; colonialism and, 30–31;
Confederate forces, 107–8, 111–16, 209–10;
democracy and, 49; equality and, 49;
historical narrative of, 30–31; Lame Bull's
Treaty and, 140; land ownership relating
to, 180–81, 183–84, 222; Mississippi Valley
during, 30–31; North Carolina and, 112–15;
secession and, 111–12, 113; South Carolina
and, 111–12; Texas and, 209–10; Union
forces, 83–85, 209–10. *See also* Indigenous
Civil War experience

American exceptionalism, 38
American Land League, 189–90
American Revolution: Mexican independence
and parallels to, 63–67; Native Americans
in, 111–12
American South: in American Civil War, 30–31,
239–40; city sovereignty in, 239–40; Indian
Removal Act and, 109–11; Reconstruction in, 47; sustaining Indigenous South,
1830–1860, 109–11; Thomas Legion in,
107–8, 111–16; transition of, 109
American West: expansion into, 136–40,
146–48; Gold Rush and, 15–16, 63, 140–41,
226–27, 230; public land in, 181–82
annexation: of Alaska, 52, 177; of Canada,
44–52, 74; of Cuba, 30–31, 51; of Mexico,
52–53; of Oregon, 136; of Texas, 32, 65,
163–64, 169n5, 213
annexationists, 30–31
Apaches, 155–56, 160, 163–64, 166
architectural inner spaces, 83, 91–98
Arista, Mariano, 162
Armitage, David, 38
Aron, Stephen, 183–84
Articles of Confederation, 42
Atlantic history: Atlantic Revolutions in, 36–37;
historical narratives of, 27, 30
Aubert, Francois, 86
Australia, 39, 191
ayuntamiento and land ownership, 222–30

Baldwin, J., 237
Bancroft, A. L., *244*
Banks, Nathaniel P., 46
Barry, Charles, 88
Bayou Lacombe Choctaws: in American Revo-
lution, 112; Indian Removal Act and, 110–11;
Indigenous Civil War experience for, 109,
116–22, 124n11, 126n19
Beckert, Sven, 255
Belcourt, George, 207
Belich, James, 9, 178
Bender, Thomas, 28, 68

Bennett, Charles Fox, 73

Bernal, Candalario, 230–31, 236

Bird, James "Jemmy Jock," 136

Blackfoot, 13, 148n3; "civilizing" for, 135–36; Indigenous politics and, 132–48; Lame Bull's Treaty and, 133, 134–40, 146–48, 149n11; territory and homeland, 134; Treaty Seven and, 132–33, 140–45, 147–48; "Whoop-Up Trail" and, 140–41

"Boat Regatta at Ottawa" (*Harper's Weekly*), 87, 87–88

Boomtowns, 140

borderlands: borderland rebels, 203–8; changing flags, 208–10; Cortina and Riel parallels on, 202–15; free trade and, 210–15; republicanism and, 202, 203–8, 210–15; sovereignty and, 200–15

borderland studies, 13

borders: nation-state and, 13; territorialization and, 154

Bosse, Abraham, 81, 82

Brading, David, 70

Brady, Mathew, 84

Brazil, 257; British Empire and, 42, 48, 50; slavery in, 42, 48

Briones, Juana, 223–24

British East India Company, 32

British Empire, 1, 252; in Australia, 39; Brazil and, 42, 48, 50; British North American colonies and, 39–40, 42–53; in Canada, 9, 38, 41–54, 70–75; Greece and, 40; in India, 43; internal home rule granted by, 39–40; Little Englanders of, 39–40; media on, 40–41, 43; monarchism and Canadian political culture, 41–42; opposition to, 44–50; popular support for, 42–44, 50–53; power and, 8–9; Quebec Resolutions of 1864 and, 40; race and, 40, 51–53, 56n30; socioeconomic class and, 42–43; sovereignty in, 38; structure of, 8–9; taxes in, 39–40; United States and, 44; women in, 49–50

British nationality, 9

British North American colonies: British Empire and, 39–40, 42–53; as hemispheric anomaly, 36–37; Imperial Law of British North America and, 74

British World perspective, 37

Broderick, Daniel, 239

Brown, George, 74

Bryant, Wilbur, 209

Bryce, James, 186

Burbank, Jane, 6

Burlamaqui, Jean-Jacques, 209

Burnett, Peter, 239–40

California: Alta California, 222–25, 233; city sovereignty in San Francisco, 220–45; Gold Rush in, 226–27; land ownership in, 186, 226, 226; slavery in, 239–40; territorialization and, 160–61, 165; Union admission, 228

Canada, 1; agriculture in, 178–80; American Civil War and, 45–46, 50, 143; annexation, United States, and, 44–52, 74; "Boat Regatta at Ottawa," 87, 87–88; British Empire in, 9, 38, 41–54, 70–75; British World perspective on, 37; capitalscapes in, 87, 87–89, 96–99, 98; civil war in, 61–63, 70–75; "creole dream" in, 63, 70–75; expansion of, 133–34, 142–43, 145–48; free trade and, 72, 215–16; French Canadians, 43, 51–53; funding by, to British Empire, 43; future research on, 53–54; hemispheric approach to, 36–37, 41–42; identity in, 43–44; Indigenous politics in, 132–48; labor rights in, 48; Latin America and, 36–37, 50; media in, 40–41, 43, 46, 87–88; military protection for, 40; monarchism and Canadian political culture, 41–42; opposition to British Empire in, 44–50; Ottawa's Parliament Hill, 88–89; popular support for British Empire in, 42–44, 50–53; Quebec independence from, 38; Quebec Resolutions of 1864 and, 40; race and ethnicity in, 51–53; railroads in, 142–43, 145; Reconstruction and, 46–47; religion and, 48–50, 52; repatriation in, 209; Riel and borderlands of, 202–15; slavery and, 45; sovereignty in, 9, 36–41, 47–48, 53–54, 200–1; taxes in, 39–40, 71, 73; Treaty of Guadalupe Hidalgo and, 72; Treaty Seven in, 132–33, 140–45, 147–48; women in, 49–50

Canadian Confederation (1867), 1, 9, 10, 62; in capitalscapes, 96–98; Indigenous politics in, 11; nation-building and, 70–75

Canadian constitution (1867), 9, 38, 39–41

Canadian Illustrated News, 97–98, 98

Canadian West, 142–43, 146–48

capitalism, 2; agriculture and, 14, 179, 185–87; development of, 26–28; historical narratives of, 26–28; labor and, 186; land ownership and, 191; Native Americans and, 28; in North America, 26–28; secession and, 15;

slavery and, 26–27, 30–31; sovereignty and, 14–16

capitalscapes: in Canada, *87*, 87–89, 96–99, *98*; of Capitol Square, Richmond, 89–90, *90*; in *Frank Leslie's Illustrated News*, 88; of "Grand Review at Washington," 83–85, *84*; iconography and, 88; inner spaces of, 83, 91–98; Lincoln and, 85; in Mexico, 82–83, 85–87, *86*, 89, 93–96, *95*; monuments and, 89, 100n16; patriotic imagery in, 80–83; of Richmond, Virginia, 89–90, *90*, 93, *94*; in *Southern Illustrated News*, 89; of Washington, D.C., 90–93, *92*, 100n18

Capitol Square, Richmond, 89–90, *90*

captive economies, 29–30

Cartwright, Richard, 44

Catholic Church, 48–49, 207; Mexico and, 9, 64, 65, 67, 68–69

Chakrabarty, Dipesh, 27–28

Chang, David, 252

Chihuahua, 156–60, *158*, *159*, 172nn32–33, 173n53, 174n60

church-state relations, 48–50; in Mexico, 61–62, 64, 65, 67, 68–69

citizenship: changing, 208–10; "citizen soldiers" and, 113, 114–15; Fourteenth Amendment and, 69–70; Mexican naturalization and, 227; Native Americans and, 110, 112; race and, 37, 51–53; Radical Republicans and, 51; sovereignty and, 13–14

"citizen soldiers," 113, 114–15

The City of San Francisco v. the United States, 235–40

city sovereignty: in American Civil War era, 220–47; in American South, 239–40; government authority and, 221–22, 230–35; land ownership and, 220–21; in San Francisco, 220–47; slavery and, 239–40; territoriality and, 221

"civilizing": for Blackfoot, 135–36; Indigenous Civil War experience and, 114–15, 128n46; land ownership and, 188

civil war: in Canada, 61–63, 70–75; in Mexico, 63–70; nation-building and, 61–76; in North America, 61–63, 75–76; power imbalance and, 253; Treaty of Guadalupe Hidalgo and, 63; in United States, 66–70. *See also* American Civil War; *specific civil wars*

Clark, William Smith, 181

Clayton, John M., 161

Clement Ordinance, 243–44

Cobb, Amanda, 121

colonial experience, 71; Bayou Lacombe Choctaws and avoiding colonial conflict, 109, 116–19, 124n11, 126n19

The Colonial History of the City of San Francisco (Dwinelle), 235

colonialism, 1; abolition and, 29–30; American Civil War and, 30–31; San Francisco and, 235; slavery and, 30–31; Spanish, 7, 207–8, 211–12. *See also* British Empire

colonization, 12; decolonization, 6; imperialism and, 8, 254

Colson, G. Q., 227

Comanches, 155–57, 163, 164, 168

Confederate Congress, 89–90

Confederate forces, 209–10; Eastern Cherokees and, 112–16; Indigenous Civil War experience and, 107–8; Thomas Legion, 107–8, 111–16

Conness, John, 244

Constitution, United States: Constitution Convention, 221; Fourteenth Amendment and, 69–70; hemispheric approach to, 42; Thirteenth Amendment of, 30, 69, 93

constitutional crisis: in Mexico, 65, 66–69; slavery and, 64, 66; Treaty of Guadalupe Hidalgo and, 63–70; in United States, 64, 66–70

Cooper, Frederick, 6

Cordero, José, 156

Cortina, Juan, 15; borderland rebels and, 203–8; citizenship of, 209–10; early life of, 203; on land ownership, 204; nation-state and, 202–11, 214–15; proclamations and language of, 205–6, 208; republicanism of, 205–8; Riel's parallels to, 202–15; Texas Rangers and, 204

"creole dream," 63, 70–75

Crowfoot, 141–42

Cuba, 10, 256; annexation of, 30–31, 51

Culbertson, Alexander, 136, 139

Cumming, Alfred, 135, 139

Davis, Jefferson, 31, 32, 85, 89–90, 114

Davitt, Michael, 189

Declaration of Independence, U.S., 38, 49

Declaration of the Rights of Man and Citizen (1789), 3

decolonization, 6

De Haro, Francisco, 227, 241

de la Rosa, Luis, 161–62, 173nn44,49

DeLay, Brian, 11–12, 157
democracy: American Civil War and, 49; equality and, 49; nationalism and, 255
Dempsey, Hugh, 144
Denny, Cecil, 142
Díaz, Porfirio, 204
disease: malaria, 118; Native Americans and, 118, 140, 145; smallpox, 140
Domar, Evsey C., 190–91
Dominion Lands Act (1872), 178–79
Douglas, Stephen, 31, 67, 181, 239
Doyle, Don, 256
Dred Scott v. Sandford (1857), 57
Dwinelle, John, 235–37

Eastern Band of Cherokee Indians (EBCI), 107–8, 123n4
Eastern Cherokees: Confederate forces and, 112–16; Indian Removal Act and, 109–11; Indigenous Civil War experience for, 107–9, 111–16, 120–22, 123n4, 127n29, 129n58, 130n79; Thomas, W. H., and, 112–15, 127n29, 129n58; Thomas Legion and, 111–16
EBCI. *See* Eastern Band of Cherokee Indians
economic sovereignty, 38
economy: agriculture and, 14, 178, 179–80, 185–86, 193–94; Lame Bull's Treaty and, 136–38; land ownership and, 186, 192–93; nationalism and, 255–56; republicanism and, 211–15; slavery and, 64, 66, 69
Eddy, M. C., 228, 229
education, 181–82, 185
emancipation, 29, 49–50, 256
Emerson, Ralph Waldo, 63
empire: nation and, 5–7, 11; power in, 6–7. *See also* British Empire
Enlarged Homestead Act (1909), 188–89
Enlisted Labor Association, 191
equality: American Civil War and, 49; democracy and, 49; land ownership and, 185–86
ethnicity. *See* race and ethnicity
Europe: land ownership in, 183, 189–90; sovereignty in, 4, 183; state and, 4
Evans, Frederick W., 190

federalism, 6–7
Fenians, 50, 74
A Few Words on the Hudson's Bay Company (Isbister), 212–13
Field, Stephen J., 237, 238, 246, 249n44
Figueroa, José, 225, 236
Fitz, Caitlin, 36

flag culture, 81–82
Foner, Eric, 51
forced labor regimes, 29
Ford, Patrick, 189
Fort Atkinson Treaty, 136
Fort Laramie Treaty, 136
Fourteenth Amendment, 69–70
France, 1, 3, 177
Frank Leslie's Illustrated News, 88, 93, 94, 100n18
freehold ownership. *See* land ownership
Free Soil movement, 181–85, 190
free trade: borderlands and, 210–15; Canada and, 72, 215–16; republicanism and, 210–15
French Canadians, 43, 51–53
Friedmann, Harriet, 191
fur trade, 132, 137–39

Gadsden Purchase, 163–64
Gardner, Alexander, 84
Garrison, William Lloyd, 212
General Allotment Act (1887), 187
George, Henry, 185–86, 188, 189, 190
Gettysburg Address, 70
globalization, 14, 251
Gold Rush, 15–16, 63; in California, 226–27; San Francisco and, 226–27, 230; Treaty Seven and, 140–41
Gómez Farías, Valentín, 65
González-Quiroga, Miguel Ángel, 174n58
government authority: *alcalde*, 225–28, 246; city sovereignty and, 221–22, 230–35; federal intervention and, 230–35; land ownership and, 222, 230–35; in San Francisco, 230–35, 240–45
"Grand Review at Washington" (*Harper's Weekly*), 83–85, *84*
Grand Trunk railway, 48
Greater Reconstruction, 13–14
Greece, 40
Grijalva, Don Guadalupe, 160
Grijalva, María del Rosario, 160

Hamilton, Alexander, 42
Hanlon, David, 252
Harper's Weekly: "An Alabama Regiment Marching through Capitol Square, Richmond," 89–90, *90*; "Boat Regatta at Ottawa," 87, 87–88; "Grand Review at Washington," 83–85, *84*; "Interior of the New Dome of the Capitol at Washington," 91, *92*, 93; "Scene in the Grand Plaza of the City of Mexico," 85–87, *86*

Harrison, Benjamin, 187
Hart v. Burnett, 237–39, 245–46
Hauptman, Laurence, 123n6
Hawaii, 192, 252
Hawes, Horace, 227–28
hemispheric approach, 36–37, 41–42
historical narratives: of American Civil War, 30–31; of Atlantic history, 27, 30; of capitalism, 26–28; nation-building and, 25–26, 30–33; outside national framework, 251–57; of Pacific history, 31–32; of slavery, 28–30; transnationalism and, 252–53; of United States, 25–33
Hobbes, Thomas, 81, *82*
Hobsbawm, Eric, 255
Holy Roman Empire, 5
Homestead Act (1862), 69, 178–79, 181–82, 191, 193
Hudson's Bay Company, 137, 145, 212–13, 214–15
Humphreys, Clement, 233
hunting, 135–38, 141–42, 144–45, 184
Hurd, Thomas Gladwin, 43
Hyde, George, 227

iconography, 88
identity: in Canada, 43–44; nation-building and, 70; social, 13–14, 40
Illinois Central Railroad, 31
Illustrated London News, 88
imperial adventurism, 31
imperialism: colonization and, 8, 254; Mexico and, 9–10; in nation-state, 6–8; sovereignty and, 6–7; by United States, 12
Imperialistas, 93–95
Imperial Law of British North America, 74
India, 39, 43
Indian Enfranchisement Act (1869), 187
Indian Removal Act (1830): American South and, 109–11; Bayou Lacombe Choctaws and, 110–11; Eastern Cherokees and, 109–11; Indigenous Civil War experience and, 107–10, 123n4
Indian Rights Association, 187
Indian Territory, 107–8, 110, 112–13, 123n4, 136, 194
Indigenous Civil War experience, 123n6–8; for Bayou Lacombe Choctaws, 109, 116–22, 124n11, 126n19; "civilizing" and, 114–15, 128n46; Confederate forces and, 107–8; for Eastern Cherokees, 107–9, 111–16, 120–22, 123n4, 127n29, 129n58, 130n79; Indian Removal Act and, 107–10, 123n4; Indig-

enous sovereignty and, 116, 120–22, 130n79, 131n80; sustaining Indigenous South, 1830–1860, 109–11; Thomas Legion and, 107–8, 111–16; in war's aftermath, 119–22
Indigenous politics: Blackfoot and, in Canada, 132–48; in Canadian Confederation, 11; Fort Atkinson Treaty and, 136; Fort Laramie Treaty and, 136; Lame Bull's Treaty and, 133, 134–40, 146–48, 149n11; livestock thefts and, 154–57, *158*, 160, 165–68, 171n31; state-making and, 13; territorialization and, 13, 164–66; Treaty Seven and, 132–33, 140–45, 147–48; in United States, 11–13, 134–40, 145–48
Indigenous sovereignty, 12–13; Indigenous Civil War experience and, 116, 120–22, 130n79, 131n80; Mexican Indian raids and, 153–68
industrialization, 64; land ownership and, 186–87
Industrial Relations Commission, 186–87
inheritance, 191–92
"Interior of the New Dome of the Capitol at Washington" (*Harper's Weekly*), 91, *92, 93*
Internal home rule, 39–40
international politics, 2, 3
Investigative Commission, 156–60, *158, 159*, 171n31, 172nn32,38, 173n53
invisible sovereign states, 4
Ireland, 189–90
Irish-Americans, 50, 53, 74
Isbister, William, 212–13
Izecksohn, Vitor, 256–57

Jackson, Andrew, 64, 112, 239
Jefferson, Thomas, 42, 49
Johnson, Andrew, 30, 47, 93
Joseph, Abraham, 40
Josephy, Alvin P., 184
Juárez, Benito, 3, 69, 85–87, *86*, 95, 204
Judiciary Act (1789), 238–39

Kelley, George Foster, 220
Kolchin, Peter, 254, 256
Kramer, Paul, 7

labor: agriculture and, 14, 66, 186, 191, 194–95; Canada labor rights, 48; capitalism and, 186; Enlisted Labor Association, 191; forced labor regimes, 29; land ownership and, 31, 190–91, 193–95
Laird, David, 143, 144

Lame Bull's Treaty: American Civil War and, 140; Blackfoot and, 133, 134–40, 146–48, 149n11; economy and, 136–38; on hunting, 135–38
Lanctot, Médéric, 48–49
Land and Labor in the United States (Moody), 186
Land Commission, U.S., 222, 230–36
land ownership: abolition and, 181, 182; agriculture and, 179–92; American Civil War relating to, 180–81, 183–84, 222; American Land League and, 189–90; *ayuntamiento* and, 222–30; in California, 186, 226, *226*; capitalism and, 191; in *The City of San Francisco v. the United States*, 235–40; city sovereignty and, 220–47; "civilizing" and, 188; economy and, 186, 192–93; Enlarged Homestead Act and, 188–89; equality and, 185–86; in Europe, 183, 189–90; freehold ownership, 180, 181–95; Free Soil movement and, 181–85, 190; General Allotment Act and, 187; government authority and, 222, 230–35; in *Hart v. Burnett*, 237–39, 245–46; Homestead Act and, 181–82, 191; industrialization and, 186–87; inheritance and, 191–92; in Ireland, 189; labor and, 31, 190–91, 193–95; land monopolies and, 185–89, 192; Mexican land grants and, 222, 231–32; in Mexico, 222–30; Morrill Land-Grant Act and, 181–82; national expansion and, 192; National Reform Association and, 190; Native Americans and, 183–84, 187–88, 190, 194–95; Northwest Ordinance on, 183; of Outside Lands, 243–44; Preemption Act and, 234–35; public lands and, 181–82; in Pueblo Case, 232–38, 241–44; race, ethnicity, and, 181, 190–91, 204; Radical Republicans and, 187, 190; railroads and, 186; in San Francisco, 220–47; settlement and, 180, 182–85, 187, 188–92; slavery and, 181, 190–91; sovereignty and, 14, 15–16, 179–95; Spain and, 222–25; squatters and, 230, 234–37, 241–42, 245; taxes and, 183, 189–90; Treaty of Guadalupe Hidalgo and, 225–27; Van Ness Ordinance and, 242
land speculation, 246
language, 4, 205–6
Latin America, 252; Canada and, 36–37, 50; War of the Triple Alliance in, 50. *See also* Brazil
Leavenworth, Thaddeus, 227
Lee, Robert E., 70, 118
Lenin, V. I., 194

Leonhard, Jörn, 254–55
Leviathan (Hobbes), 81, *82*
Lewis and Clark expedition, 32
L'Heureux, Jean, 141
liberal nationalism, 255–56
Lincoln, Abraham, 3, 8, 31, 45, 47, 68, 69, 201, 220; on agriculture, 180; capitalscapes and, 85; Gettysburg Address by, 70
Little Dog, 138
Little Englanders, 39–40
livestock thefts: Indigenous politics and, 154–57, *158*, 160, 165–68, 171n31; territorialization and, 165–68
Louisiana Purchase, 32, 169n6
Love, Eric T., 52
Lumbee Indians, 128n44

Macdonald, John A., 3, 53, 143
MacKay, Charles, 43
Macleod, James, 142, 143–44
Madison, James, 221
Maier, Charles, 6, 80, 201, 215n2, 254
Making a New World (Tutino), 28
malaria, 118
Marx, Karl, 49, 191
Maximilian I, 3, 85–86, 93–96
Mazzini, Giuseppe, 3
McGee, Thomas D'Arcy, 41–42, 47–48, 50, 53
McPherson, James, 68
media: on British Empire, 40–41, 43; in Canada, 40–41, 43, 46, 87–88. *See also Harper's Weekly*
Medicine Calf, 141, 144
Medill, Joseph, 47
Melbourne, William, 72
mercantilism, 211–12
Métis, 206–7, 212, 214–15
Mexican-American War, 157, 213, 232
Mexican independence, 63–67
Mexican Indian raids: Indian incursions, 155–56, *159*, 167–68, 170n21, 171n30, 173n44; Indigenous sovereignty and, 153–68; Investigative Commission and, 156–60, *158*, *159*, 171n31, 172nn32,38, 173n53; livestock thefts and, 154–57, *158*, 160, 165–68, 171n31; United States and, 156, 161–68
Mexican land grants, 222, 231–32
Mexican naturalization, 227
Mexican Republic (1867), 1, 225–26
Mexico, 1; *alcalde* authority in, 225–28, 246; annexation of, 52–53; capitalscapes in,

82–83, 85–87, *86*, 89, 93–96, *95*; Catholic Church and, 9, 64, 65, 67, 68–69; Chihuahua, 156–60, *158*, *159*, 172nn32–33, 173n53, 174n60; church-state relations in, 61–62, 64, 65, 67, 68–69; civil war in, 63–70; constitutional crisis in, 65, 66–69; Cortina and borderlands of, 202–15; imperialism and, 9–10; *Imperialistas* in, 93–95; Indian incursions in, *159*, 167–68, 170n21, 171n30, 173n44; Indigenous politics in, 11, 170nn19–21; Indigenous sovereignty in, 153–68; invasion, of 1940s, 32; land ownership in, 222–30; nation-state in, 10; *Palacio Nacional* in, 85–86, 94–95; Reform Laws in, 69; Reform War in, 61–62; Rio Grande in, 165–66; slavery and, 161–62; Sonora, 156–60, *158*, *159*, 172nn32–33, 173n53, 174n60; sovereignty in, 153–54; Spain and, 211–12, 222–25; taxes in, 213–14; territorialization and, 154, 160–61, 164–68, 169n5, 173n55, 174n59; Treaty of Guadalupe Hidalgo and, 63–67, 161–63, 225–27; Treaty of La Mesilla and, 163–64; United States and, 44, 52–53, 136–37, 154, 157, 160–61, 213, 232; *Zócalo* complex in, 93–95

"Mexico. 26 juin." (*Le Monde Illustre*), *95*, 95–96

Midway Islands, 52

migration, 14, 108

Mission Dolores, 222–24, *223*, 225, 231, 233

Mississippi Valley, 30–31

Missouri Compromise, 64, 67

monarchy, 4–5, 41–42

Le Monde Illustre, *95*, 95–96

monopolies, 212–13; land, 185–89, 192

monuments, 89, 100n16

Moody, William, 186

Morrill Land-Grant Act (1862), 181–82

Morse, Omar, 180, 186

nation, 1; empire and, 5–7, 11

nationalism, 3; danger of, 254–55; democracy and, 255; economy and, 255–56; growth of, 6; liberal, 255–56; nation-state and, 254–55; state-making and, 10–11; in United States, 12

nationality: British, 9; social identity and, 13–14, 40

national loyalty, 40–44, 70, 75, 112–13, 208–10

National Reform Association, 190

nation-building: Canadian Confederation and, 70–75; civil war and, 61–76; Cortina and Riel parallels on, 202–15; historical narratives and, 25–26, 30–33; identity and, 70; in North America, 61–63, 75–76; race and, 37, 51–53; slavery and, 256–57; socioeconomic class and, 37; sovereignty and, 202–3; of United States, 25–33

nation-state, 5; borders and, 13; Cortina and, 202–11, 214–15; defining, 1–2, 4; imperialism in, 6–8; in Mexico, 10; nationalism and, 254–55; Riel and, 202–10, 214–15; territoriality and, 201

A Nation Without Borders (Hahn), 8

Native Americans: in American Revolution, 111–12; Apaches, 155–56, 160, 163–64, 166; capitalism and, 28; citizenship and, 110, 112; Comanches, 155–57, 163, 164, 168; disease and, 118, 140, 145; EBCI, 107–8, 123; General Allotment Act and, 187; Indian Enfranchisement Act and, 187; Indian Removal Act and, 107–11, 123n4; Indian Rights Association and, 187; Indian Territory and, 107–8, 110, 112–13, 123n4, 136, 194; land ownership and, 183–84, 187–88, 190, 194–95; "Peace" Indians, 155–56; power and, 28. *See also* Blackfoot; Eastern Cherokees; Indigenous Civil War experience; Indigenous politics; Indigenous sovereignty; Mexican Indian raids

Native captives, 29–30

New Mexico, 160–61, 165

New Spain, 211–12, 213, 238

Ngai, Mae, 252–53

Noé, José Jesús, 227, 230, 236, 242

non-state actors, 4

North America: Atlantic history of, 27, 30; capitalism in, 26–28; nation-building and civil war in, 61–63, 75–76; Pacific history of, 31–32. *See also* British North American colonies; *specific countries*

North Carolina, 112–15

Northern Pacific Railway, 137, 145

North-West Mounted Police (NWMP), 141–42, 144

Northwest Ordinance (1787), 183

North-West rebellion, 204–5, 214–15

NWMP. *See* North-West Mounted Police

Ochoa, Antonio, 210

Old Sun, 144

"The Opening of Parliament" (*Canadian Illustrated News*), 97–98, *98*

Oregon, 66, 136

Osiander, Andreas, 5

Osterhammel, Jürgen, 6, 88

Otero, Mariano, 63, 70
Ottawa capitalscapes, 96–98
Ottawa's Parliament Hill, 88–89
Outside Lands, 243–44

Pacific history, 31–32
Pacific Railroad Acts, 69
Palacio Nacional, 85–86, 94–95
Papineau, Louis-Joseph, 44
patriotic imagery, 80–83
"Peace" Indians, 155–56
Peace of Westphalia, 5
Peachy, A. C., 228, 231, 233–34
Pembina, 214
Perry, Arthur Latham, 182
political geography, 221, 238
politics: agriculture and, 14; international, 2, 3; world political organization, 4
Polk, James K., 32, 49, 136, 239
Polley, John B., 241
"popular sovereignty" doctrine, 67, 181
Populism, 185
Porter, David Dixon, 85
Postel, Charles, 185
Potter, John F., 46
Potts, Jerry, 144
power: British Empire and, 8–9; in empire, 6–7; imbalances, 252–53; Native Americans and, 28; sovereignty and, 7, 8
Preemption Act (1841), 234–35
property rights. *See* land ownership
public lands, 181–82
Pueblo Case, 232–38, 241–44

Quebec independence, 38
Quebec Resolutions of 1864, 40

race and ethnicity: British Empire and, 40, 51–53, 56n30; Canada and, 51–53; citizenship and, 37, 51–53; land ownership and, 181, 190–91, 204; nation-building and, 37, 51–53; sovereignty and, 40
Race over Empire (Love), 52
racism, 47
Radical Republicans: citizenship and, 51; land ownership and, 187, 190; during Reconstruction, 47
railroads, 178–79; in Canada, 142–43, 145; Grand Trunk railway, 48; Illinois Central Railroad, 31; land ownership and, 186; Northern Pacific Railway, 137, 145; Pacific Railroad Acts, 69

Ramos, Raúl, 170n19
Rauchway, Eric, 191
Reciprocity Treaty (1854), 45–46
Reconstruction, 33, 255; in American South, 47; Canada and, 46–47; Greater Reconstruction, 13–14; Radical Republicans during, 47
Red River, 203–4; Métis, 206–7, 212, 214–15; rebellion, 204–5, 214–15
Reform Laws, 69
Reform War, Mexico, 61–62
religion: Canada and, 48–50, 52; United States and, 49–50. *See also* Catholic Church; church-state relations
repatriation, 209
republicanism: borderlands and, 202, 203–8, 210–15; of Cortina, 205–8; defining, 215n3; economy and, 211–15; free trade and, 210–15; mercantilism and, 211–12; of Riel, 206–8
Richardson, Guillermo, 233–34
Richmond, Virginia, 89–90, *90*, 93, *94*, 101n26
Riel, Louis, 15, 217n11; borderland rebels and, 203–8; citizenship of, 209; Cortina's parallels to, 202–15; early life of, 203–4; nation-state and, 202–10, 214–15; North-West rebellion and, 204–5, 214–15; proclamations and language of, 206; republicanism of, 206–8
Rio Grande, 165–66
Rodd Commission, 171n31
Rombout, Melissa, 96
Rouquette, Adrien, 116, 118
Rupert's Land, 46
Russia, 1, 177

San Francisco: Bancroft's map of, *244*; in *The City of San Francisco v. the United States*, 235–40; city sovereignty and land ownership in, 220–47; colonialism and, 235; county map, *233*, *244*; federal intervention in, 230–35; first lots in, 227–30, *229*; Gold Rush and, 226–27, 230; government authority in, 230–35, 240–45; in *Hart v. Burnett*, 237–39, 245–46; Land Commission and, 222, 230–36; Mexican *ayuntamiento* and, 222–30; Mission Dolores, 222–24, *223*, *225*, 231, *233*; official map, by Eddy, *229*; Pueblo Case, 232–38, 241–44; settlement in, 222–24, *223*; in *Townsend et al v. Greeley*, 238–39, *240*; Treaty of Guadalupe Hidalgo and, 225–27; Van Ness Ordinance in, 242; Yerba Buena Cove, 224, *224*–25, 231–34, 241–43
Sassen, Saskia, 201

"Scene in the Grand Plaza of the City of
    Mexico" (*Harper's Weekly*), 85–87, *86*
science and agriculture, 185
Scott, Rebecca, 256
secession: American Civil War and, 111–12, 113;
    capitalism and, 15; sovereignty and, 3, 15
Seed, Patricia, 183
settlement: agriculture and, 178–79, 184–85,
    188–89; land ownership and, 180, 182–85,
    187, 188–92; in San Francisco, 222–24, *223*
settler-nationalists, 12–13
Seward, William, 32, 45
Sheehan, James, 7
Sister Republics (Fitz), 36
slavery, 8, 10, 14, 49, 256; abolition of, 29–30,
    181, 182; age of emancipation and, 29;
    agriculture and, 64, 180–81; in Brazil, 42,
    48; in California, 239–40; Canada and, 45;
    capitalism and, 26–27, 30–31; chronologies,
    29–30; city sovereignty and, 239–40; colo-
    nialism and, 30–31; constitutional crisis and,
    64, 65; economy and, 64, 66, 69; expansion
    of, 30–31; historical narratives of, 28–30;
    land ownership and, 181, 190–91; literature,
    28–30; Mexico and, 161–62; Missouri Com-
    promise and, 64, 67; nation-building and,
    256–57; Thirteenth Amendment and, 30, 69
smallpox, 140
Smith, Adam, 211–12
Smith, Kirby, 114
Smythe, William Ellsworth, 189
social identity, 13–14, 40
socialism, 48–49
socioeconomic class: agriculture and, 185–86;
    British Empire and, 42–43; nation-building
    and, 37
Sonora, 156–60, *158*, *159*, 172nn32–33, 173n53,
    174n60
Sota, Maria, 230–31
South Carolina, 111–12
Southern Illustrated News, 89
sovereignty: agriculture and, 178–95; border-
    lands and, 200–15; in Canada, 9, 36–41,
    47–48, 53–54, 200–1; capitalism and, 14–16;
    capitalscapes and sovereign imaginary,
    80–99; citizenship and, 13–14; city sov-
    ereignty in era of American Civil War,
    220–47; confederation and, 3; defining, 2–4,
    7, 16–17, 37–39; economic, 38; in Europe,
    4, 183; imperialism and, 6–7; international
    politics and, 2, 3; land ownership and, 14,
    15–16, 179–95; language and, 4; in Mexico,

153–54; migration and, 14; nation-building
    and, 202–3; "popular sovereignty" doctrine,
    67, 181; power and, 7, 8; property rights and,
    15–16; race and, 40; secession and, 3, 15;
    state-making and, 10–11, 13–14; taxes and,
    39–40; territorialization and, 165, 177–78;
    transnationalism and, 14; tribal, 38. *See also*
    Indigenous sovereignty
Spain, 63–64, 65; land ownership and, 222–25;
    mercantilism and, 211–12; Mexico and,
    211–12, 222–25
Spanish colonialism, 7, 207–8, 211–12
squatters, 230, 234–37, 241–42, 245
state: defining, 2, 3–4; Europe and, 4
"The State Convention at Richmond, Va, in Ses-
    sion" *Frank Leslie's Illustrated News*, 93, *94*
State House of Capitol Square, 89
state-making, 7; Indigenous politics and, 13;
    nationalism and, 10–11; sovereignty and,
    10–11, 13–14
Stern, Steve, 27–28
Stevens, Isaac, 135, 136–40

taxes: in British Empire, 39–40; in Canada,
    39–40, 71, 73; land ownership and, 183,
    189–90; in Mexico, 213–14; sovereignty and,
    39–40
Taylor, Bayard, 183
Taylor, Zachary, 162
Tenorio, Mauricio, 62
territoriality, 200–1, 215n2; city sovereignty and,
    221; nation-state and, 201; political geogra-
    phy and, 221, 238
territorialization: borders and, 154; California
    and, 160–61, 165; Indigenous politics and,
    13, 164–66; livestock thefts and, 165–68;
    Louisiana purchase and, 32, 169n6; Mexico
    and, 154, 160–61, 164–68, 169n5, 173n55,
    174n59; New Mexico and, 160–61, 165; Rio
    Grande and, 165–66; sovereignty and, 165,
    177–78; Treaty of Guadalupe Hidalgo and,
    63, 65–66; Treaty of La Mesilla and, 163–64.
    See also annexation
Texas: American Civil War and, 209–10;
    annexation of, 32, 65, 163–64, 169n5, 213;
    Cortina and, 203–4, 207–8
Texas Rangers, 204
Thirteen Colonies, 36, 44
Thirteenth Amendment, 30, 69, 93
Thirty Years War, 5
Thomas, William Holland, 112–15, 127n29,
    129n58

Thomas Legion, 107–8; Eastern Cherokees and, 111–16

Thompson, T. Phillips, 47–48

Thring, Henry, 40, 56n30

Townsend et al v. Greeley, 238–39, 240

transnationalism, 4, 14, 251–53

transnational studies, 61–62

Treaty of Guadalupe Hidalgo: Canada and, 72; civil war and, 63; constitutional crisis and, 63–70; land ownership and, 225–27; Mexico and, 63–67, 161–63, 225–27; San Francisco and, 225–27; territorialization and, 63, 65–66; United States and, 63–67, 161–63, 225–27

Treaty of La Mesilla, 163–64

Treaty Seven: Blackfoot and, 132–33, 140–45, 147–48; confusion over, 144–45; Gold Rush and, 140–41; territory, 132–33

tribal sovereignty, 38. *See also* Indigenous sovereignty

Tupper, Charles, 43

Turner, Frederick Jackson, 28, 192

Tutino, John, 28

Union forces, 83–85, 209–10

unionists, 210

United States, 1; British Empire and, 44; Canada, annexation, and, 44–44–52, 74; civil war in, 66–70; constitutional crisis in, 64, 66–70; expansion of, 44–45, 52–53, 133–34, 136–41, 145–48, 192; geographical area and size of, 169n6; historical narratives of, 25–33; imperialism by, 12; Indigenous politics in, 11–13, 134–40, 145–48; Lame Bull's Treaty and, 133, 134–40, 146–48, 149n11; Land Commission, 222, 230–36; Mexican Indian raids and, 156, 161–68; Mexico and, 44, 52–53, 136–37, 154, 157, 160–61, 213, 232; nationalism in, 12; nation-building of, 25–33; Reciprocity Treaty in, 45–46; religion and, 49–50; repatriation in, 209; settler-nationalists in, 12–13; Treaty of Guadalupe

Hidalgo and, 63–67, 161–63, 225–27; Treaty of La Mesilla and, 163–64; Treaty Seven in, 132–33, 140–45, 147–48; wars of rebellion and, 32–33. *See also* American Civil War; *specific topics*

Van Ness Ordinance, 242

Varon, Alberto, 205

Vatel, Emer de, 209

Veblen, Thorstein, 178

Vela, Isidro, 210

Victoria (Queen), 41–42, 46

Vioget, Juan, 224, *224*, 236

Virginia State Assembly, 89

Wakefield, Edward Gibbon, 191

War of 1812, 64

War of the Triple Alliance, 50

Washington, D.C.: capitalscapes of, 90–93, *92*, 100n18; "Interior of the New Dome of the Capitol at Washington," 91, *92, 93*

Washington, George, 89

water and irrigation, 188–89

Weber, Max, 3

Webster, Daniel, 162, 183

West, Elliott, 13–14

Westminster Palace complex, 88

"Whoop-Up Trail," 140–41

Williams, John, 238

Williams, William Appleman, 195

Wilmot, David, 139

Witgen, Michael, 217n11

wolf poison, 144

women, 49–50

Wood, Orrin S., 47

world political organization, 4

Yerba Buena Cove, *224,* 224–25, 231–34, 241–43

Zamora, Teodoro, 210

Zócalo complex, 93–95

RECONSTRUCTING AMERICA
Andrew L. Slap, series editor

Hans L. Trefousse, *Impeachment of a President: Andrew Johnson, the Blacks, and Reconstruction.*

Richard Paul Fuke, *Imperfect Equality: African Americans and the Confines of White Ideology in Post-Emancipation Maryland.*

Ruth Currie-McDaniel, *Carpetbagger of Conscience: A Biography of John Emory Bryant.*

Paul A. Cimbala and Randall M. Miller, eds., *The Freedmen's Bureau and Reconstruction: Reconsiderations.*

Herman Belz, *A New Birth of Freedom: The Republican Party and Freedmen's Rights, 1861 to 1866.*

Robert Michael Goldman, *"A Free Ballot and a Fair Count": The Department of Justice and the Enforcement of Voting Rights in the South, 1877–1893.*

Ruth Douglas Currie, ed., *Emma Spaulding Bryant: Civil War Bride, Carpetbagger's Wife, Ardent Feminist—Letters, 1860–1900.*

Robert Francis Engs, *Freedom's First Generation: Black Hampton, Virginia, 1861–1890.*

Robert F. Kaczorowski, *The Politics of Judicial Interpretation: The Federal Courts, Department of Justice, and Civil Rights, 1866–1876.*

John Syrett, *The Civil War Confiscation Acts: Failing to Reconstruct the South.*

Michael Les Benedict, *Preserving the Constitution: Essays on Politics and the Constitution in the Reconstruction Era.*

Andrew L. Slap, *The Doom of Reconstruction: The Liberal Republicans in the Civil War Era.*

Edmund L. Drago, *Confederate Phoenix: Rebel Children and Their Families in South Carolina.*

Mary Farmer-Kaiser, *Freedwomen and the Freedmen's Bureau: Race, Gender, and Public Policy in the Age of Emancipation.*

Paul A. Cimbala and Randall Miller, eds., *The Great Task Remaining Before Us: Reconstruction as America's Continuing Civil War.*

John A. Casey Jr., *New Men: Reconstructing the Image of the Veteran in Late-Nineteenth-Century American Literature and Culture.*

Hilary Green, *Educational Reconstruction: African American Schools in the Urban South, 1865–1890.*

Christopher B. Bean, *Too Great a Burden to Bear: The Struggle and Failure of the Freedmen's Bureau in Texas.*

David E. Goldberg, *The Retreats of Reconstruction: Race, Leisure, and the Politics of Segregation at the New Jersey Shore, 1865–1920.*

David Prior, ed., *Reconstruction in a Globalizing World.*

Jewel L. Spangler and Frank Towers (eds.), *Remaking North American Sovereignty: State Transformation in the 1860s.*

CPSIA information can be obtained
at www.ICGtesting.com
Printed in the USA
LVHW052225030320
648868LV00007B/994